Buddhist America

CENTERS, RETREATS, PRACTICES

Edited by Don Morreale

Foreword by Jack Kornfield

John Muir Publications
Santa Fe, New Mexico

Sabbe Sankhara Anicca Ti: "All composite things are impermanent." This fundamental teaching applies as well to the Buddhist centers listed in this book. New centers are opening every day, while others fold, or move, or change leaders or phone numbers. Every attempt has been made to verify the information presented herein. Almost all of it was provided by the centers themselves or by their headquarters, so that we feel reasonably confident that this is the most up-to-date guide to this subject available at this time. If you discover inaccuracies, or if you know of a center that we have failed to list, please be kind enough to let us know so that we can update it in the next edition.

To contact Buddhist America, please write to:
Don Morreale
Conspiracy of Silence Productions
1220½ East 20th Avenue
Denver, Colorado 80205
(303) 894-8006

Printed in the United States of America
First edition September 1988

Cover illustration by Jim Finnell
Design by Joanna Hill
Interior cutout motifs by Paul Briggs

Published by:
John Muir Publications
P.O. Box 613
Santa Fe, NM 87504

Library of Congress Cataloging-in-Publication Data

Buddhist America.

1. Buddhism—North America. 2. Spiritual life (Buddhism) 3. Buddhist centers—North America—Directories. 4. Temples, Buddhist—North America—Directories.
I. Morreale, Don, 1947-
BQ724.B83 1988   294.3'0973   88-61655
ISBN 0-912528-94-X

Distributed to the book trade by:
W.W. Norton & Company, Inc.
New York, New York

This book is dedicated to my two original
spiritual teachers,
The Rev. Samuel O. Morreale and
Eufemia Azzolina Morreale
and to the memory of my brother
David Lawrence Morreale

The wise person learns from life itself; the fool waits for the perfect weather. The wise person learns from all schools of Buddhism; the fool will cling to one and despise the others—for the wise man knows that any viewpoint or opinion whatsoever is only a changing condition, and with its cessation there is peace.

—Ven. Ajahn Sumedho Bhikkhu

We Americans can no longer look outside ourselves for peace and happiness. We have reached the limits of our external expansion. It is now time to listen to and practice the principles of the *Buddhadharma*, to turn our energy inwards, and to discover that the search for paradise that has always brought people to America ends ultimately in the discovery and the purification of one's own mind.

—Bhikshu Heng Chau

All Dharmas agree at one point.

—Atisha

Contents

Is Buddhism Changing in North America?

BY JACK KORNFIELD

Something new is happening on this continent. Buddhism is being deeply affected by the spirit of democracy, by feminization, by ecological values, and by the integration of lay life. A North American vehicle is being created. Already this vehicle draws on the best of the roots, the trunk, the branches, the leaves, the blossoms, and the fruits—all the parts of Buddhism; and it is beginning to draw them together in a wise and supportive whole.

One day an old woman who lived in New York went to her travel agent and asked him to get her a ticket to Tibet.

"Tibet!" he exclaimed, "That's a long and difficult journey. You usually go to Miami for the winter. Why not just go there?"

"I must go see The Guru," she replied.

She got a ticket, flew to India, disembarked at the airport in Delhi, and went through all the difficulties of Indian customs. When asked where she was going, she said, "To Tibet, to see The Guru."

After this her journey continued by train across India to Gangtok, the capital of Sikkim. Here she secured a border pass and traveled by bus up to the Tibetan border, where the guards again asked where she was going and again she replied, "I must go see The Guru."

They told her, "You can only say three words to him."

She replied, "I know, I know. I must go anyway."

She then journeyed with her bags across the Tibetan plateau by bus, by jeep, by horse caravan, and finally came to a large mountain with a monastery at the top. There was a long line of pilgrims, and she joined the line. After three days of waiting, it was her turn.

The guard at the door reminded her, "only three words now."
"I know, I know," she said.

She entered the grand chamber, and there sat The Guru, a lama with a wispy beard, wearing maroon robes. She sat down opposite him and looked directly at him. After a silent period she simply said, "Sheldon, come home."

This is the task of North American Buddhism: to bring the heartfelt practices and awakening of the Buddha home to our native soil and contemporary times in a useful way. In this chapter I wish to reflect on how Buddhism may change as it is adapted to our North American cultures.

Eighteen years ago as a monk practicing in Southeast Asia, I wrote *A Brief Guide to Meditation Temples of Thailand* (World Federation of Buddhists Book Series, no. 44) to help other Westerners who were

Ceremony at Taungpulu Monastery, Boulder Creek, California, in which these four Westerners were sanctioned as teachers by the late Ven. Mahasi Sayadaw. *Front row, left to right:* Sharon Salzberg, Joseph Goldstein, Jack Kornfield, Jacqueline Schwartz-Mandell. *Back row, left to right:* U. Aggadhama, U Silananda, Mahasi Sayadaw, U Janaka U Kelatha.

coming to practice in Asia find appropriate monasteries, teachers, and circumstances for their study. I've recently learned that that little guide was one of the inspirations for this book as well.

It is remarkable that already there is enough history and breadth to the movement of American Buddhism to have a book as wide-ranging and encompassing as this one. In watching this movement bring Buddhism to life in America, I've seen its struggles, its difficulties, and the great joy and understanding that it has brought into thousands of people's lives.

As "Sheldon" comes home, as Buddhist practice comes to America, it is changing. As in its evolution in Japan, China, and Tibet, there are already new forces, flavors, and qualities in its practice. In Asia practice has been characterized by a renunciatory and monastic tradition. Whether in Thailand, Tibet, or Japan, most of the best of Buddhist practice has been preserved in monasteries, kept alive by older monks in situations removed from the everyday society around them. For centuries in Asia, Buddhism has had a monastic, masculine, ascetic, and somewhat patriarchal flavor.

While many generations of us have benefited greatly from excellent training in these monasteries (and we certainly hope that a number of well-run and non-sexist monasteries for monks and nuns will grow in this country, providing opportunity for those who wish to experience the life of renunciation), it appears that monasteries with monks and nuns will not be the major focus of Buddhism in America. Instead, there is a shift in focus taking place, and it is the lay community which is at the center of practice here.

In the Theravada tradition that has brought Vipassana practice to America, and to some extent in the other major traditions of Zen and Vajrayana Buddhism, several forces for the integration and opening of the Buddhist tradition are at work. The three key themes which I have noticed in the past fifteen years are:

Democratization

In Asia Buddhism was primarily hierarchical and authoritarian. Wisdom, knowledge, and practice were handed down from elders to juniors, and the running of monasteries and the *sangha* (community of practitioners) at large rested in the hands of a small core of senior monks. What they decided was the way things were, and there was no questioning of their authority; students just followed. In North America, where our cultures are at heart much more democratic, this has begun to change. Western Buddhists are trained to think and understand for themselves and are less suited to the hierarchical models of Asia. At present in Western Buddhist communities there are strong forces for democratization, participation in decision making by the whole community; and rather than a hierarchical structure, there is a structure of mutual support and appreciation. This will be a great vitalizing factor and a major change in Buddhism as it evolves in our country.

Feminization

The second, and perhaps most important, force affecting Buddhism in America has been the force of feminization. In Asia, through the monasteries and older monks, Buddhism has been primarily a masculine and patriarchal affair, masculine by virtue of the fact that it has been men who have preserved and transmitted it, and more deeply masculine in that its language and traditions have been predominantly in the masculine mode. Buddhism has been a practice of the mind, of *logos*, of understanding through striving and attainment, of gaining enlightenment through conquering oneself. All of these elements—the mind, logic, striving, the patriarchal structures that did not allow for a full participation of women and that discounted the feminine values—are now being confronted by the powerful force of feminine consciousness that is growing in Western culture. This consciousness is already bringing about a softening and an opening of the Buddhist spirit and practice that will allow for strength of mind and the masculine element, but also for the tenderness and earthiness of the feminine. Not only is there a clear movement to abandon the superficial structures, sexism and patriarchy, but there is a more profound movement to develop the Dharma as a practice of relationship to the body, the community, and the earth, and to stress interdependence and healing rather than conquering or abandoning.

Integration

The third major theme as Buddhism develops in the West is integration. In Asia Buddhism was primarily characterized by monasteries, ashrams, caves, and temples; and ordinations of priests, monks, hermits, and forest dwellers, all of which involved withdrawal from worldly life, and which created circumstances of simplicity and renunciation for practice. The rest of the Buddhists, the great majority of lay people, did not actually practice meditation, but remained devoted supporters of the monks. However, here in the West, the lay people are not content to be only the devotional supporters of other people's practice. Almost all North American students involved want to actually practice the path of liberation. The most frequently asked question of my fifteen years of teaching has been: How can we *live* the practice in our American lives? Our practice will emphasize *integration*, not a withdrawal from the world, but a discovery of wisdom within the midst of our lives. North American Buddhists have already begun to develop means to integrate and live the practice as householders, as family people, as people with jobs who still wish to partake of the deepest aspects of the Dharma— not through running away to caves, but by applying the practice to their daily lives.

All of these things, along with the integration of modern Western psychology, are becoming important themes and forces for Buddhist practice as it approaches the twenty-first century in North America and the West. This adaptation is taking place much more quickly here than it did in China and Tibet. For example, when Buddhism went from India to China, it underwent many centuries of integration with an indigenous Chinese culture steeped in Confucian and Taoist values before it became a part of the Chinese way. Here, because of the speed of communication and the rapid pace of our culture, development of a unique North American Buddhism, instead of taking centuries, may become apparent in only decades.

It is not always an easy process, and it has been a struggle for many of us—Buddhist teachers and students alike—to sort out what is valuable and ought to be preserved from what is merely a "container," a structure which could be more suitably reshaped or cast off. Personally, I have struggled with this a great deal and have, at times, become very frustrated. Like a number of other Dharma teachers, I have come close to quitting the Buddhist tradition to do my practice alone, without being a part of organized Buddhism. Here I'm not speaking of the discipline of the *Vinaya* for renunciates, nor of the place for rules of silence and celibacy in practice, nor of precepts, forms of bowing, or ceremonies, nor of the hardships and surrender that are, in fact, valuable parts of spiritual practice. What I have struggled with are the limitations of Buddhism as an organized religion, with the sectarianism and attachments of many of the students and teachers involved, the territoriality, the patriarchy, and the excessive life-denying tendencies of practice which can leave *it*, and some students, disconnected from their hearts.

For me, this same struggle began in Asia. While traveling and practicing there, I discovered that Buddhism is a great religion just like any other—Christianity, Judaism, Hinduism, or Islam. I saw that the majority of Buddhists in Asia do not actually practice. At best, they go to temple devotionally, like to church, once a week for a sermon or to hear a few moral rules or to leave a little money to make some merit for a better birth in the next life. In fact, even among the monasteries of such countries as Thailand, Burma, Sri Lanka, and Japan, I discovered that only a fraction of the monks and nuns actually practice—perhaps only five or ten percent. The rest are priests (some very kindly) who study and learn the scriptures (preserving the tradition, but rarely practicing it), or are school teachers or village elders who perform ceremonies and live a simple existence. Others are monks, who become part of a whole hierarchy of bishops, and archbishops and councils of elders, who are usually more involved in the organization of the religion than the practice of liberation taught by the Buddha.

It was inspiring and refreshing to finally discover that there is a small group of monasteries (perhaps six hundred out of thirty-five thousand) where the actual practices of liberation are kept alive and open to sincere followers of the Buddha's Way. Even after discovering this, it remained necessary to separate the universal teachings from the cultural container, and to overlook the problems and difficulties of certain teachers and practice temples which were "mixed bags," where good practice was mixed with power trips, blind allegiance, or other delusions. Perhaps this sorting out process is always necessary for the maturing of us as spiritual students.

The struggle has been more than worth it, for what has been clear all along is that the heart of the Buddha's awakening is still an island of sanity in a world of delusion and suffering. What an extraordinary vision he had that night under the Bodhi tree. How unutterably marvelous that one person could sit down and see into the truth of life so deeply, with such great clarity, and with such overwhelming compassion, and that this one night's vision would have the power to affect one and a half billion human beings on this earth for twenty-five hundred years. All of us involved in Buddhist practice have been touched by the depth and immediacy of this vision and inspired to continue in the face of both the external and the internal difficulties that are a part of any genuine spiritual path.

In order to have access to these teachings, there were some important lessons I had to learn. One of the first was how to take what's good. I had a teacher in one Burmese monastery, where I practiced intensively for more than a year, who was renowned as a master of certain Vipassana meditation practices. I had come there from the monastery of Ajahn Chah, who was a teacher of impeccable simplicity, straightforwardness, and wisdom. In this new Burmese monastery, the cottage I was given was the most beautiful one, for I was the only Western monk there at the time. Unfortunately, the cottage was also right next to one of the teachers. This teacher was a slob. His robes dragged on the ground, and he smoked cigars. He used to throw rocks at the dogs who were getting into his flower garden and yell at monks who were misbehaving. He spent a great deal of time gossiping with the nuns and the monks. And I was supposed to practice there! I would close my eyes and meditate, and because the instructions he gave me were excellent, after a number of days I began to experience deeper meditations and wonderful results. As the weeks went by, I would close my eyes and meditate, have new, important understandings, and then open them to begin walking meditation. But as soon as I began to walk, I would see this teacher yelling at a monk, or throwing rocks at a dog, or sipping his tea and belching while he smoked his cigar, and think, "I can't learn from such a person. He's a slob. He's not enlightened. I want a better and wiser teacher." Then I would go back and close my eyes and start to sit, and again the fruits of the practice would show themselves; clarity, understanding, and insight would arise. Then I would open my eyes and see him again and wonder what I was doing there. It went back and forth like this for quite a few weeks. I suffered tremendously from the tension.

Finally, it dawned on me that it wasn't necessary to imitate this teacher, that I could simply take from him what was good. He was an excellent guide for inner meditation. He gave me wonderful interviews every day and knew quite well how to fine-tune my Vipassana practice. And as for the rest, I could leave it for him. If he had some level of realization, which he must have had to guide my practice, I could take advantage of it, and if his realization didn't encompass many other parts of his life, so be it. What a relief to learn that one can take what is good and leave the rest.

It will take a great deal of courage on the part of North American Buddhists to face the areas where Buddhism, in its structures and practices, is not working. To make a place for the Dharma that is open and true, we will need to look honestly at such difficult issues as abuse of power and authority, alcohol, sexuality, money, and at our political and social responsibilities. Already upheavals over teacher behavior and abuse have occurred at dozens (if not the majority) of the major Buddhist and Hindu centers in America. If we respond with courage, these very upheavals can focus our attention on those aspects which will need more consciousness and help us build the practice in such areas as sexuality and human relationships, where the expression of Buddhist tradition has been weak or medieval. Similarly, we have to examine ourselves. So many of us come to practice wounded, lonely, or in fear, wanting a loving family as much as enlightenment. That is fine, for we can use the power of practice and the *sangha* to support, heal, and awaken. However, many people also get stuck perpetuating their neuroses in Buddhism itself, abusing practice as a means of escape, using

Buddhism to hide from difficult parts of their lives, trying to create an idealistic world, not dealing with growing and living in the world as mature individuals. The strength of our Dharma will depend on the honesty with which we address these issues and our ability to preserve what is good and leave the rest.

Many of us who have helped bring Vipassana practice to America have initially simplified the practices we've learned and attempted to bring the clearest, most straightforward version of Buddhist practice to the West. We left much of the ritual, Eastern culture, and ceremony behind in Asia. That is not because we don't value it (in fact, I'm a great lover of ritual myself), but we felt it was unnecessary. It seemed to us that for our time and culture the simplicity and straightforwardness of mindfulness practice itself would speak best to the heart of North Americans. And, in fact, the very simplicity of our retreats, without foreign costumes, rituals and bowing, or the necessity of joining an organized church, has appealed to many thousands of people over the years. Naturally, there are those who prefer or benefit from practice which includes more ritual and sacred ceremony. Fortunately, the plurality of Buddhism will provide that, too.

What matters is to find a genuine path of practice and do it fully, to take a practice and go to the very depths of it, which means to go to the very depths of one's own being. We must each find a practice that inspires us and follow it over and over again in whatever fashion makes it come alive in our body, in our heart, and in our mind. Through doing this, we rediscover the greatness of heart, the truth, and the mystery which were discovered by the Buddha and which he declared openly and made available to anyone who wishes to practice.

Such practice, the practice of liberation, is not exclusive. There is no one tradition, one way, or one particular kind of practice which will awaken people. Although systematic practice seems most beneficial for our time, there are many ways to realize truth. Even though D.T. Suzuki was a foremost exponent of Zen, he wrote that many more Buddhists were liberated through the heartfelt practices of Chinese devotional Buddhism than through all of the insight of Ch'an and Zen put together. In the traditional Pali Buddhist scriptures, most of the people who were awakened did not become so through the systematic process of meditation, but were opened by simply hearing the universal truths proclaimed by the Buddha. When the Buddha spoke of the ever-present truth of impermanence, people became enlightened. As the Buddha spoke of the true happiness and freedom which come only from letting go and non-attachment, those beings who listened and were ready were awakened. Yet these truths are universal and are also held in other great traditions; enlightenment or liberation is never the possession of any one great teacher or lineage.

What is wonderful about Buddhism is the clarity and directness of the Buddha's expression of enlightenment and the great number of skillful means which he taught to enable others to realize it. In his forty-five years of teaching, and during the twenty-five hundred years which have followed, a wide range of practices for liberation have been taught, encompassing many lands and many cultures. The Buddha himself taught hundreds of techniques of awareness practice, of concentration meditations, of discipline and surrender. Since his time, the great masters who have followed have elaborated even more fully. Now that these techniques are all coming to America, how can we sort through all of them, how can we understand them as presented in a book such as this?

Some of the history of Buddhism is, unfortunately, also a history of sectarianism. Zen masters put down other Zen masters. Lamas defend the turf of their own Tibetan sects, waging spiritual—if not actual—warfare with one another. The Sri Lankans or Burmese or Thai take a dim view of one another's practice. Buddhism has become divided into greater and lesser, more and more vehicles. This sectarianism has existed since the time of the Buddha himself, and since the day he died there have been sects which have developed based on the realization and expression of different aspects of the Dharma. This is certainly present in current Buddhism. Sectarianism is based on the idea that "our way is best," and its divisiveness is actually rooted in misunderstanding and fear. As the Third Zen Patriarch put it, "Distinctions arise from the clinging needs of the ignorant. There is one Dharma, not many." Or as a contemporary Buddhist poet, Tom Savage, puts it in another way: "Greater vehicle, lesser vehicle, all vehicles will be towed at owner's expense."

The many practices of Buddhism are like paths up a mountain, outwardly different approaches that are appropriate for different personalities and character types. Yet, through skillful guidance and skillful teachers, many of these paths can be used to lead one to universal vision at the summit of the mountain.

A story is told of the Buddha which will help in understanding this. It takes place while the Buddha is standing in a grove at one of his monasteries. A visitor remarks about how tranquil and beautiful the scene is with so many monks in such a composed manner. The Buddha points to his great disciples and the students gathered around them. He notes that there are many ways that people are practicing. Pointing to the wisest of his disciples, Sariputta, he observes, "Those who have the propensity to practice through wisdom are gathered there with my wisest disciple, Sariputta. And there is my disciple Maha Mogallana, foremost in psychic powers. Those whose propensities draw them to use psychic powers as a part of their path to realization are gathered with Maha Mogallana. There is my great disciple Upali, master of the Vinaya and the discipline, and those whose tendencies would benefit by that way of practice are gathered with him. There again is another great disciple and another group of students," and so on. It is not important to judge one practice against another; in fact, this is a detriment to practice. Our task is simply to find a practice that touches our heart and to undertake it in a committed and disciplined way.

Kindness of Heart, Inner Stillness, and Liberating Wisdom

Our understanding of different practices is also helped by seeing the structure of the entire spiritual path, by understanding its essence and how it brings about human happiness and freedom. The essential path taught by the Buddha has three parts to it. The first is *kindness of heart*, which is practiced by a combination of virtue and generosity. The second is *inner stillness* or *concentration*. The third aspect of all Buddhist practice is the development of *liberating wisdom*. All Buddhist practices

are ways of developing virtue that entails the non-harming of other
beings and a generosity of heart. There are ways of developing concentration, steadiness, stillness, clarity or depth of mind; and there are ways
of developing insight or wisdom, a wise relationship to the whole body
and mind, and the freedom that comes from it. These three aspects of
practice themselves are but means to the final freedom of the heart. As
the Buddha himself said, "The purpose of my teaching of the holy life
of the Dharma is not for merit, nor good deeds, nor rapture, nor concentration, nor insight, but the sure heart's release." This and this alone
is the reason for the teaching of the Buddha. The purpose of all these
practices of virtue, kindness, non-harming, generosity, concentration,
steadiness of mind, and the understanding and wisdom that arises, is to
bring us to freedom.

Buddhism has also evolved and changed in its expression of the
Dharma that is its core. As many Buddhist schools developed over the
centuries, they shifted in direction from a dualistic approach to a nondualistic one. The earlier forms of Buddhism expressed the path of practice in primarily a renunciatory way, seeing the body and sexuality as
impure and the mind and spirtitual thoughts as pure, stressing the necessity of withdrawing from the world to embrace a life of solitude as a
monk or a nun, emphasizing the need to get out of the rounds of rebirth
to the cessation of *nirvana*, and so forth. As the nondualistic expression
of Buddhism (which was also taught by the Buddha) grew in predomi-
nance, the emphasis shifted to the interdependence of all life and the
importance of discovering *nirvana* in the midst of *samsara*, or a liberation from greed, hatred, and delusion in this very life and on this very
earth.

This nondualistic spirit of Dharma is particularly important in our
times, in a world of turmoil threatened by the nuclear arms race and
ecological disaster. The mind is able to create such weapons and disas-
ters only when it has split off from the heart and the body. If the mind
were connected with the heart and the body, with this earth, with children, with cycles of nature, it would not be possible to plan abstractly
the mathematics of nuclear arms or the destruction of our ecology. A
nondualistic understanding, and the wisdom of interdependence, com-

passion, and non-greed which it teaches, is essential for the very survival of our earth.

Lama Govinda uses the image of a seed and a tree as a nondualistic way of illustrating the variety of Buddhist practices available and presented in this book. Two thousand five hundred years ago, Siddhartha Gotama, through his extraordinary realization, planted a seed of timeless wisdom and compassion. Over the centuries the seed has grown and produced an enormous and wonderful tree, which has a trunk and branches, flowers and fruit. Some people claim that the roots are the true Buddhism; others claim, "No, it's the fruit or the flowers"; still others say, "No, it's the great trunk of the tree," or "the fruit of Vajrayana," or "the roots of Theravada Buddhism." In fact, all parts of the tree support one another. The leaves give nourishment back to the roots; the roots draw moisture and minerals, bringing nourishment up to the leaves, and they in turn provide support for the flowers and the fruit. It is all part of the whole, and to understand that is to see the creative and dynamic forces that were set loose from the seed of the Buddha's awakening.

Historically, all major religions, including Buddhism, have contained a basic tension—one which persists as Buddhism comes to America. This is the tension between tradition or orthodoxy and adaptation or modernization. Many people involved in Buddhism see it as their purpose and their duty to preserve and sustain the *sutras*, the tradition, the practices just as they were handed down from the time of the Buddha. Other people have found it important to try to adapt Buddhist practice to new cultures, finding skillful means of allowing access to and understanding of the great wisdom of Buddhism, without presenting it in old, ungainly, and inaccessible forms. This tension has been present since the time of the Buddha himself. Since the first council held after the Buddha's death, there have been those great teachers whose main purpose was to preserve, as literally as possible, the practice, style, and teaching of the Buddha, without losing any aspect of the original expression of the truth. At the same time, there have been other masters and teachers who have seen the need to adapt, to translate, to reconnect these teachings. Both of these ways, like the great tree of Lama Govinda, are parts of a whole. The ability to adapt Buddhism without losing its essence is dependent on the depth of the tradition that has been preserved. Yet awakening new followers and gaining support for the preservation and depth of practice must come through the translation and creativity of those who have made practice truly alive in new cultures and new times. Each part depends on the other. The very diversity of views, schools, and teachings is the health of Buddhism, keeping it vital and true.

In the twenty years of my own study, practice, and teaching of Vipassana practice, of Theravada Buddhism, I have come to recognize very clearly that our tradition contains both—masters who emphasize close adherence to the twenty-five hundred years of Buddhist tradition and masters who insist that practice must also be *practical*, as alive today as it was at the time of the Buddha. After helping to found one center (Insight Meditation Society, Barre, Massachusetts) devoted almost exclusively to traditional retreat practice, we are now founding a center with a broader purpose and are becoming part of a large community in California. Spirit Rock Center (Insight Meditation West in Marin County, California) will offer teachings that balance the traditional and integrative aspects of practice. On the one hand, Insight Meditation West will be a center that preserves a depth of practice through ten-day and three-month retreats, traditional study, a monastery, and so forth. On the other hand, the key need to integrate practice into our times will also be addressed. The experience of sitting a meditation retreat may be compelling and wonderful, but now how do we actually live it? How do we bring not just our minds to the practice, but also make that practice alive in our hearts and in our bodies as well? To address this question, at our new center we will also have teachings on right livelihood and service, on right speech and communication, as well as more emphasis on the development and expression of compassion in all aspects of life—through Buddhist peace work, through family life, through ecology. As in many other Buddhist centers, it is becoming clear to us that our practice is not just sitting, not just study, not just belief, but encompasses how we actually live, how well we love, and how much we can let go of our small self and care for this earth and all beings.

As Buddhism comes to North America, a wonderful new process is happening. All of us, as lay people, as householders, want what was mostly the special dispensation of monks in Asia: the real practice of the Buddha. American lay people are not content to go and hear a sermon once a week or to make merit by leaving gifts at a meditation center. We, too, want to *live* the realizations of the Buddha and bring them into our hearts, our lives, and our times. This is why so many Americans have been drawn to the purity of intensive Vipassana retreats, or to the power of Zen *sesshin*, or even to the one hundred thousand prostrations and three-year retreats of the Vajrayana tradition. Somehow we have an intuitive sense of the potential of human freedom and the heart of basic goodness, the timeless discovery of the Buddha.

We are drawn not just to study it and understand it, but to practice it, realize it, and live it in our lives. Practice always involves a great deal of struggle, for it means confronting ourselves, our fears, our territoriality, and our need for security. When we practice with devotion and a love for truth, we can each find the timeless freedom and compassion of the Buddha in our very own heart. To do this skillfully, we can use the raft of Buddhism to the shore of liberation, but we must never mistake the raft for the shore. At its best, there are elements of questioning, investigation, integrity, and freshness in North American Buddhism, which Zen master Suzuki-Roshi observed when he said:

> Here in America we cannot define Zen Buddhists the same way we do in Japan. American students are not priests and yet not completely laymen. I understand it this way: that you are not priests is an easy matter, but that you are not exactly laymen is more difficult. I think you are special people and want some special practice that is not exactly priest's practice and not exactly layman's practice. You are on your way to discovering some appropriate way of life.[1]

While teaching and practicing in North America, I am also learning from the cross-fertilization of Buddhist traditions and from the privilege of having access to great masters in the Tibetan and Zen traditions. Even though my own heart has found its home in the simplicity of

1. Suzuki-Roshi. *Zen Mind, Beginners's Mind*. (New York: John Weatherhill, Inc., 1986), p. 133.

mindfulness practice, I discover myself teaching this "*Hinayana* practice with a *Mahayana* mind." Over the years I've shifted my teaching from an initial emphasis on effort and striving to one of opening and healing. Many students come to practice wounded, conditioned to closing off and hating parts of themselves. For them, striving perpetuates their problems. Instead, by awakening the heart of kindness and inspiring a love of truth, there arises a very deep motivation for practice. This heart-centered motivation brings together loving kindness, healing, strength, and clarity in an interdependent way. Understanding and practicing with this spirit of interdependence brings the deepest realization and keeps alive in us the awakening of the Buddha.

I do not want to be too idealistic. There are many problems that Buddhist communities must face—unhealthy structures, unwise practices, and so forth. Still, something new is happening on this continent. Buddhism is being deeply affected by the spirit of democracy, by feminization, by ecological values, and by the integration of lay life. A North American vehicle is being created. Already this vehicle draws on the best of the roots, the trunk, the branches, the leaves, the blossoms, and the fruits—all the parts of Buddhism; and it is beginning to draw them together in a wise and supportive whole.

Let me end with a story that illustrates this. Several years ago we had the privilege of a visit to the Insight Meditation Society by His Holiness, the sixteenth Gyalwa Karmapa, head of the Kagyu sect of Tibetan Buddhism. His Holiness Karmapa came during one of our three-month retreats. He sat on a gilded throne in our meditation hall, surrounded by one hundred and fifty yogis and students to whom he gave a Dharma talk and ceremonial blessing. As a teacher of the retreat, I sat in the front row next to a sixty-eight-year-old woman from Calcutta named Dipa Ma Barua, who is one of the most highly attained and realized yogis in Theravada Buddhism. She was a visiting master who had developed the highest levels of insight practice and all the great concentration practices of compassion and loving kindness. Because she did not speak English, as Karmapa's Tibetan was being translated into English by *his* translators, that English was in turn translated into Bengali by *hers*.

After hearing a wonderful talk by Karmapa on the Buddhist Four

Dipa-Ma visiting Insight Meditation Society, Barre, Massachusetts, in the fall of 1980. Photo courtesy of Jacqueline Mandell.

Noble Truths and on the great teachings of compassion and emptiness,
Dipa Ma turned to me, put her hand on my knee, and exclaimed with
delight, "He's a Buddhist!" As an Indian Buddhist she had been to
Bodh Gaya for twenty years, lived right across the street from the Tibetan temple, and had seen tens of thousands of Tibetan pilgrims and
Tibetan lamas at the Bodhi tree in India during the many years of her
practice; yet she had never heard their teachings in translation and had
never really understood that they, too, were Buddhists.

The Tibetans, the Burmese, and the Japanese have been hidden from
one another for centuries through the heights of mountainous terrain,

through the barriers of their cultures, and by the shields of their languages. These traditions, and masters such as Chogyam Trungpa, Rinpoche, and Suzuki-Roshi, or His Holiness Karmapa and Dipa Ma, or Joshu Sasaki-Roshi and Kalu, Rinpoche (who as the story goes met at an airport in Arizona one year without their translators and could only sit there, hold hands, and smile at one another for an hour), are finally meeting one another in the great melting pot of our North American cultures. And now a new generation of North American teachers is continuing the process.

In this book and in the West we are seeing the awakening of the Buddha, and the statues of the Buddha are smiling very broadly, with the wisdom of Tibet, India, Japan, Thailand, Burma, and America all joined in. For every practitioner it is a privilege to be a part of this process and a wonderful adventure to see what we will make of it.

Jack Kornfield was trained as a monk in the monasteries of Thailand, India, and Burma; for the past fourteen years he has been teaching Vipassana meditation retreats throughout the world. A founding teacher of the Insight Meditation Society and of Spirit Rock Center, he is a psychologist, a father, and an author whose books include Living Buddhist Masters *(Boulder: Prajna Press, 1983),* A Still Forest Pool, *with Paul Breiter (Wheaton: Theosophical Publishing House, 1985), and* Seeking the Heart of Wisdom, *with Joseph Goldstein (Boston: Shambala, 1987). He currently resides in Woodacre, California.*

A Lotus Blooms in the Mouth of the Dragon

This meal is the labor of countless beings; let us remember their toil.

 In Zen temples and centers around the globe, these words are recited at mealtimes, inviting followers of the Way to reflect upon the interdependence of all living beings. The teeming earth nurtures seed planted by farmers who have tilled the soil with machines made by other human hands and minds. Others harvest it, while still others package it, market it, purchase it, prepare it, serve it, and so on. This teaching comes to mind in connection with this book. I do not think of myself as its author, for in truth it has been the labor of countless beings. What I hoped to do was to provide the Buddhist community in North America with an opportunity to write its own book, to collaborate in representing itself to the non-Buddhist community and to *itself* as well, for it is a sad fact that there is little awareness among Buddhists of the practices of other Buddhist traditions, and precious little effort towards communication among the *sanghas*.

In addition, the sheer proliferation of teachings, approaches, and styles is often bewildering to people who are just becoming interested in Buddhism and who wish to know which of the paths is most suitable for them. So one of the intentions of this book is to bridge the communications gap among Buddhist *sanghas*—as well as between Buddhists and the larger community—by unraveling some of the mystery surrounding the practices of each tradition.

What has struck me in the course of this work is the extent to which Buddhist meditation has taken root on this continent. Twenty years ago when I first went in search of a Zen master, there was only a handful of centers, concentrated in the bigger cities on each coast. To my knowledge there were none in Colorado. Today there are more than twenty

in this state alone, and on beginners nights and at introductory workshops they are packed. Glance through the listings in this book and you
will find *dharmadhatus*, Zendos and sitting groups, and lamas, monks,
and lay teachers tucked away in the most unlikely places. Kearney, Nebraska, Eureka Springs, Arkansas, and Ouray, Colorado, come to mind.
And Des Moines, Iowa, and Reno, and Cleveland, and Tulsa, and
Nashville, not to mention Kinmount, Ontario, Whitehorse, Yukon Ter-
ritories, and Anchorage, Alaska.

There is, I believe, a mistaken notion abroad, primarily among the
larger centers that flourished during the seventies but have since fallen
on leaner times, that Dharma on this continent is already in decline.
This could not be further from the truth. Dharma has come home quite
literally, and one is no longer compelled to *leave* home in search of a
true teacher or a vital practice center. The Buddhist "movement" has
become a *regional* phenomenon. It is pervasive, and it is quietly trans-
forming our North American cultures. *This* is the Golden Age of Buddhism! Right *here*! Right *now*! Evidence: a few weeks ago on Larry
King's nationally syndicated talk show, a caller phoned in to ask guest
Ralph Nader if he had read Roshi Philip Kapleau's book on vegetarianism and the non-harming of animals. What occurred to me while
listening spellbound in my car was that neither host nor guest felt con-
strained to define Zen to themselves or to the national listening audi-
ence. It was simply taken for granted that everybody knows what it is.
And just today I came upon an article in *Time* magazine about a nonsectarian meditation club in the Pentagon, the goal of which is "to link
enough individual 'peace shields' to protect humanity by their unified
force." "Love," says club president Edward Winchester, "is the ultimate
first strike capability."[1] When Dharma hits the late-night talk show air-
waves and reaches the inner sanctums of the Pentagon, you can be certain that the lotus has blossomed in the mouth of the dragon.

Actually, the listings in this book constitute only a fraction of the true
number of Buddhist groups in North America. I have limited the listings to those groups which actively promote, teach, or at least encour-

1. "Peace Shield at the Pentagon, a new SDI." *Time*, 131 (25 April 1988).

age the practice of meditation. For every meditation center listed here, there is another that for some reason was not included. For example, although a surprising number of ethnic meditation temples did respond to our questionnaire, a greater percentage did not, perhaps out of shyness due to limited facility with the English language, or else out of the conviction that their principal duty is to their own ethnic constituencies. As the Asian minorities become acculturated, this situation will no doubt change, and these changes will be reflected in future editions of this book. The potential for the expansion of the Buddha's teaching is limitless here, but for now we must respect the wishes of our Asian brothers and sisters in the Dharma.

Another lacuna exists in the listings for Theravada centers. Although there are comparatively fewer of them listed herein, this does not necessarily reflect the true picture. Vipassana practice in its native (Asian) context tends to be something of a solitary enterprise. Here on "Turtle Island," practitioners attend group retreats, often in rented facilities under the guidance of teachers who have been invited to lead them, and then go home to practice on their own. A network has arisen of loosely structured Vipassana meditation groups who meet in the homes of like minded individuals. Most of these aggregations are not aligned formally with any one teacher or center, and they "arise and cease" in fairly fluid fashion. Information about them can be found in an excellent publication called *Inquiring Mind: A Bi-annual Journal of the Vipassana Community* (P.O. Box 9999, North Berkeley Station, Berkeley, CA 94709). *Inquiring Mind* regularly features an updated list of informal sitting groups throughout the United States and Canada, and since it is published bi-annually, it is a much more reliable source of information on the subject than this book could ever be.

In addition, many of the principal centers in the Mahayana, Vajrayana, and Buddhayana traditions have information on similar sitting groups which practice according to their respective teaching lines. Please write to them. They will be happy to furnish you with names, addresses, and phone numbers.

The inspiration to create this book came when I was studying meditation in the monasteries of Thailand in 1986. My first week there, confused and lost, I happened upon an invaluable little volume entitled *A Brief Guide to the Meditation Temples of Thailand*, written by one Sunno Bhikkhu (who turned out to be Jack Kornfield in a former incarnation as a monk).[2] Clearly, a need exists on this continent for a similar guide-book, and much gratitude is due to Jack, not only for the initial in-spiration, but for the ongoing support both he and all of the Insight Meditation Society and Insight Meditation West teachers have given this project.

A further influence on the structure and content of this book came from Philip Kapleau-Roshi of the Rochester Zen Center, a redoubtable old boatman in whose ship many have crossed over. Roshi Kapleau's highly acclaimed book *The Three Pillars of Zen* provided the inspiration for soliciting the retreat narratives. The narratives themselves were pro-vided by practitioners of every lineage from all over North America and were contributed free of charge. In fact, all who worked on this book did so out of the kindness and generosity of their hearts. In the tradition of *Dana* that has sustained the Buddha's teaching in its long and un-blemished history, all authors' profits accrued from the sale of this book will go towards the establishment of meditation retreat scholarships or other Dharma related charities. A deep bow of gratitude to all who submitted essays and photographs.

Before leaving the subject of inspiration, let me acknowledge a debt to the Ven. Eido Tai Shimano-Roshi, a Dharma friend who's "long-distance-*Ronin*-disciple" it has been my priviledge to be. It was this shining monk who some twenty years ago taught me how to sit. And though I have not been a formal student of his for many years, he has displayed an uncanny knack for popping up in my life at critical mo-ments and pointing out the direction I need to take, often long before I am ready to accept his advice. Several years ago Roshi suggested that I visit every Dharma center in the country. "Investigate them thor-oughly," he advised, "Do Dharma combat." (He had, I am sure, his own reasons for suggesting this course of action, but I think that he wanted me to get the spiritual wanderlust out of my system once and

---

2. Sunno Bhikkhu. *A Brief Guide to the Meditation Temples of Thailand*. World Federa-tion of Buddhists Book Series, Number 44.

for all.) I went to Thailand instead, but here I am, three years later, having done exactly as he suggested. . . . Well, sort of.
Roshi-Sama, old friend . . .
Hands together palm to palm,
Gratitude knowing no bounds.

"Oh Buddhas and Bodhisattvas, Abiding in All Directions . . ."

It is often said that once you truly embark upon the Path to Liberation, Buddhas and Bodhisattvas will spring up on every hand to aid you. Having set out upon the path of "book writing *samadhi*," vast armies of Buddhas and Bodhisattvas have indeed stepped forward. Of the countless beings who have contributed time and energy towards the completion of this book, here are a few of whom I am aware.

Joye Smith has given magnanimously of her time and expertise, initially helping to formulate and produce the questionnaire and, on the other end of the process, helping to input the data onto computer disks, a nightmare that she has borne with grace and good humor.

Very special thanks as well to the Venerable Sisters of the Chan Nhu Buddhist Pagoda, of Lakewood, Colorado. Sister Martha Dharmapali and Sister Nora both helped to prepare the data for input, proof the copy, stamp envelopes, make suggestions, confirm the existence of elusive Dharma centers, and so on, always cheerfully and efficiently. Sister Martha contributed one of the first-person accounts in the Theravada section. Sister Nora, by the way, makes a mean sour dough bread; she gave me a lovely batch of starter—a most excellent gift.

Freddi Bosco, a Denver poet, newspaper essayist, and pal for over twenty years, sat with me at his kitchen table night after night sifting through some fifteen hundred names and addresses of Buddhist practice centers, temples, libraries, and schools, an Augean task that simply could not have been accomplished without his kind assistance.

Thanks are also due to Judy Cross for innumerable favors to this project, not the least of which was the donation of a sizable chunk of her spring vacation to type the Vajrayana narratives. And I am indebted to Nicole Langley (of Tri-Tek) for her computer expertise and willingness to drop everything and jump in at the last minute to help us meet our deadline.

Pat Meyer, a long time friend and Dharma compatriot, has helped in countless ways. Her sound advice throughout this project has done much to define the scope—and shape the content—of this book. Pat also contributed the introductory article on Mahayana Buddhism.

The following Bodhisattvas acted as contact persons in major cities around the United States and Canada:

Bruce Alexander—Vancouver, British Columbia
Lisa Bardwell—Ann Arbor, Michigan
Ven. Koten Benson—Vancouver, British Columbia
Rev. Nobuyoshi Fukushima—Liaison for the ethnic Soto Zen temples of Hawaii
Ven. Zenson Gifford—Toronto, Ontario
Lou Hart—Northern California
Marge Jayne—Portland, Oregon
Charlotte Kramer—Atlanta, Georgia
Ven. Paul Anzan Lee-Sensei—Ottawa, Ontario
Mimi M. Maduro—Portland, Oregon
Kamala Masters—Maui, Hawaii
Donna McKintyre—Vajradhatu network of affiliate centers
Wally Muszynski—Chicago, Illinois
Rosalie Post—Boston, Massachusetts
Loren Rivers—Honolulu, Hawaii
Dr. Christopher Robinson—Edmonton, Alabama
Virginia Robinson—Anchorage, Alaska
Bob Ryan—Chicago, Illinois
Maggie Seeley—Santa Fe, New Mexico
Ven. Dharman Shakya—Boston, Massachusetts
Kris Stenzel—New York, New York
Greg Tzinberg—Seattle, Washington
Andy Weaver—Liaison for Karma Thegsum Choling affiliates
Terry Yamada—Southern California

Deeply felt appreciation and gratitude to all who submitted first-person retreat narratives, and to those who wrote the introductory articles at the beginning of each chapter. Their names are listed in the table of contents and in the by-lines of their articles.

Special thanks to my editors at John Muir Publications, Steven Cary and Ken Luboff, to designer Joanna Hill, and to copy editor Ann Mason.

The following helped in ways sundry, great and small: American Buddhist Congress, Jamie Baraz, Jim Bedard, Paul Briggs, John Bradley, Bruce Burkhardt, Lani Carroll, Ven. Heng Chau-Bhikshu, Frederic Cloyd, Annee Corey, Linda Cressman-Burrill, Minke DeVosse, Mark Diament, Patsy Dixon, Tony Duff, Christer Ekstrom, Bea Ferigno, Rick Fields, Marcey Fink, Terri Fish, Barbara Gates, Nina Hagen, Ruth-Inge Heinze, Deirdre Henneman, Amy Henry, Ven. Danan Henry, Judy Hiatt, Ed Hill, Susan Horigan, Jonathan Hulsh, Ven. Anek Imphitak-Bhikkhu, Bill Karellis, Paul Kay, Arnold Kottler, Sister Kho Chan Nhu, Mr. Kitti, Jack Kornfield, Kim Long, Tim Lyons, Jacqueline Mandell, Susan Madden, Nicolee Jikyo Miller, Cindy and Sam Morreale, Sherwyn Morreale, Gina Metzger, Charles Nash, Wes Nisker, Rev. Kanya Okamoto, Valerie Pachini, Ann Palm, Ph.D., Dr. Chuen Phangcham, Sam Rose, Brenda Ryan, David Sanford, San Francisco Zen Center Staff, Tom and Cissy Severance, Bob and Donna Schrei, Eric and Helen Shaffer, Ven. Heng Shun-Bhikshu, Marla Silver, Marilynne Solomon, Jackqueline Stockin, Ven. Ajahn Sumedho-Bhikkhu, Ven. U Surruttama-Bhikkhu, Ven. Pirom Thammapiramo-Bhikkhu, Vajradhatu Computer Services, Carl Varady, Ven. Vivekananda-Bhikkhu, Peter Volz, Hank and Marlene Wilhite.

"Lotus in the Fire: Prison, Practice, and Freedom" by John Daido Loori first appeared in *The Ten Directions* 7, no. 2 (Fall/Winter 1986), the newspaper of Zen Center, Los Angeles.

"Graduating from Buddhism: An Interfaith Retreat with Thich Nhat Hanh" by Christopher Reed, was previously published in the *Buddhist Peace Fellowship Newsletter* 9, no. 2-3 (Fall 1987).

"East Moving West: Theravada Buddhism Grows in Great Britain" by Amaravati Buddhist Community first appeared in *Inquiring Mind* (Winter 1988 issue), copyright © by Amaravati Publications.

We wish to thank all of these excellent publications for their cooperation in allowing us to reprint these articles.

And finally, to all who took the time to fill out the questionnaire and to those of you who wrote letters of encouragement, many thanks.

"May all sentient beings enjoy happiness and the root of happiness.
Be Free from suffering and the root of suffering.
May they not be separated from the great Happiness devoid of suffering.
May they dwell in the great equanimity free from passion and aggression and ignorance."[3]

DON MORREALE
Conspiracy of Silence Productions

3. From the "Bodhisattva Vows for Mahayana Students," translated by the Nalanda Translation Committee and recited at centers affiliated with Vajradhatu.

The Four Noble Truths and the Eightfold Path

BY DON MORREALE

Shortly after his great Enlightenment under the Bodhi tree, the Buddha delivered a sermon to five colleagues in the Deer Park at Sarnath. Known as the "Turning of the Wheel of the Dharma," the discourse contains all the major tenets of the Tathagata's teaching. Despite differences in approach, technique, and style, Buddhists everywhere agree on these basic points of doctrine.

The Four Noble Truths

I. Dukkha: The Truth of Suffering

All life is suffering. To be sure, the word "*dukkha*" means suffering in the ordinary sense of the term, but it also carries with it a variety of connotations which amplify this commonly held interpretation. *Dukkha* means literally "a wheel not running true on its axis" and suggests discomfort, disharmony, dissatisfaction. "Birth, aging, sickness, and death are painful," proclaimed the World Honored One. "Enduring what you hate, separation from what you love, and cravings which are not satisfied are all equally painful. In short, any condition which springs from attachment is suffering."

II. Samudhaya: The Truth of the Origin of Suffering

Suffering is rooted in *Tanha*—thirst, desire, craving. There are, according to the Buddha, three fundamental objects of desire. These are:

1) Gama Tanha   Desire for sensual gratification.
It is this grasping after satisfaction that leads one to rebirth, for in

the end all thirst must be slaked, all desires fulfilled—whether in this life or the next.

2) *Bhava Tanha*   The desire to exist.

3) *Vibhava Tanha*   The desire not to exist.

III. Nirodha: The Truth of the Cessation of Suffering

There is a way out of this dilemma. Simply stated, your suffering will cease as soon as you stop craving. Let go of desire for anything whatsoever, whether it be food, wealth, fame, companionship, or sensual attachment. The objects of desire are not at issue; it is the *function* of craving that must be eradicated. The Path to Liberation is much different from ordinary ways of being in the world, since it is not a question of getting and keeping, but of giving and letting go—not a grasping fist, but an open hand.

IV. Magga: The Path Which Leads to the Cessation of Suffering

Having diagnosed the disease, the Great Physician now prescribes the course of treatment. This is the Noble Eightfold Path, also called the "Middle Way," since it avoids the extremes of self-indulgence and self-mortification.[1]

Panna or *Prajna* (Wisdom)
1) Right Understanding
2) Right Aspiration

Sila (Moral Integrity)
3) Right Speech
4) Right Action or Conduct
5) Right Livelihood

Samadhi (Concentration, or One Pointedness of Mind)
6) Right Effort
7) Right Mindfulness
8) Right Meditation

1. For a more complete explanation of the Four Noble Truths and the Eightfold Path, please read *What the Buddha Taught* by Walpola Rahula (New York: Grove Press, 1974).

Although the conventional translation for the Pali word *Samma* ("right") has been used here, in fact it has the richer connotations of "complete, balanced, harmonious, and perfect."

This, then, is the essential teaching of the Buddha.

PART I

Theravada

The Path of Mindfulness

Theravada: Thus Have I Heard

BY BHIKKHU SURUTTAMA

With this direct seeing and knowing that everything is imperma-
nent—arising only to instantaneously dissolve—comes an equally
deep knowledge of the unsatisfactoriness of conditioned reality, its
inability to deliver on its promises, its incapacity to provide any
kind of lasting satisfaction or permanent happiness, and its lack of
any secure refuge.

What the Buddha Taught:
The Dhamma—Path to Liberation

It is said that the Buddha looked upon the world and saw people everywhere striving to be happy, wanting and working to be free from suffering, but unclear about how to realize these goals. He saw that in their confusion and ignorance, they were pursuing paths which were incapable of providing the lasting satisfaction, happiness, and peace that they sought. He saw people pursuing paths that would ultimately end in suffering. Thus, out of great compassion, he began to teach.

For forty-five years he taught the Dhamma, the laws and principles by which the universe operates—the means by which happiness and suffering come into being, and the truth of suffering and the means by which one can put an end to it. He taught the paths which lead to worldly happiness: happiness in relationships, health and long life, success, wealth, beauty, respect, power, knowledge, and a happy rebirth. He also taught about the paths which lead to suffering: to worldly failure, failed relationships, illness, ill repute, ignorance, poverty, premature death, and to an unhappy rebirth.

The Buddha further taught the paths which lead to specific states of

extraordinary consciousness, such as states of complete unity and oneness, states pervaded with infinite love and unbounded compassion;
states of infinite consciousness and a higher, more silent, and empty
domain of Nothingness—spaces of unimaginable peace. He taught all
of this out of his own direct knowledge and experience, not as theory;
and he taught the specific practical means by which to attain these
results.

Because the Buddha's teaching was grounded in direct knowledge
and experience, he knew, too, the one essential flaw and failure of each
of these realms and the kinds of happiness possible, even the highest
states of extraordinary consciousness. What he saw and knew is that
they are and always will be impermanent. Because they are conditional,
born out of and dependent on conditions, they will all end. He thus
knew that they were incapable of providing lasting happiness. He saw
further that the happiness they do provide often leads to craving and
attachment which, in turn, lead to more suffering when conditions
change.

Thus, seeing the suffering in the world, the Buddha made known, in
precise detail, the Path leading to the complete end of all suffering, the
Path of Liberation. "Just as all of the waters in all the oceans have but
one taste, the taste of salt," he declared, "so, too, all of my teachings
have but one taste, the taste of Liberation." He strongly encouraged
people to embark upon this Path which leads to the end of suffering
through the permanent uprooting of craving, aversion, and delusion
from the heart/mind. He made known, in precise detail, a direct and
practical method by which this can be accomplished—the Eightfold
Path of Liberation. The eight factors which are the Path can be grouped
into three aspects: 1) *Sila* (virtue, integrity) includes the factors of Right
Action, Right Speech, and Right Livelihood; 2) *Samadhi* (concentration, meditation) includes the factors of Right Effort, Right Mindfulness, and Right Concentration; and 3) *Panna* (wisdom) includes the
factors of Right View and Right Thought or Aspiration.

It takes but little reflection to realize how extraordinary it is to even
hear of the possibility of permanently freeing the heart/mind from all
greed, aversion, and delusion in this life, thereby putting an end to all
suffering. Such a possibility never occurs to most people, much less the

learning of a precise method for doing so. To hear of the opportunity for such a Liberation opens a whole new domain of possibility, an entirely new perspective from which to live one's life.

It is precisely this Liberation that is the final goal of the Theravada teaching and practice. Essential in the Path to this Liberation is Vipassana/Satipatthana[1]—insight meditation, established in the four domains of mindfulness.

The four domains of mindfulness that lead to Liberation are: 1) the body 2) feeling (pleasant, unpleasant, and neutral feeling, both physical and mental) 3) types of consciousness, and 4) types of mental and physical phenomena. Mindfulness in other domains, e.g., business, relationships, or family, can enhance performance and bring happiness in those domains without necessarily leading to Liberation. The complete practice of Vipassana is outlined in the *Maha Satipatthana Sutta*.[2]

Origins of Theravada

First Great Council of the Theras

Following his decease and *Parinibbana*,[3] the Buddha's five hundred foremost living disciples, all *Arahants* (fully enlightened beings), convened as the First Great Council of the *Theras* (elders—from which comes the word Theravada). The Venerable Maha-Kassapa presided over the Council. The purpose of the Council was to preserve the entire body of Buddha's teachings with accuracy and precision. For this rea-

---

1. The terms "*Vipassana/Satipatthana*" are from Pali, the language in which the Buddha's teachings were originally recorded. Because there is no adequate English translation of these terms, and because they so precisely describe the method, I have chosen to retain and use the Pali throughout this essay. The same is true for certain other key terms, such as "Dhamma," the Sanskrit spelling of which is "Dharma."

2. For a translation and explanation of the practice outlined in this *sutta*, see the Ven. Nyanaponika Thera's outstanding book *The Heart of Buddhist Meditation* (York Beach: Samuel Weiser, Inc., 1965). It is also available from the Vihara Book Service (an excellent source for Dhamma books). For books by mail, write: Vihara Book Service, Washington Buddhist Vihara; 5017 16th Street N.W.; Washington, D.C. 20011. They publish an extensive free catalogue of their books-in-stock.

3. *Parinibbana* means complete Liberation from the cycle of birth, death, and suffering through the final extinguishing of its causes.

son, Ven. Ananda, the Buddha's faithful attendant, was chosen to answer Maha-Kassapa's questions about the Buddha's discourses. Ananda was uniquely qualified for this role. By agreement with the Buddha, he was either present at or given a summary of the Buddha's discourses. Further, the Buddha acknowledged Ananda as being The Guardian of the Dhamma and among the foremost of his disciples in perfection of memory and in precise and intuitive grasp of how to correctly teach Dhamma.

The entire body of knowledge preserved by the First Great Council of the Theras, plus its later commentary, comprises over twenty thousand pages. Known as the Pali Canon, it is an extraordinarily complete and precise body of knowledge which includes a vast and deep range of individual teachings, methods, practices, and *yanas* (vehicles)[4] for monks, nuns, and lay people. It is this body of knowledge and commentary that is the foundation and guide for the Theravada.[5]

Primary Significance Given to the Vinaya

The *Vinaya* is the Buddha's teaching of the behavior and speech most conducive to the permanent uprooting of all greed, aversion, and delusion. It is formally expressed as the *bhikkhus'* (monks') rules and guidelines for living. The *Vinaya* formulates a way of living that makes the *bhikkhu's* life vibrantly alive and authentic, creating the greatest possibility for complete Liberation (Arahantship) in this life.

It is sometimes mistakenly assumed that the *Vinaya* is not critically important to lay people, since only *bhikkhus* are expected to fully conform to the *Vinaya's* teachings. The Buddha regarded the living of the

4. Following the Buddha's strong encouragement to put an end to the cycle of birth and death, many people in Theravada pursue the Path to complete Liberation in this very life. Some monks, nuns, and lay people in the Theravada tradition, however, postpone their Liberation for countless aeons, aspiring to become Teaching Buddha's themselves. These aspire to the Path of the *Bodhisattva*, using the vehicle in the Theravada tradition known as the *Mahabodhiyana*, the Vehicle of the Great Enlightenment (the Enlightenment of a Teaching Buddha).

5. A complete English translation of the main works of the Pali Canon, with some commentary also translated, is available from the Pali Text Society. Translations of individual works, from publishers such as the Buddhist Publication Society, Kandy, Sri Lanka, are available through the Vihara Book Service.

Vinaya as being the protector of the integrity and accuracy of the Dhamma after he was gone; and he said that Dhamma/Vinaya would be the teacher to his followers then. He therefore emphasized that the length of the life of the Dhamma and Path to Liberation is dependent upon the *Vinaya*. He spoke of disrespect and disregard for the *Vinaya*, by renunciates and lay people, as being one of the key causes for the disappearance of the authentic Dhamma and for the arising of a counterfeit Dhamma.[6] Thus, when asked by the Ven. Maha-Kassapa, "Which shall we recite first, the discourses of the Buddha or the *Vinaya?*" the Enlightened beings of the First Great Council agreed that, "Because it is the life-blood of the Dispensation of Dhamma, let us recite the *Vinaya* first."[7]

Teachings Are for All People

The Buddha's teachings in Theravada are for all people—monks, nuns, laymen and laywomen alike—whether living in seclusion in forests or caves, or living in the midst of the city devoting their lives to service and opening the doors of Liberation to others. Since the time of the Buddha, through the commitment of many teachers, the teachings have been made extensively available to people in all walks of life and in many nations.

Theravada has never been either an exclusively monastic tradition or an exclusively lay tradition, but has come forward throughout history, in India and in Southeast Asia, as a Dhamma family, with renunciates and householders living in harmony and mutual appreciation and support. The essential discourse on Satipatthana, (mindfulness meditation), for instance, was said to be first given by the Buddha to both renunciates and lay people of the Kuru village; and even today,

6. See the Buddha's discourse on "False Dhamma," recorded in the *Samyutta Nikaya* 16, p. 13. A very readable English translation is available from Vihara Book Service (see above) under the title of *Samyutta Nikaya Anthology*, Wheel Series, no.s 318—321, *Samyutta Nikaya* 3, pp. 25, 26, 99. See also the outstanding book *The Splendor of Enlightenment* (Bangkok: Mahamakut Rajavidyalaya Press, 1976) for several powerful extracts from the Buddha's discourses on these issues. (Available from Vihara Book Service.)

7. The authority chosen in the Council to recite the Buddha's teachings of the *Vinaya* was the Ven. Upali, acknowledged by the Buddha as being the most accomplished in his complete and penetrating grasp of the *Vinaya*.

though many monks and nuns meditate and teach meditation and Dhamma, the overwhelming majority of meditators in Burma, Sri Lanka, and Thailand are lay people. The tradition of householders teaching Dhamma also extends back to the time of the Buddha.

In establishing Dhamma in the West, it is important to understand how Dhamma is lived in the East. Professors Robinson and Johnson describe this well in their book *Buddhist Religion*:

> Recently, excellent empirical studies have described the Buddhist religion as it exists today in the Theravada countries of Southeast Asia. . . . Buddhism exists as a religious practice in which lay and monastic Buddhists take equal part. By studying this empirical material, we see that Buddhism has a life of its own in the practical everyday world. . . . We should keep in mind the whole religious life of Buddhists.[8]

This integration of the Dhamma into daily life in the East is important. This is especially so in light of the tendency in the West to fragment the Dhamma, taking only what is culturally familiar. To do so is to miss the opportunity to realize the power of Dhamma as an integrated whole, with mutual empowerment between renunciates and householders.

The Importance of the Monastic Opportunity to Householders

The Training of Teachers   Since the time of the Buddha, there have been lay people who have renounced the household life and lived their entire lives as *bhikkhus* under the *Vinaya*. By supporting these renunciates and the monastic way of life, householders have provided themselves with Dhamma and meditation teachers who have thus been able to devote twenty, thirty, forty, or more years totally to the study, practice, and mastery of Dhamma and meditation. Because of the lay support, and because of the willingness and commitment of these renunciates to live fully under the *Vinaya* throughout their lives, devoting themselves singlemindedly to Dhamma and meditation, they have been able to teach and to maintain the channel of continuity that has pre-

---

8. Richard H. Robinson and Willard L. Johnson, *Buddhist Religion: A Historical Introduction* (Belmont: Wadsworth Publishing Co., 1982).

served the Buddha's teachings and the Path to Liberation for more than twenty-five hundred years.

One well-known recent example of this, and of the impact that such mutual support can have, is the combined work of a committed group of householders and the late Ven. Mahasi Sayadaw and his successor, the Ven. U Pandita Sayadaw. The householders created a meditation center in Rangoon, Burma, and invited Mahasi Sayadaw, a *bhikkhu* and outstanding meditation instructor of our time, to become its spiritual head. Ven. Mahasi Sayadaw accepted responsibility for the center and its growth; opened the center to foreigners, including Westerners; and further inspired the creation of a network of over three hundred additional centers in Burma, as well as many centers abroad. The Ven. U Pandita Sayadaw had the primary responsibility for training meditation teachers and for guiding meditators, and between 1949 and 1988 the centers in Burma alone are estimated to have trained approximately two million householders in insight meditation.

This is but one of many examples of the cooperation between *bhikkhus* and householders throughout Southeast Asia, the kind of cooperation that is now beginning in America; working together, they preserve and make available in-depth practice and training in Dhamma. Seeking such in-depth training, increasing numbers of Western meditators and meditation teachers, living as *bhikkhus*, nuns, and lay meditators, are undertaking practice and study at monasteries in Burma, Thailand, and Sri Lanka. And many Asian *bhikkhus* from these countries, as well as from Cambodia and Laos, have quietly begun to teach and to establish monasteries in America.

The Opportunity for Householders to Ordain   The Buddha is said to have declared the opportunity to ordain and live as a *bhikkhu* under the *Vinaya* to be one of the five most rare and precious opportunities throughout time, and he opened this possibility to all classes and races of people without distinction. In supporting a monastic practice, lay people have kept open and easily available to themselves the opportunity to become monks or nuns at some point in their lives—either for short periods, or for their entire lives. Throughout Southeast Asia, almost all men, and many women, have taken advantage of this opportunity to ordain and have taken robes for varying periods of time.

Whether we in America will have this option will depend on whether we clearly understand its nature, and on whether we create and protect it for ourselves and for others.

One might mistakenly think that such an opportunity could only exist in Asia; but in England, householders and an American *bhikkhu* trained in Thailand, the Ven. Ajahn Sumedho, have worked together to establish four monasteries and two nunneries. These now train over fifty-five Western *bhikkhus* and many Western nuns, as well as offer teaching and meditation to the neighboring communities. Hundreds of lay people, both householders and those living a renunciate lay life, are actively involved in the programs, operations, and support of these monastic Dhamma centers; and many more have benefited from their existence and teaching.

Traditional training in meditation and Dhamma is thus gradually being made accessible to many people through the mutual support and commitment of lay people—both those who remain in the household life and those who have left the household life to live as *bhikkhus* and nuns.

The Foundation of Sila

Whatever one's path, the practice of Dhamma is built upon a foundation of *sila*—virtue, integrity, and purity of both behavior and speech. Without the foundation of *sila*, one's life and mind become filled with agitation and regrets—obstructions to clarity, tranquility, and insight. Thus, *sila* creates the space in which the entire Path of practice can unfold.

Sila should not be confused with externally imposed commandments. Rather, it is the voluntary undertaking of commitments that harmonize our actions and speech with the principles by which the universe operates, thereby bringing harmony, peace, and happiness to our lives and minds.

The Precepts

The level and quality of consciousness with which one lives life or undertakes the practice of meditation depends upon one's virtue or *sila*. The level of *sila* chosen depends upon each individual. Since the time of the Buddha, householders have had a wide range of options in *sila* (virtue) for pursuing their practice of Dhamma. The basic foundation for harmonious daily living is created by undertaking the precepts (commitments) to abstain from killing, stealing, sexual misconduct, lying, and intoxicants (alcohol and intoxicating drugs). These are traditionally referred to as The Five Precepts and were considered by the Buddha to be the essential foundation and support for one's human existence.

Those who wish to further simplify, calm, and refine their state of consciousness, for example during a period of intensive meditation, may choose to undertake additional precepts, such as the Eight Precepts or Ten Precepts. These may be undertaken for whatever period of time one chooses. In Southeast Asia, for example, householders usually undertake the Eight Precepts during periods of intensive meditation practice and on certain days of each month.

Ordination

If one wishes formal ordination, initially as a *samanera* (novice), or later full ordination as a *bhikkhu*, then one must seek out qualified *bhikkhus* who understand and live by the *Vinaya* to conduct those ordinations.

Meditation (Bhavana)

Within the space created by the fulfillment of basic *sila*, one then undertakes training in meditation. The word "meditation" is actually a rather inadequate translation of the Pali word *bhavana*, which literally means "bringing forth," or cultivating and developing. In *bhavana*, that which is brought forth and developed are the mental qualities of confidence, effort, clear mindful awareness, concentration, and wisdom.

This mental development (*bhavana*) is similar in many ways to developing a muscular, flexible, well-toned body—a body that is vibrant and healthy. If we develop the muscles of the body in a systematic and consistent way, they become strong and useful, capable of doing many things. If we neglect using and exercising the muscles, they become weak and may atrophy or degenerate. It is like this, too, with the mind and mental qualities such as mental effort, concentration, and mindful awareness. If exercised and developed in a systematic and consistent way, these mental qualities become powerful, capable, and supportive of our well-being. The mind thus trained becomes clear and flexible, vibrant and alive in a totally new way. If neglected, however, the mind becomes weak, and a slow process of mental atrophy or degeneration may occur. *Bhavana* can reverse this kind of mental deterioration and develop the power, vibrancy, and clarity of mind necessary to realize enlightenment.

Two types of Meditation (Bhavana)   The Buddha taught two broad types or branches of *bhavana*: *Samatha* (tranquility meditation) and *Vipassana* (insight meditation).[9] The first, *samatha*, generally takes a single object as the exclusive focus of concentration and ignores all other phenomena that arise. The meditator aims for increasing levels of stillness and one-pointedness of mind, centering only on this single object. As the mind becomes increasingly withdrawn and secluded from all other stimuli, one may eventually attain a state of absorption or *jhana*. Examples of the kind of object of meditation one may choose for *samatha* practice include: the breath; internal mental images of a color, of light, of space, or of the human body or its constituent parts; feelings of loving kindness or compassion directed toward various beings; reflections on the qualities of the Buddha, or on one's generosity; or in other traditions, mantras or visualizations.

Eight basic levels of absorption may be systematically developed; the first four may be developed through a progressive discarding of coarser elements of consciousness, and the latter four through an inclining of the mind toward increasingly more refined, peaceful, and empty states of consciousness. Once developed, the states of absorptive consciousness can be mastered through persistent practice and cultivation.

These states can bring great peace, happiness, purity, and power of mind; and the Buddha taught them as a way to prepare the mind for insight meditation. They are not, however, permanent and do not, of themselves, lead to complete Liberation. In other words, by themselves the *jhanas* and tranquility meditations do not have the power to uproot greed, aversion, and delusion permanently from the mind. For this permanent Liberation of the heart/mind, it is not necessary to exclude all phenomena from consciousness, but rather to see into the nature of all

9. For a thorough introductory explanation of both types of meditation, see Amadeo Sole-Leris' superb book *Tranquility and Insight* (Boston: Shambhala, 1986).

phenomena with penetrating wisdom; and for this, *Vipassana/Sati-patthana* (insight meditation in the four domains of mindfulness) is necessary.

Essential Differences   It is important to understand the basic differences between the two forms of meditation. In order to clarify one essential difference, it is useful to understand the distinction between realities that are filtered or conditioned by concepts, and actual momentary realities known at the level of bare perception. An illustration can help to clarify this distinction. If we stretch out our arm and look at what is attached to the end of the arm, what do we see and feel? A "hand." But at the level of bare perception, what is present is really only momentary patterns of color and form, associated with physical sensations of heat, heaviness, tingling, pressure, and so forth. The mind, however, conceptually filters and interprets these actual bare perceptions as "a hand."

The objects of focus in the *samatha* (tranquility meditation) are similarly filtered through concepts, or are mental representations ("*re*-presentations") of realities, or are mental images; but they are not the direct, bare perceptions of actual, *momentary* realities themselves. In insight meditation (Vipassana) the objects of focus *are* the actual, underlying, momentary realities themselves—realities of materiality, mind, and mental phenomena.

With the "hand" illustration in mind, it is easier to further clarify this distinction. Take, for example, the breath, which can be used either as an object in tranquility meditation or as an object in Vipassana (insight meditation). Using the breath as an object in tranquility meditation, one may focus on the *general experience* of sensations of "the breath" (like feeling "the hand" in the above illustration). One does *not*, however, clearly know the *constant arising and dissolving* of the actual, *momentary sensations* in each instant. If these discrete, *momentary sensations* were made the object of focus, the meditator would have hundreds of rapidly arising and dissolving sensations as objects, but would not have the one seemingly stable object of focus necessary to gain absorption (*jhana*).

By contrast, when one uses the breath as an object in Vipassana (insight meditation), one may take precisely the actual *momentary sensa-*

tions, which are constantly arising and passing away in each instant, as the primary object. Further, one may include in awareness whatever other physical and mental phenomena become predominant, rather than excluding them as in tranquility meditation.

So to review, the use of a single exclusive object of focus—as well as the use of images, mental representations, and conceptually-conditioned objects—distinguishes tranquility meditation from insight meditation (Vipassana). In Vipassana the primary objects of focus are not exclusive and are not the appearance, image, or representation of realities; they are, rather, the actual underlying, momentary realities themselves—realities of materiality, mind, and mental phenomena. Only the direct experiential knowledge of reality has the power to lead to the permanent Liberation of the heart/mind. Why is this so?

Conceptually-filtered objects, images, or representations of reality usually create the *illusion* of stability and permanence, thereby concealing their essential nature. By contrast, actual underlying realities allow insight into their essential and universal nature—into their impermanence and their emptiness.

To understand how this is crucially relevant to our lives and to our Liberation, it is useful to elaborate at this point.

Trapped in the "Story" of Life

We are all familiar with the "story level" of reality: I was born in _____, had _____ kind of relationship with my parents, grew up in _____, went to school at _____, met and married _____, worked as a _____, had a family, grew old, and died. End of chapter. But is that it? Is that all there is?

This story level of reality traps us and binds us within it, obscuring its actual nature and blocking our knowledge and vision of something more, of something deeper and more profound, of another domain of possibility.

The story level is totally conditioned by conceptual and perceptual filters (recall the above example of "a hand"). When operating on the story level of reality, seeing through filters of concept and conceptually interpreting what we see may not be a problem. In fact, it is necessary for survival in the world. We need to know that a red light means

STOP, and not simply know the bare perception of the color red. Conceptually-conditioned perception and interpretation become quite a serious problem, however, when we seek to liberate our heart/mind from the cycle of suffering.

When we seek Liberation, we then begin to see the extent to which concepts and images dominate our lives, filtering and interpreting everything we see, depriving us of direct and clear contact with reality. We begin to see that we have become stuck in a filtered, interpreted, illusory perception of reality. We come to know that we have taken illusion and appearance to be real while actually seeing only shadows of reality. We understand that this is the source of the vague feeling, sometimes present at even the best of times, that "something is missing."

When we lose direct contact with reality, we become increasingly lost in concepts, story, drama, and thought. Our lives then seem to go by at an ever-increasing pace as we grow older, and our patterns of perception, thought, and behavior become more automatic and stereotyped. We drive to work or to the store lost in thought, without ever really being aware of the journey. We lose our ability to be truly present and aware in each NOW. Concepts and images are thus gradually woven into and become the story of our lives, and we live trapped in this increasingly deadened world as our life slips quickly by.

What are the causes of this entrapment within illusion and story, and what are the obstructions to clear knowledge and vision? And what is the way out?

The Buddha pointed to the three root conditions of craving, aversion, and ignorance (delusion) as the source of suffering and of perpetual spinning within the story level. Of these three root mental conditions, it is ignorance that conceals and distorts the actual nature of conditioned reality, and it is precisely this ignorance that must be penetrated by wisdom if we are to be free.

Vipassana/Satipatthana Meditation Can Free Us From the Cycle of Suffering

In order to free ourselves from the painful and ceaseless cycle of living in concept and ignorance, inner tranquility and clarity need to be established first. *Samatha* (tranquility) meditation can help us to attain a temporary inner peace and clarity. But to completely dissolve the problem of suffering, one needs to get to its roots—to eliminate suffering at its *source*.

To get at the source, one must penetrate beneath the surface story level of reality and see clearly and directly the root of the problem of human suffering. It is just this cutting through the story level of life that Vipassana/Satipatthana (insight meditation in the four domains of mindfulness) is designed to do.

Ordinary light scattered about a room enables us to see in an ordinary way. But if we take the same light and harmonize and focus it into a laser, it can then pierce through steel. It is like this, too, with the mind. Ordinary mental effort, concentration, and awareness allow us to see things in an ordinary way. But if we take the same qualities of mental effort, concentration, and awareness, and systematically harmonize and focus them, we can elevate them to a new level. Just as the laser can cut through steel, so the mind, developed in this way, can pierce and cut through the surface, or story level, of reality. The mind then comes into direct contact with realities that lie beneath the surface level of our ordinary perception—beneath the story level in which we usually live our lives.

When this happens, we begin to know things as they really are, to perceive the actual characteristics of each phenomenon in the mind/body process. At first, we see only the individual characteristics of each phenomenon that arises. As we continue to watch, however, moment after moment, day after day, week after week, the perception becomes increasingly refined, clearer, and more subtle. As this happens, a deep wisdom begins to develop in the heart, on a far deeper level than that of our ordinary discursive intellect, and on a far deeper level than our ordinary understanding. We begin to perceive the universal nature of all phenomena of mind and body. The heart begins to see and learn at the deepest level that all conditioned phenomena are impermanent.

With this direct seeing and knowing that everything is impermanent—arising only to instantaneously dissolve—comes an equally deep knowledge of the unsatisfactory nature of conditioned reality, it's inability to deliver on its promises, its incapacity to provide any kind of lasting satisfaction or permanent happiness, and its lack of any secure refuge. Conditioned reality is seen as mere empty phenomena of materiality and mind—ceaselessly arising and passing away beyond our control and totally devoid of any "self" or "substance" behind the process. With the ripening or maturing of this wisdom, the heart/mind becomes dis-"illusioned," dis-"enchanted," thus seeing the absolute hopelessness of finding a stable or permanent happiness in anything conditioned; the heart's grasping and craving for pleasure and its aversion to the unpleasant ceases. It enters into a profound equanimity and detachment out of which the heart/mind can open to the unconditioned.

With the first opening to the unconditioned, the mind is permanently freed from the obstructive mental factors of wrong view and doubt. It is plunged into the stream of Dhamma and destined, in no long time, to reach complete Liberation—the final and permanent freeing of the heart from the mental defilements of greed, aversion, and delusion. The heart is thereby established in the unshakable happiness, peace, and knowledge of Liberation. One is then able to effectively work for the ultimate benefit of others, bringing to them the gift of the Dhamma and the Path to the end of suffering.

The Dhamma stands as an open gate inviting the wise to come and see for themselves. Everything depends on whether the effort is made.

> Having entered upon this Path you will come to the end
> of your suffering. Having seen this for myself, I
> proclaimed this Path which removes all thorns.
>
> —The Buddha

Bhikkhu Suruttama is an American monk who was ordained in 1983 by the Ven. Taungpulu Sayadaw at Taungpulu Monastery in Boulder Creek, California. He has practiced in the United States and Burma.

War and Catharsis:
Letting Go of Vietnam*

BY LLOYD BURTON, Ph.D.

. . . It had been eight years since my return from Vietnam when I
attended my first Vipassana retreat. At least twice a week for all
those years I had sustained the same recurring nightmare common
to many combat veterans: dreaming that I was back there, facing
the same dangers, witnessing the same incalculable suffering; waking suddenly, alert, sweating, scared . . .

Teachers

Vipassana (insight) meditation retreats have been a regular feature of California's spiritual landscape since 1974. It was in that
year that several long-time Western students of Southeast Asian
Theravada teachers returned to the United States to start sharing their practice.

Teachers such as Mahasi Sayadaw and U Ba Khin in Burma, Anagarika Munindra and S.N. Goenka in India, and Ajahn Chah in Thailand
had trained serious Western students in this ancient, simple, yet surprisingly challenging approach to Buddhist meditation which formerly
had been practiced and transmitted almost exclusively by the Southeast
Asian monkhood.

The earliest West Coast Vipassana retreats were held in summer
camps and campgrounds deep in the forests of rural California. Led by
Joseph Goldstein, Jack Kornfield, and Sharon Salzberg—who had all
spent years as senior Vipassana students in India, Burma, and Thai-

*Insight Meditation West, Woodacre, California

land—these early retreats created an immediate following for insight meditation practice.

Similar enthusiasm greeted the teachings on the East Coast. In 1975 students of Joseph, Jack, and Sharon founded the Insight Meditation Society and retreat center at Barre, a small town in western Massachusetts. For the next several years, IMS served as "home base" for these Western teachers as they travelled nationally and internationally, leading increasingly frequent retreats on both North American coasts, at several sites in between, and abroad.

As the West Coast *sangha* continued to grow, in the early 1980s Jack Kornfield moved his permanent residence to northern California. Jamie Baraz, a senior student, Jack, Joseph, and some of their Asian teachers also began to offer instruction at West Coast Vipassana retreats.

Today there is a full schedule of Vipassana retreats held annually in northern and southern California. In 1985 West Coast students of Jack, Joseph, and Sharon founded Insight Meditation West, a loose affiliate of IMS in Barre. In addition to coordinating the two-week retreats which Jack, Joseph, Sharon, and Jamie lead in California (as well as those taught by some other Vipassana teachers, such as Christopher Titmuss), IMW is also in the process of developing a retreat center on four hundred acres of ranch land in rural Marin County near San Francisco.

As of this writing, retreats led by these teachers are held at secluded, well-appointed retreat facilities rented from other spiritual groups in Santa Rosa (about sixty miles north of San Francisco) and near Joshua Tree National Monument, in the desert about one hundred miles east of metropolitan Los Angeles.

The Retreat and the Practice

Except for introductory weekend or one-day sittings, a typical IMW-sponsored Vipassana retreat is from ten to fourteen days duration. Most of these retreats are open to beginning and advanced students alike, but one or two a year are now usually designated only for those students who have already attended at least three such retreats. Depending on the facility, retreat size may range from sixty to one hundred and fifty students.

Most retreats begin with arrival and check-in in the afternoon. After sharing a light, vegetarian evening meal (only vegetarian food is served— non-dairy available on request), the retreat opens with the taking of five precepts and introductory meditation instruction. Students vow to refrain from 1) killing or knowingly harming any being 2) sexual misconduct (defined for retreat purposes as any sexual contact—men and women are housed separately, although all students meditate and eat together) 3) taking that which is not given 4) ingesting intoxicants and 5) heedless speech (defined for retreat purposes as any unnecessary speech). From the time precepts are taken, retreats are held in silence; the only exceptions are meditation instruction and discourses by the teachers, questions after discourses by students, and personal interviews between teachers and students, held privately and periodically during the course of the retreat.

A typical retreat day begins with rising about 5 : 00 A.M., followed by an early morning sitting and by walking meditation (about forty-five minutes each), breakfast at 7 : 00, and meditation instruction at 8 : 00. After instruction, and questions and answers, most of the rest of the day is filled with alternating forty-five to sixty-minute periods of sitting and walking meditation, punctuated by lunch at 11 : 30 (the sensory high point of the day), an after-lunch rest period, and tea and fruit at 5 : 00 P.M.

After another sitting, at 7 : 00 P.M. one of the teachers (retreats are usually co-led by at least two) offers a discourse on some aspect of the teaching of the Buddha, insight meditation practice, or the application of teachings to daily life. This is also an opportunity for students to raise questions about these issues.

Vipassana practice is deceptively simple, yet perhaps because of its very simplicity, surprisingly difficult for some students to master. Unlike some practices which use a word, visualization, or concept to focus the mind, in Vipassana the object of meditation is the mind itself.

For the first two or three days of the retreat, the emphasis is simply on steadying and calming the mind to the point where it can begin to focus on its own activity. Using awareness of the breath as an "anchor," students gradually develop the continuity of inner attention necessary to observe more carefully and minutely the nature of the mind/body process.

The alternating periods of sitting (relaxed but upright, spine straight, hands folded or otherwise at rest) and walking (a slow, mindful practice in which students focus microscopic attention on the lifting, moving, and placing of each foot during each step) are intended to enable the development of this continuous, ever-deepening inner awareness. Later in the retreat, the scope of attention is gradually broadened to encompass bodily sensations, emotional states, thoughts, and then the mind itself as it observes these phenomena.

Personal Experience

But why undergo such deep, reflective training? What good does it do? What purpose does it serve? There are probably as many answers to these typically Western questions as there are Vipassana students. Joseph, Jack, Sharon, and Jamie urge students to come to retreats with no pre-conceptions as to what they will gain or what the experience will or should be like. Once released from such expectations, it becomes easier to see more clearly what is going on inside in the moment.

For this reason it is not possible to describe what a "typical" insight meditation retreat experience is like. Instead, I can only recount what my own experience of retreats has been; these experiences will explain why I have continued to do this practice for the last thirteen years.

The early days of my first retreat were a veritable symphony of hindrances: aversion to the discomfort of prolonged sitting, attraction to certain other students (complete with lurid tantric fantasies), sloth, torpor, restlessness, excruciating boredom, and real doubts about the wisdom of enduring what, for me, seemed like a self-imposed spiritual boot camp.

But what gradually began to occur was a deep psychic relaxation—a relaxation which permitted the mind to observe pleasant thoughts, feelings, and sensations without clinging to them; to observe painful, emo-

tionally charged thoughts about my life without reacting against or re-
treating from them; and to accept the experience of other hindrances as
the normal responses of conditioned consciousness.

As the mind relinquished its censor-like control over the flow of experience and the relaxation became deeper, however, more painfully
charged visions began to emerge from the recesses of memory—mostly
related to my experiences in Vietnam. I had served as a field medical
corpsman with Marine Corps ground forces in the early days of the war,
in the mountainous provinces on the border between what were then
North and South Vietnam. Our casualty rates were high, as were those
of the villagers we treated when circumstances permitted.

It had been eight years since my return from Vietnam when I attended my first Vipassana retreat. At least twice a week for all those
years I had sustained the same recurring nightmare common to many
combat veterans: dreaming that I was back there facing the same dangers, witnessing the same incalculable suffering; waking suddenly, alert,
sweating, scared.

At the retreat the nightmares did not occur during sleep. They filled
the mind's eye during the day—at sittings, during walking meditation,
at meals. Horrific wartime flashbacks were superimposed over a quiet,
redwood grove at the retreat center; sleeping students in the dormitory
became body parts strewn about a makeshift morgue on the DMZ.

What I gradually came to see was that as I relived these memories as
a thirty-year-old spiritual seeker, I was also enduring for the first time
the full emotional impact of experiences which as a twenty-year-old
medic I was simply unprepared to withstand. Through private interviews with the teachers at the retreat and through my own continued
inner exploration, I began to realize that the mind was gradually yield-
ing up memories so terrifying, so life-denying, and so spiritually erod-
ing that I had ceased to be consciously aware that I was still carrying
them around. I was, in short, undergoing a profound catharsis, by
openly facing what I had most feared and had therefore most strongly
suppressed.

At the retreat, I was also plagued by a more current fear: that having
released the inner demons of war, I would be unable to control them—
that they would now rule my days as they had my nights. But what I ex-

perienced instead was just the opposite. The visions of slain friends and dismembered children gradually gave way to other half-remembered scenes from that time and place: the entrancing, intense beauty of a jungle forest a thousand different shades of green; a fragrant breeze blowing over beaches so white and dazzling they seemed carpeted by diamonds.

What also arose at the retreat for the first time was a deep sense of compassion for my past and present self: compassion for the idealistic, young would-be physician forced to witness the most unspeakable horrors of which mankind is capable, and for the haunted veteran who could not let go of memories he would not acknowledge he had.

Since that first retreat, the compassion has stayed with me. Through practice and continued inner relaxation it has grown to sometimes encompass those around me as well—when I'm not too self-conscious to let it do so. And while the memories have also stayed with me, the nightmares have not. The last of the sweating screamers happened in silence, fully awake, high atop a meditation cushion somewhere in northern California over a decade ago.

Lloyd Burton has been a student of Jack Kornfield and Joseph Goldstein since 1975. He has a Ph.D. in Law and Public Policy, and teaches at the University of Colorado. He is the former chairman of the Board of Directors of Insight Meditation West. In 1966 and 1967, he served as a field medical corpsman with the 3rd Marine Division in the Republic of Viet Nam.

---

*"Whatever You Think it is, it Isn't"**

BY SISTER MARTHA DHARMAPALI

"If you have come to the center to be enlightened," Ajahn Sobin admonished us, "or to experience blissful states, special powers, deep tranquility—you can all forget it!"

"If you learn one thing in this class, remember that wherever you go, whatever you do, investigate everything. Whatever you think it is, it isn't." This was wise counsel from an old English teacher of mine, and a dictum which can be applied to my first encounter with an intensive Vipassana (insight meditation) retreat. It wasn't at all what I expected.

Ajahn Sobin Namto is telling our group of fledgling insight meditators that mindfulness is to be regarded as a tool of spiritual training and that "meditation" is not our goal. "If you have come to the center to be enlightened," he admonishes us, "or to experience blissful states, special powers, deep tranquility, you can all forget it! Coming here is solely for the purpose of discovering the unknown, dark territory of the mind. Look deeply into the mechanism of the stress-pain-frustration cycle. See its birth and death, moment-to-moment, in the present. Your duty as a meditator is singular: develop continuous, complete, and correct mindfulness."

We are to study with him for three full days, both individually and as a group, the theory of Vipassana meditation and some basic Buddhist doctrines. Only after this initial period of study will we begin the actual practice of meditation. Since he prefers to work with small groups, each

* A traditional Thai Vipassana Retreat at Wat Buddhawararam, Denver, Colorado.

of us will receive personal attention; he will interview us once or twice a day.

A long questionnaire is first completed, followed by an equally lengthy personal interview. We become familiar with the "road map" of the *Mahasi Sayadaw* technique, which consists of becoming conscious of the rising and falling of the abdomen in breathing, noting when the mind wanders off into thought or is distracted by sound, and then focusing again on the rising and falling. Ajahn further refines it to include mindful bowing, the mindful placing of the hands as one begins ones meditation, the precise pivot of the foot as one turns in walking. The details of body-mindfulness go on and on—meticulously and precisely elaborated while remaining faithful to the method. Nothing is added for our "entertainment," although exceptions may be made for the physical capabilities of the meditator.

Ajahn thoroughly explains how to focus on objects of mindfulness. What is an object of mindfulness? What is the right object, the wrong object? Consciousness can only have one object at a time, although the rapidity of mind deceives us into believing we see, think, touch, etc. all at once. So we learn, slowly, knowing that it is essential to focus object-by-object, step-by-step. Our teacher is extremely careful about establishing a firm foundation for beginners, for if we don't understand mental and physical objects, practice will be distorted and incomplete. He also teaches us the Four Noble Truths of suffering, the cause of suffering, the fact that it can be eradicated, and the means whereby this can be accomplished. We ask many questions, but we will not know whether the Buddha's teaching is correct until we enter insight meditation and verify it from our own personal experience.

After three days of instruction, we feel confidence in the training and in our teacher, and we are ready to begin the practice. Ajahn initiates us into this phase of our training through a simple ceremony called "on entering practice." It isn't essential that we participate, but it is a custom in many Southeast Asian Vipassana centers, and through it a bond is established between teacher and meditator for the duration of the retreat. In this ceremony, the meditator formally requests instruction and invites correction. Recalling the Buddha's own struggle and his indomitable perseverance, it fortifies us for the arduous journey that lies ahead. Emotion surges when I read in the ceremony booklet that those who enter training "have not lived in vain." Silently, I repeat this phrase and feel that this is the turning point in my life.

During the ensuing seventy-two hours, momentary concentration follows mental and bodily movements fairly well. Of course, there are giant gaps . . . sleepiness, impatience. Sometimes I can focus on them, sometimes not. Again and again, Ajahn admonishes us to follow the technique to the letter in order to develop *continuity* of practice. The method will, of course, eventually be dropped, but not until it has been thoroughly assimilated.

There are no scheduled breaks in the routine, no exercise periods except walking mindfully in meditation. We stay indoors for the next few weeks and undergo twenty hours of practice, night and day. Other volunteers fully care for our needs. No work is given to us in the temple; we are not to do anything complicated and thus lose mindfulness. Each of us has a private room, and we practice there or in the meditation hall, not necessarily as a group. Feelings of gratitude surge, and even these, I am later to discover, remove me from the present moment and are seen as one of the subtle Ten Defilements of Insight. The game-playing mind plays on!

I am having difficulty with tension. Everything feels stiff, structured, artificial. I can't remember where I put things. Sometimes I am able to maintain the method by labeling my state of mind "confusion." But what am I supposed to do next? I ask Ajahn why this is happening. He tells me that concentration is too high and not balanced with mindfulness—a very common problem for beginners. People who have naturally high concentration, performers and persons from other spiritual disciplines in which single-pointed concentration is emphasized—usually have an excess of concentration for insight work. Sometimes they understand the necessity of lowering it, and Ajahn can help them. "One is tempted to run down the road of concentration," he explains, "because one naturally wishes to leave suffering behind and quickly experience tranquility. But mindfulness is always low when concentration is high. . . . So, just mentally 'touch' the object and let it go." He urges me to find skillful means for dealing with this problem. I decide to walk faster and speed up all movements slightly. It works. Mindfulness improves.

Eating is a revelation, and it often takes hours to complete a meal mindfully. A burst of taste . . . and then nothing. On retreat you begin to realize that you have never before truly *tasted* with any real awareness. Ajahn calls us in individually for private interviews. Often it's an hour long, especially for beginners. Like a physician, the experienced teacher knows what is happening with you simply by the way you walk into the room. I sit down slowly, step by step. Since mindfulness disperses rapidly when speaking, I speak word by word, eyes guarded, following through with the technique. (This is no *break* in practice.) A palpable feeling of interest, warmth, and compassion resonates in the room. It's difficult to gauge what is important to report; what may be important to you may turn out not to be so earth-shaking to the teacher, and vice versa. At first Ajahn's questions are simple, but as the days pass, they become more precise, more probing: "Do you have doubts? . . . Let's talk about them. . . . Are you distracted by sounds? . . . Can you focus on mental states? . . . What is sitting? . . . What knows sitting? . . . Who is sitting? . . . Why are you sitting? . . . Has anyone ever seen sitting? . . . What causes you to change posture? . . . Labeling can stop as soon as convenient; the object in consciousness has already passed while applying a label. It's only a name, a concept." As needed, the instructions are increased or changed. I mindfully bow, rise slowly, and leave the room.

The next day something breaks. Tension lifts and mindfulness seems to run by itself like a finely tuned automobile going along on a level road. It has the satiny quality of dough being kneaded under your hand. Everything is easier. Mindfulness and concentration have struck a balance, and my mind is as clear as drops of water falling into a pond and rippling out. Lines from Buddhist texts float into mind, and I understand them in a new way.

The days move on rapidly. I stop comparing: *this* is a good day; *this* is a bad day. For the first time in my life, even in the midst of fear, boredom, and agitation I feel safe and complete. Rather than the usual response of avoiding or suppressing these defilements, Ajahn instructs us to welcome them as they sizzle and dance in the mind. The fire of mindfulness burns them up. This is freedom . . . moment by moment.

But then, later in the retreat, this tranquility is shattered, and my mind is filled with a strange fear of ordinary things: cups, tables, and the stirring of the trees outside. Then the fear subsides and is replaced with a maddening, incessant mental chatter, like birds of prey picking away. It's a nightmare, but I'm awake. Everything is moving too fast. I can't focus clearly, and mindfulness is weak. The pitch black August night reflects my lightless mind. I report to Ajahn late at night. He says I should have come to see him sooner if I couldn't manage. "This is really a sign of progress," he encourages, "Things are beginning to stir up. It's uncomfortable for you now, but stay with it. It does not matter if mindfulness is weak or strong. Just be there, in the present. Just watch."

Can I go on? Yes, I can. I go back to my cushion and sit down. "Touch-and-go. . . . Just focus and forget it." My teacher's words echo through my troubled psyche, and the long night wanes.

A friend, a Buddhist teacher, once told me that enlightenment is as easy or difficult as turning your hand. Reflecting back upon that first episode of fumbling practice, I realize now that it was the hardest work I had ever attempted; it was the work of an invalid or a baby learning to sit, stand, walk, eat, talk—but all observed with uncommon clarity. Many years have passed since that early training. My life is much better now; every moment is precious. How did I manage to live all those years without this training? Well, I did . . . but not very well. Truly, the Dharma protects those who practice it.

Sister Martha Dharmapali (Martha Sentnor) is a Buddhist nun from New York City who is interested in helping create a contemporary Western order of nuns. Her special field of study is the early Buddhist sangha. She has practiced Vipassana meditation for over ten years and has lived in Theravada and Mahayana temples. She currently resides at the Chan Nhu Buddhist Pagoda, a women's Dharma center in Lakewood, Colorado.

Enough Is Enough*

BY JANET HOWEY

So many times I have hiked through the woods, noticing the sounds for a brief moment and commenting absentmindedly on how pleasant they are, missing all of the magic. Yet here I could barely tolerate the fullness I felt.

Ten days of silence. No talking, television, radio, reading, or writing. No caffeine, alcohol, sex, or exercise. All this I had agreed to, and although the anticipation occasionally gave me cold feet, I was fairly sure I was ready.

We met in a converted seminary in western Massachusetts to learn about Theravada Buddhism and to practice Vipassana, or insight meditation. The traditional teachings described three purposes of the practice: to open what is closed, to balance the reactive mind, and to investigate what is hidden. As the practice deepened, the practitioner could look forward to greater self-acceptance, to increased ability to be present in the moment, and to a heightened capacity for compassion.

So, robbed of the usual distractions, I joined the others in exploring that elusive and chaotic phenomenon so inadequately called "the mind." A teacher cautioned that this was not a "bliss trip," and that our search for insight would lead us through valleys as well as to peaks and plateaus.

Between the 5:00 A.M. wake up bell and 10:00 P.M. we spent approximately eleven hours in either sitting or walking meditation. Our instructions were the following:

*From Insight Meditation Society, Barre, Massachusetts

"When you are sitting, pay attention to your breath at one point in your body."

I chose my abdomen.

"Feel it rising and falling, rising and falling. As soon as you notice your mind wandering, label what it is doing, accept it, and come back to your breath."

The walking meditation was the same, only instead of paying attention to the breath, we were supposed to pay attention to the moving limbs as we walked very slowly, fifteen steps in one direction and then back, over and over—silently noting the lifting, moving, placing.

Just an instant after the first meditation began, my mind flew off. . . . *Oh God, ten days of this, how will my body make it. . . . Did I cover all my bases at work? . . . I hate what that woman did three years ago, and if she ever does it again, I know what I'll say. . . . Is Dad really dead, or if I call him will he answer the phone? . . . I wonder how many Christmas cards I'll get and if the carrier will remember to hold my mail. Thinking, thinking, rising and falling, rising and falling. Boy, what a garbage dump my mind is—remembering, projecting, defending, complaining, setting the world straight in no uncertain terms.*

"When you note where you have gone, note it gently, with affection and acceptance. Your mind is conditioned, and it behaves like a two-year-old. When it wanders off, delight in its ability to move; then bring it back firmly, but do not punish it. Do this over and over and over. It will never lose its tendency to wander; you will never lose your ability to bring it back."

I tried in a softer tone. *Anger, anger, rising and falling.* My jaw quivered, and my neck ached. *Bitterness, envy, self-doubt.* Tears floated in the corners of my eyes. *Rising and falling, rising and falling.* The bell rang, and slowly I opened my eyes, now noticing more color and form in the room than I had when I sat down. As I stood, I felt each movement—the texture of my wool blanket as I removed it from my shoulders, the slight variation in the level of the floor as I walked across thin mats to leave the hall.

And so it continued. Each journey of the mind into some dark corner was an adventure in self-acceptance, a confrontation with the urge to escape; each comforting memory or engaging fantasy was a temptation to indulge the mind's tendency to wander from the present.

"There are five hindrances to the practice: attachment, aversion, laziness, restlessness, and doubt. Treat these mind states with the same gentleness you bring to all the others, but make a special note of them."

These were my companions, all five of them, throughout the retreat. Walking, sitting, eating, working.

"Pay attention. Directly experience everything you do."

But walking at a snail's pace is so boring.

"Boredom arises from inattention. Break the walk into smaller parts; feel the heel get light as the ball gets heavy; feel the stretch in the arch and know in which order the toes leave the floor."

My walking seemed to be a pattern of endless dull steps. Later I noticed that when my weight shifted from the heel to the ball, it also shifted from the instep to the outside of the foot. And I was fascinated.

Three times during the retreat we met in small groups for an hour with a teacher. These sessions were reassuring, for I discovered that everyone struggled as I did, and no one had glimpsed enlightenment.

"I keep falling asleep," I said.

"See if you can become aware of the moment just before you begin to doze. As you practice, you will get closer and closer to the precise moment. Then take a deep breath or try sitting up straighter. If you still fall asleep, try to notice the precise moment when you wake up."

"The only thing I've felt for three days is anger. How do I stop being angry?"

"Is it all right with you that you're angry? Are you trying to stop your anger? Don't try to stop it. Become curious about it. How do you know you're angry? Where in your body do you feel it, and what happens to that feeling when you bring your attention to it?"

My mind never ceased its busyness, but I developed some partial skill at noting its contents with interest, amusement, even tenderness. Then the still places between the meanderings began to come a little more frequently and stay a little longer. They made room for my defensive crusts to flake a bit, and gradually I became more aware of the others in the group. We were grateful for each other's commitment to be here, and we formed a bond which was expressed by a patience and courtesy not diminished by silence.

The simple, vegetarian meals were abundant and satisfying, and as the days went by I needed smaller and smaller amounts to fill me. I saw the food's color, felt its texture, tasted its flavor. Eventually it took me at least a full hour to finish a small meal, and I began to be aware of the extraordinary gift of food production and preparation.

An hour each day was spent on a work assignment; mine was in the kitchen. Systematically and without compulsion I cleaned every spot off the counters, feeling the texture of the cloth and noting the back and forth motion of my hand as I worked. After finishing I was deeply satisfied and really did understand that all work is honorable when you bring your full presence to it.

During the middle of the week I walked into the woods behind the buildings. The snow was fresh, and the totality of sights, sounds, smells, and textures was more than I could absorb. Closing my eyes and noting each mind state arise and pass, I heard the noise in my head recede and the sounds of nature grow louder. The constant wind, whistling *fortissimo* and *dolce*, played background music for the woodpecker's tapping, the snapping of twigs, the birds' singing, and the rustling of small creatures in the bushes. I was surprisingly aware of the power of this symphony. So many times I have hiked through the woods, noticing the sounds for a brief moment and commenting absentmindedly on how pleasant they are, missing all of the magic. Yet here I could barely tolerate the fullness I felt.

It seemed strange that in this environment, which would normally be seen as one of deprivation, it was so easy to experience having enough: enough food, enough time, enough space, enough company. And in the still places between the mind's flurries, there was more than enough sensation—in fact almost more than I could tolerate. It is so tempting to stampede the senses with television, radio, dessert, sex, crowds—

only to be left dissatisfied and in search of more stimulation. Yet as I sat in the meditation hall and heard an orchestra play the sound that silence makes, or waited with excitement to discover just how long it would be until my next inhalation, I was astounded at the precision of my senses and at what was available to them without even moving.

But after returning to the walking meditation, I became restless and depressed. *What happened to the magic?*

> *"All mind states, like everything else, arise and pass. When we accept this, we can stop resisting the natural order of things and learn to live with more presence and skill."*

That man walking over to my left, he's very attractive, he's not wearing a wedding ring, what would it be like to sleep with him, he looks so sensitive, a bit too beatific, though, I don't buy it, besides, at his age if he's not married it's because he's either gay or too scared to make a commitment, so he comes here to convince himself he's on a higher plane. Whew! Lifting, moving, placing . . . from crush to disgust in under thirty seconds. Lifting, moving, placing, lifting, moving . . . laughing.

On the last afternoon we broke the silence to introduce ourselves. There were one hundred and twenty-five of us altogether, including lawyers, housewives, engineers, artists, businessmen, students, retirees, and those who were unemployed. Projections and fantasies disappeared, and romances and vendettas dissolved, as my previously silent companions acquired personalities, motives, and histories. I chattered through dinner but then felt lost and ill at ease. Returning to the silence of the meditation hall, I found about twenty-five others who were also presumably uncomfortable with the noise. I experienced a pounding headache, a deep flush and perspiration in my face, and an angry abdomen. *Rising and falling, rising and falling.* Tears broke into strong sobs, and I was filled with remorse—for not tasting the meal, for not paying attention, for letting a life experience slip by without being conscious of it. That is the way I eat every day, but at that moment I realized how much I had missed and what a loss it was. I cried with the ache of leaving this silent world of awareness for the other world, where the temptation is so great to fall into a noisy sleep.

"Be gentle with yourself as you leave here. Do not expect to be as present in your daily life as you have been on retreat. You will have to make choices to protect yourself. But try to be a little more mindful; try to make your actions count."

Four of us shared a car back to Boston. Conversation was tentative and soft-spoken, as if we were afraid that the hard sound of our voices might shrink us back to our smaller selves and shatter the silent ties that had felt so comfortable. Looking out the window I noticed the shape and color of every house, heard the hum of the engine increase as the driver accelerated, and felt my body moving with the motion of the car, rising and falling, rising and falling.

Janet Howey has been a participant in Vipassana sitting retreats since 1982. She is a personnel administrator for an alternative energy services company in Portland, Oregon, which has been her home for the past eighteen years. She writes short stories and essays for her own pleasure.

Sitting Ten Weeks: A Chronology*

BY YESHUA MOSER

I experience things as though for the first time; seeing the sun rise, eating an orange, walking, smelling the rain, feeling the water as I wash my hands, opening my eyes—all for the first time. Often these states arise after a particularly difficult sitting. At these times the joy and wonder I feel are indescribable.

Every year, beginning in September, the Insight Meditation Society of Barre, Massachusetts, conducts a three-month Vipassana meditation course. The course is limited to one hundred participants (called yogis) and is team taught by the IMS staff instructors, along with some guest teachers. The following is a thumbnail chronology of ten weeks of intensive Vipassana practice by one participant in the 1987 retreat.

First Week

I experience withdrawal from all my accustomed sensory stimulation—no TV, radio, books, friends to talk to, telephones, newspapers . . . none of the stuff I "fill" my time and mind with. This leads to lots of confusion, frustration, and mental pain. Just what *am* I supposed to do? Oh, yeah . . . watch the breathing process . . . that's all? *For three months?* I'll *never* make it!

Second Week

On top of my mental confusion, there is now physical discomfort and restlessness. Unaccustomed to long hours of sitting and slow walking,

*From Insight Meditation Society, Barre, Massachusetts

I develop intense knee and back pains. My mind tells me that I might be doing "unacceptable physical damage" and I had "better stop NOW." However, the instruction is to look into the sensations that make up the pain and see their basically unstable components. Not yet having enough concentration to do this for long makes this an extremely difficult time for me.

Third Week

By the middle of this week my concentration is building, and I can sit for longer periods of time. The mind now becomes very creative. I feel as though I am living inside a TV set with a random channel selector. Here's the movie channel, now sports, how about current affairs? M-TV keeps cranking away in the background . . . all those favorites from yesteryear. Daydreams, plans, schemes, memories make for many hours of rich entertainment (but little *attainment*) in the meditation hall. Gradually my mind becomes tired of the several hundred grade B movies it is churning out.

Fourth Week

Now body and mind are becoming more workable. The mind is still busy, but somehow I don't feel so identified with it. Restlessness in the body is dying down, and all those pains from the first weeks don't seem so solid after all.

Fifth and Sixth Weeks

As I look at the experience of "body," what I begin to see is a composite of points of pressure, warmth, coolness, and tension. The spaces in between are filled in by the mind, and this filling in process begins to fall away. What I have, instead, is a collection of sensations, some subtle, some intense, but all of them in a state of change. So just what do I "have?"

Sixth and Seventh Weeks

The body sits very still now, and I feel a subtle sense of enjoyment in my practice. The body is now experienced as a field of sensations, in the middle of which thoughts arise. I experience something like a plane in front of me, where mind objects float up like bubbles, bursting when touched with the sharp point of awareness. My sense of identification with thought, my most intimate of belongings, is beginning to slip.

Eighth and Ninth Weeks

All the component parts that make up my sense of "I" are now becoming clearly seen. There are sensations in the body, there are thoughts, there is awareness of these, but there does not appear to be anything else—no "I" or "self" in this continual stream of changing phenomena. I experience things as though for the first time; seeing the sun rise, eating an orange, walking, smelling the rain, feeling the water as I wash my hands, opening my eyes . . . all for the first time. Often these states arise after a particularly difficult sitting. At these times the joy and wonder I feel are indescribable.

Last Week

I'm getting deeply into the practice, but the course is almost over. During this week the mind becomes increasingly more active, with thoughts revolving around the retreat's impending conclusion. I experience anticipation and anxiety; I can't wait to tell my friends about this, but what exactly *can* I tell them?

The retreat is over. Looking back over my experience, I begin to see the effect it has had on my life. I can see its effect in the feedback I get from friends about a quiet calmness I have, or in the way they feel they get my full attention. I notice how much more quickly I drop attachments that previously would have put me, or kept me, in conflict. Sometimes I find myself stopping in the middle of some hurried task to savor the experience of the moment. Although personality changes are wonderful, I no longer see the changing of my personality as the final goal. And the more I practice, the more I feel that I'm just about to begin.

> May all beings hear the Dhamma
> May all beings awaken

Yeshua Moser has been practicing Vipassana for five years. When not sitting in meditation, he can be found working for social change and nonviolent insurrection.

With Goenka

BY PHIL ALTERMAN

The course description itself sounded brutal. Ten days? Ten hours of sitting meditation per day? Men and women separated? Complete silence for the entire ten days? Were they kidding? Some vacation!

I attended my first Vipassana meditation course on a lark. I decided to go because an old friend whom I wanted to see had called and invited me along. I figured once I was there I would talk her out of attending, and we would have a nice little vacation. Fortunately, things didn't go as planned.

I approached this first course in Vipassana as a virtual neophyte to meditation and with a strong cynical streak about anything having to do with Eastern religions, mysticism, and gurus. I had briefly dabbled in Transcendental Meditation in college in the early seventies, but I had had no exposure to any Buddhist philosophy whatsoever, let alone meditation techniques.

I registered through the mail and received a pamphlet entitled *The Art of Living: Vipassana Meditation* by S.N. Goenka. It briefly explained the philosophy behind the meditation technique, the course structure, its daily schedule, policies, and goals. I had expected to receive a flowery magazine with strange symbols all over it containing glossy photos of a bearded guru, his followers kneeling on the floor around him with ecstatic expressions on their upturned faces.

Vipassana, a Pali word defined as "to see things as they really are," was described as "The Art of Living," a technique for gaining insight into the reality of the human experience. It explained that human suffering arose from "negativities" or "defilements" in the mind, which could be eradicated by a simple process of observation. The technique was based upon the discovery that whenever "any defilement arises in the mind, simultaneously two things start happening at the physical level. One is that the breath loses its normal rhythm. . . . And at a subtler level, some kind of biochemical reaction starts in the body—some sensation." It was the blind reaction to these sensations that multiplied one's misery and caused suffering. The meditation technique consisted of training the mind to observe these sensations with a balanced mind, without reaction. This "choiceless" observation, Mr. Goenka explained, would allow the mental defilements to pass away, purifying the mind and allowing one to experience joy, compassion, and love.

While I wasn't entirely sure what Goenka meant by "defilements," "negativities," or "sensations," I was certain that I had my share of complexes that got in the way of happiness. Moreover, I had experienced "physical feelings" (sensations?) which sometimes seemed to arise out of nowhere and which had a great effect on my mental equilibrium. The theory thus seemed quite logical. My cynicism was even further alleviated when Vipassana was described as completely nonsectarian, beneficial to all regardless of one's religious and philosophical beliefs.

While the philosophy and goals of the course sounded alright to me, the course description itself sounded brutal. Ten days? Ten hours of sitting meditation per day? Men and women separated? Complete silence for the entire ten days? Were they kidding? Some vacation! However, not really intending to remain for the entire course anyway, I filled out the registration card and sent it in. Besides, it wouldn't cost me anything. There was no charge for these courses. They were run entirely on the donations of former students who wished to make the Vipassana experience available to new students.

A few weeks later I arrived at the meditation site clutching my newly purchased *zafu* (meditation cushion). During registration I was asked to fill out a written questionnaire asking about my previous meditation experience and whether I had any mental or physical problems the teacher should know about. I was also asked to acknowledge that I had read the "Code of Discipline" and agreed to abide by all of its rules and regulations for the duration of the course.

The "Code of Discipline" required one to follow five precepts:
1. To abstain from killing.
2. To abstain from stealing.
3. To abstain from all sexual activities.
4. To abstain from telling lies.
5. To abstain from all intoxicants.

In addition, students were required to observe "noble silence" during the course. The only communication allowed was with the teacher and management. There was to be no physical contact with anyone—the sexes were to be segregated—and no religious practices of any kind were permitted. Smoking was prohibited, and even reading and writing were out of bounds.

These rules, it was explained to us, while seemingly severe, were designed to diminish any distractions and to ensure that other students were not disturbed during the course. This would allow one to give a fair trial to the technique in its purest form. Students were encouraged to immediately seek clarification from the teacher if the practical reasons for the rules were not clear.

As I signed the registration form, I wondered what I was getting myself into. My friend seemed determined to try the course, and by this time there seemed to be no backing out. And as if to seal my fate, just before the course began one of the management staff encouraged each of us to take a vow of determination to remain for the entire ten-day course. In this way we could give it a fair trial. If we weren't willing to do so, it was suggested that we not even begin. Well I had come this far, and so I swore an oath to myself to try.

After registering I was shown my living quarters, which consisted of a room I would share with four other male students. (The female living quarters were located on the other side of the camp, ensuring the segregation mentioned in the rules.) At about sunset a bell rang, summoning us to the meditation hall. Approximately three hundred students gathered outside the hall. Students who had taken courses previously were asked to enter first. Entering with the new students a few minutes later, I found a place in the back of the hall and sat down.

The hall was large, about the size of a tennis court. Males and females sat on opposite sides of the hall with a long, narrow walkway between the two groups. In the front on a raised platform, sat the teacher,

Mr. Goenka, seated cross-legged on a small cushion and wearing a simple white shirt. He began chanting in a low, melodious voice in a language I did not understand. A few minutes later he addressed the group in English.

He explained that we had gathered to practice the ancient art of Vipassana meditation as taught by the Buddha more than twenty-five hundred years ago. He briefly reviewed the rules and asked the students to take refuge in the Buddha, the Dhamma (the Path of Enlightenment as taught by the Buddha), and the *sangha* (the community of meditators). After doing so in both Pali (the language in India during the time of the Buddha) and in English, Goenka began giving instructions.

He told us to find a seated position on the floor that felt comfortable. No particular posture, such as the lotus position, was required. It was a good thing, as I could barely cross my legs. The most important thing to keep in mind, he pointed out, was to keep a straight back and neck, since this would be helpful in the long run. While meditating we were to keep our eyes closed in order to avoid distractions.

We had been seated about thirty minutes and already my back was beginning to hurt. I couldn't imagine how I would be able to sit there for ten days. But I looked around the hall at the other students, and they didn't seem to be much different than I. If *they* could do it, I supposed that I could, too.

When the introduction was over, the teacher asked us to close our eyes and to focus our entire attention on the small area around the nose above the upper lip, up to the area inside the nostrils. We were told to concentrate on the flow of breath as it passed over this small part of the body. The normal, natural breath—without any effort to control it—was to be the focus.

I began concentrating on my breath and quickly became aware of its flow as it passed through my nostrils: cold as it entered, warm as it left. While my mind raced with a million thoughts, I tried to remain focused on this "feeling" of the breath. I soon realized that it was not going to be easy. My mind constantly wandered off into a quagmire of thought: "What am I doing here? . . . I wish I had eaten more for dinner. . . . My aching back. . . . Did I lock my car? . . . I can't wait for breakfast!" *Anything* except the breath!

In a comforting, reassuring manner, Goenka instructed us to gently bring our attention back to the breath when we discovered that the mind had wandered. After some time, we were told to relax and to retire to our rooms for the evening. I wasn't too encouraged, although I did notice that my back pain didn't seem to be such a problem if I was concentrating on the breath. Maybe I could get through the course after all.

The sound of a bell fluttered through the woods the next morning. With sleep-encrusted eyes, I looked at my watch. Four o'clock, I thought, guess they're serious about the schedule. I slowly got up, washed, and made my way to the meditation hall. Most of the students were already in their places, immersed in the task of observing the breath as Goenka had instructed. I sat down and did the same.

I struggled with my "monkey mind," as Goenka called it, for the next four days. Sometimes it would wander away from the breath for hours. Then I would "come-to" and realize how little control I actually had over my own mind. Slowly I noticed that it was becoming quieter, and I was able to focus on the breath for longer periods of time. These stretches of focused attention were peaceful and relaxing, like an oasis in a desert of confusion.

Each evening Goenka delivered a discourse in which he slowly revealed the theory of Vipassana, unraveling just enough of the puzzle each lecture so that we could understand the meditation instructions he had given thus far. Goenka is a very dynamic, and sometimes humorous, speaker, and I found myself looking forward to his discourses with great anticipation. My mind was filled with questions. And though he was speaking to the entire group, it seemed that every evening he somehow knew what I was thinking and would address those questions that were foremost in my mind.

The fourth day, we were told, was to be an important one. For it was on this day that we would be taught the "art of Vipassana." Having struggled with my "monkey mind" and aching back for three days, I was anxious for it to arrive. What could this mysterious Vipassana be? What was this field of *panna*, or wisdom, that Goenka kept referring to? In the afternoon of the fourth day, we were instructed by Goenka to begin meditating using the technique of *anapannasati* or focusing on the breath. He began chanting in his low and powerful voice. He then told us that to practice Vipassana it was necessary to keep the body as still as possible. Any movements would disturb the mind's concentration.

Suddenly he directed us to switch our attention from the breath to a small area at the top of the head and to observe any sensations which might be occurring in that small, two or three-square-inch part of the body. We were to simply be aware, in a choiceless fashion, of any sensation—from pain to itching, from gross to subtle—which appeared in that part of the body.

I was surprised by the instruction. This was the field of *panna*? What did the top of my head have to do with wisdom? Ignoring my thoughts, I focused on the top of my head as instructed. Sure enough I felt a slight tingling. Slowly Goenka guided us through each little part of the body, from head to toe, directing us to merely observe all of the various sensations. We weren't to search for any particularly blissful sensation, nor were we to avoid any painful ones that we came across during our survey of the body. The secret was to learn how *not* to react, to keep the mind balanced, regardless of the type of sensation. "Let nature take its course," he kept reminding us, instructing us to focus on *anicca* (impermanence, or in this case the constant flux of physical sensations in the body).

By the time we had completed our survey of the entire body (this took well over an hour), I was completely flabbergasted. Though there were many parts of my body in which I was unable to feel any sensations, and though I constantly reacted to the painful ones, it felt as if a light had just gone on inside my mind. My body felt unified in some sort of electric field. I could not believe that I had lived thirty years and had been unaware of what was really going on inside this body, this *anicca*, as Goenka called it. Even more powerful was the realization that my mind was in a constant state of turmoil, reacting to these sensations. I left the hall at the end of the meditation, stunned by the world that had just opened up to me.

The next six days were spent refining the technique of scanning the body, observing this new continent of sensations that were manifesting themselves throughout the physical structure. We were taught to vary the method depending upon the quality of the mind and the sensations springing up at any particular time. Layer upon layer of sensation, some pleasurable, some very painful, seemed to rise to the surface, only to disappear after close observation.

Despite Goenka's instructions to the contrary, I often found myself searching for pleasurable sensations and trying to "push out" the painful ones. I had a particularly nasty burning pain that felt like a knife wound in the center of my back. It seemed to linger for days. The more I tried to fight it, the worse it seemed to get. As I learned to relax and simply observe it, I began to notice that this gross pain was in reality made up of many different types of subtle sensations that, when observed without reaction, would change and sometimes disappear completely. The more focused and non-reactive my mind was while observing these gross sensations, the less mental suffering in response to the pain there seemed to be. It became clear that my reaction to the pain, not the pain itself, was the source of suffering.

Each day brought new states of mind. I passed through periods when I could barely stay awake to periods of intense concentration, when nothing seemed to exist but the sensation and the process of observation. These moments brought feelings of incredible harmony and peace. I also experienced times of extreme doubt, wondering what in the world this was all about, wondering what these sensations had to do with happiness and peace of mind. Under Goenka's sometimes gentle, sometimes stern encouragement, I continued to work, and I began to feel lighter, as if the meditation was lifting a burden from my body and mind. I began to realize that all of these states of mind were merely *anicca*—constant change, appearing and disappearing as quickly as the physical sensations.

On the ninth day, we were taught another meditation technique to be used in conjunction with Vipassana. Goenka called it *Metta Bhavana* or the cultivation of loving kindness and compassion for ourselves and all living beings. Though we only practiced it for a very short period, its powerful effects brought me feelings of peace, harmony, and joy, the strength and intensity of which I had never experienced before.

By the end of the course, I felt as if I had passed through one of the most difficult ordeals of my life, and I was glad that it was over. But

I also felt that I had been given an incredible gift, a tool for self-realization that would be with me for the rest of my life.

Phil Alterman took his first course with S.N. Goenka in California in 1982. In 1984 he traveled to India for further study. He is an immigration lawyer in Denver, Colorado.

The Theravada Centers of North America

Centers are listed alphabetically first by state, then by city and, should there be more than one within a given city, by the names of the centers themselves.

ALASKA

Vipassana Meditation Group
We are a loose-knit group of practitioners who meet weekly to practice and hold weekend retreats, two to four times per year. The organizer acts as a teacher and facilitator, giving basic instruction in Theravada practice.
ADDRESS: P.O. Box 92085, Anchorage, AK 99509
PHONE: (907) 278-2910
RESIDENT DIRECTOR: Christie Niebel
AFFILIATED WITH: Autonomous
ESTABLISHED: 1986
FACILITIES: Urban meditation center
RETREATS OFFERED: Weekly practice and weekend retreats
OPEN TO: General public

ARKANSAS

Devachan Temple
Devachan is a small center in the Ozark Mountains. There is a meditation shrine hall called "Dharma Megha," which seats twenty persons. Bhikkhuni Miao Kwang Sudharma has had monastic experience in Japan, Sri Lanka, and Taiwan. Chanting in Pali and Chinese is done, and meditation practice is Ch'an (prajna) and Pure Land chanting. Counselling is available. Prajna Ch'an is given as taught by Master Hiu Wan in Taiwan; it has six subtle stages: 1) Counting breaths 2) Following the breath 3) Ceasing all thoughts 4) Contemplating 5) Return to the source 6) Purity.
ADDRESS: 5 Dickey Street, Eureka Springs, AR 72632
LINEAGE: Soto Zen, Theravada, Ch'an, Pure Land
SPIRITUAL HEAD: Bhikkhuni Miao Kwang Sudharma
RESIDENT DIRECTOR: Same
AFFILIATED WITH: Autonomous
ESTABLISHED: 1980
FACILITIES: Urban meditation center with private rooms for solitary retreats
RETREATS OFFERED: Evening meditation, chanting retreat, prostration retreat, and supervised solitary retreats are offered whenever requested.
OPEN TO: General public

CALIFORNIA

Dhammachakka Meditation Center
The Dhammachakka Meditation Center is a group of San Francisco Bay Area Meditators who organize classes and retreats for the study of Dhamma in the Theravada Tradition, under the guidance of the Ven. U Silananda, a meditation teacher and scholar from Burma. A monk for more than forty years, Ven. U Silananda came to America with the Ven. Mahasi Sayadaw in 1979 at the invitation of the IMS in Barre, Massachusetts. Mahasi Sayadaw chose U Silananda and one other monk to remain in America to serve the needs of the Burmese community here

Bhikkhuni Miao Kwang Sudharma seated in front of
Devachan Temple, Eureka Springs, Arkansas.

and to spread Dhamma in this country.
His knowledge of the *Abhidhamma* is
well known, especially among Theravada
monks. He is now sharing this knowledge
with Western students. The Dhammachakka Meditation Center is currently as-
sembling materials for a correspondence
course that will make the *Abhidhamma*
accessible to Western students.

ADDRESS: 2321 Russell #3A, Berkeley,
CA 94705 (Mailing address: Box 206,
2124 Kittredge Street, Berkeley, CA
94702)

PHONE: (415) 531-1691; (415) 849-3791
SPIRITUAL HEAD: Ven. U Silananda
(Burmese)
RESIDENT DIRECTOR: Same
AFFILIATED WITH: Autonomous
ESTABLISHED: 1982
FACILITIES: Various rented facilities for
classes and meditation retreats
RETREATS OFFERED: Extended Vipas-
sana courses twice a year. One-day
retreats almost every month.
OPEN TO: General public

Sayaji U Ba Khin / Vipassana Foundation

Please see California Vipassana Center, Occidental, California, for more information.
ADDRESS: P.O. Box 9426, Berkeley, CA 94709

Taungpulu Kaba-Aye Monastery

Established in 1981 by the Ven. Taungpulu Sayadaw, TKA is a monastic meditation center in the redwood forests of the Santa Cruz Mountains, available for all who wish to learn and practice Vipassana meditation in a peaceful and natural setting. Meditation instruction is available, and daily interviews with the teacher may be arranged. We maintain two meditation halls, one in the monastery and one in the peace pagoda, which was consecrated in 1983. Comfortable rooms and nutritious meals are provided.
ADDRESS: 18335 Big Basin Way, Boulder Creek, CA 95006
PHONE: (408) 338-4050; city center: (415) 282-3124
SPIRITUAL HEAD: Ven. Hlaing-Tet, Sayadaw (Burmese)
RESIDENT DIRECTOR: Rina Sircar (Burmese). Rina Sircar is a Ten Precept nun and practitioner of meditation for over thirty years. She is professor of Graduate Buddhist Studies at the California Institute of Integral Studies.
AFFILIATED WITH: This is organizational headquarters.
ESTABLISHED: 1981
FACILITIES: Country monastic retreat center. We also maintain a small, urban meditation center in San Francisco.
RETREATS OFFERED: Vipassana courses, "Days of Mindfulness," weekend sittings, supervised solitary retreats. Schedule at the monastery: Daily sittings mornings and evenings, Saturday

sittings 1:00–5:30 P.M.; weekend group retreats two or three times a year. At the city center there are all-day sittings once a month.
OPEN TO: General public

Bodhi Dhamma Society

We study Buddhist literature in group discussions and have lectures at our monthly meetings. A Vipassana meditation retreat is conducted once a year.
ADDRESS: 182 East Miramar Avenue, Claremont, CA 91710
PHONE: (714) 624-7712
LINEAGE: Thai Theravada
AFFILIATED WITH: Autonomous
ESTABLISHED: 1982
FACILITIES: Rented facility
RETREATS OFFERED: Yearly Vipassana meditation course
OPEN TO: General public

California Buddhist Vihara Society

The California Buddhist Vihara Society was founded in July 1977 by a group of Sri Lankan Buddhists in the San Francisco Bay Area. The society exists to provide a center for the traditional religious practices of Theravada for Buddhists who live in this state, as well as to foster a better understanding of the Buddha's teachings among the American people. The society's founding president is Ven. Madawala Seelawimala. A Theravada scholar-monk who practiced Buddhism for twenty years in Sri Lanka, he was invited to the United States by the Buddhist Churches of America to better acquaint Buddhists in this country with the Theravada tradition. Presently he is teaching at the Institute of Buddhist Studies, Berkeley.
ADDRESS: 4797 Myrtle Drive, Concord, CA 94521
PHONE: (415) 845-4843

Pagoda at Taungpulu Kaba-Aye Monastery, Boulder Creek, California.

SPIRITUAL HEAD: Ven. Madawala Seelawimala Mahathera (Sri Lanka)
RESIDENT DIRECTOR: Same
ESTABLISHED: 1977
FACILITIES: We meet at different places
in the Bay Area.
RETREATS OFFERED: Meetings are held
at least once a month in different places
in the Bay Area for the convenience
of the members. Dhamma classes and
classes for meditation and other mental
exercises will be arranged soon. Members are free to meet with Ven. Seelawimala at 2717 Haste Street, Berkeley,
CA. Phone (415) 849-2383 for individual
consultation. He is also available to
speak before any religious or educational group.
OPEN TO: General public

Theravada Buddhist Society of America

This society is a nonmembership organization, founded in 1979 by Burmese immi-
grants. A very small group meets daily at
7:00 P.M. for a one-hour meditation
sitting.
ADDRESS: 68 Woodrow Street, Daly
City, CA 94014.
PHONE: (415) 994-8272
LINEAGE: Burmese Theravada

SPIRITUAL HEAD: U Silananda
(Burmese)
RESIDENT DIRECTOR: U Silananda. At
present there are three Theravada
monks in residence.
AFFILIATED WITH: Autonomous
ESTABLISHED: 1979
FACILITIES: Urban meditation center
RETREATS OFFERED: One-day, weekend,
and longer Vipassana retreats; daily
meditation sittings from 7:00 to 8:00
P.M.; *Abhidhamma* class Fridays from
6:00 to 7:30 P.M.; Sunday class for
children from 4:00 to 5:00 P.M.
OPEN TO: General public

Vipassana Dhura Society

Located on Big Bear Mountain, near San
Bernardino, a comfortable forty-foot
cabin, situated in a pine forest, is available
for two to three self-reliant meditators
who have several years of regular Vipassana practice. Permission for solo retreats
is given after an interview with Ajahn
Sobin. The cabin is available for spring,
summer, and fall months. The cost is $14
daily, including room and board. Ajahn
Sobin maintains close contact with retrea-
tants. The society also conducts a yearly
Vipassana tour of Thailand, where medi-
tators may practice at selected temples.
ADDRESS: 1125 Chickasaw Lane, Fawn-
skin, CA 92333 (Mailing address: P.O.
Box 355, Fawnskin, CA 92333)
PHONE: (714) 985-0832
LINEAGE: Vipassana meditation based
on Mahasi Sayadaw line
SPIRITUAL HEAD: Ajahn Sobin S. Namto
(Thai)
RESIDENT DIRECTOR: Same
AFFILIATED WITH: Autonomous
ESTABLISHED: 1985
FACILITIES: Cabin in pine forest for
solitary retreats

RETREATS OFFERED: Individual and
small group retreats
OPEN TO: General public

Wat Buddha Godam

Anyone is welcome any time. Phra Tham-
massonthorn speaks excellent English.
ADDRESS: Box 634, 7445 Streater Ave-
nue, Highland, CA 92346
PHONE: (714) 864-6070
LINEAGE: International Meditation Cen-
ter; Vietnamese, Cambodian, Laotian,
Thai
SPIRITUAL HEAD: H. Ven. Dr. F. Kham-
piro (Thai)
RESIDENT DIRECTOR: Phra Khru Sathit
Thammassonthorn (Thai)
AFFILIATED WITH: Autonomous
ESTABLISHED: 1979
FACILITIES: Urban meditation center
RETREATS OFFERED: None currently
OPEN TO: General public

Los Angeles Buddhist Vihara

The first Sunday of each month we have a
Dhamma class for children. On each full
moon day there is a service from 8:00
A.M. to 4:00 P.M. consisting of a sermon,
discussion, and recitation of the Ten
Precepts.
ADDRESS: 1147 North Beechwood Drive,
Hollywood, CA 90038
PHONE: (213) 464-9698
LINEAGE: Sri Lankan Theravada
SPIRITUAL HEAD: Ven. Ahangama
Dhammarama
RESIDENT DIRECTOR: Same
AFFILIATED WITH: Autonomous
ESTABLISHED: 1978
FACILITIES: Urban meditation center
with solitary retreat facilities available.
RETREATS OFFERED: Insight medita-
tion; weekend retreats; meditation

classes every Tuesday and Friday evening from 6:00 P.M. to 7:00 P.M.
OPEN TO: General public

Dhamma Dena Desert Vipassana Center

Dhamma Dena is a high desert sanctuary encircled by mountains and illuminated by the constant change of color. It is a silent, meditative space, permitting insight and discovery of communion with all life. Since we live in close relationship with our desert environment, water conservation is practiced. Accommodations are very simple. Vegetarian meals are served. Self-retreats and formal group retreats in Vipassana meditation are available under the guidance of Ruth Denison. During retreats we observe silence and the basic training precepts, refraining from 1) harming living beings 2) taking what is not given 3) unskillful speech 4) sexual misconduct (during retreat periods celibacy is observed) and 5) intoxicants and drugs.
ADDRESS: 65620 Giant Rock Road, Joshua Tree, CA 92252 (Mailing address: HC-1, Box 250, Joshua Tree, CA 92252)
PHONE: (619) 362-4815
LINEAGE: Sayagyi U Ba Khin (Burmese)
SPIRITUAL HEAD: Ruth Denison (American)
RESIDENT DIRECTOR: Ruth Denison (American)
AFFILIATED WITH: Autonomous
ESTABLISHED: 1977
FACILITIES: Desert retreat facility
RETREATS OFFERED: Solitary as well as weekend retreats, nine-day, two and three-week Vipassana courses
OPEN TO: General public

The Khemara Buddhikarama

ADDRESS: 20622 Pioneer Boulevard, Lakewood, CA 90715
PHONE: (213) 860-9664
LINEAGE: Cambodian Theravada
AFFILIATED WITH: Autonomous
FACILITIES: Urban meditation center with residency program
OPEN TO: General public

Metropolitan Vipassana

Metropolitan Vipassana is a newly formed division of the Sayagyi U Ba Khin Memorial, a nonprofit corporation in the state of California. Progressive elements of insight discourses and rapidly-advancing meditation instruction are given one night a week for five consecutive weeks, requiring individual daily practice at home. Overcoming personal pain is a modern-day, secondary advantage of awakening insight.
ADDRESS: 14713 La Mesa Drive, La Mirada, CA 90638
PHONE: (714) 521-3046
LINEAGE: U Ba Khin (Burmese)
SPIRITUAL HEAD: U Ba Khin (Burmese)
RESIDENT DIRECTOR: Robert H. Hover (American)
AFFILIATED WITH: Autonomous
ESTABLISHED: 1970
FACILITIES: We meet any place available
RETREATS OFFERED: Ten-day retreats, lectures, and instruction
OPEN TO: General public

Buddha Sasana Foundation

The Buddha Sasana Foundation was established to further the teachings of the Buddha as instructed by the late Ven. Mahasi Sayadaw of Burma. The foundation is under the direct guidance of Mahasi Sayadaw's successor, Ven. U Pandita Sayadaw,

Senior Teacher at the Mahasi Center in Rangoon. This classic Theravada tradition emphasizes a unique combination of the deep practical understanding of Satipatthana Vipassana meditation together with a comprehensive study of Buddhist texts. The central vision of the foundation is to develop a meditation center that will allow interested individuals to complete, in this country, a thorough course of training in traditional Dhamma theory and practice, under the guidance of Sayadaw and in forms appropriate to the American cultural transmission of *Buddhadhamma*. Satipatthana Vipassana can be described in the following way:

> *Satipatthana Vipassana* meditation, as taught by the late Mahasi Sayadaw, emphasizes the continuity of moment-to-moment awareness of all physical and mental phenomena that comprise experience. The primary objects of concentration and mindfulness are the physical elements (rising and falling of the abdomen during sitting, or lifting and placing of the feet during walking); mindfulness of nonphysical elements (mental states, thoughts, perceptions, etc.) is also cultivated. The sequence of meditative experience involves (1) the recognition of the object in the field of awareness; (2) the deliberate mental noting of the object; and (3) the observation or experience of the object through its duration. (This, too, is the format for reporting during the every-other-day interview with the meditation teacher.) With diligent and continuous practice, this formal processing of all our mental and physical experiences leads to progressively deeper insights into the essential characteristics of all things: impermanence, infelicity, and unsubstantiality. An alternating schedule of sitting and walking sessions (forty-five minutes to an

hour) is scheduled some thirteen to fourteen hours a day, with two meals before noon. Activities such as speaking, reading, writing, listening to tapes, etc. are squarely discouraged as impediments in the cultivation of continuous awareness.

ADDRESS: 45 Oak Road, Larkspur, CA 94939
PHONE: (415) 924-6447
LINEAGE: Mahasi Sayadaw
SPIRITUAL HEAD: Sayadaw U Pandita (Burmese)
RESIDENT DIRECTOR: Alan Clements (American)
AFFILIATED WITH: Autonomous
ESTABLISHED: 1985
FACILITIES: Urban meditation center
RETREATS OFFERED: Several ten-day and annual six-week Vipassana retreats offered yearly from April to September
OPEN TO: General public

Burma Buddhist Monastery

Burma Buddhist Monastery (Dhammadaya) is a residential center for Burmese Buddhist monks under the direction of the Ven. U Pyinnya Wuntha and exists primarily to serve the needs of the Burmese ethnic community of Los Angeles. However, the temple is open to the general public for meditation in the evenings from 6:00 to 7:00 P.M. Instruction in insight meditation is available after evening services.

ADDRESS: 115 South Commonwealth Avenue, Los Angeles, CA 90004
PHONE: (213) 382-9477
SPIRITUAL HEAD: Ven. U Pyinnya Wuntha (Burmese)
RESIDENT DIRECTOR: Same
AFFILIATED WITH: Autonomous
ESTABLISHED: 1980
FACILITIES: Urban monastic residence for monks only. Private rooms for soli-

tary retreats. No overnight accommodations.

RETREATS OFFERED: Supervised solitary one-day retreats; daily sitting 5:00 to 6:00 A.M. and 6:00 to 7:00 P.M.

OPEN TO: General public welcome for evening meditation

Dharma Vijaya Buddhist Vihara

The Dharma Vijaya Buddhist Vihara was founded on April 20, 1980 by a group of Sri Lankan Buddhists. Since its inception the Vihara has been maintained and promoted by Sri Lankan and other Eastern and Western Buddhists, as well as non-Buddhist friends from many national and cultural backgrounds. Five venerable monks from Sri Lanka conduct the day-to-day activities and render guidance for those seeking the services of the Vihara. On Fridays and Sundays, 7:00 to 9:00 P.M., instruction in meditation is given, followed by a Dhamma talk based upon the teachings of the Buddha. When possible, weekend intensive meditation retreats are organized. People of any tradition or background are invited to attend.

ADDRESS: 1847 Crenshaw Boulevard, Los Angeles, CA 90019

PHONE: (213) 737-5084

LINEAGE: Theravada (Sri Lankan)

SPIRITUAL HEAD: Ven. Walpola Biyananda (Sri Lankan)

RESIDENT DIRECTOR: Same

AFFILIATED WITH: Autonomous

ESTABLISHED: 1980

FACILITIES: Urban meditation center and meditation hall. Main shrine room available for meditating in solitude.

RETREATS OFFERED: Shorter Vipassana courses are offered intermittently.

OPEN TO: General public

Gay Buddhist Group

The teacher of the Gay Buddhist Group, Norman McClelland (Vajra Dharma),

holds a B.A. and an M.A. in anthropology, with a specialty in oriental cultures. He received his *Upasaka* (lay ordination) in 1981 from the International Buddhist Meditation Center in Los Angeles, and his *Dharmacari* (higher lay ordination) in 1982 from the Dharma Vijaya Buddhist Vihara in Los Angeles. He is a full-time elementary school teacher in Los Angeles.

ADDRESS: P.O. Box 27565, Los Angeles, CA 90027

PHONE: (213) 461-5042

LINEAGE: Theravada

SPIRITUAL HEAD: Vajra Dharma (Norman McClelland)

RESIDENT DIRECTOR: Same

AFFILIATED WITH: Autonomous

ESTABLISHED: 1985

Wat Thai of Los Angeles

A group meditation retreat is held the first week of each month (Friday evening through Sunday evening). All-night meditation (*nesatchikanghathudong*) is conducted on Buddhist holidays.

ADDRESS: 8225 Coldwater Canyon Avenue, North Hollywood, CA 91605-1198

PHONE: (818) 785-9552

LINEAGE: Thai Vipassana

SPIRITUAL HEAD: Ven. Thepsophon, Lord Abbot (Thai)

RESIDENT DIRECTOR: Phra Kru Setthakit and Phra Maha Prakob

AFFILIATED WITH: Autonomous

ESTABLISHED: 1972

FACILITIES: Urban meditation temple

RETREATS OFFERED: Short Vipassana meditation retreats monthly

OPEN TO: General public

Dharma Foundation

The Dharma Foundation sponsors Vipassana meditation retreats, classes, and teachings in the Theravada tradition. A plurality of Vipassana teachers present different styles and emphases within the framework of mindfulness practice. Some focus on more traditional teachings of liberation through intensive practice, while others emphasize integrating mindfulness and basic Dharma principles in daily life, and involvement in the world. There is a year-round program of intensive retreats of varying lengths for new and old students. The Dharma Foundation is affiliated with Insight Meditation West (IMW), which is in the process of establishing a center in Marin County, California. When IMW is completed, Dharma Foundation retreats in the Bay Area will be held there while facilities will be rented in other locations. We teach insight (Vipassana) meditation, adapted from the Burmese teacher Mahasi Sayadaw. Other techniques are also taught, depending on the teacher, but all have in common the development of mindfulness.

ADDRESS: 6169 Harwood Avenue, Oakland, CA 94618
PHONE: (415) 655-9623
LINEAGE: Major Theravada practice lineages of Mahasi Sayadaw, Ajahn Chaa, and others.
SPIRITUAL HEAD: Jack Kornfield, Joseph Goldstein, Sharon Salzberg, Christopher Titmuss, Christine Feldman, Jamie Baraz, and others.
RESIDENT DIRECTOR: Jack Kornfield and Jamie Baraz
AFFILIATED WITH: Sister of Insight Meditation West and Insight Meditation Society
ESTABLISHED: 1982
FACILITIES: Facilities are rented throughout the West Coast for retreats; sitting groups meet regularly around the Bay Area.
RETREATS OFFERED: One-day, five-day, and weekend sittings; women's spirituality retreats, peace weekends, and approximately six ten-day or longer retreats.
OPEN TO: General public

International Meditation Center–USA

Please see International Meditation Center–USA, White Marsh, Maryland, for a description.
ADDRESS: P.O. Box 13314, Suite 111, Oakland, CA 94661

California Vipassana Center

California Vipassana Center provides Vipassana meditation in the tradition of Sayagyi U Ba Khin, as taught by S. N. Goenka and his assistant teachers. The center offers ten-day meditation courses conducted in "Noble Silence." In order to learn this technique, it is necessary to attend a complete ten-day course, during which the student first develops increased concentration, which is then used as a means to examine his/her own mental and physical nature. By doing so, the student gains the insight and detachment necessary to free him/herself from unwholesome qualities such as greed, anger, and fear. As these unwholesome qualities are weakened and then eliminated, the latent wholesome qualities of mind—love, compassion, joy, and equanimity—begin to develop. A ten-day course provides mental training of profound and practical value in everyday life. Introductory videos are available as well as the booklets *The Art of Living: Vipassana Meditation*, by S. N. Goenka, and *Introduction to Vipassana Meditation*, which defines Vipassana in the following way:

> Vipassana means "To see things as they really are"; it is the process of self-purification by self-observation. One starts by observing the natural breath to concentrate the mind. With this sharpened awareness one proceeds to observe the changing nature of body and mind and experiences the universal truths of impermanence, suffering, and egolessness. This

truth—realization by direct experience—is the process of purification. (From: *Introduction to Vipassana Meditation*).

ADDRESS: P.O. Box 510, Occidental, CA 95465
PHONE: (707) 874-3031
LINEAGE: Sayagyi U Ba Khin (Burmese)
SPIRITUAL HEAD: S. N. Goenka (Indian)
RESIDENT DIRECTOR: Rotating assistant teachers
AFFILIATED WITH: Vipassana International Academy/S. N. Goenka
ESTABLISHED: 1985
FACILITIES: Country retreat facility
RETREATS OFFERED: Ten-day Vipassana courses. Three-day *Ana-Pana*
OPEN TO: General public

Nama-Rupa

Nama-Rupa was established as a nonprofit organization to facilitate the public availability of Dhamma teaching and activities, with particular emphasis on Theravada traditions. In a conveniently located urban meeting place, weekly meditation sittings and scheduled *Sutta* and *Abhidhamma* classes are held—taught in English by experienced and knowledgeable Asian teachers. Teaching monks from various affiliations are welcome to visit and teach in an environment devoted to the dispensation of Dhamma. Additional activities include the distribution of Dhamma materials (tapes, etc.) and fund-raising for Asian monasteries. Nama-Rupa was conceived to help "counter-balance" the emphasis on formal sitting practice many Westerners develop as they pursue Satipatthana Vipassana meditation. Though *Sutta* and *Abhidhamma* classes begin with a forty-minute sitting, using traditional objects of concentrated awareness (such as the sensations of breath at the nostrils or of the

rising and falling of the abdomen), the teaching of classic Pali texts and chanting is meant to round out the devotional and intellectual dimensions of Dhamma practice. No attempt is made to duplicate the abundant retreat opportunities locally provided by fellow Bay Area groups (e.g. Dhammachakka, Dharma Foundation, Taungpulu Kaba-Aye), but rather Nama-Rupa seeks to be a neutral, supplemental forum for Dhamma learning.

ADDRESS: 10 Arbor Street, San Francisco, CA 94131
PHONE: (415) 334-4921
SPIRITUAL HEAD: (None)
RESIDENT DIRECTOR: (None permanently)
AFFILIATED WITH: Autonomous
ESTABLISHED: 1987
FACILITIES: Urban meditation center
RETREATS OFFERED: Weekly sittings and classes
OPEN TO: General public

Research Institute for Buddhalogy, Light and Color Energy, Inc.

The founder of the institute, Ven. V. B. Dharmawara, teaches Vipassana, or insight meditation, based on Maha Satipatthana, which investigates the physical body, feeling, mind and mind-objects. He has taught meditation in India, where he lived for forty-five years, and in various other parts of the world. Here in the United States, he has been teaching meditation to students at Claymont School for Continuous Education, Charleston, West Virginia, since 1974 and conducting short nine-day courses in various states. Ven. Dharmawara instructs beginners to start their meditation and concentration-of-mind by means of *Kasinas*, consisting of light of different colors, earth, air, and water. Students then progress to concentration on the rising and falling of the abdomen, as taught by Ven. Mahasi Saya-daw of Burma, or on the breath directly (as instructed in *Visuddhi Magga*). The Research Institute welcomes students for long-term study.

ADDRESS: 3732 East Carpenter Road, Stockton, CA 95205
PHONE: (209) 943-2883
LINEAGE: Theravada
SPIRITUAL HEAD: V. B. Dharmawara
RESIDENT DIRECTOR: Same
AFFILIATED WITH: Autonomous
ESTABLISHED: 1980
RETREATS OFFERED: Shorter Vipassana courses and bi-monthly nine-day courses
OPEN TO: General public

Ordinary Dharma

At Ordinary Dharma our intention is to integrate formal Vipassana training with a practical approach to life in the world. We offer workshops, weekly classes, and instruction in Vipassana meditation. We practice sitting and walking, using a synthesis of styles adapted from Southeast Asia (chiefly Mahasi). We also coordinate the Buddhist Peace Fellowship in Los Angeles.

ADDRESS: 247 Horizon Avenue, Venice, CA 90291
PHONE: (213) 396-5054
LINEAGE: Burmese/Thai Vipassana
SPIRITUAL HEAD: Christopher Reed (British)
RESIDENT DIRECTOR: Same
AFFILIATED WITH: Autonomous
ESTABLISHED: 1981
FACILITIES: Urban meditation center
RETREATS OFFERED: A "Day of Mindfulness," weekend sittings, and Vipassana retreats five or six times annually.
OPEN TO: General public

Insight Meditation West

IMW is establishing a Dharma center, the core of which is Vipassana meditation

from the Theravada tradition. A plurality of Vipassana teachers present different styles and emphases within the framework of mindfulness practice. Some focus on traditional teachings of liberation through intensive practice, others on integrating mindfulness and basic Dharma principles in practical ways in daily life, and involvement in the world. There is a year-round program of intensive retreats of varying lengths for new and old students. These are currently co-sponsored by Dharma Foundation in rented facilities. Once the center is completed, there will be other Dharma related activities offered, such as classes, lectures, dialogues, and workshops. Opportunities for families with children to practice will be given. The completion of all the buildings depends on funds. Donations are appreciated and can be sent to the address below.

ADDRESS: P.O. Box 909, Woodacre, CA 94973
PHONE: (415) 456-8940
LINEAGE: Mahasi Sayadaw, Ajahn Chaa, Taungpulu Sayadaw, Buddhadasa-Bhikkhu, and others
SPIRITUAL HEAD: Jack Kornfield, Joseph Goldstein, Christopher Titmuss, Sharon Salzberg, Jamie Baraz, Christina Feldman, and others.
RESIDENT DIRECTOR: Jack Kornfield and Jamie Baraz
AFFILIATED WITH: Sister of Insight Meditation Society and Dharma Foundation
ESTABLISHED: 1981 informally, 1985 formally.
FACILITIES: Country retreat facility. At present we rent facilities throughout the West Coast and are building a center on a 412-acre property in West Marin, California.
RETREATS OFFERED: Approximately six one to three-week intensive Vipassana retreats per year, several one-day and weekend sittings, "Days of Mindfulness," and other programs which in-

Proposed meeting hall for Spirit Rock Center, Woodacre, California.

clude family retreats, peace retreats, study classes, and other ways of integrating practice into daily life.
OPEN TO: General public

COLORADO

Boulder Vipassana Group
The Boulder Vipassana Group meets once a week in a member's home for sitting practice.
ADDRESS: 745 32nd Street, Boulder, CO 80303
PHONE: (303) 449-3361
LINEAGE: Vipassana
RESIDENT DIRECTOR: Lu Wright
AFFILIATED WITH: Autonomous
FACILITIES: Member's home
OPEN TO: General public

Vipassana Meditation Group
Weekly classes are open to everyone (Buddhist and non-Buddhist, men and women). We offer sitting, walking, Dharma, and chanting. "My main vision in life" writes Lucinda Treelight Green, "is to co-create a Buddhist women's spiritual retreat center and community—who

knows where—within three to five years." Please contact us if interested.
ADDRESS: P.O. Box 6386, Colorado Springs, CO 80934
PHONE: (719) 685-5870
LINEAGE: Theravada
SPIRITUAL HEAD: Ruth Denison
RESIDENT DIRECTOR: Lucinda Treelight Green, Ph.D.
AFFILIATED WITH: Dhamma Dena Desert Vipassana Center, IMS, IMW
ESTABLISHED: 1986
RETREATS OFFERED: One-day and half-day retreats. Weekly classes
OPEN TO: General public

Insight Meditation Institute
Insight Meditation Institute functions as a contact for Vipassana meditators in the Rocky Mountain Region. We provide information about Vipassana, as well as instruction in the practice, when desired. Members gather occasionally for meditation and mutual support. We do not maintain facilities nor a regular schedule of activities, but meet in the homes of members as the need arises.
ADDRESS: 2324 Grape Street, Denver, CO 80207

PHONE: (303) 321-3572
LINEAGE: Mahasi Sayadaw
RESIDENT DIRECTOR: Keith Meagher
AFFILIATED WITH: Autonomous
ESTABLISHED: 1979
FACILITIES: Members' homes
RETREATS OFFERED: None
OPEN TO: General public

Wat Buddhawararam

Wat Buddhawararam is a Buddhist temple
housing a group of Thai monks who serve
the ceremonial needs of Denver's Southeast Asian immigrant community. Monks
conduct services and sit in meditation every morning and evening. The resident
meditation master, Ven. Vivekananda-
Bhikkhu, invites all interested American
people to join the monks in meditation
and to participate in insight meditation.
Retreats are held three times each year. All
teachings and meditation courses are offered free of charge.
ADDRESS: 1801 Julian Street, Denver,
CO 80221
PHONE: (303) 433-1826
LINEAGE: Theravada (Thai)
SPIRITUAL HEAD: Ven. Dr. Vivekananda
(Thai). The Ven. Dr. Vivekananda has
been a Buddhist monk since 1946. In
his native Thailand he studied with the
Ven. Buddhadasa-Bhikkhu and with
Ajahn Chaa before journeying to Ran-
goon, Burma, for intensive training un-
der the Mahasi Sayadaw. Dr. Vivekan-
anda teaches insight meditation based
upon mindfulness of the breath.
RESIDENT DIRECTOR: Same
AFFILIATED WITH: Autonomous
FACILITIES: Urban meditation center,
Thai Buddhist temple.
RETREATS OFFERED: Seven-day medita-
tion course three times a year in July,
August, and September. Daily medita-
tion and service morning and evening.
OPEN TO: General public

DISTRICT OF COLUMBIA

Buddhist Vihara Society

Ven. Bhante Henepola Gunaratana
teaches Vipassana meditation at the Washington Buddhist Vihara and at the Bhavana Center in West Virginia. At the Vihara, he teaches meditation daily and at
the Bhavana Center, in summer. Also he
conducts periodic retreats. His courses
run from seven days to ten days. All these
courses are open to the public.
"Vipassana meditation is a systematic
method of cultivating mindfulness of
the body, feelings, consciousness, and
Dhamma. This is the system taught by the
Buddha. It is preserved in the *Mahasati-
patthana Sutta* (foundations of mindfulness). Vipassana meditation leads to purification of mind, to overcoming grief and
sorrow, pain and suffering, to treading the
path to liberation from *samsara* and to attaining *nibbana*. Vipassana, the way of
mindfulness, is the only path to liberation
from *samsara*."—H. Gunaratana
ADDRESS: 5017 16th Street, Northwest,
Washington, DC 20011
PHONE: (202) 723-0773
SPIRITUAL HEAD: Ven. Dr. H. Gunara-
tana (Sri Lankan)
RESIDENT DIRECTOR: Same
AFFILIATED WITH: Sasana Sevaka
Society
ESTABLISHED: 1966
FACILITIES: Urban meditation center
with a country retreat facility in West
Virginia.
RETREATS OFFERED: Short Vipassana
courses. Monthly retreats.
OPEN TO: General public

Vietnamese-American Buddhist Association

Also known as Jetavana Vihara or Chua
Ky Vien, the Vietnamese-American Buddhist Association is a small city monastery
and meditation center of the Theravada

tradition. Ten-day Vipassana retreats are offered four times a year, and the monastery is open for informal sitting the rest of the time. Meditation is taught mainly according to the Mahasi Sayadaw system. Instruction is available in English.
ADDRESS: 1400 Madison Street, Northwest, Washington, DC 20011
PHONE: (202) 882-6054
LINEAGE: Theravada (Vietnamese)
SPIRITUAL HEAD: Ven. Khippapanno (Vietnamese)
AFFILIATED WITH: Autonomous
ESTABLISHED: 1982
FACILITIES: Urban meditation center
RETREATS OFFERED: Ten-day Vipassana retreats four times yearly.
OPEN TO: General public

FLORIDA

Bodhi Tree Dhamma Center

This one-acre suburban center offers weekly Vipassana sittings, monthly half-day retreats, and periodic longer intensives. Visiting teachers from both the Theravada and Zen traditions are invited to lead retreats and give public lectures. A healthy specimen of the Bodhi tree grows on the grounds, a fine setting for walking meditation. The center's bookstore offers meditation texts and supplies imported from Asia. Classes in meditative movement are also offered.
ADDRESS: 11355 Dauphin Avenue, Largo, FL 34648
PHONE: (813) 392-7698
SPIRITUAL HEAD: Visiting teachers
RESIDENT DIRECTOR: Jim and Jeanne Cameron
AFFILIATED WITH: "We are independent, but we have a loose affiliation with Dhammachakka Meditation Center and Washington Buddhist Vihara."
ESTABLISHED: 1982
FACILITIES: Urban meditation center. ("Call us suburban—we're in a busy metropolis, Tampa Bay, population one million, but we have quiet, one-acre grounds.")
RETREATS OFFERED: Short Vipassana courses. Combination Rinzai/Soto sesshin, a "Day of Mindfulness," weekend sittings, classes in meditative movement (e.g., Hatha Yoga and Tai Chi). Half-day retreats every month on full moon; one-day retreats quarterly; one-week retreat once a year.
OPEN TO: General public

Insight, Inc. and Miami Insight

ADDRESS: 1525 Northeast 142nd Street, North Miami, FL 33161
PHONE: (305) 895-7334
LINEAGE: Mahasi Sayadaw (Burmese)
RESIDENT DIRECTOR: Bob and Jackie Leshin
AFFILIATED WITH: Autonomous
ESTABLISHED: 1976
FACILITIES: A private home
RETREATS OFFERED: Extended Vipassana retreats on weekends and holidays
OPEN TO: General public

Buddha Sasana Vihara

ADDRESS: 1085 Plaza Comercio Drive, Northeast, St. Petersburg, FL 33702
PHONE: (813) 576-9209
LINEAGE: Theravada
RESIDENT DIRECTOR: The Ven. Sasana Vamsa
AFFILIATED WITH: Autonomous
ESTABLISHED: 1987
FACILITIES: Solitary retreat facilities. Residency program.
OPEN TO: Members only

HAWAII

Vipassana Hawaii

Steven Smith and Michele McDonald offer instruction and guidance in the Mahasi Sayadaw tradition of Satipatthana (mindfulness) Vipassana (insight) meditation, and also teach Shamatha (concentration) practices, such as loving kindness, compassion, sympathetic joy, and equanimity. This is done by way of Sunday sittings, which include instructions, and one hour of silent practice, followed by a Dhamma Talk. Each month one full day of mindfulness practice is offered. Periodically there are weekend and ten-day retreats given on Oahu, Maui, or the Big Island.

From time to time, studies are offered in basic Buddhist psychology, Pali, and in cultivating the forces of purity of mind that are conducive to moral harmony and integrity within the world in which we live. Satipatthana (Mindfulness) Vipassana (Insight) can be defined in the following way:

> Mindfulness and concentration are developed and strengthened by focusing one's attention on a primary object, namely, the rise and fall of the abdomen. Simultaneously, one gives a precise mental notation to each phase of the breath's movement (beginning, middle, and end). During this process it is natural for secondary objects— sounds, smells, bodily sensations, thoughts, emotions—to arise in the field of awareness. When such objects become prominent, one must again observe them precisely and concurrently. When the secondary object is no longer prominent, one's mindfulness should then return to the rise and fall of the abdomen. These mental notes are made with "bare attention," which is nothing more than mindfulness of each object at the precise moment of its occurence. That is to say that each object is noted without condemning or clinging; just allowing; reflecting, like a mirror, only what is in front of it.

ADDRESS: 882 Nenelea Street, Haliimaile, HI 96796

PHONE: (808) 572-0137
LINEAGE: Ven. Mahasi Sayadaw and Ven. U Pandita Sayadaw
SPIRITUAL HEAD: Ven. Sayadaw U Pandita
RESIDENT DIRECTOR: Steven Smith and Michele McDonald. The teachers have had extensive training and are also on the teaching staff of Insight Meditation Society, Barre, Massachusetts. Steven Smith has had training as an ordained monk. Occasionally other teachers are invited to teach at the Vipassana Hawaii Center. All instruction and studies are offered to beginners and to advanced students alike.
AFFILIATED WITH: Thathana Yeiktha, Rangoon, Burma (Mahasi Monastery)
ESTABLISHED: Incorporated in 1987; sitting groups started approximately in 1977.
FACILITIES: Urban meditation center with a rented country facility available for retreats
RETREATS OFFERED: Supervised solitary retreats. Monthly "Day of Mindfulness"; quarterly weekend, and once yearly ten-day retreats.
OPEN TO: General public

ILLINOIS

Wat Dhammaram

Wat Dhammaram came into being on May 17, 1976. Although young in years, the temple is mature in its program initiatives. Programs such as Buddhist Sunday School, daily morning and evening meditation open to the public, short Vipassana courses, and so on have been established. Wat Dhammaram issues two journals and also publishes booklets and pamphlets from time to time.

ADDRESS: 7059 West 75th Street, Chicago, IL 60638
PHONE: (312) 594-8100
LINEAGE: Theravada

SPIRITUAL HEAD: Phra Rajratanaporn (Thai)
RESIDENT DIRECTOR: Ft. Chuen Phangcham (Thai)
AFFILIATED WITH: Autonomous
ESTABLISHED: 1976
FACILITIES: A separate room in our own building is provided for group meditations; facilities for solitary meditation are available.
RETREATS OFFERED: Vipassana course conducted once a year, usually in January
OPEN TO: General public

Buddhadharma Meditation Center

The Buddhadharma Meditation Center is an institution dedicated to spiritual discipline and the realization of higher knowledge. It emphasizes the application of Dharma to life as one progresses along the path of the Buddha and his enlightened disciples. The BMC holds the Pali Tripitaka as its source of inference but is also open to other thoughts and theories without prejudice as to denomination. It runs an excellent Sunday Dharma school as well as weekend services and meditation sittings and retreats; it has a regular newsletter, Dharma discussions, and is involved in teaching Buddhism and meditation in several other states in the United States. Dr. Phra Sunthorn also accepts invitations to teach and conduct retreats at other centers. He travels widely and is a well-known meditation master.
ADDRESS: 7201 South Cass Avenue, Darien, IL 60559
PHONE: (312) 960-5359
SPIRITUAL HEAD: Dr. Phra Sunthorn Plamintr (Thai)
ESTABLISHED: 1986
FACILITIES: Urban meditation center. We also plan to remodel existing facilities for group meditation.

RETREATS OFFERED: Three-month Vipassana retreats are under consideration. We offer short Vipassana courses, weekend sittings, supervised solitary retreats, and a meditation tour to Thailand. Dates for meditation retreats throughout the year vary.
OPEN TO: General public

Burmese Buddhist Association

Burmese Buddhist Association of Chicago was formed in 1984. The main objective was to establish a Burmese Buddhist Temple in Chicago with resident monks who would be able to perform religious ceremonies according to Burmese custom. The association has now bought a building which will be used as a residence for the monks.
ADDRESS: 15 West 110 Forest Lane, Elmhurst, IL 60126
PHONE: (312) 941-7608
LINEAGE: Burmese Buddhist
SPIRITUAL HEAD: Ven. U Panawuntha (Burmese)
RESIDENT DIRECTOR: Ven. U Thondaya (Burmese)
AFFILIATED WITH: International Organization of Burmese Buddhist Sanghas
ESTABLISHED: 1987
FACILITIES: Urban meditation center with facilities for solitary retreats
RETREATS OFFERED: Short course in Vipassana meditation
OPEN TO: General public

IOWA

Vipassana Sitting Group

We meet Wednesdays at 7:00 P.M. at the Thoreau Center, 2920 Kingman Boulevard, Des Moines, Iowa 50311.
ADDRESS: C/O Ray Hock, 1920 40th Place, Des Moines, IA 50310
LINEAGE: Theravada
RESIDENT DIRECTOR: Ray Hock

AFFILIATED WITH: Autonomous
RETREATS OFFERED: Weekly meditation
OPEN TO: General public

MARYLAND

Burman–American Buddhist Association/Mengala Rama Buddhist Vihara

A small, urban monastery supported by the Burman–American Buddhist Association, which serves the Burmese Community in the Washington, D.C. area. Under the direction of Ven. Kaba Aye Sayadaw U Pannadipa, the monastery offers a program of weekend and seven-day Theravada Vipassana meditation retreats, principally in the tradition of the Mahasi Sayadaw, though other techniques are taught as well. These retreats are open to all. Additionally, space is available for solitary retreats. The monastery publishes books on the theory and practice of Buddhism, and lectures on Buddhist topics are given from time to time.
ADDRESS: 1708 Powdermill Road, Silver Springs, MD 20903
PHONE: (301) 439-4035
LINEAGE: Burmese Theravada, Mahasi Sayadaw and other methods of Vipassana
SPIRITUAL HEAD: Mahasi Sayadaw
RESIDENT DIRECTOR: Ven. Kaba Aye Sayadaw U Pannadipa
AFFILIATED WITH: Autonomous
ESTABLISHED: 1982
FACILITIES: Urban meditation center; monastery in the city with solitary retreat facilities.
RETREATS OFFERED: Weekend and seven-day Vipassana retreats, and solitary retreats
OPEN TO: Burmese community and the general public

Cambodian Buddhist Society, Inc.

ADDRESS: 13800 New Hampshire Avenue, Silver Springs, MD 20902
PHONE: (301) 622-6544
SPIRITUAL HEAD: Ven. Oung Mean (Cambodian)
FACILITIES: Urban meditation center
RETREATS OFFERED: Vipassana retreat once a year for three months
OPEN TO: General public

Wat Thai Buddhist Association of Washington, D.C.

Located on five acres of land near the nation's capitol, Wat Thai is the residence for five monks from Thailand. It is supported by Buddhists in the District of Columbia, Maryland, Virginia, Delaware, and from all over the United States. Besides Thai diplomatic officials, those who frequent the temple are mostly students, who, in comparison with those in other big cities, are not numerous. The temple is quiet most of the day and on most days of the week. Its activities concentrate mainly on the observance and celebration of annual Buddhist holy days and Thai traditional holidays. The temple also welcomes inquiries from devoted lay persons and interested occasional visitors. It provides answers and explanations on various points of the Buddha's teaching and on meditation, both in theory and practice.
ADDRESS: 13440 Layhill Road, Silver Springs, MD 20906
PHONE: (301) 871-8660
LINEAGE: Theravada Buddhism (Thai)
AFFILIATED WITH: Autonomous
ESTABLISHED: 1974
FACILITIES: Urban meditation temple and monastic residence
RETREATS OFFERED: Depends on the occasion
OPEN TO: All Buddhists

International Meditation Center—USA

IMC-USA is a nonprofit religious organization whose purpose is to promulgate the teachings of the Buddha, including the practice of Vipassana Meditation as taught by the late Sayagyi U Ba Khin of Rangoon, Burma. The group is currently engaged in developing a center which will be located in southeastern Pennsylvania, easily accessible to all major East Coast cities. Currently ten-day and weekend retreats are being offered on both East and West coasts by United States resident teachers and Sayama and Saya U Chit Tin. Ten-day retreats involve three and one-half days of the practice of *Anapanasatti* (mindfulness of the breath), followed by Vipassana Meditation to develop one's own understanding of impermanence, unsatisfactoriness, and non-self. The training aims towards the cultivation of *Sila* (morality) through virtuous living, *Samadhi* (concentration) through the practice of *Anapanasatti* (meditation on the breath) and *Pannya* (wisdom), which develops through the practice of Vipassana (insight) meditation by means of which an understanding of *Anicca* (impermanence), *Dukkha* (unsatisfactoriness), and *Annata* (non-self) arises naturally.

ADDRESS: P.O. Box 314, White Marsh, MD 21162
P.O. Box 13314, Suite 111, Oakland, CA 94661
PHONE: (301) 461-8946
LINEAGE: Sayagyi U Ba Khin
SPIRITUAL HEAD: Sayama and Saya U Chit Tin (Burmese)
RESIDENT DIRECTOR: Michael Kosman, Dave Young, Craig Storti
AFFILIATED WITH: Sayagyi U Ba Khin Memorial Trust, England
ESTABLISHED: 1984
FACILITIES: Rented facilities at present but in the process of purchasing country retreat site

RETREATS OFFERED: Four ten-day courses a year and one weekend retreat per month
OPEN TO: General public

MASSACHUSETTS

Insight Meditation Society

The Insight Meditation Society is located on eighty-five acres in the quiet countryside of central Massachusetts. IMS provides a secluded environment for the intensive practice of Vipassana (insight) meditation. Silence and a daily sitting schedule are maintained at all times. A typical retreat day would start at 5:00 A.M. and end at 10:00 P.M., with the entire day spent in alternating periods of silent sitting and walking meditation. Teacher-supervised retreats may vary in length from two to nine days, to three months. The guiding teachers of IMS are Joseph Goldstein, Sharon Salzberg, Jack Kornfield, and Christina Feldman. Other teachers living in the United States and abroad are invited to lead retreats on a regular basis so that a wide range of teachings within the Vipassana tradition are represented. IMS also offers the opportunity for individuals to do self-retreats if they have had experience in the practice of insight meditation described in the following way:

Learning to observe experience from a place of stillness enables one to relate to life with less fear and clinging. Seeing life as a constantly changing process, one begins to accept pleasure and pain, fear and joy, and all aspects of life with increasing equanimity and balance. As insight deepens, wisdom and compassion arise. Insight meditation is a way of seeing clearly the totality of one's being and experience. Growth in clarity brings about penetrating insight into the nature of who we are, and increased peace in our daily lives.

ADDRESS: Pleasant Street, Barre, MA 01005

PHONE: (617) 355-4378

SPIRITUAL HEAD: Joseph Goldstein, Sharon Salzberg, Jack Kornfield, Christina Feldman

RESIDENT DIRECTOR: Teaching staff rotates.

AFFILIATED WITH: Autonomous

ESTABLISHED: 1975

FACILITIES: Country retreat facility with facilities for solitary retreats

RETREATS OFFERED: Three-month Vipassana retreat, shorter Vipassana courses, weekend sittings, supervised solitary retreats. Except for two weeks in January, the center is open year-round.

OPEN TO: General public

Cambridge Insight Meditation Center

The Cambridge Insight Meditation Center is a nonresidential urban center for the practice of insight meditation. The center provides an environment where contemplative life can be developed and protected amidst the complexities of city living. It serves as a place where a growing community can come together to learn, support, and deepen practice. CIMC offers group sittings, classes, retreats, talks, special programs, and social activities. A particular emphasis of CIMC is the integration of mindfulness in sitting practice with mindfulness in all aspects of everyday life.

ADDRESS: 331 Broadway, Cambridge, MA 02139

PHONE: (617) 491-5070

SPIRITUAL HEAD: Larry Rosenberg

RESIDENT DIRECTOR: Larry Rosenberg

AFFILIATED WITH: Autonomous

ESTABLISHED: 1985

FACILITIES: Urban meditation center

RETREATS OFFERED: "Days of Mindfulness," daily and weekend sittings. Retreats are given about twice a month.

OPEN TO: General public

Vipassana Meditation Center

Vipassana Meditation Center offers Vipassana meditation as taught by S. N. Goenka. Intensive silent retreats are open to the general public. The usual course format is ten days. Introductory weekend courses are also offered, as well as longer advanced courses. The center operates under the close guidance of S. N. Goenka. Most courses are conducted by authorized assistant teachers. There is no charge for the teaching. Donations are accepted from participants only to cover room, board, and other operating expenses. There are affiliated centers or organizations in California, the Northwest, Canada, Europe, Australia, New Zealand, Japan, Nepal, and India. The following describes a typical retreat:

In a ten-day retreat, meditators begin by undertaking the Five Precepts of moral conduct as the basis for their practice. They work to concentrate the mind by focusing attention on natural breath at the entrance of the nostrils. Once sufficient concentration is established, they proceed to the technique of Vipassana proper: They explore their mental and physical nature by moving attention systematically throughout the body, dispassionately observing the physical sensations that naturally occur. This ever-deepening introspection sets in motion a process by which the past conditioning of the mind is eliminated layer by layer. The course concludes with the practice of *metta-bhavana*, the mental sharing with others of the benefits meditators have gained by their practice.

ADDRESS: Shelburne-Colrain Road, Shelburne Falls, MA 01370 (Mailing address: P.O. Box 24, Shelburne Falls, MA 01370)
PHONE: (413) 625-2160
LINEAGE: Vipassana Meditation in the tradition of Sayagyi U Ba Khin, as taught by S. N. Goenka.
SPIRITUAL HEAD: S. N. Goenka (Indian)
RESIDENT DIRECTOR: No resident teachers; numerous American assistants conduct courses on a guest basis.
AFFILIATED WITH: There are other organizations with the same teaching, but there is no "parent" group, as such.
ESTABLISHED: 1982
FACILITIES: Country retreat facility
RETREATS OFFERED: Approximately thirty ten-day courses a year in North America.
OPEN TO: General public

MICHIGAN

Mrs. Sarnsethsiri's Vipassana Sitting Group

Mrs. Sarnsethsiri is a Thai woman who teaches meditation in several states, as well as in Europe and Thailand. She offers meditation instruction and conducts retreats in her home. A beginner's class is held every Saturday afternoon at 1:00 P.M. (or at other times by appointment). In extended retreats she is often joined by Thai monks and meditation masters from the surrounding area. Dhamma tapes and books are available, which are either loaned or given out free of charge. Mrs. Sarnsethsiri writes: "There have been several American friends who have come to join in Vipassana meditation practice. The results are beginning to show in their daily lives, and some have even started to teach meditation in their own homes."
ADDRESS: 2427 Hunt Club Drive, Bloomfield, MI 48013

PHONE: (313) 644-7403
LINEAGE: Vipassana (Thai)
SPIRITUAL HEAD: Traipitra Sarnsethsiri
RESIDENT DIRECTOR: Same
AFFILIATED WITH: Autonomous
ESTABLISHED: 1985
FACILITIES: In home. Solitary retreat facilities available.
RETREATS OFFERED: Four or seven-day Vipassana courses
OPEN TO: General public

MISSOURI

Heartland Insight Meditation

This is an informal organization that serves to support the growth of Zen and Vipassana practice in the central Midwest. Students and interested persons are referred to established centers or upcoming retreats. Gregg (Khemacara) Galbraith, a student of Vipassana in the Burmese tradition since 1973, provides teaching and counselling services.
ADDRESS: 427 South Main Street, Carthage, MO 64836
SPIRITUAL HEAD: None
RESIDENT DIRECTOR: Gregg Khemacara Galbraith (American)
AFFILIATED WITH: Autonomous
ESTABLISHED: 1982
FACILITIES: None
RETREATS OFFERED: Sittings. Weekend retreats occasionally.
OPEN TO: General public

NEW MEXICO

Las Vegas Vipassana

Bob and Dixie Ray recently settled in Las Vegas after having operated the Chicago Meditation Center for many years. They are organizing insight meditation retreats in the New Mexico area and hope to establish a meditation center in the forseeable future. They welcome requests for information about Vipassana meditation and retreats and will give instruction to all who wish to learn.

ADDRESS: 818 7th Street, Las Vegas, NM 87701
PHONE: (505) 454-1671
LINEAGE: Vipassana (Burmese-Thai)
SPIRITUAL HEAD: None
RESIDENT DIRECTOR: Bob and Dixie Ray
AFFILIATED WITH: Chicago Meditation Center
ESTABLISHED: 1988 in New Mexico
FACILITIES: Private home
RETREATS OFFERED: Seven-day vipassana retreat; two-day nonresidential retreat.
OPEN TO: General public

Community Meditation Center of Santa Fe

Shelly Young teaches Vipassana meditation, emphasizing the "Body Scanning" technique adapted from the Burmese teacher U Ba Khin. Beginning classes and retreats are offered on a regular basis. Shelly specializes in the application of Vipassana to eating disorders and other addictions.

PHONE: (505) 438-0116
SPIRITUAL HEAD: Shelly Young
RESIDENT DIRECTOR: Same
AFFILIATED WITH: Community Meditation Center of Los Angeles
ESTABLISHED: 1982
FACILITIES: Urban meditation center
RETREATS OFFERED: Monthly one-day and annual ten-day retreats
OPEN TO: General public

NEW YORK

The Metta Foundation

The Metta Foundation was established to provide access to Vipassana meditation and Buddhist teachings in the Theravada

tradition. In addition to weekly meditation, extended retreats, and Dhamma talks, the group sponsors visits by teachers from Sri Lanka, Thailand, and elsewhere. The Metta Foundation has embarked upon the Buddhist Text Computer Project, entering into computer format the entire Pali Canon. The Foundation maintains an extensive library and is also involved in limited translation and publishing activities. A group sitting is held Wednesday evenings at 8:00 P.M. at the center. Meditation instruction is available. All of the group's activities are open to the public and are offered free of charge.

ADDRESS: Nelson Lane, Garrison, NY, 10524
PHONE: (914) 424-4071
LINEAGE: Theravada
SPIRITUAL HEAD: None
RESIDENT DIRECTOR: Gregory Kramer
AFFILIATED WITH: Autonomous
ESTABLISHED: 1979
FACILITIES: Country retreat facility
RETREATS OFFERED: Weekly Wednesday evening sittings; one to seven-day Vipassana retreats.
OPEN TO: General public

New York Buddhist Vihara

This is a religious center teaching the principles and practices of Theravada Buddhism. The resident monks offer instruction in Buddhist philosophy and meditation and are available as speakers for educational and religious institutions. We welcome Buddhists of all traditions, friends of Buddhism, and visitors. Instruction and guidance are given without charge and are offered as a gift of the Dhamma. The shrine room at New York Buddhist Vihara is a special place for devotional and meditational use. The focus of the shrine room is the serene Buddha image, sculpted by a monk from Sri

Lanka. A reference library of over a thousand books is available and covers many aspects of Buddhist thought and practice.
ADDRESS: 84–32 124th Street, Kew Gardens, NY 11415
PHONE: (718) 849-2637
LINEAGE: Theravada
SPIRITUAL HEAD: Ven. Mahathera Kurunegoda Piyatissa (Sri Lanka)
RESIDENT DIRECTOR: Same
AFFILIATED WITH: Gangaramaya, Colombo 2, Sri Lanka
ESTABLISHED: 1980
FACILITIES: We have a meditation room and main hall at the temple.
RETREATS OFFERED: Short Vipassana courses, chanting retreat, supervised and unsupervised solitary retreats, *Abhidhamma* class, Dhamma *Desanas,* children's class, monthly Dhamma program. Retreats held every Saturday afternoon.
OPEN TO: General public

Vajiradhammapadip Temple, Inc.

The temple's activities can be summarized as follows: 1)Perform Buddhist ceremonies for all types of religious occasions. 2) Educate and disseminate to the general public Buddhist religious practices and doctrines. Sunday School is provided for American-born Thais. The curriculum includes Thai language, folk dance, and martial arts. 3) Provide and maintain an English-Thai library of over two thousand books on Buddhism. The collection includes the full *Tripitaka* (Buddhist Canon) in Thai, Pali, and English. 4) Teach and help develop personal tranquility through *Samma Arahang* meditation. 5) Give guest lectures on Buddhism as requested.
ADDRESS: 75 California Road, Mount Vernon, NY 10552
PHONE: (914) 699-5778; 699-7737

LINEAGE: Theravada Buddhism (Thai)
SPIRITUAL HEAD: Somdejphra Ariyavongsakatanan, Patriarch (Thai)
RESIDENT DIRECTOR: Phramaha Siripong Ariyavangso
AFFILIATED WITH: The Council of Thai Bhikkus, USA
ESTABLISHED: 1975
FACILITIES: Urban meditation center; solitary retreat facilities.
RETREATS OFFERED: Seven-day tranquility development (*Samma Arahang*) retreat. Group meditation available daily (7:00 to 9:00 P.M.) at the temple.
OPEN TO: General public

NORTH CAROLINA

Durham Yoga and Meditation Center

John A. Orr is a former Theravada Buddhist monk ordained in Thailand. For the past eight years he has been leading Vipassana retreats, ranging from a weekend to ten days, at various centers in the United States and Europe. He has lived in Durham, North Carolina, for the last five years, offering weekly yoga and meditation classes in various community centers and at Duke University, and extended retreats at a local camp and at other retreat facilities in the area. "I feel," he writes, "that there is a community of people practicing meditation here, but as yet we don't have a building of our own. There is a center without a center, if you will." Plans for the immediate future are to find a space to be called the Durham Yoga and Meditation Center.
ADDRESS: 1214 Broad Street #2, Durham, NC 27705
PHONE: (919) 286-4754
LINEAGE: Vipassana (Thai)
RESIDENT DIRECTOR: John A. Orr (American)

68

THERAVADA

AFFILIATED WITH: Autonomous
ESTABLISHED: 1985
FACILITIES: Homes of friends
RETREATS OFFERED: Vipassana weekends, seven and ten-day retreats.
OPEN TO: General public

OREGON

Eugene Vipassana Group

"Our Eugene Vipassana Group celebrated its second anniversary in February 1988. We meet once a week, starting with a fifteen-minute walking meditation and then sit for forty-five minutes. Once a month we follow the meditation with a potluck supper and discussion group with prearranged topics such as 'Why do we meditate?', suffering, 'How can we help?', money, sex, and parents. There is no leader in our group. We are all equals and share responsibilities. We started the group in order to have a *sangha* of loving friends to support us in our practice. We are delighted with the warmth and laughter that we share before and after our sessions and with the family-like feeling that has grown among us. We now have between seven and ten people regularly attending our meditations, and at our second anniversary meditation and potluck party there were twenty people. Meditation is alive and well in Eugene!"
ADDRESS: 2441 Emerald, Eugene, OR 97403
PHONE: (503) 683-6280
LINEAGE: Theravada
SPIRITUAL HEAD: None
RESIDENT DIRECTOR: None
AFFILIATED WITH: Insight Meditation Society
ESTABLISHED: 1986
FACILITIES: Urban meditation center
RETREATS OFFERED: One and two-day Vipassana retreats
OPEN TO: General public

Columbia Sangha

The Columbia Sangha is an informal group, varying in size between six and fifteen people. We sit weekly for forty-five minutes and are planning to begin some all-day sits. All the members of this *sangha* have had some training in Vipassana.
ADDRESS: 2501 Southeast Madison, Portland, OR 97214
PHONE: (503) 234-3219
LINEAGE: Vipassana
FACILITIES: Members' homes
RETREATS OFFERED: We attend retreats at other centers.

RHODE ISLAND

Buddhist Temple of New England

This temple is grounded in the Buddha-Dhamma-Vinaya, which includes Shamatha and Vipassana meditation practice for all people. The temple offers morning and noon chanting, discourses, and preaching, daily. Open to all.
ADDRESS: 178 Hanover Street, Providence, RI 02907
PHONE: (401) 273-0969
LINEAGE: Theravada (Cambodian)
SPIRITUAL HEAD: Maha Ghosananda (Cambodia)
RESIDENT DIRECTOR: Same
AFFILIATED WITH: World Federation Of Buddhists
ESTABLISHED: 1980
FACILITIES: Urban meditation temple; country retreat facilities.
RETREATS OFFERED: *Vedananupassana* (feeling insight meditation)
OPEN TO: All people

TENNESSEE

The Buddhist Temple

We are closely associated with the Mahasi Yeiktha of Burma.

ADDRESS: 230 Treutlan Street, Nashville, TN 37207 (Mailing address: P.O. Box 121191, Nashville, TN 37212)
PHONE: (615) 254-6108; 297-9860
LINEAGE: Vipassana
SPIRITUAL HEAD: Ven. Siccavumsa (Burmese) and Ven. Ratanaseeha (Sri Lankan)
RESIDENT DIRECTOR: We have monks from Sri Lanka, Burma, Laos, and Cambodia and hope to get some Mahayana and Vajrayana monks soon.
AFFILIATED WITH: Autonomous
ESTABLISHED: 1982
FACILITIES: Urban meditation center
RETREATS OFFERED: Short Vipassana courses given irregularly
OPEN TO: General public

TEXAS

Southwest Vipassana Association

ADDRESS: 3936 Travis Street, No. 9, Dallas, TX 75204
PHONE: (214) 528-5715
LINEAGE: Vipassana/U Ba Khin Tradition
SPIRITUAL HEAD: S. N. Goenka
AFFILIATED WITH: Vipassana Meditation Center, Shelburne Falls, Massachusetts
ESTABLISHED: 1987
FACILITIES: SVA organizes courses from time to time at campsites and other locations.
RETREATS OFFERED: Ten-day Vipassana courses led by assistant teachers of S. N. Goenka
OPEN TO: General public

UTAH

The Last Resort

As a bed and breakfast service we offer a unique environment. Our solid log home in the mountains of southern Utah can accommodate up to twelve people comfortably. We overlook the incredible view of Sunset Cliffs at an elevation of 8,700 feet. As an alternative to the usual fare and mood, we serve gourmet vegetarian food, and the space is very conducive to relaxation, yoga, and other practices. With our work, we follow the seasons and the natural flow of our energy. Winter is a natural time to turn inward. To start the new year off right, we have a five or ten-day Vipassana Meditation Retreat. We also utilize the precision art of i yoga to ease muscle tension. This retreat is in total silence. No pleasures of this world can compare to the inner stillness of deep meditation.
ADDRESS: P.O. Box 6226, Cedar City, UT 84720
PHONE: (801) 682-2289
LINEAGE: Vipassana/Burmese tradition
SPIRITUAL HEAD: Abhilesha and Pujari
RESIDENT DIRECTOR: Pujari
AFFILIATED WITH: Autonomous
ESTABLISHED: 1984
FACILITIES: Country retreat facility for group and solitary retreats
RETREATS OFFERED: Five and ten-day Vipassana retreats
OPEN TO: General public

WASHINGTON

Washington Buddhavanaram

ADDRESS: 4401 South 360th Street, Auburn, WA 98002
PHONE: (206) 927-5408
LINEAGE: Theravada (Thai)
SPIRITUAL HEAD: P Suwat Suwajo
RESIDENT DIRECTOR: Smai Harnseetthi
FACILITIES: Ethnic temple and monastic center with facilities for solitary retreats
OPEN TO: General public

Cloud Mountain

Cloud Mountain is a rural retreat center in southwestern Washington State, available to Buddhist groups as a site for intensive meditation practice. The center has hosted short (weekend to ten-day) Zen, Vipassana, and Tibetan Buddhist retreats, and is open to groups of any tradition for contemplative purposes. Cloud Mountain has worked closely with Dharma Friendship Foundation in Seattle to sponsor long-term (three-month and one-year) Shamatha retreats (using meditation practices for the development of mental concentration and equanimity) led by Tibetan Lama Ven. Gen Lamrimpa from Dharmasala, India, and American teacher B. Alan Wallace.

ADDRESS: C/O Anna and David Branscomb, Cloud Mountain, 373 Agren Road, Castle Rock, WA 98611
PHONE: (206) 274-4859
SPIRITUAL HEAD: None
RESIDENT DIRECTOR: None
AFFILIATED WITH: Autonomous
ESTABLISHED: 1984
FACILITIES: Country retreat facility
RETREATS OFFERED: Please see the above description.
OPEN TO: General public

Dhiravamsa Foundation

A Thai *Vipassanacarya*, Dhiravamsa teaches a holistic consciousness through insight meditation (Vipassana), voice dialogue, and body awareness, blended with Dharma teachings and transformational psychology. This center offers a daily meditation session, chanting, movement to music, and bodywork. Short (ten-day), as well as long, retreats are strongly emphasized. Vipassana, as taught by Dhiravamsa, is based on the Buddha's Satipatthana. It is a way of openness where there is no question of exclusion or control. The focus throughout is on developing

and enlarging simple, nonverbal and nonjudgmental awareness and pure insight into realities as well as unrealities. Our retreats consist of long sittings, interspersed with short periods of walking meditation and gentle bodywork.

ADDRESS: 1660 Wold Road, Friday Harbor, WA 98250
PHONE: (206) 378-5787
LINEAGE: Buddha
SPIRITUAL HEAD: Dhiravamsa
AFFILIATED WITH: Autonomous
ESTABLISHED: 1982
FACILITIES: Country retreat facility with solitary retreat space
RETREATS OFFERED: Shorter Vipassana courses and weekend sittings are conducted throughout the summer and early fall.
OPEN TO: General public

Heartsong Sangha

A "group-managed *sangha*," we function as a support group for individual practice and for applying Buddhist teachings in daily life. A sitting and discussion is held every Wednesday evening at 7:30 P.M., which is open to the public.

ADDRESS: 6015 Greenwood North, Seattle, WA 98103
PHONE: (206) 782-1438
LINEAGE: An amalgam of groups
SPIRITUAL HEAD: None
RESIDENT DIRECTOR: None
AFFILIATED WITH: Autonomous
ESTABLISHED: 1984
FACILITIES: Urban meditation center
RETREATS OFFERED: By arrangement
OPEN TO: General public

Northwest Vipassana Association

We are primarily a contact organization which functions to sponsor and organize Vipassana courses in the tradition of Sayagyi U Ba Khin, as taught by S. N. Goenka and his assistant teachers. The organization maintains the Northwest Dhamma Retreat House on Whitby Island, where introductory talks, weekly group sittings, and self-courses of varying lengths are given.

S. N. Goenka and his assistant teachers lead Anapanna and Vipassana courses of three days, nine days, ten days, twenty days, thirty days, or fifty days in length. This is a nonsectarian practice, and there is no charge, but grateful, old students may provide Dhamma service or make donations towards someone else's course, if their means and volition permit. Introductory talks are given the second Monday of each month and weekly sittings each Tuesday. Periodic self-courses are also offered.

ADDRESS: 1156 North 78th, Seattle, WA 98103
PHONE: (206) 523-2967
LINEAGE: Sayagyi U Ba Khin as taught by S. N. Goenka and his assistant teachers.
SPIRITUAL HEAD: S. N. Goenka (Hindi, born in Burma)
RESIDENT DIRECTOR: All teachers and assistant teachers teach throughout the world.
AFFILIATED WITH: We have many centers throughout the world.
ESTABLISHED: 1983
FACILITIES: Country retreat facility and official meditations at approved places. Solitary retreat facilities available.
RETREATS OFFERED: Weekend sittings and various lengths of self-courses. Eight retreats were conducted in 1987.
OPEN TO: General public

WEST VIRGINIA

Bhavana Society

The Bhavana Society's forest meditation center offers newcomers and experienced meditators alike the opportunity to study and practice Vipassana meditation under the guidance of Ven. H. Gunaratana and Bhante Yogavacara Rahula. Monthly weekend retreats are offered, along with several ten-day courses each year. The center is located on thirteen secluded acres about two hours from Washington, D.C. Plans call for facilities to allow for training of Americans who wish to enter the Theravada (monastic) Sangha, as well as laymen wishing to practice for extended periods in a forest setting.

ADDRESS: Back Creek Road, Highview, WV 26808 (Mailing address: Route 1, Box 218-3, Highview, WV 26808)
PHONE: (No phone yet)
SPIRITUAL HEAD: Ven. Dr. H. Gunaratana (Sri Lankan)
RESIDENT DIRECTOR: Bhante Yogavacara Rahula (American)
ESTABLISHED: 1983
FACILITIES: Country retreat facility
RETREATS OFFERED: Short Vipassana courses; weekend sittings. We plan to establish solitary retreats soon.
OPEN TO: General public

Theravada Centers—Canada

ALBERTA

Light of the Dhamma

Light of the Dhamma is a nonprofit Theravada Buddhist Society. Activities range from introductory workshops in Vipassana meditation to extended residential retreats running from three to ten days in length and which may include seminars and study sessions on *Abhidhamma* philosophy. Either local or international resource persons participate. A newsletter, *Sati*, publishes details three times yearly. Membership is $10 annually. A lending library is available.

Meditation retreat at Bhavana Society, High View, West Virginia.

ADDRESS: 1511 Rio Terrace Drive, Ed-
monton, Alberta, Canada T5R 5M6
LINEAGE: Theravada
ESTABLISHED: 1980
FACILITIES: Urban retreat center, meet-
ings in member's home. Lending library
available.
RETREATS OFFERED: Three, five, seven,
and ten-day Vipassana retreats
OPEN TO: General public

British Columbia

Dhamma—A Theravada Buddhist Society

Anagarika Dhamma-Dinna teaches the
Abhidhamma philosophy. Vipassana teachers such as Ven. Piyadassi Mahathera,

Ven. Nyanasatta Mahathera, Ven. Balan-
doda Ananda Maitreya, Ven. Ajahn So-
bin, and others have been invited repeat-
edly. As a result several manuscripts are
awaiting publication.
ADDRESS: R.R. 1, Halfmoon Bay, B.C.,
Canada V0N 1Y0
PHONE: (604) 883-2643
LINEAGE: Sumatipala Maha Thera (Sri
Lankan)
SPIRITUAL HEAD: Sumatipala Maha
Thera
RESIDENT DIRECTOR: Anagarika
Dhamma-Dinna (Buddhist nun)
AFFILIATED WITH: Autonomous
ESTABLISHED: 1976
FACILITIES: Hermitage; facilities for
solitary retreats for very special students
only; rented hall for Vipassana retreats.

RETREATS OFFERED: Week-long Vipassana retreats, "divine abidings," *Abhidhamma* (Buddhist psychology) studies.
OPEN TO: Generally by invitation

Vipassana Foundation

Assistant teachers of S. N. Goenka offer ten-day courses in Vipassana meditation in the tradition of U Ba Khin. Local activities also include weekly and all-day sittings. Introductory evenings are regularly held. A permanent facility is in the planning stages.
ADDRESS: 95 West 23rd Avenue, Vancouver, B.C., Canada V5Y 2G8
PHONE: (604) 879-9791
LINEAGE: U Ba Khin line (Burmese)
SPIRITUAL HEAD: S. N. Goenka
RESIDENT DIRECTOR: Visiting assistant teachers
AFFILIATED WITH: V.I.A.
ESTABLISHED: 1982
FACILITIES: Group sittings at a student's country retreat property, and rental camps.
RETREATS OFFERED: Ten-day Vipassana courses, one-day sitting for experienced students
OPEN TO: General public

ONTARIO

Toronto Mahavihara

Inaugurated in July of 1978, Toronto Mahavihara is the first Theravada Buddhist center in Canada. At its inception, the service of the Vihara was limited to catering to the spiritual needs of Theravada Buddhists in Canada. However, as Theravada Buddhists are traditionally never satisfied with merely serving themselves, we have extended our services even to the non-Buddhist public by offering courses in the theory and practice of Buddhism. It is our sincere hope that these courses will make a real contribution to the Canadian public, not only in enriching its culture but also in helping build a physically and mentally healthy society. Meditation is held Saturday mornings from 8:00 to 10:00 A.M. A Dhamma class for adults who seek a thorough understanding of the original teachings of the Buddha is conducted on Saturday afternoons from 3:00 till 5:00 P.M.
ADDRESS: 3595 Kingston Road, Scarborough, Ontario, Canada M1M-1R8
PHONE: (416) 269-5882
LINEAGE: Sri Lankan Theravada
SPIRITUAL HEAD: Bhante Punnaji
RESIDENT DIRECTOR: Bhante Punnaji
AFFILIATED WITH: Autonomous
ESTABLISHED: 1978
FACILITIES: Urban meditation center and Buddhist temple with a book store
RETREATS OFFERED: Buddhist meditation retreats off and on
OPEN TO: General public

Vipassana Meditation

ADDRESS: 85 Thorncliff Park Drive, Apt. 2302, Toronto, Ontario, Canada M4H 1L6
LINEAGE: Gotama Buddha via U Ba Khin
SPIRITUAL HEAD: Goenka (Burmese-Indian)
RESIDENT DIRECTOR: Eve Hoch
AFFILIATED WITH: Dhammagiri (India)
ESTABLISHED: No establishment. No organization.
FACILITIES: Country retreat facility and group sittings in homes
RETREATS OFFERED: Three-month retreat, weekend retreats, and shorter Vipassana courses as taught by S. N. Goenka. These retreats are on-going in Shelburne Falls, Massachusetts.
OPEN TO: Students only. One becomes a student at first retreat or course.

PART II

Mahayana

The Path of Compassion

Mahayana: The Path of Compassion

BY PATRICIA CHRISTIAN-MEYER

All beings, without number, I vow to liberate.
Endless blind passions I vow to uproot.
Dharma gates, beyond measure, I vow to penetrate.
The Great Way of Buddha I vow to attain.

These are the *Four Great Bodhisattvic Vows*, the cornerstone of Mahayana Buddhism. The first time I heard these vows chanted, with all their innate energy, I was entranced. The first time I tried chanting them myself, I was intimidated by their magnitude: save all beings? become a Buddha? Good lord, what I wanted from Zen was relief from all the stresses and unhappiness in my life, not sainthood!

Because this book is a guide to meditation and retreat facilities, this overview of the Mahayana branch of Buddhism will take a hands-on practical approach. We'll forego the intricate philosophical and theological aspects in favor of showing you what fundamental attitudes and beliefs you may expect to find if you wander into a Mahayana center: What is *Mahayanism*? What do *Mahayanists* believe? And how does this differ from the other branches of Buddhism?

Bodhisattvahood

The word "*Mahayana*" means "great vehicle" and refers to the fact that the Mahayana branch developed in order to make the attainment of Buddhahood accessible to all beings, as opposed to a select few. The Mahayana tradition is often compared to a very broad river, able to accommodate all manner of boats—fast or slow, large or small, humble or luxurious. Most Mahayanists are generally tolerant of divergent modes of behavior, and it was the Mahayana tradition which enabled Buddhism to spread outside of India, because of its willingness to assimilate cultural elements which were new or foreign to it. The Mahayana tradition developed in Nepal, Tibet, China, Korea, and Japan; although it exhibits very definite cultural traits in each instance, nevertheless it is still very easily identifiable as Mahayana because of the basic doctrines which all hold in common.

The Mahayana doctrines are not so much changes from those which preceded them as they are a shift in emphasis. Think of the development of the Mahayana tradition as a twist of the Buddhist kaleidoscope—all the parts are still there, they just form a different pattern. Mahayana shares all the basic doctrines of Buddhism with the other major denominations, but each emphasizes and interprets those doctrines a little bit differently. The most basic tenet of Mahayana Buddhism is that of the *Bodhisattva*. A Bodhisattva is a person who combines compassion with the wisdom which had been emphasized as the most desirable trait in the Theravada tradition. Where the previous ideal had been the *arahat*, who attained individual liberation, now the new ideal became the Bodhisattva, a being who vows to forego the joy of Nirvana until *all* beings have been enlightened (as in the first vow). In order to become a Bodhisattva, something more was needed than had been previously taught; now the emphasis became the path one follows to develop compassion along with one's wisdom—the "Six Paramitas" (Perfections): generosity, morality, patience, perseverance, meditation, and wisdom. Again, these "perfections" are not a repudiation of the original Eightfold Path of the Buddha, but rather a new emphasis on certain aspects of that path.

Sunyata: Emptiness

Long before the Buddha started preaching the Four Noble Truths, various philosophical schools in India had investigated and debated the proposition of *sunyata* or Emptiness. But in the Mahayana School, the

concept of Emptiness was given very strong emphasis as the fundamental nature of *all* reality. It was re-defined and expanded to be all-
inclusive; now even thoughts and concepts were perceived as fundamentally empty, arising from a primal void which was seen as an active
and positive force, rather than as a negation. When even Nirvana came
to be included in Emptiness, the Mahayana School had made the
breathtaking leap to the clarity beyond all dualistic thinking: if everything is Emptiness, then everything is one and the same. The *absolute*
equals the *relative*; *samsara* (the suffering of the world) equals Nirvana
(the extinction of the suffering of the world). True reality was thus held
to be the knowledge or perception which is experienced before the perception of duality—not a "oneness," but a "not-two-ness." In the Mahayana tradition, there is no way to state simply the true nature of reality—it is considered indefinable.

The Mahayana Emerges

The Mahayana as a recognizable tradition began approximately five
hundred years after the Buddha's time, or around the year A.D. 1 in our
Western calendar. As early as one hundred years after the Buddha's
death there were already arguments among the *sangha* having to do
with interpretation and implementation of the Buddha's words, and the
first split in the group—the *Mahasanghikas*—were definite forerunners
of the Mahayana; this school emphasised the spirit, rather than the letter, of the law. By A.D. 1, a number of major points of dissension had
developed: the "orthodox" forms had ossified and were perceived as
degenerate by the laity; various and competing philosophical schools
had developed within Buddhism; foreign influences were being encountered in both northern and southern India; and, most importantly,
the laity was demanding a larger role in the religion. Mahayana developed as a "solution" to these "problems," with emphasis on the belief
that *all* beings had the potential to attain Nirvana.

From the very start, adherents of the Mahayana tradition claimed that
they were really only revealing doctrines which had previously been
considered "too sacred" to be made known to the laity. The rise of

the Mahayana led to a tremendous flowering of Buddhist literature. It must be remembered that the Buddha—like Christ, Confucius, and Socrates—left not one single word written in his own hand. His words were transmitted through oral tradition and were not actually put into written form until long after his death. So, it is possible that the Mahayana, as well as the Vajrayana after it, represented a gradual shift of the line which divided the "secret" teachings from the "common" ones.

Resilience

Anicca, or change, is a basic tenet of Buddhism, and the Mahayana spread rapidly into other countries because of its emphasis on the need to accommodate changing circumstances and conditions. Thus, while Theravada monks were forbidden by their *Vinaya*, or Rule, to practice medicine, Mahayana monks believed compassion was more important. Like Christian missionaries long after them, they found medicine an apt vehicle for spreading their beliefs. Also, the emphasis on changing conditions made it easier for the Mahayana to assimilate the religious traditions of other cultures. In Tibet it first completely replaced the Theravada tradition and then merged with the indigenous religion (Bon) to eventually develop into an entirely new branch of Buddhism, the Vajrayana, with its emphasis on magic and the esoteric. In China it adopted aspects of Confucianism and Taoism and, with the arrival of Bodhidharma from India in approximately A.D. 500, developed the *Ch'an* (meditation) sect—a uniquely practice-oriented, rather than scholastic, approach to attaining "the Great Way of Buddha." *Ch'an* Buddhism eventually merged again with a devotional sect in China. But before that happened, *Ch'an* was carried into Korea and Japan, where it again merged with indigenous elements in each place.

In Japan the *Ch'an* sect became the *Zen* sect, which stressed direct perception of the true nature of reality; scripture was relegated to a distant second in importance. More attention will be given to Zen in a bit. For now, let's finish looking at the spread of Mahayana Buddhism and the different forms it acquired in Japan. In the twelfth century, devotional sects dedicated to the mythical Buddha Amida arose in Japan. These sects taught that Nirvana could be attained through the repetition of the name of Amida Buddha. Like the "Jesus Prayer" promulgated by the pilgrim in the Christian tradition, the *Amida* sects strove to take the individual beyond dualistic perceptions through intense concentration on one specific word or phrase, to the exclusion of all else. The Pure Land Sect was founded in 1175 by Honen and the *Jodo Shinshu* in 1173 by Shinran, who made Buddhism even more accessible to the laity by doing away with the monastic tradition entirely.

The Rise of Zen

The Mahayana sect of most interest in this book is the Zen sect, because of its emphasis on meditation and retreats. As much as possible, the standard Zen terms will be avoided here and their nearest English equivalents used instead, for the sake of making an admittedly difficult training system more accessible. "Zen" is the Japanese word for the Chinese "*Ch'an*," which itself is a transliteration of the Sanskrit word *dhyana*, roughly translatable as "meditation." Zen traces its founding as a distinct path back to Bodhidharma, who travelled from India to China around A.D. 500 and emphasized meditation and its resultant direct perception as a reaction against the extreme scholasticism of the Chinese Buddhism he encountered. Zen maintains that it is a secret doctrine transmitted orally from the Buddha to his disciple Mahakashyapa and hence directly from one mind to another, rather than in written texts. "Teaching beyond teaching; no leaning on words and letters" is how Zen often describes itself.

Chinese *Ch'an*, which reached its peak in the T'ang Era (A.D. 618–907), eventually split into five sects, of which only two survived. These are best known today by their Japanese names: *Soto* and *Rinzai*. Again, the difference lies solely in emphasis, not in essence. *Rinzai* Zen was brought to Japan at the start of the thirteenth century by Eisai and revitalized by Hakuin some four hundred years later. *Soto* Zen reached Japan in the thirteenth century with the great master Dogen. Zen peaked in Japan during the Kamakura Period (A.D. 1192–1333), the age of the Samurai, warriors who were greatly attracted to Zen's austere discipline. In the early twentieth century, a Zen teacher named Sogaku Harada-roshi studied in both the *Soto* and the *Rinzai* traditions and then proceeded to blend them into a dynamic new tradition, generally called the "Harada-Yasutani Line" today. This new lineage has had a profound effect on Zen in North America.

Zen Training

There are five important elements in Zen training: the student, the teacher, the attitude, the method, and the result. Only the method differs from Zen sect to Zen sect.

In Zen the student sets the pace and the teacher applies his or her methods accordingly. What does this mean for someone who wants to look into Zen training? It means, first and foremost, that one must have a thorough knowledge, on a psychological level, of oneself. Because a Zen student is very much on his or her own, because the Zen manner of meditation is so intense and powerful, and most of all because any meditation which is wholeheartedly practiced will, by its very nature, lead to some sort of "altered state of consciousness," it is important that the beginning student have a basically healthy psyche—Zen is *not* a type of psychotherapy and should not be used as such. Know how you react under pressure; know your ability to persevere in adversity; know your main strengths and weaknesses; and especially know what it is you want to attain.

Finding a Teacher

The second important element of Zen training is the teacher, and finding the right one is a subject which has inspired volumes of advice. Lineage is considered important because one must be sure that one's teacher is competent to handle what is likely to arise in the course of training.

Furthermore, a teacher can only take a student as far as that teacher himself or herself has gone; after that, the student must again make a decision—whether to be content with that level of development, or to seek another teacher. One should, therefore, investigate a number of teachers and their styles *before* making any commitments; once one becomes a formal student of a specific teacher, one's "shopping around" should cease—at least for a number of years. All meditation paths have their peaks and valleys, so there are bound to be "dry spots" where a student feels no progress is being made; the important thing in Zen is to be able to distinguish between a dry spot and a dead end—and the only way to do that is to go through a number of dry spots.

Developing the Right Attitude

The third element of Zen is attitude. Zen places its emphasis on the Buddha's insight into the cause of human suffering (the Second Noble Truth)—attachment. And so Zen training is specifically designed to foster a spirit of nonattachment in the student. It does this by driving the student, as directly as possible, past dualistic thinking, believing that if the true nature of reality is clearly perceived, such perception will dissolve attachment. How can one cling to something one knows is essentially nonexistent, the momentary result of constantly changing circumstances? How can one fear such a fleeting shadow? Do you want to see clearly and live freely? Are you willing to let go of everything—including your self—to do so?

Soto or Rinzai? Two Paths Up the Mountain

It is in the methods of each Zen sect that you will find the greatest diversity. The *Soto* sect, for example, places its primary emphasis on sitting meditation (*zazen*), which is practiced facing the wall in the meditation hall, and sees no dualism between practice and enlightenment. Since the Buddha said all creatures are whole and complete from the very beginning, it is not a matter of "attaining" anything outside ourselves (how can a Buddha become a Buddha?), but rather of slowly deepening our awareness of what we already are. The *Soto* approach to other meditation activities, such as chanting and walking meditation, tends to be a very slow, conscious one, emphasizing intense concentration on the present moment.

Rinzai training, on the other hand, has a somewhat bombastic approach, driving the student beyond his or her dualistic thinking as quickly as possible and as forcefully as necessary. Chanting and walking meditation tend to be very fast, sitting meditation is done with one's back to the wall of the meditation hall (considered more demanding), and an "encouragement stick," applied to the student's back to rouse and deepen meditation energies, is an essential part of the training.

One of the most important tools of *Rinzai* training, however, is the "koan," a sort of Zen riddle which is absolutely insoluble with logic or reason. One of the best known koans, for example, is "What is the sound of one hand?" The first koan appeared in China in 1125, and they now number in the thousands. A koan, skillfully assigned by a teacher and wholeheartedly embraced by a student, will quickly drive that student past all dualism. Because it is such a powerful device, one should *never* work on a koan unless it is assigned by a teacher and one's efforts are then monitored in periodic private interviews with the teacher. One can only "solve" a koan (called "penetrating" or "seeing through" the koan) by intense concentration to the point where small ego-self is abandoned and one is totally identified with the koan.

In the Harada lineage, the methods of both the *Soto* and the *Rinzai* sects are blended and mixed according to the temperament of the teacher and the needs of the students. However, koan practice is generally the norm, and chanting and walking meditation are usually at a medium speed. Primary emphasis is often placed on the initial "breakthrough" of the student, rather than on advanced work.

Dwelling in *Samadhi*

What "results" can be expected from Zen training? The very word "results" is anathema in Zen, but it is useful here. Zen training leads to true freedom. Zen emphasizes seeing the true nature of reality by means of an intensity of meditation training which is designed to lead one to a complete letting go of one's small ego-self in order to see—*and ulti-mately act*—freely, spontaneously, beyond duality. One's entire way of perceiving changes and one's actions then flow from that new level of perception. One is "free" from one's problems, not because one has found "solutions," but because one sees them differently. *Samadhi* is a word used to describe the state of one who is existing on this level of perception, but it is a much misused word. *Samadhi* does not just refer to a state in formal meditation, although that is its most common use. Rather, one who has trained well in Zen lives every moment in a *samadhi*-like state: that is to say, the person does all of his or her tasks from a center of inexhaustible energy, an energy which fairly glows in its detachment from our normal, petty ways of thinking and acting. Such a person moves from washing the dishes to writing a poem, to eating, to driving a car, to sleeping, without becoming entangled in liking or disliking the tasks, without becoming bogged down in past failures and future hopes, always fully aware of exactly what must be done and then totally immersed in *just* doing it. Such a person lives as freely and as naturally as the sun shines down its light and warmth— because he or she can do nothing else. This is why Zen holds that there is nothing to be "attained" or "accomplished." Living in this way is as extraordinary as breathing. As Thomas Merton says in the Christian tradition, "The simplest and most effective way to sanctity is to disap-pear into the background of ordinary everyday routine." Or as Zen has it, "When hungry, just eat; when tired, just sleep." But how many of us live that way?

Ultimately, this entire essay has been nothing but empty words— words to be used as signposts at the start of a journey and then dis-carded in favor of the actual, personal experience of the journey. Bon voyage!

Patricia Christian-Meyer has been a student of Zen Buddhism since 1978. Formerly a vice president in an international corporation, she served as Roshi Philip Kapleau's secretary and research assistant in 1986. She is presently working as a freelance writer and business consultant in St. Louis, Missouri.

One Hand Clapping in Cleveland*

BY MIKE BONASSO

---

*Sensei hurls at us the words of encouragement he will repeat so
many times during this* sesshin: *"Testify it! TESTIFY IT! To
know is* not *to testify! Testify it! You have heard the sound of two
hands clapping." He claps both hands. "Now, what is the sound of
one hand clapping? Sit down!"*

 Rohatsu Sesshin is what I call a "commuter *sesshin.*" Since most
of our *sangha* is comprised of working people, a week of continuous sitting isn't very practical. So we sit for two hours in
the morning starting at 5:30 A.M. and two hours a night, each
day for a week. Our sitting must be very concentrated and sincere to
make up for not being able to sit for fifteen or sixteen hours a day like
our Dharma friends at monasteries.

It is chilly and windy as *sesshin* begins, and the days are getting
shorter and shorter. The darkness of the Zendo is broken only by the
altar lights and candles. Most of us are fatigued as we begin our sitting.
Once we are all seated on our cushions, Sensei Ogui takes his place on
the platform along with the *Ino* and *Gyorin*. We sit for half an hour.

"BONG!" As the gong sounds, we *gassho*, fix our cushions, and prepare for *kinhin*. We conduct our slow walking meditation around the
Zendo with a little more energy than we had when we first got here,
and by the time we return to our cushions after chanting the mantra
Mu, we are fully awake.

The second sitting begins. After a few minutes Sensei Ogui, in a
voice that is soft but at the same time strong, relates the story of Sid-

---

*Rohatsu Sesshin at Zen Shin Sangha at Cleveland Buddhist Temple, Euclid, Ohio

dhartha Gautama, the prince who became a Buddha. In simple words, Sensei tells of the struggle the young prince experienced under the Bodhi tree until, on the morning of December 8, he attained the supreme Enlightenment. Then we are given the koan with which we will struggle during this *Rohatsu Sesshin*: "The sound of One Hand Clapping."

Sensei then hurls at us the words of encouragement he will repeat so many times during this *sesshin*: "Testify it! TESTIFY IT! To know is *not* to testify! Testify it! You have heard the sound of two hands clapping." He claps both hands. "Now, what is the sound of *one* hand clapping? Sit down!"

With a will, we all begin to work on this old, honored koan. As we work, the *Junkei* respectfully approaches the incense burner and takes the *Keisaku* in hand. Slowly, precisely, the *Junkei* begins a circuit of the Zendo. Those who wish to have the *Keisaku* administered, *gassho* to the *Junkei*, who *gasshos* also. "CRACK . . . CRACK! CRACK . . . CRACK!" Then silence. Each one of us struggles with our koan.

"BONG!" Again we *gassho* and fix our cushions. Then three great bows, foreheads touching the floor, hands raised above our ears in thankfulness and respect. *Sutra* chanting. We honor the *Three Treasures*, recite the *Heart Sutra*, and take the vows of a Bodhisattva. After chanting we offer incense and sit in chairs, awaiting Sensei Ogui. He tells us to make a sincere effort during this *Rohatsu Sesshin* and bids us a good morning as we leave for our various homes and workplaces.

And so it continues.

As the week progresses fatigue is forgotten. All that remains is "the sound of one hand clapping." Beating it to death! Beating it to death! I remember thinking that we might as well have been at a monastery; we've had to get up at four o'clock in the morning, shower and get ready in silence, eat quickly, and drive in silence along dark and lonely roads to the Zendo. Those morning drives become *kinhin*, or whatever the word for "driving meditation" is. Red light (*the sound of one hand clapping*), green light (*the sound of one hand clapping*), Exit 49 (*the sound of one hand clapping*), Speed Limit 55 (*the sound of one hand clapping*), and so on.

Each morning and evening fewer words are exchanged as we arrive

Koshin Ogui-Sensei, Zen Shin Sangha, Cleveland Buddhist
Temple, Euclid, Ohio.

at the Zendo. Each sitting is more intense than the last, something
everyone can feel but no one needs to acknowledge. Sensei Ogui:
"Dainin said you must sit on your cushion and STRIVE! As you
continue with your efforts, *zazen* energies will build up. Testify it!
TESTIFY IT!"

There is more driving back and forth between the Zendo and the
day's activities—more automotive *kinhin*, eyes horizontal, "the sound
of one hand clapping" being delved into more and more deeply. Something is happening . . . being lost? Found? What? Dark mornings and
dark nights blend into one another. What day is it? Who cares?

Chanting is becoming more intense. *Enmei Jukku Kannon Gyo*, the
ten phrase, life prolonging *Kannon Sutra* thunders through the Zendo!
At its end we shout "MUUUUUUUUUUUUUUUUUUUUU!" *Zazen*
energies have certainly built up! At the end of each sitting we chant

"*Namu Dai Bosa*" (becoming one with the Bodhisattva spirit) and "*Nam An Da Bu*" (becoming one with infinite wisdom and compassion). Each time there is more feeling in our chanting, a manifestation of our common effort.

Sensei Ogui: "As we approach the end of this *Rohatsu Sesshin* 1987, if any thought arises, DROP IT! DROP IT! DROP IT!" Effort continues . . . the koan begins to burn a hole in my stomach. I'm going to beat it to death if it's the last thing I do! WHAT IS THE SOUND OF ONE HANDCLAPPINGTHESOUNDOFONEHANDCLAPPINGTHE SOUNDOFONEHANDCLAPPINGTHESOUNDOFONE HANDCLAPPING?

As the *sesshin* nears its end, Sensei Ogui's tone is a mixture of understanding and sternness. Quietly, but firmly, he encourages us to devote ourselves to understanding this koan. Each of us meets him in *dokusan* only once during *sesshin*. I wait outside the Zendo door for the sound of the small gong that signals Sensei is ready to see me. As it sounds, I walk through the door, approaching the incense burner. I make a great bow to the Buddhas and Bodhisattvas, bow to Sensei, and sit down. He tells me that the most important thing is to keep up my sincerity. He asks me to demonstrate the sound of two hands clapping, and I comply. Then he asks me to show him the sound of one hand clapping. I demonstrate my current understanding. He says simply, "You may continue to work on it" and excuses me.

Five-thirty in the morning. It's the next-to-last morning of *sesshin*. Working, working, working. The atmosphere in the Zendo seems almost stonelike, and I feel as though I'm all alone among statues in a great museum. The first sitting and *kinhin* are over, and it is nearly time for the *Junkei* to administer the *Keisaku*, when Sensei rises from his cushion, grabs the "encouragement stick," and proceeds to use it on everyone in the Zendo whether they ask for it or not. His approach is like a great windstorm bearing down upon us. Swiftly he is behind me, touching my shoulder with the stick. I *gassho* and bend forward. "CRACK-CRACK! CRRRAAACCK . . . CRRRAAACK!" The force of the blows to my shoulders practically knocks the wind out of me. Dazed, I *gassho* and the windstorm blows on to the next cushion. Later Sensei remarks, "The sitting was very solid today."

December 8 . . . the final day of *Rohatsu Sesshin* 1987. "Bodhi Day." It's early morning, not unlike the one on which an Indian prince saw the morning star and became Buddha. The-sound-of-one-hand-clapping is having its front door beaten and kicked on. "Open up, damnit, open up!" Sensei, implacable on his cushion, says "Your mind must *become* this koan and, at the same time, must guard against other thoughts like a wall of iron . . . AAAUUUURRRRRRRRRRGGGGGHHH!" This powerful roar galvanizes me. I *must*! I *must*! I *must*! WHAT . . . IS . . . THE . . . SOUND . . . OF . . . ONE . . . HAND . . . CLAPPING? Over and over, and over. Come *ON*! . . . WHAT . . . IS . . . THE . . . SOUND . . . OF . . . ONE . . . HAND . . . CLAPPING?

Suddenly, like a car on cruise control, the effort continues of its own accord. It keeps going and going and going. Without any effort it sweetly becomes NAM AN DA BU NAM AN DA BU NAMAN-DABU NAMANDABU NAMANDABU. And then I know. And then it is felt. And then it is clear. And then it is all.

Mike Bonasso has been studying at Zen Shin Sangha since 1986 and is also a member of Cleveland Buddhist Temple (Jodo Shinshu). He is a radio news-man and is married, with "no kids, two cats."

Finding the Middle Way in Ann Arbor*

BY SCOTT MERWIN

The Buddha recognized that we have no other tool than our own body with which to achieve enlightenment. If we foolishly destroy it through extreme practice, we destroy our only chance at gaining freedom from delusion.

I live in East Lansing, Michigan, and regularly travel an hour to the Zen Buddhist Temple in Ann Arbor, where I have been training under the Ven. Samu Sunim since December 1982. Sunim is the founder and president of the Zen Lotus Society, which also has a temple in Toronto and a strong community in Mexico City. He was born in Korea and received his Buddhist training there. Our training in the Zen Lotus Society is largely based on the Korean Zen tradition, although, of course, it has been Westernized to a degree. The three main spiritual practices are sitting meditation, chanting, and prostrations.

Retreats led by Sunim include private interviews during the morning and evening meditation periods. Meditation sessions consist of thirty-minute rounds of sitting, with ten-minute breaks in between. Sunim usually gives a talk at the end of evening meditation. During all retreats there is no talking unless absolutely necessary. People are instructed to keep their eyes down and to concentrate on practice at all times.

With daily practice, and frequent participation in retreats, my commitment to Buddhism has steadily grown over the last five years. My ability to train well during a retreat has also developed slowly, but measurably, over the years.

*Korean *sesshin* at Zen Lotus Society, Ann Arbor, Michigan

Ven. Samu Sunim, president and founder, Zen Lotus Society, Ann Arbor, Michigan.

My first retreat was positive only in that I learned that it is serious
business, and hard work, too. The energy and beauty of a group of
people doing nothing but unbroken spiritual practice is so inspiring
that one can train more effectively in retreat than at any other time.
However, because these retreats are so demanding, there is an element
of risk involved. Mental stability and good physical health are key factors in withstanding the rigorous discipline and hardships one must
often undergo in Zen training.

I had taken three beginner's classes at the temple before I participated in my first retreat. A five-day *Yongmaeng Chongjin* (literally "to leap like a tiger while sitting still") was being held, and the resident priest invited me to participate, even if only for a day or two. I was quite excited at this prospect and made plans to come for one day. Like virtually all Western Zen beginners, I had read books about Buddhism for a long time before I ever resolved to seek formal training. For years I had read about extended retreats and imagined participating in what I regarded as the highest human endeavor. I arrived for evening meditation and was so excited all I could do was watch myself and the others as though we were all actors in a movie. After an hour or so this wore off, and I began to practice resolutely, following my breath as carefully as I could. This resolve also wore off after about an hour. I was left with my same old self, my same sloppy mental habits, my painful legs that were un-trained in sitting. We sat for four forty-minute periods with short breaks in between. Formal sitting ended at 10:00 P.M. I resolved to try again in the morning.

We rose at 4:00 A.M. and began sitting, once again for forty-minute periods. In misery I sat and watched the two pipes on the wall in front of me. Second after second in silence. Minute after minute. I concen-trated on my breath a little, but most of all I wished it were noon so I could go home. At 7:30 A.M. the early morning sitting ended. At 9:00 A.M. we assembled again in the *Sonbang* (meditation hall) for four more periods of sitting. I sat it out in a delirium of pain, distraction, and fatigue, and went home at noon. I was absolutely flabbergasted at how physically and mentally demanding the experience had been. And this was just one day of it!

A month later I again found myself in retreat, this time for two days. By now I had attended seven beginner's classes. I was fully aware that the retreat would be profoundly difficult and was prepared for this. I carefully followed my breath and did my best to concentrate on it when I was distracted.

During the work period following breakfast, I was assigned to clear the snow and ice from the walkway and steps. It was a brilliant morning with a shining blue sky and fresh snow, and I felt great joy in continuing my practice while I swept away the snow. It was also a relief to be physically active, and I enjoyed the crisp air. That afternoon I was as-

signed to cut up wood for the stove with Tosim, a long time student of
Sunim. I was tired and developed a nasty headache, but I watched Tosim just keep working and concentrating like nothing was special. He
hardly seemed like any superman, and I figured if he could do it, I
could, too. This was my first experience of the inspiration we often
unintentionally give to one another during retreat. And work, I discovered, is no different than sitting in meditation. Each moment presents
itself to us. We can choose to bring to it the best attention we can
muster, or we can simply squander it by just getting through it.

Before evening sitting we had a snack; I ate quite a bit and felt mi-
raculously better. My headache completely cleared, and I felt fresh
again. There was another lesson in this for me: no matter how good or
bad you feel at any given moment in retreat, it isn't permanent.

I completed the retreat, but by Saturday night my upper back was so
tired I could hardly sit up on my cushion. I finished hunched over in a
daze of pain but was proud to have made it nonetheless.

During the summer of 1983, I attended my first five-day *Yongmaeng
Chongjin*. The evening rest period at this retreat was only five hours,
and I had great difficulty with fatigue, particularly during morning sittings. No matter how earnestly I tried to follow my breath, I just got
drowsier, and drowsier. At one point I glanced back at Sunim and tried
to imagine how it must feel to have thirty years of hard practice behind
you. Suddenly, my mind quieted, my eyes cleared, and the tiredness fell
away. It was like waking up from a bad fever. I sat with a feeling of pure
suchness in the morning quiet.

I struggled through the next five days trying to make a good effort,
but all in all I felt like a lousy student. However, I also knew that I had
at least tried hard.

During the next year, I continued practicing and in the summer of
1984 participated in my second *Yongmaeng Chongjin*. At this one I at
least seemed to have my wits about me. Sunim had encouraged all of
us to do extra practice, so after the mid-day meal I did fifty prostrations,
and then another fifty before retiring that night. My energy at this retreat was quite high, and I felt calmer, less fearful of the difficulties than
I had been before.

A few days into the retreat I began to notice a strange tingling sensation in my left hand, and my legs grew a little heavy. I felt OK, though, and attributed it to the heavy physical labor of temple renovations, the hundreds of prostrations, and little sleep. Throughout the retreat I had many moments of suchness, feelings of wonder and joy at reality and my oneness with it. As I lay down to sleep on the night before it ended, I felt almost nostalgic, wishing it could go on forever.

When I returned home, the tingling sensations continued, and the heaviness in my legs worsened slowly. I assumed I must have somehow pinched some nerves in my back and legs. A week later I saw a neurologist for an examination. By then nearly all strength in my lower left leg was gone, and I had a multitude of tinglings and other strange sensations. The strength gradually returned, and eventually I could walk normally again, but some weakness and the tingling remained. After weeks of tests I was finally diagnosed as having multiple sclerosis.

Since 1984 I have not fully participated in a *Yongmaeng Chongjin* or a two-day retreat, although I have done several one-day retreats. Since apparently the rigors of *Yongmaeng Chongjin* triggered the attack of multiple sclerosis, I have been trying to come up with the perfect balance between throwing myself completely into a retreat on the one hand, and avoiding too much stress on the other. In the Spring of 1987 I participated in *Yongmaeng Chongjin* but slept away from the temple for my standard eight hours each night. This has proved to be an excellent compromise. I deeply enjoy putting my everyday concerns behind me and practicing ceaselessly. The time in retreat feels absolutely precious, and all my old fears and difficulties are no distraction. In fact, when I do face difficulties from boredom and daydreaming, I am able to accept them as I would any other experience of the moment, which sooner or later will pass. It is said that the Great Way is neither easy nor difficult to those who do not care either way. This has been my experience.

I have tried to take guidance from the Buddha's example when he gave up severely austere practices and promoted a Middle Way as the wisest spiritual path. The Buddha recognized that we have no tool other than our own body with which to achieve enlightenment. If we foolishly destroy it through extreme practice, we destroy our only chance at gaining freedom from delusion. I believe it is important to strike a level of practice that we can sustain. I have seen many people over the years become disillusioned and drop away, feeling like failures. What a pity. Retreats are priceless opportunities to cultivate ourselves.

Scott Merwin has been training in Korean Zen Buddhism since December 1982, and is a student of Samu Sunim. He is married, has one child, and currently works for the state of Michigan.

"The Wind That Blows Through Our Bodhi Tree Blows Through the Bodhi Tree at Magadha"*

BY CARL VARADY

The ocean breeze blows the cloud ships overhead as we wait to meet the old boss face to face. As best we can, we will try to strike a spark together and illuminate our fundamental ground.

 On the first evening of our *sesshin* at Koko An in Honolulu, Aitken-Roshi instructs us:

> As you know, Dogen Zenji described realization as the "fallen away body and mind." Other teachers have called it "forgetting the self." *Sesshin* is a time when we practice this forgetting for five or seven days. We don't know if today is the second day or the fourth day, unless we are reminded. We don't know whether the next meal will be dinner or supper. We don't know whether the bell is about to ring or whether we have just sat down. Each moment is full and complete, the empty universe itself.

As we complete our sitting and Roshi retires, we chant the *Four Vows* together and the thirty or so of us scurry to the bathrooms and then to our respective sleeping quarters. Some sleep in the various bedrooms of the old house or newer cottage; others, including me, lie down to rest on the cushions in the Dojo. There is often a light breeze at night, and it is still and quiet. I set my alarm for 3:30 A.M. I am a food server and must get up early to make morning tea. I find a round cushion of just

---

* *Sesshin* at Koko An Zendo, Honolulu, Hawaii

the right firmness for my head and close my eyes. Our *sesshin* has now begun, and all the nervous energy of the day fades into the night as we bring our collective effort to bear in our practice, just as our ancestors in the Dharma have done in the past.

The alarm sounds its tiny beep-beep. I am already awake, worrying about the tea. How long will it take to boil? Will it cool in time to drink at 4 : 30 A.M.? Just in case I oversleep, I've left the alarm on. To my relief, the tea boils and cools in plenty of time. I join the exercise period, and we gather on the large, wooden porch outside to stretch and bend in our own preferred ways. The morning air is cool and sweet.

The bell sounds and calls us to our seats. I make the tea offering, placing the tiny, white cup filled with the pale, green liquid on the altar and make a full bow. My fellow server and I then pour the hot tea into each person's small cup, and all share tea at the sound of the bell after the bow. Another bow and the empty cups are wrapped in their brown cloths and returned to their places between each person's large cushion and the wall, and we all begin our *zazen*. Backs erect, thirty of us are sitting the first morning round of our *sesshin* together in the long living room and dining room of this faithful old house, now empty of all but the neat, black sitting cushions lining the walls, with the altar at one end.

Near the end of the first round, and at the same time daily thereafter, we hear Roshi's footsteps coming from the cottage, along the walk, up the stairs on the porch, and into the Dojo to inspect the troops. During this *kentan*, we all place hands palm to palm, and Roshi makes a bow to each of our four leaders—Dojo monitor, timer, lead chanter, *dokusan* line monitor—as he circles the room with hands palm to palm to all of us.

As the wind rustles through our fifth generation Bodhi tree in the garden outside, Roshi says:

> The wind that blows through our Bodhi tree blows through the Bodhi tree at Magadha. The ancient figure seated beneath it is none other than yourself. Settle there as your ancient koan. Settle into your timeless *Mu*.

We settle into *Mu* together as Roshi leaves the Dojo, walks to the cottage, and prepares to meet us individually in the *dokusan* (private interview) room, which is named for Yasutani-Roshi's calligraphy hanging there, *Sunyata*: "Emptiness." *Dokusan* is announced verbally by the *dokusan* monitor in the morning, as a bell would wake our neighbors who live very close by. We walk outside to form a seated line on the porch. Some of us get in line immediately, others wait for some inner voice telling them the time is right. The first person in line stands at the bottom of the porch stairs as the Bodhi leaves and seeds fall from above, one after the other. It is raining gently, and the birds sing noisily as it gets lighter. All of us in line work to maintain our practice as the world around us begins to stir. The barking dogs, radio alarms, toilet flushes, car engines, and helicopters begin to float together with the bird songs in the fragrant tropical air.

The *dokusan* room door opens, and it's my turn. I walk, flip-flop, flip-flop, with my hands folded against my heart, which beats a little harder as I go to face my teacher. As I close the door behind me and enter the small room, I am thankful for this privacy. After a full bow I take my seat. The candle is melting, and wax is running down the humble, little blue chest that serves as the altar. I am comforted by the Kannon (Avalokiteshvara) figure upon it and the picture of Robert Olson: a student and friend of Roshi's whom Roshi continues to remember after his death in this touching way. We conclude our visit, and I make a full bow and return to the Dojo as another student quietly takes my place.

At the sound of the clappers I go to the kitchen to set up for serving breakfast. Silently we put the food in containers and on trays and wait for 6:30 A.M. When that time comes, I'm standing before the *umpan*—the beautiful, flat bronze gong emblazoned with mythical gryphons—and the timer strikes the bell to signal breakfast. Each person carefully unwraps and spreads their bowls and, after the *sutras* are chanted, we serve the food, being careful not to spill it. A bit of dry food is placed in the offering dish, and everyone eats in silence. Each day less food is eaten, and our job becomes less demanding and more coordinated.

After the meal is over, we pour tea. The bowls are washed, wrapped, and returned neatly to their places. A bit of the waste water is offered by each person to the "thirsty spirits' bowl" that is passed from one person to the other. The work period then begins. All through the house food preparation and cleaning are going on busily around us as my fellow server and I begin our meal outside on the long porch.

We have been told that, as servers, we need not chant the meal *sutras*, but we choose to do so anyway and find that this chanting is a very bright moment for both of us in our *sesshin*. We finish our meal, make our water offering, bow, and go off for a brief rest.

Daily *sutras* are chanted at 8:30 A.M. The sounds are round and full as we follow the staccato of the wooden drum and warm tones of the round gong played by our lead chanter. We finish with the *Four Vows*, three full bows, and then walking *zazen*. During the morning rounds of our silent sitting and walking *zazen*, the neighboring world around our Dojo is filled with sounds of wind, laughter, rain, birdsongs, arguments, power tools, music, and the clamoring of our dinner cook. Sometimes I catch myself before drifting off to chase some fantasy; other times I am far away when the bell sounds to remind me of my true home. We rise and bow to each other before circling the room slowly, walking and breathing *Mu*.

Roshi is present and sits with us in the Dojo each day during these morning rounds of *zazen*. His presence on his cushion and in our line, as we circle the Dojo in walking *zazen*, encourages us to maintain our attention. Before leaving the Dojo he says to us, "You must exercise patience with your practice. Patience is not endurance. It is loving acceptance—loving acceptance of your own practice."

Again the clappers call us to prepare the food for serving. At 11:30 A.M. I strike the *umpan* with the venerable wooden mallet that has been repaired with glue and screws after cracking from years of service. Bowls are spread, *sutras* are chanted, and we serve our fellow students and begin to develop a feel for who will want seconds, who likes rice, who doesn't like vegetables, and who wants extra juice. On the middle day of our retreat, we receive a treat of some kind after the meal—often a cake or cookie. For me, this is the gastronomical and psychological reward for our half-week of hard practice and encouragement for our time ahead. It is especially welcome as a small, but significant, kindness which we all enjoy and know silently that we all enjoy.

It's getting warmer, and I treat my body to a refreshing shower after lunch. After showering I go out on the porch and stretch my back, which is older and stiffer it seems, and rest a bit before the afternoon sitting.

The large bell sounds at 1:30 P.M., calling us back to our cushions.

My co-server makes the tea offering, and we all share tea. At 2:00 the timer strikes the bell and asks us to prepare for *teisho*—Roshi's daily Dharma talk. His rickety, rattan chair and the small, wooden lectern are put in place; visitors who are not attending *sesshin* quietly join us through the front door, and Roshi takes his seat facing the altar after making three full bows. We chant "Opening the Dharma," and Roshi clears his throat, reads the material upon which his talk will be based—often a koan—and then asks us to sit comfortably. His exposition is cogent, direct, and often spiced with wry humor, which makes us laugh and creates a closeness in the group, as the cloak of seriousness is pulled aside by our shared mirth. Roshi ends his discourse, and we chant the *Four Vows* in Japanese, in reverence to our immediate predecessors in the Dharma. After three full bows the chair and lectern are returned to their former place, and we walk together in *zazen*. The bell sounds, and we take our seats awaiting the bells that announce our afternoon *dokusan* with our teacher. The Roshi rings his silvery sounding hand bell from the *dokusan* room, and the *dokusan* monitor answers with the full sound of her bell. We proceed as before, each attempting to sense when the time is "right," and each working sincerely to maintain our practice. The ocean breeze blows the cloud ships overhead as we wait to meet the old boss face to face. As best we can, we will try to strike a spark together and illuminate our fundamental ground; the cardinal watching over us in the Bodhi tree as we cross his territory calls "Here I am."

At 4:30 P.M. we read together the *Shodoka*, written by Yoka Daishi (Yung Chia), an outstanding disciple of the Sixth Patriarch of Zen, Eno (Hui-neng). *Shodoka* is Yoka Daishi's exposition of Zen practice and enlightenment and is recited throughout the Zen world. Its total commitment to heartfelt practice and its beautiful images of our ancestors' struggle to realize the way, bring tears to my eyes as I read. I do not know where these tears come from, but they flow naturally without concern for their source. The clappers sound again after the reading has ended, and we prepare to serve supper: soup, bread, cheese or nut butter—more like an afternoon snack, although all are free to eat their fill.

After supper there is a short rest. Then the large bell calls us again to

our cushions, and we begin our evening *zazen*. The sounds of the busy
world around us fade into the cool night air that wanders through our
Dojo and relieves the heat and perspiration of the long afternoon. Our
head monitor gives us words of encouragement to keep our practice
focused and alive. I have almost been dozing on my cushion but am
roused to attention as Roshi's small, silver bell calls in its high soprano,
and the large bell answers in its tenor to announce the evening *dokusan*.
We strike no sparks this time, and I return again to my place to continue
the task. Owning my practice as best I can, I no longer stray so far into
the dark water of self-criticism but reassure myself that my practice is
my own, full and complete no matter how focused or scattered. I continue to try to nurture the soil of this practice so that this small *Mu* can
breathe and grow.

Roshi enters the Dojo for the evening ceremonies. We chant Hakuin
Zenji's *Song of Zazen*, "All beings by nature are Buddha. . . . This very
place is the Lotus land, this very body the Buddha." We chant the *Four
Vows* and make three full bows as the small bell sends its clear tone off
into the night.

Roshi gives us our final encouragement of the evening:

> The conviction that "this very body is the Buddha" is our inspiration
> in Zen practice. I am all right from the very beginning. Practice this
> rightness *as if* you really know that you are all right. This is the ancient
> Hindu way of practicing *as if*—and it becomes true. This is not a Polly-
> anna practice; Shakyamuni was a human Buddha; you are a human
> Buddha. Settle into your practice in that right place.

Roshi leaves the Dojo, and we bow to each other and prepare for
sleep or find an unobtrusive place to continue our *zazen* into the dark
night, until it is time to rest.

---

*Carl Varady has been a practitioner of Zen since 1981 and a student of Robert
Aitkin-Roshi and member of the Diamond Sangha since 1985. He lives and
works in Boulder, Colorado, where he is an assistant city attorney. As a law
student at Wayne State University, Detroit, Michigan, he worked in a steel
mill. In addition to Zen, he is a student of Aikido.*

Jade Flute Plays in Yellow Crane Pavilion*

BY KEN KING (VEN. TAEWOO)

We are told that three things are required: Great Faith, Great Doubt, and Great Provocation.

Waking up at 2:30 A.M., those of us who deliver papers go to Lake Forest to work. It is raining lightly. Silently putting newspapers in bags, I examine my koan. "Jade Flute is Playing in the Yellow Crane Pavilion." If a note is heard, it shouldn't be jade; if no note is heard, it shouldn't be a flute—so what is it? I put the papers in a basket on a golf cart and after loading it, go to deliver them.

What is the Jade Flute?

The rain stops before I finish, so on returning I jog three miles in a nearby park.

What is the Jade Flute?

I shower and have breakfast, eating silently, examining.

What is the Jade Flute?

We chant for one hour; I feel the *Ki* energy building. We chant the *Heart Sutra* and the *Thousand Arm Sutra*. Who is chanting? Who is listening?

And what is the Jade Flute?

After chanting we sit facing the walls of the Dharma room. I examine the koan and re-examine the "examination codes" from previous koans. When I answered *Sumeru Mountain*, Master Myo Bong expressed the answer succinctly in an "examination code," and I am to review that code and the others as a background for understanding the new koan. Self-nature mind is functioning purely when examining the truth of the

---

*Winter retreat at Western Son Academy, Irvine, California

Ven. Master Hye Am (1886–1985), successor of the seventy-sixth Korean Son
Patriarch Venerable Master Mann-Gong of Dok Son Mountain. In 1984, when
he had lived twenty years longer than Buddha, this old good and wise one left
Korea for America to repay all Buddhas by directing the seeing of self-nature.
His disciple Myo Bong S'nim carries on his work.

examination code, and automatically the answer comes. We are told that
three things are required: Great Faith, Great Doubt, and Great Provocation. We get up to walk slowly around the room to stretch tired legs,
but keep the concentration going. At noon we eat "temple style," using
four bowls while remaining at our seats, but facing the center of the
room. Rice soup and vegetables are served and after eating silently, we

clean the bowls and rinse them out. Continuing to ask "What is the Jade Flute?" I pour the rinse water into the large bowl being passed around, put my four bowls away, and wait for all to finish.

After lunch I take a walk, quietly reflecting, "How are we to understand sound and color?" "Jade Flute is Playing in the Yellow Crane Pavilion." I return and take my seat for the afternoon sitting.

After the Dharma talk I go in to speak with Master Myo Bong. I bow to him and then tell him what has occurred to me. He says "Not bad. Examine more." I go to have tea and some apple quarters which someone has cut up. Then after tea we do the evening ceremony. I push down in the lower abdomen, and the chanting is strong. "Who is chanting? Who is Listening?" During the day at times when I have been chanting or sitting or jogging, various thoughts arise in the mind, memories of past events, such as driving along a certain road, or anticipations of future events or projects or even fantasies. At such times we are to notice the thoughts arising but not to fight them, and to bring the attention back to the chanting or the koan. This is called "tending the Ox."

We finish the chanting. Then we sit until bedtime. I lie in bed on my side examining "What is the Jade Flute?" I fall asleep. My alarm goes off at 2:30 A.M. It is not raining.

Ken King (Ven. Taewoo, "Great Ox") has been with Western Son Academy since 1982. He has a master's degree in philosophy and sold real estate before becoming a fully ordained monk in the Korean Chogye Order. He reads and translates Greek and Chinese and is working on a translation of the Surangama Sutra. *He is presently helping to establish a new center near Carmel, California.*

---

*"Two Arrows Meeting in Mid-Air"**

BY DOROTHY MOKUREN ROBINSON

It's taken me all these years to forget about the Zen of washing walls and cleaning toilets, and just do the job.

Our group of lay Buddhists is small, and almost all of us have full-time jobs. Twice a year we pack up all of our temple paraphernalia and head twenty miles out of town to a retreat center which, from Friday evening until Sunday afternoon, will be our Zen monastery. We appoint a "chief junior," who will keep the retreat on schedule, assign people to work projects, lead the mealtime ceremonial, and wake us up in the morning with his jangling bell. One of us becomes "chief cook" and another his assistant. Yet another will start and end the sitting periods and intone the ceremonies. Presiding over all are the "priors," the abbots of our temporary monastery— Roshi Kyogen and Reverend Teacher Gyokuko Carlson.

I arrive early on Friday evening and select a bunk in one of the four-person sleeping rooms surrounding a large room, which we have emptied of furniture and transformed into a Zendo. We begin the retreat with two half-hour sitting periods. We sit facing the wall in the dimly-lit Zendo. "Don't try to think, don't try not to think." This is our style of pure *zazen*. This evening I draw together my mental forces, concentrating energy in a quiet place to carry me through a weekend of effort. Then we sing vespers, still facing the wall in the dimness. There is a short tea during which we are admonished to maintain silence and concentration throughout the retreat; then we are off to bed, to rest for our 6:00 A.M. rising.

---

*Winter retreat at Oregon Zen Priory, Portland, Oregon

Sleep is long in coming, and then suddenly it is morning. Silently we take our seats in the Zendo in the pre-dawn dark and cold. There are two periods of meditation, and when the sun has risen there is a morning service. The lights come on, altar candles are lit, and we turn to face the room and our fellow trainees. Cued by the ding of the little signal bell, we do six full prostrations, touching our foreheads to the floor, then take our seats and chant the scriptures while the priests offer incense at the appropriate times. The Soto Zen ceremonial has been translated not only into English but also into Gregorian plain chant in our lineage. The music suits my taste in devotions, so the morning service is my favorite part of the retreat day, no matter how long it takes. When it is over, we spend a half hour cleaning bathrooms while others prepare breakfast. How difficult it is to do even this kind of work without one's ego getting involved. It's taken me all these years to forget about the Zen of washing walls and cleaning toilets, and just do the job.

Then the bell is rung, and we gather silently at the breakfast table. The "chief junior" leads the recitation as we pass the food down the long tables, serving ourselves and then sitting in meditation until everyone is ready. We lift our bowls in offering and begin to eat, each paying attention only to his own food. After consuming oatmeal, we say the closing verse and then line up to wash our own dishes and return them to our places at the table. How good even plain food seems when it is eaten in this fashion.

A work period follows breakfast. Though I am one of the senior members, I have not escaped responsibility. I am to lead the sewing projects, making meditation cushions and repairing a frayed bowing mat. In our tradition work is both a means of training and a measure of one's attainment. What have all those hours of *zazen* done for you? Are you really putting aside your ego on your meditation cushion if you cannot also put it aside when you work? What do all your preferences, your impatience, and your personal conflicts say about your inner self? I feel my teachers' eyes on me throughout the day as I interact with the other retreatants.

The retreat settles into a routine: sitting, lectures, teas, work, ceremonies, meals, and silent rest periods. The tautness of *sesshin* is never broken. I think back to earlier retreats when I was a green trainee. It

Statue of the Bodhisattva Manjusri, Oregon Zen Priory, Portland, Oregon.
Photo courtesy of Dorothy Mokuren Robinson.

was a struggle to get through them: long hours, winter cold, the unaccustomed proximity of other people, my fearful and somewhat high-
strung nature. But *zazen* held revelations! I felt real progress then,
bought with my suffering. I'm harder to impress now. I've learned to
dress for the cold, and I've gained some self-confidence. I do not feel
that I've really gotten into this retreat. I decide to talk to my teacher
about it.

So into *sanzen*—informal spiritual counselling with one of the
priests. I put my name on the signup list for Reverend Teacher to come
and get me during one of the work periods. By the time the interview
comes up, though, there have been a few more periods of meditation,
and I feel the energy beginning to flow. So we discuss a problem I've
been having in my daily life and arrive at an approach for deepening my

training while addressing it. It's so good to have a teacher who knows me and understands how my koan presents itself in my life! But I'm saving a question for *Shosan*, the teaching ceremony which will take place this evening.

Shosan is the high point of the retreat. After evening meditation, the lights come on, incense is offered, and the Roshi stands before the altar in proxy of the Buddha. Each of us has sharpened our meditation into a single succinct question. One by one we approach, kneel, and ask it with all our concentration. The Roshi, from his meditation, answers back. It is "like two arrows meeting in mid-air," as one of the scriptures puts it. Sometimes the answers are grave, sometimes humorous, but they are helpful for the one who asks and also for those who are witnesses. My turn! I kneel and ask, "How can I free myself from self-love and self-hate?" The answer comes back," "Let the self that loves and the self that hates have a little talk. Perhaps some mixing is in order." Everyone grins, and I rise, bow, and return to my place. When *Shosan* has ended, we do vespers. Afterward I take the question and the answer into my sleep.

Sunday. After breakfast and the morning's work and sitting, there is a festive ceremony commemorating the Buddha's enlightenment. Festivals are fun. I scatter tissue-paper lotus petals as we proceed around the hall singing. The retreat lightens as it ends. The final event is the midday meal, for which the cooks have outdone themselves. There is even dessert. It is at this meal that we break our silence with convivial conversation, as we joke about things that happened during the retreat. It is over. And we're relaxed, happy, full, and tired.

Dorothy Mokuren Robinson has been meditating at the Oregon Zen Priory since 1981. She is a computer software engineer and is interested in Celtic music.

Open the Window of Mind . . . Joy of a Fresh Spring Breeze*

BY DO WON-SUNIM

The willow glows with a yellow green light
Spring bird-songs fill our ears,
and with these gentler winds the massive trunk no longer creaks.

 Kyol Che is the Korean name for the ninety-day retreat held twice a year (winter and summer) in Korea and here at Providence Zen Center since 1980. *Kyol Che* means "tight Dharma." It is a time for intensive practice. Silence is maintained except for functional talking, for one on-one interviews with the teacher twice weekly, and for one or two Dharma Talks a week. Participants can do one to four three-week intervals, and there is an intensive week in the middle when a 12:00 P.M. to 2:00 A.M. practice period is added. Over the years this schedule has undergone some modifications, but generally it has meant rising at 4:45 A.M. and practicing through most of the day until bedtime at 9:40 P.M.

The day begins energetically with fifteen minutes of bowing, followed by sitting meditation from 5:30 to 7:00 A.M. Forty-five minutes of chanting rouses our energy and wakes us up.

Breakfast is followed by a period of work and then more sitting until the formal lunch at noon. After lunch the group takes its longest break of the day—almost one hour.

The practice begins again at 1:30 and lasts until 4:30. These sitting stretches are thirty to forty minutes long with ten minutes of walking

*Kyol Che at the Providence Zen Center, Providence, Rhode Island

meditation in between. Some afternoons there is a long walking meditation outside. A light, formal supper is served at 5:30, followed by chanting from 6:30 to 7:30, and sitting again until 9:30 when the evening builds to a crescendo with one final effort as we chant together for ten minutes.

Kyol Che represents a rare opportunity to simplify the structure of our lives. Once outward distractions have been minimized, the focus of our attention can more readily return to mind functioning. To me, as a new student, *Kyol Che* sounded wonderful—a perfect time to hunker down with the caprices of mind that were hindering a clearer, more energetic, and compassionate experience of life.

I lie awake for a little while before the bell and listen to the stirrings of those still asleep and those beginning to wake up. Outside in the woods and on the pond, the sounds are still too quiet to hear. On some mornings it's hard to get up and on others it's easy and natural. In any case, there is no choice, since we all sleep together here on the Dharma room floor. It's time to get up, roll up our mats and sleeping bags, put them away, and use the bathrooms quickly. Then we meet back at our seats for bows. I'll try again today to be here for bows—or at least for some of them. So far I've only been able to manage about one-eighth of the 108 full prostrations that are expected of us every morning.

Interviews today. Good! A break for the old knees and back. But then there's that damn koan. George gave me this one four months ago and *still* no clarity about it.

> Heh! Cut the crap!
> Stay with this moment!
> *"What is this?"*

How can I sit really deeply when there is this person next to me sneezing for the twentieth time? Once more . . . just one more time, and I'll scream!

Oh God! The pain is too awful! Surely we've sat longer than the scheduled time. Is the head Dharma teacher sleeping, or is she simply torturing me? I've read stories about this—teachers purposefully mak-

Entry gate to Providence Zen Center, Cumberland, Rhode Island.

ing you sit longer to push your limits. Well, it's *damned* inconsiderate. Don't they know how painful this is? Clack! The wooden clappers. Oh! Right on time. Thinking again.

Okay. Just walk around this room. One step at a time. Whoops! Off into a fog of thought . . . and back again . . . to this step, and this step.

Breakfast. Bananas *again*? I want something more substantial. And some variety. Boy, when this thing is over I'm going to the Swiss Alps for cheese fondue and salad with that wonderful house dressing and wine and chocolate mousse and coffee . . .

Gradually there is change. Small inroads into complaining, wanting mind. Periods of a deep inner quiet.

> Light changing on the floor
> as a cloud passes overhead.
> The small bruise on an apple
> tastes of slightly hard cider.

Outdoor walking meditation, Winter Kyol Che, Providence Zen Center.

Bowing! At times it is just the body moving. Up and down. And it's not just me; this whole group moves as one body. Is this it? When I finish here, I'll give a Dharma Talk about this experience. This is what practice is all about. Whoops! How many bows have we done? There are countless ways to lose *this* moment, even in periods of wonderful insight and profound feeling.

Interview time again. A bell rings, and it's my turn. Getting up, walking quietly to the room, closing the door . . . holding this question carefully. The teacher probes and tests, and again I have no answer. Back to my place, and as I sit down . . . *Oh! That's it! Of Course!* The answer comes . . . so simple, so obvious.

> Open the window of mind
> ever so slightly
> . . . joy of a fresh spring breeze.

A new koan. There's no handle on this one. No matter how I look at it, twist it, or turn it, it's just a smoothly polished metal ball . . . no place to catch hold. Arghhh! Impossible! Let it go!

"What is this?"

And so it goes. Sitting, walking, chanting, bowing, day after day. How many now? Sixty-five? That willow out there. I sense it's pale, green buds beginning to swell. The cold creaks of winter winds give way to billowing gusts which carry warmth. More frequently now the days are downright balmy. Today after lunch the sweatshirt comes off. Down to a tee-shirt, I walk to a solitary spot in the woods to sit and look and listen and to add my own chanting to the sounds of the forest. The big rock I sit on now *gives* warmth more often than draws it from me.

Eighty-three days! One week left. Can't believe it. All these days and minutes are suddenly (?) drawing to a close. Feelings mix. Anticipation: soon I will see family and friends and *talk* with them. Wistful sadness: these increasingly precious moments on the cushion will soon be over.

So "What is this?"
Let's not waste this time!

And this group. I know next to nothing about anyone's life history, yet some strong bond has grown here through sharing this effort together. The idea of one body/mind has given way to a fuller *experience* of one body/mind, so much more complete than the idea and yet so ordinary, too.

And "What is this?"
Breath and the changing light.

There is still pain at times, but the flow of the day—its rhythm—is smoother. There are still many koans left unanswered. This, too, is part of the rhythm.

The willow glows with a yellow green light.
Spring bird-songs fill our ears,
and with these gentler winds the massive trunk no longer creaks.

Tomorrow it will end. Tonight many of us sit later and rise earlier, a trend that has gradually increased these last few weeks. Though all of our old habits remain, they seem softer. The raw energy of beginning has given way to a more supple movement as a group. Air of opened mind jives with mild, fresh breeze of spring.

Today we finish.
Yet, even so, stay with it!
And even still "*What is this?*"

Movement of light, of season, of bodies through the day. Each of us offers a stick of incense, and any merit earned, to all sentient beings. We pack our bags, and hug, and speak, and move on.

Do Won-Sunim has been practicing Zen since 1980. In 1985 she became a nun in the Chogye Order. She has studied in monasteries in Korea and currently lives and works at the Providence Zen Center.

The Mahayana Centers of North America

Centers are listed alphabetically first by state, then by city and, should there be more than one within a given city, by the names of the centers themselves.

ALASKA

Anchorage Zen Center

Anchorage Zen Center offers weekly zazen meditation with a short service. We usually have two sesshins a year, led by Katagiri-Roshi or a priest from the Minnesota Zen Meditation Center. We are participating in the Buddhist studies course offered by MZMC. Newcomers are welcome.
ADDRESS: 2401 Susitna, Anchorage, AK 99517
PHONE: (907) 248-1049
LINEAGE: Soto Zen (Japanese)
SPIRITUAL HEAD: Dainin Katagiri-Roshi (Japanese)
RESIDENT DIRECTOR: None
AFFILIATED WITH: Minnesota Zen Meditation Center
ESTABLISHED: 1986
FACILITIES: Urban meditation center
RETREATS OFFERED: Two-day sesshins
OPEN TO: General public

Han-Ma-Um Zen Center

Hai Ill is a priest of the Chogye sect, who is in America to establish a Korean Zen center for Anchorage Korean people and other interested Buddhists. She is currently learning English, so at this time teaching American students is difficult. But everyone is welcome for meditation.
ADDRESS: 1805 Karluk Street, Anchorage, AK 99501
PHONE: (907) 278-9228 or Virginia at (907) 333-6554
LINEAGE: Chogye (Korean Zen)
SPIRITUAL HEAD: Dae Haeng
RESIDENT DIRECTOR: Hai Ill
FACILITIES: No retreats offered at this time
OPEN TO: General public

Khawachen Dharma Center

Khawachen is a small nonsectarian center in Anchorage, Alaska. Members meet weekly for sitting practice in a home, where our permanent shrine room is set up. Once or twice a year we invite different lamas to come to Alaska for several weeks or a month and give us teachings. Our membership is spread over a large geographical area, and weekly attendance is usually no more than ten people, but when a teacher comes that number triples. Teachers we have invited in the past are: Lama Karma Rinchen, Zasep Tulku, Geshe Tsultrim Gyeltsen, Gyaltrul, Rinpoche, Katagiri-Roshi, and Lama Tashi Namgyal.
ADDRESS: 1520 Orca Street, Anchorage, AK 99501
PHONE: (907) 279-0377 (Contact Denise Lassaw or Ngodup Paljor)
LINEAGE: "Remay" (Mahayana Tibetan)
SPIRITUAL HEAD: Ngodup Paljor
RESIDENT DIRECTOR: Same
AFFILIATED WITH: Autonomous
ESTABLISHED: 1979
FACILITIES: Member's home

RETREATS OFFERED: When a visiting lama is here, we offer retreats—usually two to four days long.
OPEN TO: General public

ARIZONA

Zen Desert Sangha

No description available.
ADDRESS: 2238 East Hedrick Drive, Lot C, Tucson, AZ 85719
PHONE: (602) 323-9654
LINEAGE: Sanbo Kyodan (Japanese)
SPIRITUAL HEAD: Robert Aiken-Roshi
RESIDENT DIRECTOR: None, but Nelson Foster visits regularly
AFFILIATED WITH: Diamond Sangha
ESTABLISHED: 1983
FACILITIES: Member's home
RETREATS OFFERED: Weekend Zazenkais
OPEN TO: General public

CALIFORNIA

Berkeley Buddhist Priory

Founded in 1973, the Berkeley Buddhist Priory is a Buddhist church in the Serene Reflection Meditation tradition. The Prior is Rev. Master Jiyu-Kennett, who is also the Abbess of Shasta Abbey in Mt. Shasta, California. The Priory is affiliated with the Order of Buddhist Contemplatives, whose headquarters is Shasta Abbey, and is a matsu-ji of Shasta Abbey, meaning that the Priory is Shasta Abbey in the Bay Area. The Priory's meditation hall is open to the public for meditation between the hours of 9 : 00 A.M. and 7 : 00 P.M. Tuesday through Saturday. Guests are also welcome to attend scheduled meditation periods, services, lectures, and retreats. In addition to the meditation hall, the Priory has a Buddhist library and a Buddhist supplies and book shop.

ADDRESS: 1358 Marin Avenue, Albany, CA 94706
PHONE: (415) 528-2139
LINEAGE: Soto Zen (Japanese)
SPIRITUAL HEAD: Rev. Master Jiyu-Kennett
RESIDENT DIRECTOR: None
AFFILIATED WITH: Shasta Abbey, Mt. Shasta, California
ESTABLISHED: 1973
FACILITIES: Urban meditation center
RETREATS OFFERED: One-day retreat on one Sunday per month
OPEN TO: Retreats open to anyone who has attended an introductory meditation instruction class.

Berkeley Zen Center

The Berkeley Zen Center, or Berkeley Zendo as it is called informally, is a place where people may practice zazen together daily with the support of the Zen Center Community under the guidance of an ordained priest. The center was established in 1967 by the late Japanese Zen Master Shunryu Suzuki-Roshi with the help of one of his American disciples, Mel Sojun Weitsman. It is a lay community based on the teachings of the Soto Zen Buddhist tradition. The center moved to its present location in September 1979. It is under the direction of Mel Weitsman in cooperation with the practicing members and is supported by membership dues and contributions. The membership includes people from all walks of life and nearly every age group. There is a small residential community living at the center, but most members live outside the center, in Berkeley and the surrounding area. "Zazen" (meditation) is the hub around which the practice turns. Our ordinary daily activity as it is extended from zazen is the field where practice finds its full expression. Each member is free to decide the degree of participation which is

118   MAHAYANA

compatible with his or her other
responsibilities.
ADDRESS: 1931 Russell Sreet, Berkeley,
CA 94703
PHONE: (415) 845-2403
LINEAGE: Soto Zen
SPIRITUAL HEAD: Sojun Mel Weitsman
RESIDENT DIRECTOR: None
AFFILIATED WITH: Autonomous
ESTABLISHED: 1967
FACILITIES: Urban meditation center
with accommodations for solitary re-
treat—only on a time-limited basis.
RETREATS OFFERED: Long Soto Zen
sesshin three times a year, day and
weekend sittings each month
OPEN TO: General public

Empty Gate Zen Center
Empty Gate Zen Center is affiliated with
Kwan Um Zen School, headed by Zen
Master Seung Sahn. Practice emphasizes
meditation, *kung-an* work, and living to-
gether as means of overcoming the "I, me,
my" syndrome. Residency, daily practice,
and monthly retreats are offered.
ADDRESS: 1800 Arch Street, Berkeley,
CA 94709
PHONE: (415) 548-7649
LINEAGE: Chogye Order
SPIRITUAL HEAD: Zen Master Seung
Sahn (Korean)
RESIDENT DIRECTOR: None
AFFILIATED WITH: Kwan-Um-Zen
School
ESTABLISHED: 1978
FACILITIES: Urban meditation center
RETREATS OFFERED: Chanting retreat,
Korean Zen sesshin (Yong Maeng Jong
Jin); offered monthly.
OPEN TO: General public

Tassajara Zen Mountain Center
Tassajara Zen Mountain Center is a Buddhist monastic community where lay and
ordained men and women practice to-

gether. Although it is closed during the
winter months to nonresidents, from early
May until the beginning of September
Tassajara is open to the public. Besides an
ongoing student schedule, plus special retreats and workshops, we offer full guest
accommodations for those who wish to
vacation at Tassajara. Information on the
guest season may be obtained from the
City Center Office in San Francisco. The
Guest Student Program provides an opportunity to experience Zen Buddhist
monastic life in the context of the Tassajara Guest Season. Guest students follow
a daily schedule which includes three periods of meditation and seven hours of
work. Most work during the summer involves caring for guests. Opportunities are
available for group and private discussion
with senior practice leaders at Tassajara.
Lectures for students are scheduled regularly. Our work week is four days long,
with free time between breakfast and evening zazen on every fifth day. Guest students should plan to stay at least five days
and may stay up to six weeks or longer.
During the first week in the program, the
fee is $5.00 per night. Guest students stay-
ing longer than a week receive free room
and board after the first week while they
are participating in the full-time medita-
tion and work schedule. For further information on becoming a guest student at
Tassajara, please call or write to: Zen Cen-
ter, 300 Page Street, San Francisco, CA
94102 (415) 863-3136.
ADDRESS: Carmel Valley, CA 93924
(Mailing address: Zen Center, 300 Page
Street, San Francisco, CA 94102)
PHONE: (415) 863-3136
LINEAGE: Soto Zen (Japanese)
SPIRITUAL HEAD: Reb Anderson and
Mel Weitsman
RESIDENT DIRECTOR: Katherina Thanas
AFFILIATED WITH: San Francisco Zen
Center
ESTABLISHED: 1960

FACILITIES: Country retreat facility with accommodations for solitary retreats.
RETREATS OFFERED: Sesshin, one-day retreat; three-month practice period
OPEN TO: General public

Vietnamese American Buddhist Association

Ven. Thich Phap Chau teaches an integral Zen grounded in the doctrines and disciplines of both the Rinzai and Pure Land sects, which includes koan practice and chanting the name of Amita Buddha. Vietnam Temple offers a daily schedule of meditation and chanting with periodic weekend and seven-day retreats open to members.
ADDRESS: 12292 Magnolia, Garden Grove, CA 92541
PHONE: (714) 534-7263
LINEAGE: Rinzai
AFFILIATED WITH: Autonomous
ESTABLISHED: 1980
FACILITIES: Urban meditation center with country retreat facility
RETREATS OFFERED: Three-month Vipassana retreat and weekend sittings
OPEN TO: General public

Hsi-Lai Temple

The temple has a large and complete faculty of monks, nuns, and lay persons—all masters in various aspects of Buddhism—as well as a thriving group of disciples. These masters have undergone extensive training in oriental Buddhist universities and monasteries. The approach is nonsectarian, with the emphasis being on living life as a Bodhisattva. Mindfulness, Lin-chi (Rinzai), Ts'al-tung (Soto), Nien-fo' (chanting Buddha's name), Mantra/Tantra practice, Sutra chanting, and others are taught. The temple offers a wide variety of instructions (personal and class), daily *puja* service, and daily open meditation. It also offers a variety of re-treat schedules and facilities for private retreats. Periodic monk, nun, novice, and lay ordination, as well as Bodhisattva precepts, are given. Weddings, funerals,.and counselling are also available. All services are open.
ADDRESS: 3456 South Glenmark Drive, Hacienda Heights, CA 91745 (Mailing address: P.O. Box 5248, Hacienda Heights, CA 91745)
PHONE: (818) 961-9697
LINEAGE: Nonsectarian
SPIRITUAL HEAD: Hon. Hsing Yun (Chinese)
RESIDENT DIRECTOR: Ven. Hsing Kuang Shin (Chinese)
AFFILIATED WITH: Autonomous
ESTABLISHED: 1978
FACILITIES: Urban meditation center with accommodations for solitary retreats
RETREATS OFFERED: Shorter Vipassana courses, Soto Zen sesshin, Rinzai Zen sesshin, chanting retreat, weekend sittings, supervised or unsupervised solitary retreats; offered monthly.
OPEN TO: High-level retreats restricted; others open to general public

Western Son Academy

Master Myo Bong S'nim and all the resident monks and nuns deliver newspapers in the morning between 2:30 and 6:00 A.M. This is part of the practice as well as a means of providing income. In Irvine there are two resident Dharma Teachers. A nun, Young Cho, a Chinese from Ecuador, has been a resident for two years and has permission to give meditation instruction. The monk Tae Woo, an American who has been in residence for four years, has also been given permission to give meditation instruction. We hold retreats in each of our centers, all urban. We are seeking a meditation retreat place in the mountains of Wyoming or Colorado. We hold winter and summer one-hundred-day

retreats, including sitting and chanting (*ki do*). We hold regular weekend retreats, and the centers are open 365 days a year for all who wish to study.
ADDRESS: 2 Hopkins, Irvine, CA 92715
PHONE: (714) 786-9586
LINEAGE: Lin Chi-Chogye
SPIRITUAL HEAD: Myo Bong S'nim (Korean)
RESIDENT DIRECTOR: Young Cho (Ecuador)
AFFILIATED WITH: Autonomous
ESTABLISHED: 1975
FACILITIES: Urban meditation center currently buying a country retreat facility
RETREATS OFFERED: Rinzai Zen sesshin, chanting retreat, weekend sittings, one-hundred-day retreats twice a year.
OPEN TO: General public

Hsi-Fang Temple

This is a branch of the Hsi-Lai Temple of Hacienda Heights, California. We conduct daily *puja* and open meditation.
ADDRESS: 7460 Girard, Suite 2, La Jolla, CA 92037
PHONE: (619) 459-9209
LINEAGE: Nonsectarian
SPIRITUAL HEAD: Hon. Hsing Yun (Chinese)
RESIDENT DIRECTOR: Revolving system assigned by Hsi-Lai Temple
AFFILIATED WITH: Hsi-Lai Temple of Hacienda Heights, California
ESTABLISHED: 1983
FACILITIES: Urban meditation center
RETREATS OFFERED: Soto Zen sesshin, Rinzai Zen sesshin, chanting retreat, a "Day of Mindfulness," weekend sittings; offered monthly.
OPEN TO: General public

Kanzeon Zen Yoga Center

Kanzeon offers daily practice in Zen meditation and a precise, mindful ap-

proach to Yoga Asana and Pranayama. Practice at this center includes Buddhist Shamatha/Vipassana meditation, Iyengar style Hatha Yoga, workshops in the Alexander Technique, Hakomi, and Vinyasana Yoga. The center also conducts regular Zen-Yoga retreats of from one to seven days in length.
ADDRESS: 20 Magnolia, Larkspur, CA 94939 (Mailing address: 25 Deer Run, Corte Madera, CA 94925
PHONE: (415) 924-5322
LINEAGE: Rinzai Zen
AFFILIATED WITH: Autonomous
ESTABLISHED: 1984
FACILITIES: Urban meditation center using rented retreat facilities
RETREATS OFFERED: Zen meditation, Hatha Yoga retreats, one to seven days.
OPEN TO: General public

Zen Buddhist Temple Zen Center of Long Beach

Our "Zen Buddhist Temple" is a residential building in the middle of a quasi-ghetto area of Long Beach. Long ago the living and dining rooms were transformed into a permanent Zendo that accommodates up to twenty people facing the wall. Occasionally there is overflow into Matsuoka-Roshi's bedroom. Our *sangha* numbers approximately thirty-five to fifty members, half of whom make it to the temple on a weekly basis. At the festivals of O-Higan and Obon, most members get together at the temple for "services" and a potluck party. Everyone is encouraged by Matsuoka-Roshi (addressed as "Sensei"), and by one another, to "sit everyday, everyday."
ADDRESS: 1942 Magnolia Avenue, Long Beach, CA 90806
PHONE: (213) 599-3275
LINEAGE: Soto Zen
SPIRITUAL HEAD: Soyu Matsuoka (Japanese)

RESIDENT DIRECTOR: Same
AFFILIATED WITH: Headquarters
ESTABLISHED: 1971
FACILITIES: Urban meditation center; small residential building with an urban Zendo.
RETREATS OFFERED: Soto Zen sesshin, weekend sittings, three-day sesshin; offered three or four times each year.
OPEN TO: General public

Cimarron Zen Center of Rinzai-Ji

Cimarron Zen Center offers a daily schedule of chanting and meditation in the Rinzai tradition. The center is the home temple of Rinzai-ji, the umbrella organization for centers founded by the Abbot Kyozan Joshu Sasaki, from the Myoshinji School of Rinzai Zen in Japan. Meditation instruction is also available. Meditation taught at Cimarron Zen Center consists of the Diamond Posture and the complete breath, which could be summarized for beginners as being soft and quiet and, at the same time, deep.
ADDRESS: 2505 Cimarron Street, Los Angeles, CA 90018
PHONE: (213) 732-2263
LINEAGE: Rinzai Zen
SPIRITUAL HEAD: Kyozan Joshu Sasaki-Roshi (Japanese)
RESIDENT DIRECTOR: Michael Tekio Radford (New Zealand)
AFFILIATED WITH: Headquarters of Rinzai-Ji Organization
ESTABLISHED: 1969
FACILITIES: Urban meditation center with large, forty-four-seat Zendo
RETREATS OFFERED: Daily meditation Sunday 10:00 A.M.; no retreats given.
OPEN TO: General public

Dharma Sah Zen Center

Under the direction of Master Dharma Teacher Bob Moore and Abbot Glen Bradley, Dharma Sah Zen Center is the Los Angeles affiliate of the Kwan Um Zen School. The center maintains a large, two-story house with space for twelve full-time residents. There is a large Dharma room which can accommodate up to twenty-five meditators. The daily schedule includes bowing, sitting, chanting, and study at 5:00 A.M., and again at 7:00 P.M. The center conducts extended retreats, six-hour intensives on Saturdays, and a monthly introductory workshop. Zen Master Seung Sahn Soen Sa Nim visits the center periodically.
ADDRESS: 1025 South Cloverdale, Los Angeles, CA 90019
PHONE: (213) 934-0330
LINEAGE: Korean Chogye
SPIRITUAL HEAD: Zen Master Seung Sahn Soen Sa Nim
RESIDENT DIRECTOR: Master Dharma Teacher Bob Moore and Abbot Glen Bradley
AFFILIATED WITH: Kwan Um Zen School
FACILITIES: Urban meditation center
RETREATS OFFERED: Three-day retreats, six-hour Saturday morning intensives.
OPEN TO: General public

Gold Wheel Monastery

Gold Wheel is an affiliate monastery of the City of 10,000 Buddhas in Talmadge, California. The principal residents here are Bhikshunis (nuns), who give lectures twice each day on the Buddhist Sutras. Ceremonies and periods of meditation are also given and are open to the public.
ADDRESS: 1728 West 6th Street, Los Angeles, CA 90017
PHONE: (213) 483-7497
LINEAGE: Ch'an Meditation and Pure Land
SPIRITUAL HEAD: Master Hsuan Hua (Chinese)
RESIDENT DIRECTOR: None

AFFILIATED WITH: City of 10,000
Buddhas
ESTABLISHED: 1975
FACILITIES: Urban meditation center
RETREATS OFFERED: Daily meditation;
no retreats given.
OPEN TO: Daily sittings open to nuns
and monks only

International Buddhist Meditation Center

International Buddhist Meditation Center
was founded in 1970 by the late Ven. Dr.
Thich Thien-An, a Zen Master from Vietnam. The center is now directed by Ven.
Dr. Karuna Dharma, his student. We
teach an integral Zen, utilizing various
meditation techniques from Vietnam, including koan, Shikan-taza, chanting, and
visualization. Resident monks from different traditions, both Theravada and Mahayana, provide a wide variety of teachings
and practices. Weekend and single-day retreats, workshops, visiting Tibetan teachers, and Vajrayana retreats, as well as academic studies in Buddhist philosophy,
sutras, meditation, and canonical languages offer a unique program of pan-
Buddhist studies. The College of Buddhist Studies resides on its grounds, aug-
menting IBMC's practice program with
academic studies. Both Zen and Vipassana meditation are taught, and techniques such as breath practice, Shikan-
taza, meditation upon sound, visualization
and koan may be given in specific cases.
Use of chanting for gaining serenity and
concentration may also be used. Guest lamas provide instruction in various Tibetan
meditation practices. Emphasis is always
upon the development of constant awareness, to be cultivated in all situations,
both on the pillow and in daily life.
ADDRESS: 928 South New Hampshire
Avenue, Los Angeles, CA 90006

PHONE: (213) 384-0850
LINEAGE: Lieu Quan (Vietnamese Rin-
zai Zen)
SPIRITUAL HEAD: Rev. Karuna Dharma
RESIDENT DIRECTOR: Same
AFFILIATED WITH: Autonomous
ESTABLISHED: 1970
FACILITIES: Urban meditation center
with country retreat facility; residency
program available.
RETREATS OFFERED: Weekend sesshins
offered every quarter, one-day retreats
monthly
OPEN TO: General public

International Zen Institute of America

Roshi Gesshin Prabhasa Dharma, founder
and director of the International Zen Institute of America, travels around the
world to conduct sesshin, to lecture in
churches and at universities, and to represent Buddhism at many interreligious ecumenical conferences. The intensive meditation periods of five to seven-day sesshin
provide a situation where encounter with
self becomes possible. Steeped in silence,
the individual, freed from thinking and
decision making, can enter into the inner-
most recesses of self and eventually experience "seeing one's true nature."
ADDRESS: 3054 West 8th Street , Los
Angeles, CA 90005 (Mailing address: P.
O. Box 145, Los Angeles, CA 90005)
PHONE: (213) 472-5707
LINEAGE: Rinzai
SPIRITUAL HEAD: Roshi Gesshin Prab-
hasa Dharma (German)
RESIDENT DIRECTOR: Same
AFFILIATED WITH: Autonomous
ESTABLISHED: 1983
FACILITIES: Retreats are held in various
countries; rented facilities.
RETREATS OFFERED: Rinzai Zen ses-
shin, one-month retreats (Zen), instruc-

tor training programs; offered seven times per year.
OPEN TO: General public

Kanzeonji Zen Buddhist Temple

Swami Premananda (also known as Rev. Ryugen Watanabe) was born in Japan, where he received direct inspiration from Kanzeon Bosatsu, the Buddha of Compassion, to bring a new spiritual discipline to the United States: Zen Yoga. Swami Premananda teaches yoga classes at the center and provides training for yoga instructors. He also conducts zazen (sitting meditation) and is available by appointment for physical and spiritual healing and counselling.
ADDRESS: 944 Terrace 49, Los Angeles, CA 90042
PHONE: (213) 255-5345
LINEAGE: Soto Zen (Japanese)
SPIRITUAL HEAD: Rev. Ryugen Watanabe (Japanese)
RESIDENT DIRECTOR: Same
AFFILIATED WITH: Long Beach Zen Center
ESTABLISHED: 1983
FACILITIES: Urban meditation center
RETREATS OFFERED: Sesshin (usually three-day)
OPEN TO: General public

Vietnamese Buddhist Temple

No description available.
ADDRESS: 863 South Berendo Street, Los Angeles, CA 90005
PHONE: (213) 384-9638
LINEAGE: Vietnamese Zen (mix of Pure Land, Soto, and Rinzai)
SPIRITUAL HEAD: Ven. Dr. Thich Man Giac (Vietnamese)
RESIDENT DIRECTOR: Same
AFFILIATED WITH: Autonomous
ESTABLISHED: 1975
FACILITIES: Urban meditation center

RETREATS OFFERED: Weekend retreats
OPEN TO: General public

Zen Center of Los Angeles

Under the direction of Taizan Maezumi-Roshi, ZCLA maintains two practice centers. The city center is a community devoted to Zen practice. At the city center students may train full time or participate as much as is possible with work and family responsibilities. The mountain center, located in a secluded mountain setting, is set aside for those who want to pursue full-time training. During the summer we offer a three-month intensive retreat at the mountain with at least eight hours of sitting meditation per day. Both centers are also open for those who do not live in the community.
ADDRESS: 923 South Normandie Avenue, Los Angeles, CA 90006
PHONE: (213) 387-2351
LINEAGE: Soto Zen
SPIRITUAL HEAD: Maezumi-Roshi (Japanese)
RESIDENT DIRECTOR: None
AFFILIATED WITH: ZCLA is parent of over ten affiliates
ESTABLISHED: 1971
FACILITIES: Urban meditation center with country retreat facility and accommodations for solitary retreats.
RETREATS OFFERED: Soto Zen sesshin, combination Rinzai/Soto sesshin, weekend sittings; offered at least once a month.
OPEN TO: General public

Zenshuji Soto Mission

The Zenshuji Soto Mission is an organization deeply rooted within the Japanese community as well as the Soto Zen family. Zenshuji is the official North American Headquarters for Soto Zen Buddhism. Zenshuji is also the only Zen

Zenshuji, Soto Mission—the Official North American headquarters for Soto Zen Buddhism.

organization in the United States to have an authentic Japanese Soto Zen Zendo on its premises. All zazen sessions and retreats are open to the general public as well as members.

ADDRESS: 123 South Hewitt Street, Los Angeles, CA 90012

PHONE: (213) 624-8658

LINEAGE: Soto Zen

SPIRITUAL HEAD: Bishop Kenko Yamashita (Japanese)

RESIDENT DIRECTOR: Rev. Nobuyoshi Fukushima (Japanese)

AFFILIATED WITH: Autonomous

ESTABLISHED: 1927

FACILITIES: Authentic Soto Zen-style meditation Zendo

RETREATS OFFERED: Soto Zen sesshin offered twice a year and weekend sittings.

OPEN TO: General public

Jikoji

We teach the Soto Zen meditation system. Emphasis is on Shikan-taza or "just sitting."

ADDRESS: 12100 Skyline Boulevard, Los Gatos, CA 95030

PHONE: (408) 741-9562

LINEAGE: Soto Zen

SPIRITUAL HEAD: Kobun Chino Otogawa (Japanese)

RESIDENT DIRECTOR: None

AFFILIATED WITH: Autonomous

ESTABLISHED: 1983

FACILITIES: Country retreat facility with accommodations for solitary retreats

RETREATS OFFERED: Soto Zen sesshin, weekend sittings, unsupervised solitary retreats; offered six to eight times a year.

OPEN TO: General public

Los Gatos Zen Group

This is a lay group with a lay teacher, Arvis Joen Justi. The Zendo is in her private home. There is a weekly meditation schedule with weekend and/or one-day sesshin monthly for students. Interviews are offered during sesshin. Introduction and instruction for beginners is by arrangement. Zazen practice at Los

Gatos is adapted from the Zen Masters Yasutani-Roshi, Soen Nakagawa-Roshi and Maezumi-Roshi. The practice is formal but not monastic, consisting of alternate thirty-minute meditation periods: chanting, walking meditation, and bowing practice, there is koan practice for some students. This group has been active for over twenty years, with emphasis on bringing the practice into family life and the work place. There is no leadership structure.

ADDRESS: 16200 Matilija Drive, Los Gatos, CA 95030
PHONE: (408) 354-7506
LINEAGE: Soto and Rinzai
SPIRITUAL HEAD: Arvis Joen Justi
RESIDENT DIRECTOR: Same
AFFILIATED WITH: Autonomous
ESTABLISHED: 1963
FACILITIES: Zendo in private home
RETREATS OFFERED: Combination Rinzai/Soto sesshin, a "Day of Mindfulness," weekend sittings; offered monthly.
OPEN TO: General public

Zen Mountain Center

ZCLA's Zen Mountain Center, Yokoji, is a branch of the Zen Center of Los Angeles (ZCLA), under the direction of Taizan Maezumi-Roshi. In 1979, ZCLA purchased 160 acres of property in Apple Canyon nestled in the San Jacinto Mountains, 120 miles east of Los Angeles. The Mountain Center is situated at the end of a dirt road amidst pine, cedar, and oak trees. The air and water are fresh and clean. Facilities include a Zendo, a kitchen, a bathhouse, and multi-use buildings. Tents and trailers provide sleeping quarters. Electric power lines do not reach into this part of the canyon. Summer Ango (ninety-day training period) at Zen Mountain Center is a challenging and rewarding program which offers the oppor-

tunity for intense practice in a secluded mountain setting. Students may stay as briefly as one week or up to the full three months. Vegetarian meals are provided. The daily schedule includes six hours of zazen per day, a work period, study with Maezumi-Roshi, and a seven-day sesshin each month.

ADDRESS: P. O. Box 43, Mountain Center, CA 92361
PHONE: (714) 659-5272
LINEAGE: Soto Zen (Japanese)
SPIRITUAL HEAD: Rev. Hakuyu Maezumi (Japanese)
RESIDENT DIRECTOR: Same
AFFILIATED WITH: Zen Center of Los Angeles
ESTABLISHED: 1967
FACILITIES: Country retreat facility with accommodations for solitary retreats
RETREATS OFFERED: Summer ninety-day; two to seven-day retreats throughout the year
OPEN TO: General public

Mount Baldy Zen Center

Mount Baldy Zen Center, located in the San Gabriel Mountains, is an environment dedicated to the understanding and clarification of Rinzai Zen and our own beings. Under the guidance of Rev. Joshu Sasaki-Roshi, we follow the monastic-style schedule of koan study, zazen, chanting, and work. Summer and winter retreats of two to three months each include three to four intensive Dai-sesshins to test and deepen our practice. Only very committed students are encouraged to attend. All students are welcome to participate during our less formal times in the spring and fall. Our Rinzai Zen meditation is the practice of taking the formal crosslegged or lotus position and breathing fully. Through breath and form, we work to realize our own beings as the largest and smallest universe, and to realize this larg-

est and smallest universe as our own
selves. In our practice walking meditation
alternates with sitting meditation.
ADDRESS: P. O. Box 429, Mount Baldy,
CA 91759
PHONE: (714) 985-6410
LINEAGE: Rinzai Zen
SPIRITUAL HEAD: Rev. Kyozan Joshu
Sasaki-Roshi (Japanese)
RESIDENT DIRECTOR: Same
AFFILIATED WITH: Rinzai-Ji, Inc.
ESTABLISHED: 1971
FACILITIES: Mountain retreat facility
with accommodations for solitary
retreats.

RETREATS OFFERED: Rinzai Zen sesshin
and three-month training periods (sei-
chu) offered winter and summer; sesshin conducted eight times per year.
OPEN TO: General public

Shasta Abbey, Headquarters of the Order of Buddhist Contemplatives

Shasta Abbey, headquarters of the Order
of Buddhist Contemplatives, is a Buddhist
monastery in the Serene Reflection Meditation (Japanese: Soto Zen, Chinese:
T'sao-tung) tradition. Founded in 1970 by

Rev. Jiyu-Kennett, Abbess of Shasta Abbey.

At Shasta Abbey.

Rev. Roshi Jiyu-Kennett, Abbess and Spiritual Director, the Abbey has a large monastic community of both men and women training full time for the Buddhist priesthood. Training at Shasta Abbey is based upon the practice of meditation, the keeping of the Buddhist Precepts, and the integration of meditation and spiritual training with every activity within one's daily life. Shasta Abbey offers a year-round schedule of retreats and residential training for lay trainees of varying backgrounds and experience.
ADDRESS: P. O. Box 199, 3612 Summit Drive, Mount Shasta, CA 96067; address inquiries C/O Guestmaster
PHONE: (916) 926-4208
LINEAGE: Soto Zen and Chinese Mahayana

SPIRITUAL HEAD: Rev. Roshi Jiyu-Kennett (British)
RESIDENT DIRECTOR: None
AFFILIATED WITH: Autonomous
FACILITIES: Urban meditation center with country retreat facility and accommodations for solitary retreats.
RETREATS OFFERED: Number of retreats varies throughout the year but averages twice a month.
OPEN TO: General public

Kannon Do (Mountain View Zen Meditation Center)

Kannon Do follows in the tradition established by Suzuki Shunryu-Roshi. The book *Zen Mind, Beginner's Mind* was taken from lectures given at the former lo-

cation of Kannon Do when it was "Haiku Zendo." We are a nonresidential center, emphasizing daily life as practice. There is zazen daily, plus retreats throughout the year, open to all at no charge.
ADDRESS: 292 College Avenue, Mountain View, CA 94040
PHONE: (415) 948-5020
LINEAGE: Soto Zen (Japanese)
SPIRITUAL HEAD: Les Kaye (Keido)-Sensei (American)
RESIDENT DIRECTOR: Same
AFFILIATED WITH: San Francisco Zen Center (sister organization; not parent)
ESTABLISHED: 1966
FACILITIES: Urban meditation center
RETREATS OFFERED: Soto Zen retreats
OPEN TO: General public

Green Gulch Farm Zen Center
Soto Zen Practice Center is in the Suzuki-Roshi tradition and is one of three locations of the San Francisco Zen Center. Our practice emphasizes daily zazen and work on our fifteen-acre farm and garden. We have frequent practice periods, retreats, and sesshins, and a guest student program for short-term residence. Our head teacher is Abbot Tenshin Anderson; our approach is open and informal. We practice Shikan-taza, "just sitting," as taught by Dogen-Zenji and Suzuki-Roshi. Our practice has also been influenced by Thich Nhat Hanh, who usually visits us when he is in the United States. We emphasize work (farming, carpentry, cooking, gardening) as Buddha's way, and present mindfulness in daily life teachings in a series of retreats and weekend workshops.
ADDRESS: 1601 Shoreline Highway, Muir Beach, CA 94965 (Mailing address: Star Route, Saulsalito, CA 94965
PHONE: (415) 383-3134
LINEAGE: Soto Zen (Japanese)

SPIRITUAL HEAD: Tenshin Anderson-Sensei (American)
RESIDENT DIRECTOR: Same
AFFILIATED WITH: San Francisco Zen Center
ESTABLISHED: 1972
FACILITIES: Country retreat facility
RETREATS OFFERED: Soto Zen sesshin, informal one-day sittings, weekend retreats, practice periods of one to three months.
OPEN TO: General public

Ring of Bone Zendo
No description available.
ADDRESS: P. O. Box 510, North San Juan, CA 95960
LINEAGE: Sanbo Kyodan (Japanese)
SPIRITUAL HEAD: Robert Aitken-Roshi
RESIDENT DIRECTOR: None. Aitken-Roshi and Nelson Foster visit regularly.
AFFILIATED WITH: Diamond Sangha
ESTABLISHED: 1980
FACILITIES: Country, community-based Zendo
RETREATS OFFERED: Two sesshins in June; others now and then
OPEN TO: General public

The Ojai Foundation, the Foundation School
The Ojai Foundation and the Foundation School offer training sessions in mindfulness practice, Zen sesshins, and other courses and practice sessions in Buddhism, contemplative practices of other traditions, as well as seminars addressing contemporary concerns. The foundation offers a schedule of two periods of meditation daily. The resident teacher is Joan Halifax.
ADDRESS: 9739 Highway 150, Ojai, CA 93023 (Mailing address: P. O. Box 1620, Ojai, CA 93023)
PHONE: (805) 646-8343

LINEAGE: Chogye (Korean), Rinzai (Vietnamese), Vajrayana (Tibetan)
SPIRITUAL HEAD: Seung Sahn (Korean) and Thich Nhat Hanh (Vietnamese)
RESIDENT DIRECTOR: Joan Halifax (American)
AFFILIATED WITH: Providence Zen Center and the Tren Trep Order
ESTABLISHED: 1975
FACILITIES: Country retreat facility with accommodations for solitary retreats
RETREATS OFFERED: Zen sesshin, mindfulness practice, Vajrayana courses.
OPEN TO: General public

Joshu Zen Temple

This temple was established in 1970 as a community practice center for students of the Ven. Joshu Sasaki-Roshi. Under the direction of Kodo Ron Olsen, Osho, and Myosen Marcia Olsen, who live in their home next door to the temple (a renovated church), students practice zazen mornings and evenings during the week. These sittings are open to the public. Sunday mornings a talk on Zen practice is given for members. Meditation instruction for beginners may be arranged by calling the temple.
ADDRESS: 2303 Harriman, Redondo Beach, CA 90278
PHONE: (213) 374-2934
LINEAGE: Rinzai Zen
SPIRITUAL HEAD: Sasaki-Roshi (Japanese)
RESIDENT DIRECTOR: Kodo Ron Olsen (American)
AFFILIATED WITH: Rinzai-Ji at Cimarron Zen Center
ESTABLISHED: 1970
FACILITIES: Urban meditation temple with thirty-seat Zendo
RETREATS OFFERED: Only evening and morning sittings; students go to Mount Baldy for sesshin.
OPEN TO: General public

Vietnamese Buddhist Association (Chua Kim Quang)

No description available.
ADDRESS: 3119 Alta Arden Expressway, Sacramento, CA 95825
PHONE: (916) 481-8781
LINEAGE: Lin Chi Lineage (Vietnamese)
SPIRITUAL HEAD: Ven. Thich Thien Tri (Vietnamese)
RESIDENT DIRECTOR: Same
AFFILIATED WITH: Autonomous
ESTABLISHED: 1978
FACILITIES: Urban meditation center with accommodations for solitary retreats
RETREATS OFFERED: Each Sunday and by arrangement
OPEN TO: General public

Zen Center San Diego

No description available.
ADDRESS: 2047 Felspar Street, San Diego, CA 92109

Gold Mountain Sagely Monastery

There are two monks in residence here. The monastery offers a rigorous schedule of ceremonies, lectures, and meditation seven days a week. Lectures are given in both English and Mandarin by Bhikshus (monks) and Bhikshunis (nuns) trained at the City of 10,000 Buddhas in Mendocino County. On Sunday mornings the monastery conducts Dharma School classes for children ages six to fifteen.
ADDRESS: 800 Sacramento Street, San Francisco, CA 94108
PHONE: (415) 421-6117
LINEAGE: All schools are represented
SPIRITUAL HEAD: Ven. Hsuan Hua (Chinese)
RESIDENT DIRECTOR: Many international teachers

AFFILIATED WITH: San Francisco branch of City of 10,000 Buddhas
ESTABLISHED: 1959
FACILITIES: Urban meditation center with meditation hall
RETREATS OFFERED: Informal meditation daily, morning and evening; formal meditation class Saturday and Sunday from 7:30 to 9:30 A.M.; lectures twice daily; extended retreats are held at City of 10,000 Buddhas.
OPEN TO: Sittings, classes, and ceremonies are open to the general public.

Hartford Street Zen Center

Hartford Street Zen Center was founded by Richard Baker-Roshi and his disciple, Issan Dorsey, as a response to a need among gay men and lesbians for an opportunity to practice Buddhism in a context and in a manner that specifically relates to their lives. Since 1981 the center has offered a full schedule of morning and evening zazen (meditation), services, lectures, retreats, counselling, and Buddhist study classes.
ADDRESS: 57 Hartford Street, San Francisco, CA 94114
PHONE: (415) 861-6779
LINEAGE: Soto Zen
SPIRITUAL HEAD: Issan Dorsey-Sensei; Issan-Sensei is a student of Zentatsu Richard Baker-Roshi and is in the process of receiving Dharma transmission from him.
RESIDENT DIRECTOR: Same
AFFILIATED WITH: Autonomous
ESTABLISHED: 1981
FACILITIES: Urban meditation center using rented facilities.
RETREATS OFFERED: A "Day of Mindfulness" and weekend sittings.
OPEN TO: General public

San Francisco Zen Center

San Francisco Zen Center was founded to teach Dogen-Zenji's practice of silent illu-

mination, just sitting, or Shikan-taza. There is daily practice of Shikan-taza, walking meditation, or *kinhin*, bowing, and chanting. We are closed on Sundays. Retreat periods also feature formal eating practice using *oryoki* utensils. Also open to the public are lectures, classes, and study periods. Meditation instruction is offered every Saturday morning. The practice of Shikan-taza can be described as total engagement in immobile sitting. Relying on correct posture and focused awareness, we study the unfoldings of life while sitting in stillness. In this way we begin to develop heart/mind, clarify our intention, and enter the Bodhisattva Path.
ADDRESS: 300 Page Street, San Francisco, CA 94102
PHONE: (415) 863-3136
LINEAGE: Soto Zen
SPIRITUAL HEAD: Tenshin Anderson, current abbot
RESIDENT DIRECTOR: Sundry practice leaders
AFFILIATED WITH: Autonomous
ESTABLISHED: 1961
FACILITIES: Urban meditation center.
RETREATS OFFERED: Soto Zen sesshin, weekend sittings, shorter sittings once per month, sesshin about twice per year.
OPEN TO: General public

San Pao Temple

San Pao Temple is a branch of Hsi-Lai Temple. There is daily *puja* and open meditation. Many forms of meditation are taught. See description of Hsi-Lai Temple, Hacienda Heights, California.
ADDRESS: 216 17th Avenue, San Francisco, CA 94121
PHONE: (408) 942-0934
LINEAGE: Nonsectarian
SPIRITUAL HEAD: Hon. Hsiang Yun (Chinese)
RESIDENT DIRECTOR: Revolving system assigned by Hsi-Lai Temple

San Francisco Zen Center.

AFFILIATED WITH: Hsi-Lai Temple
ESTABLISHED: 1987
FACILITIES: Urban meditation center
RETREATS OFFERED: Both Soto Zen and Rinzai Zen sesshin, chanting retreat, a "Day of Mindfulness," weekend sittings; offered monthly.
OPEN TO: General public

Soto Zen Mission Sokoji

Soto Zen Mission Sokoji is a branch temple of Zenshuji of Los Angeles under the direction of Rev. Shozen Hosokawa-Sensei. The temple exists primarily to serve the needs of the Japanese-American Buddhist community. However, on Wednesday and Friday evenings and on Sunday mornings, the temple hosts a two-hour period of Zen meditation, and ses-

shin is conducted twice yearly, all of which are open to the public.
ADDRESS: 1691 Laguna Street, San Francisco, CA 94115
PHONE: (415) 346-7540
LINEAGE: Soto
SPIRITUAL HEAD: Bishop Yamashita-Roshi (Japanese)
RESIDENT DIRECTOR: Rev. Hosokawa-Sensei (Japanese)
AFFILIATED WITH: Zen Shuji of Los Angeles
ESTABLISHED: 1934
FACILITIES: Zen temple for Japanese people; Zazen in Dharma Hall; no facilities for solitary retreats.
RETREATS OFFERED: Three-day and one-day Soto Zen sesshin offered twice a year
OPEN TO: General public

Santa Barbara Buddhist Priory

We are a Zen Buddhist church and training center established to teach and practice the Zen Buddhist religion of the Order of Buddhist Contemplatives of the Soto Zen Church (Shasta Abbey). This is the serene reflection school of Buddhist practice. Although a branch of Shasta Abbey, the Santa Barbara Buddhist Priory is legally a separate corporation. We offer a schedule of daily meditation and religious services, periodic retreats, and lectures; spiritual counselling available by appointment with the prior.

ADDRESS: 509 Casitas, Santa Barbara, CA 93103
PHONE: (805) 962-3071
LINEAGE: Soto Zen (Japanese)
SPIRITUAL HEAD: Rev. Roshi Jiyu-Kennett
AFFILIATED WITH: Order of Buddhist Contemplatives at Shasta Abbey
FACILITIES: Urban meditation center
RETREATS OFFERED: One-day and weekend sesshin
OPEN TO: General public; however, participants must have received meditation instruction at the priory or at Shasta Abbey.

Sonoma Mountain Zen Center

In 1974 Sonoma Mountain Zen Center was formed to continue the Soto Zen lineage of Shunryu Suzuki-Roshi, and to make everyday Zen available to people in Sonoma County. We are situated on eighty acres of rolling hills and mountainous land, eleven miles from the town of Santa Rosa. Our *sangha* consists of a small residence of single students and families, and a larger membership joining us in Zen practice from nearby towns. Our programs include a year-long Resident Training Program, a Guest Practice Program, and a special solitary retreat program. Throughout the year we offer Zen work-

shops, meditation instruction, Dharma talks, study groups, work practice, one-day sitting, four to seven-day meditation retreats, and month-long Guest Practice in July—to accommodate the diversity of interests. We emphasize a commitment to the practice of sitting meditation (zazen) every day as a way to deepen our true nature and to actualize it clearly in our work and activities.

ADDRESS: 6367 Sonoma Mountain Road, Santa Rosa, CA 95404
PHONE: (707) 545-8105
LINEAGE: Soto Zen (Japanese)
SPIRITUAL HEAD: Jakusho Kwong-Roshi (Chinese American)
RESIDENT DIRECTOR: Same
AFFILIATED WITH: Autonomous
ESTABLISHED: 1974
FACILITIES: Country retreat facility with accommodations for solitary retreat
RETREATS OFFERED: Soto Zen sesshin: one, two, three, five, and seven-day sittings
OPEN TO: General public

Middlebar Monastery

Middlebar Monastery was founded as a Soto Zen Temple in 1956. Daino Doki MacDonough, Disciple of Hodo Tobase-Roshi, was appointed as Chief Priest by the Primate of Soto, Rosen Takashina. The temple was affiliated with Sokoji Soto Mission (San Francisco) until 1963, when the present corporation was formed and MacDonough was elevated to the rank of Roshi by Primate Takashina. Middlebar Monastery is dedicated to training Americans using traditional Soto methods with Western values and language, without transplanting Japanese culture in the process. Zazen classes are held weekdays for nonresident laymen. No retreats or facilities for women are presently available. Applicants for admission must be high school graduates, unmarried, and in good health.

Jakusho Kwong-Roshi, teacher and Abbot of Sonoma Mountain Zen Center.

ADDRESS: 2503 Del Rio Drive, Stockton,
CA 95204
PHONE: (209) 462-9384
LINEAGE: Soto Zen
SPIRITUAL HEAD: Ven. MacDonough-
Roshi, O.S.M. (American)
RESIDENT DIRECTOR: Brother James,
O.S.M. (American)

AFFILIATED WITH: Autonomous
ESTABLISHED: 1956

City of 10,000 Buddhas

City of 10,000 Buddhas is a Buddhist
Monastery which offers a rigorous schedule of practice seven days a week from
4:00 A.M. to 10:00 P.M. The schedule in-

Front gate, City of 10,000 Buddhas.

cludes at least three hours of group meditation, two-and-a-half hours of group
recitation, and a one-and-a-half-hour-long
lecture on the Buddhist scriptures each
day. There are also daily courses in Buddhist and canonical language studies,
week-long intensive recitation and meditation sessions every other month, and a
three to ten-week meditation session in
the winter. Residents gain a thorough understanding of the main teachings of all
the major schools of Buddhism, develop
skill in scriptural languages, and become
adept at a wide variety of spiritual practices. The foundation of the practice is a
high standard of ethics; all residents hold
the Five Buddhist Precepts, which pro-
hibit killing of any living being (includes
vegetarianism), stealing, sexual misconduct, lying, and taking intoxicants (including alcohol, drugs, and tobacco). Our
activities are offered through a three-year
Sangha (monastic) and two-year Laity
Training Program. The Sangha Training

Program is a partial fulfillment of require-
ments for receiving the 250 Precepts of a
Bhikshu or the 348 Precepts of a Bhik-
shuni through traditional ordination
procedures.
ADDRESS: Talmage, CA 95481-0217
PHONE: (707) 462-0939
LINEAGE: We propagate all major line-
ages in Mahayana and even Theravada.
SPIRITUAL HEAD: Ven. Hsuan Hua
(Chinese)
RESIDENT DIRECTOR: Several
Americans
AFFILIATED WITH: Dharma Realm Bud-
dhist Association
ESTABLISHED: 1959. (Federally approved
nonprofit religious and educational
corporation)
FACILITIES: Country retreat facility for
long-term resident, fully-ordained Bhik-
shus or Bhikshunis only.
RETREATS OFFERED: Soto Zen sesshin
and Rinzai Zen sesshin (traditionally
the great Ch'an [Zen] monasteries like

Hall of 10,000 Buddhas, which has more than 10,000 images on its walls.

Kao Ann and Chun Shan did not make a distinction between any of the five lineages in their practice or sessions), chanting retreat, four-week Ch'an (Zen), one-week recitation (Pure Land); offered every two months.
OPEN TO: General public

Thousand Oaks Shim Gum Do
See American Buddhist Shim Gum Do Association, Brighton, Massachusetts.
ADDRESS: 1320 White Cliff, Thousand Oaks, CA 91360
PHONE: (805) 495-7841
LINEAGE: Chogye Korean Buddhist
SPIRITUAL HEAD: Chang Sik Kim, Founding Master
RESIDENT DIRECTOR: Michael Pierce

AFFILIATED WITH: American Buddhist Shim Gum Do Association of Brighton, Massachusetts
OPEN TO: General public and members

Jo Ren Zen Center
Jo Ren Zen Center, San Diego, is a satellite of the Zen Center of Los Angeles, headed by Hakuyu T. Maezumi-Roshi. The Jo Ren Zen Center offers a weekly zazen schedule on Tuesday from 7:30– 9:15 P.M., meditation instruction, monthly talks, and one to two-day retreats; open for Sunday zazen.
ADDRESS: 246 Santa Clara Avenue, Vista, CA 92083 (Mailing Address: 707 Hygeia Ave., Leucadia, CA 92024)
PHONE: (619) 436-5747; 724-9541
LINEAGE: Soto Zen (Japanese)

SPIRITUAL HEAD: Hakuyu T. Maezumi-
Roshi (Japanese)
RESIDENT DIRECTOR: Nicolee Jikyo
Miller (American)
AFFILIATED WITH: Zen Center of Los
Angeles
ESTABLISHED: 1987
FACILITIES: Urban meditation Zendo
RETREATS OFFERED: One to two-day
retreats
OPEN TO: General public

COLORADO

Boulder Zen Center

Formal practice at the Boulder Zen Center is characteristic of traditional Rinzai
style. Early morning sitting five days a
week includes chanting, *kinhin*, and zazen. Less formal zazen is conducted two
evenings each week, and there is basic zazen instruction twice a month. Members
frequently travel to Jemez Bodhi Mandala
in New Mexico for extended retreat and
teachings by Joshu Sasaki-Roshi.
ADDRESS: P. O. Box 7283, Boulder, CO
80306
PHONE: (303) 444-5577
LINEAGE: Rinzai Zen
SPIRITUAL HEAD: Joshu Sasaki-Roshi
(Japanese)
RESIDENT DIRECTOR: None
AFFILIATED WITH: Rinzai-Ji
ESTABLISHED: 1978
FACILITIES: We rent a sitting hall from
Karma Dzong, Boulder, Colorado
RETREATS OFFERED: A "Day of Mind-
fulness," weekend sittings; weekend re-
treats every other month, one-day re-
treats every other month.
OPEN TO: General public

Denver Zen Center

The Denver Zen Center is an affiliate center of the Zen Center, Rochester, New
York, headed by Bodhin Kjolhede-Sensei;

the style of Zen practiced here conforms
to that taught at our parent center. We
have a diverse lay *sangha*; the emphasis
here is therefore upon integrating one's
Zen training into daily activities. The center's schedule combines regular formal zazen with special observances for Buddhist
holidays and ceremonies. Extended sit-
tings of from one to five days are periodically held, and introductory mini-
workshops on Zen practice are also offered throughout the year.
ADDRESS: 1233 Columbine, Denver, CO
80206
PHONE: (303) 333-4844
LINEAGE: Soto/Rinzai
SPIRITUAL HEAD: Sensei Bodhin
Kjolhede; founded by Philip Kapleau-
Roshi
RESIDENT DIRECTOR: Danan Henry
AFFILIATED WITH: Zen Center of Roch-
ester, New York
ESTABLISHED: 1974
FACILITIES: Urban meditation center
RETREATS OFFERED: Combination
Rinzai/Soto sesshin, a "Day of Mind-
fulness," weekend sittings; offered
monthly.
OPEN TO: Members only

Rocky Mountain Zen Group

Members of the group include students
of Jakusho Kwong-Roshi of the Sonoma
Mountain Zen Center at Santa Rosa, Cali-
fornia, as well as Zen practitioners who
have not yet committed themselves to a
teacher but who wish to sit in organized
Soto Zen style. Weekly practice includes
periods of sitting, chanting, bowing, *kin-
hin*, and readings.
ADDRESS: 3281 Depew Street, Denver,
CO 80212
PHONE: (303) 237-8548
LINEAGE: Soto Zen
SPIRITUAL HEAD: Jakusho Kwong-
Roshi

Zendo, Denver Zen Center.

RESIDENT DIRECTOR: None
AFFILIATED WITH: Sonoma Mountain
Zen Center
ESTABLISHED: 1977
FACILITIES: Urban meditation center
with residential facilities.
OPEN TO: General public

Colorado Mountain Zen Centers
The Japanese Soto Zen Centers of Ouray
and Montrose, Colorado, offer the practice of zazen and personal instruction. At
present we are in temporary facilities,
hoping in time to establish more permanent arrangements. Ordained in 1969, our
resident teacher has been teaching for
nineteen years.
ADDRESS: Box 49, Ouray, CO 81427
PHONE: (303) 325-4440
LINEAGE: Soto Zen (Japanese)
SPIRITUAL HEAD: Soyu Matsuoka-Roshi
(Japanese)

RESIDENT DIRECTOR: Michael Wise-
Sensei (American)
AFFILIATED WITH: Long Beach Zen
Buddhist Temple
ESTABLISHED: 1986
FACILITIES: Member's home
RETREATS OFFERED: Brief sesshins, one-
day
OPEN TO: General public

CONNECTICUT

Living Dharma Center
The teacher of the Living Dharma Center
is Richard Clarke, who has been involved
for many years in various forms of psycho-
spiritual growth and is currently also a
practicing psychotherapist. In 1967 he
began a fourteen-year period of formal
training in the Harada-Yasutani-Kapleau
line of Zen and received formal transmission into a lineage of Buddhist teachers

which is now more than twenty-five hundred years old. There are weekly sittings
on Wednesday, from 7:00–9:15 P.M.
"If the mind is free of the obstructive
fog of gratuitous thoughts, this place
where we are and this present moment
are always being accomplished, without effort. This is to be content and
grateful for our life. This wonderful
life consists in performing the duties
of our time and our place, and walking
quietly on—with a vast trust and total
forgetfulness of self."
                                    —Richard Clarke
ADDRESS: P. O. Box 513, Bolton, CT
06040
PHONE: (203) 742-7049
LINEAGE: American Soto and Rinzai
Zen
SPIRITUAL HEAD: Richard Clarke
RESIDENT DIRECTOR: Same
AFFILIATED WITH: Living Dharma Center, Amherst, Massachusetts
FACILITIES: Urban meditation center
with country retreat facility; no accom-
modations for solitary retreats
RETREATS OFFERED: Sesshin, three to
seven-day

New Haven Zen Center

We offer practice everyday and have a spe-
cial night (Wednesdays) when we all prac-
tice together. We conduct a retreat every
other month, led by teachers from the
Kwan Um Zen School. Also offered are a
public talk on the first Sunday of each
month and workshops twice a year. We
are a small group with sixteen members.
ADDRESS: 193 Mansfield Street, New
Haven, CT 06511
PHONE: (203) 787-0912
LINEAGE: Chogye Zen (Korean)
SPIRITUAL HEAD: Zen Master Seung
Sahn Soen Sunim (Korean)
RESIDENT DIRECTOR: None
AFFILIATED WITH: Kwan Um Zen
School

ESTABLISHED: 1976
FACILITIES: Urban meditation center
RETREATS OFFERED: One-day and
three-day retreats
OPEN TO: General public

DISTRICT OF COLUMBIA

The Zen Buddhist Center of Washington, D.C./ Ka Shin Zendo Genzo-Ji

Ka Shin Zendo is a group of area residents with a strong and serious interest in
the practice of Zen Buddhist meditation.
In existence since 1969, the group is incorporated as the nonprofit Zen Buddhist
Center of Washington, D.C. Basic instruction in zazen sitting meditation is offered
on Wednesday evenings. The program includes instruction in sitting postures and
meditation techniques, short periods of
formal zazen, talks on Zen Buddhism and
zazen practice, and a discussion period.
Ka Shin Zendo offers two one-day zazen
workshops per year. These workshops offer a concentrated and in-depth exposure
to Zen teachings and practice. Each workshop includes talks and discussions on
Buddhism, instruction in the physical and
mental aspects of zazen, and several
periods of meditation. "The practice of
Zen, or zazen, is a way of living atten-
tively, joyously, and spontaneously under
all circumstances."
                                    —Eido-Roshi
ADDRESS: 7004 Ninth Street, Northwest, Washington, DC 20012
PHONE: (202) 829-1966
LINEAGE: Rinzai Zen (Japanese)
SPIRITUAL HEAD: Eido Tai Shimano-
Roshi (Japanese)
RESIDENT DIRECTOR: No resident
teacher; we are a lay group.
AFFILIATED WITH: The Zen Studies So-
ciety, New York, New York
ESTABLISHED: 1971
FACILITIES: Urban meditation center

RETREATS OFFERED: Rinzai Zen weekend sesshins and monthly all-day sittings
OPEN TO: Open to anyone with *some* experience sitting.

FLORIDA

Gainesville Zen Circle

Jan Sendzimir, a senior Dharma teacher in the Kwan Um Zen School, offers a Dharma room in his home and meditation sessions (weekly or according to individual need) as support to fellow Zen practitioners interested in deepening meditation and daily practice. Monthly retreats are held in rural locations. The principal form of meditation taught is sitting Zen, though bowing (full prostrations), chanting, and walking meditation forms are shown as requested.
ADDRESS: 562 Northeast 2nd Avenue, Gainesville, FL 32601
PHONE: (904) 373-7567
LINEAGE: Kwan Um Zen School (Korean)
SPIRITUAL HEAD: Seung Sahn Soen Sa Nim (Korean)
RESIDENT DIRECTOR: Jan Sendzimir (American)
AFFILIATED WITH: Kwan Um Zen School
ESTABLISHED: 1984
FACILITIES: Urban meditation center with country retreat facility
RETREATS OFFERED: Monthly weekend retreats
OPEN TO: General public

Zen Meditation Practice Group

Spiritual Head Master the Supreme Abbot Ven. Dr. Thich Man Giac, Ven. Roshi Gesshin Prabhasa Dharma, and other world renowned Zen Masters teach participants the Buddhist doctrines and various meditative methods of the Rinzai and Pure Land traditions.
ADDRESS: 7550 Southwest 82nd Court, Miami, FL 33143
PHONE: (305) 279-9713
LINEAGE: Rinzai (Zen)
SPIRITUAL HEAD: Ven. Dr. Thich Man Giac and Ven. Roshi Gesshin Prabhasa Dharma
AFFILIATED WITH: Vietnamese Buddhist United Churches
ESTABLISHED: 1984
FACILITIES: Urban meditation center in a private residence which is dedicated to the group meeting
RETREATS OFFERED: Weekend sittings every week, three times a year under the master's guidance.
OPEN TO: General public

GEORGIA

Atlanta Soto Zen Center

Roshi Michael Elliston, who studied with Soyu Matsuoka-Roshi at the Chicago Zen center, founded the Atlanta Soto Zen Center in the early 1970s. Matsuoka-Roshi, now at the Long Beach Zen Center, visits the Atlanta Center once a year. The Atlanta Soto Zen Center has a daily schedule of meditation, with an introductory session for newcomers on Sunday mornings. A two-day intensive retreat is held the first weekend of each even-numbered month. Shikan-taza, or "just sitting," is taught to all students, who are asked to sit facing the wall, to become aware of their breathing, and to place their attention in the pit of their stomachs. Sitting periods last about twenty-five minutes, and periods of *kinhin*, or walking meditation, intervene. The Kyosaku, or warning stick—the blow of compassion—is given on request only. In addition, most sittings include the chanting of the Great Heart of Wisdom Sutra, in English.
ADDRESS: 1404 McLendon Avenue, Northeast, Atlanta, GA 30307
PHONE: (404) 659-4749

LINEAGE: Soto Zen
SPIRITUAL HEAD: Michael Elliston-
Roshi (American)
RESIDENT DIRECTOR: None
AFFILIATED WITH: Zen Center of Long
Beach, California
ESTABLISHED: 1972
FACILITIES: Urban meditation center
RETREATS OFFERED: Soto Zen sesshin,
weekend sittings; two-day sesshins ev-
ery even-numbered month.
OPEN TO: General public

Atlanta Zen Group

Members practice an integral Zen
grounded in the doctrines and disciplines
of both the Soto and Rinzai sects, as
taught by the Ven. Philip Kapleau-Roshi
and the Ven. Bodhin Kjolhede-Sensei at
the Zen Center of Rochester, New York.
The Atlanta Zen Group offers weekly formal meditation, including chanting and
taped teishos with an occasional all-day
sitting.
ADDRESS: 5141 Northside Drive, North-
west, Atlanta, GA 30327
PHONE: (404) 955-4321
LINEAGE: Soto and Rinzai
SPIRITUAL HEAD: Roshi Philip Kapleau
(founder) and Ven. Bodhin Kjolhede-
Sensei
RESIDENT DIRECTOR: None
AFFILIATED WITH: The Zen Center of
Rochester, New York
ESTABLISHED: 1973
FACILITIES: Suburban Zendo using
rented facilities
RETREATS OFFERED: A one-day week-
end sitting offered occasionally
OPEN TO: Members only

HAWAII

Soto Mission of Aiea

No description available.
ADDRESS: 99–045 Kauhale Street, Aiea,
HI 96701 (Mailing address: P. O. Box
926, Aiea, HI 96701)

PHONE: (808) 488-6794
LINEAGE: Soto Zen sect
SPIRITUAL HEAD: Shakya-muni Buddha
RESIDENT DIRECTOR: Rev. M. Kudo
AFFILIATED WITH: Autonomous
ESTABLISHED: 1918
RETREATS OFFERED: (December) Ro-
hatsu sesshin, Bon, Higan Kannon-Ko
service
OPEN TO: General public

Kauai Soto Zen Temple Zenshuji

No description available.
ADDRESS: P. O. Box 248, Eleele, HI
96705
PHONE: (808) 335-3521
SPIRITUAL HEAD: Rev. Koichi Miyoshi
RESIDENT DIRECTOR: Same
AFFILIATED WITH: Zenshuji
ESTABLISHED: 1978
OPEN TO: General public

Ewa Sotoji

The Ewa Sotoji has a membership of
about sixty-five, consisting of mostly re-
tired people. We have a monthly service
and after the service the minister gives a
sermon. We don't have a resident minister
so they come from the next town.
ADDRESS: 1137 Hulili Street, Ewa, HI
96706
PHONE: None
LINEAGE: Soto Zen (Japanese)
AFFILIATED WITH: Autonomous
ESTABLISHED: 1949
RETREATS OFFERED: Sunday morning
meditation class
OPEN TO: General public

Dharma Zen Center of Hawaii

Dharma Master Ji Kwang (Dr. Danette V.
Choi, Ph.D.) was born in Korea. She
teaches a style of Buddhism that follows
the Sutra of the Lotus Flower of the Wonderful Law and was given transmission by
the head of this denomination in Korea at

the age of eighteen. She established the Hawaii Darma Sa (Dharma Zen Center) in 1978. She calls her teaching "Social Buddhism" because she feels that all answers can be found without the total commitment of a life spent in a monastery. One need not leave or disregard the material world to find the truth in life. By keeping clear moment to moment, a person becomes unhindered. Therefore, heaven and hell and Nirvana are not somewhere else. They are here on earth. This is "Social Buddhism."

ADDRESS: 1294 Kalaniiki Street, Honolulu, HI 96821
PHONE: (808) 373-3408
LINEAGE: Lotus Sutra (Korean)
SPIRITUAL HEAD: Dharma Master Ji Kwang (Korean)
RESIDENT DIRECTOR: Same
AFFILIATED WITH: Kwan Um Zen School
ESTABLISHED: 1978
FACILITIES: Urban meditation center in a private house
RETREATS OFFERED: Usually three to four weeks
OPEN TO: Members only

Diamond Sangha, a Zen Buddhist Society

The Diamond Sangha is a Western center of the Harada-Yasutani (or Sanbo Kyodan) line of Soto Zen Buddhism. It offers both Shikan-taza and koan study in a program of daily meditation, weekly classes, frequent personal interviews, periodic sesshins of three to seven-days, and intensive training periods of four to six weeks. The teacher is Robert Aitken-Roshi, Dharma successor of Yamada Ko'un-Roshi. Two methods of meditation are taught at the Diamond Sangha: Shikan-taza and koan study. Shikan-taza, or pure sitting, is the quiet practice of finding the place of no thoughts and settling there. Koan study is also established in the

place of no thoughts but centers upon fundamental questions of life and death. Students of both practices are coached in frequent personal interviews. We seek to personalize the peace, wisdom, and compassion of the Buddha and his successors.

ADDRESS: 2119 Kaloa Way, Honolulu, HI 96822
PHONE: (808) 946-0666
LINEAGE: Sanbo Kyodan Zen Buddhist
SPIRITUAL HEAD: Robert Aitken (American)
RESIDENT DIRECTOR: Same
AFFILIATED WITH: Autonomous
ESTABLISHED: 1959
FACILITIES: Urban meditation center; a consolidated urban center with teacher's residence, office, library, meditation hall, and residence hall is under construction, using voluntary labor.
RETREATS OFFERED: Soto Zen sesshins with optional koan study, weekend sittings, four to six-week training periods; at least six sesshins per year.
OPEN TO: Members only, but visitors are welcome during daily talks.

Soto Mission of Hawaii Shoboji

"We must realize that the present moment contains the totality of time—the past, the present, and the future. Time itself is life. The eternity is hidden in this continuity of time. Each moment is irreplaceable. Even a single day which has passed cannot be relived. With this realization, therefore, we strive to live the present moment with full mindfulness."

ADDRESS: 1708 Nuuanu Avenue, Honolulu, HI 96817
PHONE: (808) 537-9409
LINEAGE: Soto Zen (Japanese)
SPIRITUAL HEAD: Bishop Gyokyei Matsuura (Japanese)
RESIDENT DIRECTOR: None
AFFILIATED WITH: Autonomous
ESTABLISHED: 1913
FACILITIES: Shoin or zazen room

Daifukuji Soto Mission

Daifukuji Soto Mission is a Soto Zen temple with a membership of 120, mostly first, second, and third generation Japanese Americans. Visitors are welcome. Rev. Keido Osada, who is learning English, teaches meditation classes every Wednesday morning. Students attempt to empty the mind and concentrate on nothing. Natural breathing in the tradition of Master Dogen is emphasized. We base our meditation on Dogen's book *Shobogenzo.*

ADDRESS: Box 55, Kealakekua, HI 96750
PHONE: (808) 322-3524
LINEAGE: Soto Zen
SPIRITUAL HEAD: Bishop Gyokyei Matsuura (Japanese)
RESIDENT DIRECTOR: Rev. Keido Osada
AFFILIATED WITH: Soto Shu
ESTABLISHED: 1914
FACILITIES: Japanese style temple, not a retreat facility; using rented accommodations.
RETREATS OFFERED: Soto Zen sesshin (every December) and meditation class every Wednesday; retreats not given.

Paia Mantokuji Mission

Rev. Shuko Ueoka writes: "I am giving out a description of . . . Paia Mantokuji Mission, which is located at the foot of Mount Haleakala, close to the ocean. . . . This temple was established by my grandfather, who arrived here as a missionary from Hiroshima Prefecture, Japan. The moment he found this place, his dreams became clear. . . . He (ventured) near and far, seeking people to come to Paia Mantokuji Mission. . . . As of the present time, we have throughout Maui some 700 Buddhist families. In the forthcoming year we plan to have at least three days a week for members to meditate, relax, and converse with one another. Meditation is good for all people if taught in the right manner."

ADDRESS: 253-C Hana Highway, Paia, Maui, HI 96779 (Mailing address: P. O. Box 207, Paia, Maui, HI 96779)
PHONE: (800) 579-8051
LINEAGE: Soto Zen (Japanese)
SPIRITUAL HEAD: Arch Bishop Renpo Niwa
RESIDENT DIRECTOR: Rev. Shuko Ueoka
AFFILIATED WITH: Eheiji Monastery
ESTABLISHED: 1921
FACILITIES: Urban meditation center
RETREATS OFFERED: Three-day sesshin and more for memorial services
OPEN TO: Members only

Wahiawa Ryusenji Soto Mission

The Wahiawa Ryusenji Soto Mission was established and organized to teach and to propagate the religious doctrines, principles, and teachings of the Soto-Shu Sect of Buddhism; and to participate in religious, educational, social, charitable, and community activities in accordance with the tenets, principles, and doctrines of Soto-Shu.

ADDRESS: 164 California Avenue, Wahiawa, HI 96786
PHONE: (808) 622-1429
LINEAGE: Soto Zen (Japanese)
AFFILIATED WITH: Autonomous
ESTABLISHED: 1904
RETREATS OFFERED: Soto Zen sesshin
OPEN TO: Members only

Waipahu Soto Zen Temple Taiyoji

Rev. Yodo Oyama, head of Waipahu Soto Zen Temple Taiyoji, teaches the public doctrines of the Soto Zen sect. The temple conducts Sunday School (U.B.A.), Japanese School—first through ninth grades, and provides monthly family service. Judo and karate classes, and Goeika (temple choir group, songs sung only for religious purposes) are also available. Bon Dance (Fukushima Yagura-gumi), Minyo

Dance, Karaoke, craft and cooking classes complete the program.
ADDRESS: 94–413 Waipahu Street, Waipahu, HI 96797
PHONE: (808) 671-3103
LINEAGE: Soto Zen (Japanese)
SPIRITUAL HEAD: Rev. Yodo Oyama (Japanese)
RESIDENT DIRECTOR: None
AFFILIATED WITH: Soto Mission of Hawaii
ESTABLISHED: 1903
OPEN TO: General public

ILLINOIS

American Buddhist Association

Founded in 1955 by Rev. Gyomay M. Kubose, the purpose of the American Buddhist Association is to "study, publish, and make known the principles of Buddhism and to encourage the understanding and application of these principles." While our tradition has its roots in Japanese Buddhism, we are an independent, nonsectarian religious organization of American Buddhists. The ABA is multifaceted, engaging in activities to promote individual understanding of Buddhism as well as to make Buddhism known to the general public through publication, educational programs, and artistic projects. Shikan-taza, adapted from the Japanese Soto Zen teacher Dogen Zenji, is practiced in combination with the Nembutsu tradition of Shinshu Buddhism.
ADDRESS: 1151 West Leland Avenue, Chicago, IL 60640
PHONE: (312) 334-4661
LINEAGE: Soto Zen (Japanese)
SPIRITUAL HEAD: Rev. Gyomay M. Kubose
RESIDENT DIRECTOR: None
AFFILIATED WITH: Buddhist Temple of Chicago
ESTABLISHED: 1955
FACILITIES: Urban meditation center

RETREATS OFFERED: Combination Rinzai/Soto sesshin offered irregularly
OPEN TO: General public

Buddhist Temple of Chicago

Founded in 1944 by Rev. Gyomay M. Kubose, the Buddhist Temple of Chicago is a nonsectarian temple in the Mahayana tradition. It is an independent religious organization with no formal administrative ties to a higher headquarters of any other Buddhist sect. Its founding principle was to establish a humanistic Buddhism based on the universal teachings of Gautama Buddha through using Western terminology to make Buddhism in America uniquely American. Everyday awareness (meditation) is emphasized in order to "see" and "accept" each being, each thing as it truly is; that is, to know the "suchness" of all things.
ADDRESS: 1151 West Leland Avenue, Chicago, IL 60640
PHONE: (312) 334-4611
LINEAGE: Shin/Zen
SPIRITUAL HEAD: Rev. Gyomay M. Kubose
RESIDENT DIRECTOR: None
AFFILIATED WITH: Shin/Zen
ESTABLISHED: 1944
FACILITIES: Urban meditation center
RETREATS OFFERED: Combination Rinzai/Soto sesshin; Buddhist Educational Center offers classes in Buddhism and Japanese cultural arts; retreats offered irregularly.
OPEN TO: General public

Buddhist Research Center of America

Dharma teacher Jang S Lee promulgates and encourages the Buddhistic way of life and compassionate love through the daily practice of Chamsun (meditation-as-is), Jinsim (prayer-as-Buddha-Mind), and Wondon (study or research into Bud-

dhism's contribution to humanistic and
Buddhanthropologic progress) in the
Unity-In-Harmony-and-Completeness
tradition of the Ven. Saints Wonhyo,
Euysang, Bojo, and Susan from Korea.
ADDRESS: 9470 North Greenwood Ave-
nue, Des Plaines, IL 60016
PHONE: (312) 296-9550
LINEAGE: Korean Buddhism
SPIRITUAL HEAD: Jang S Lee (Korean)
RESIDENT DIRECTOR: Same
AFFILIATED WITH: Autonomous
ESTABLISHED: 1981
FACILITIES: Urban meditation center
with research library
RETREATS OFFERED: Personal study and
practice—meditation, prayer, and
research.
OPEN TO: General public and members

Chicago Zen Center

The Chicago Zen Center is an affiliate of
the Zen Center of Rochester, New York.
The Ven. Bodhin Kjolhede-Sensei
(Dharma heir of the Ven. Philip Kapleau-
Roshi) is the spiritual head of the CZC.
Activities include daily formal zazen and
chanting, frequent one and two-day sesshins, and work days. On the first Monday of each month, instruction night is
held for beginners. A Buddhist study
group meets the second Wednesday of
each month. During Sunday's service, a
taped teisho by Bodhin-Sensei or Roshi
Kapleau is played. Bodhin-Sensei visits
the CZC on a regular basis. An integrated
Rinzai/Soto form of zazen, as described
by Roshi Philip Kapleau in *The Three Pillars of Zen*, is practiced at the CZC.
ADDRESS: 2029 Ridge, Evanston, IL
60201
PHONE: (312) 475-3015
LINEAGE: Integrated Soto/Rinzai
SPIRITUAL HEAD: Bodhin Kjolhede-
Sensei
RESIDENT DIRECTOR: None

AFFILIATED WITH: Rochester Zen Center, Rochester, New York
ESTABLISHED: 1972
FACILITIES: Urban meditation center.
RETREATS OFFERED: Combination Rin-
zai/Soto sesshin, one, two or four-day
sesshins per year; approximately two
weekend sittings each quarter.
OPEN TO: Members only; general public, if experienced in sesshin or other intensive meditative retreats.

Zen Buddhist Temple of Chicago

Founded in 1949 by Rev. Dr. Soyu Matsuoka-Roshi, this is the oldest existing
Soto Zen temple in the United States.
Current abbot of the temple, Rev. Kongo
Langlois-Roshi, is an officially recognized
Zen Master by both Soto and Rinzai sects
of Zen. The temple provides beginning
instruction and continuing practice at four
weekly services, conducts monthly weekend sesshin, and trains disciples for the
priesthood. There are four ordained
priests and approximately twenty disciples. The temple has initiated more than
two hundred people as Zen Buddhists.
Priests are available for special services
such as weddings, funerals, and initiations. A free catalog of meditation aids
and supplies is available.
ADDRESS: 865 Bittersweet Drive, North-
brook IL 60062
PHONE: (312) 272-2070 or 2071
LINEAGE: Soto Zen (Japanese)
SPIRITUAL HEAD: Rev. Kongo Langlois-
Roshi, Abbot. Abbot Kongo-Roshi was
ordained a roshi of the Soto school in
1971 by Soyu Matsuoka-Roshi and has
since received the "Seal of Transmission" written by Asahna Sogen, Primate of the Rinzai sect. Kongo-Roshi
teaches in the Soto tradition, with a
special emphasis on the practical application of Zen to daily life. His tremendously insightful personal guidance has

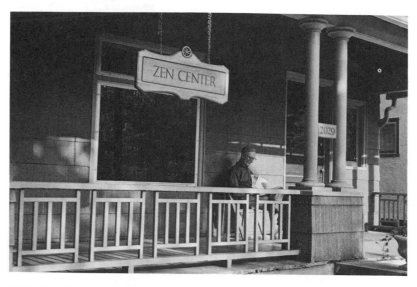

Philip Kapleau-Roshi on a visit to Chicago Zen Center. Photo courtesy of Ken Lee.

been invaluable to his disciples and temple members alike.
RESIDENT DIRECTOR: Rev. Suirin Raymond Witham and Rev. Zenku Jerry Smyers
AFFILIATED WITH: Autonomous
ESTABLISHED: 1949
FACILITIES: Urban center only; everyone is encouraged to do as much zazen as possible in their own homes.
RETREATS OFFERED: Soto Zen sesshin first weekend of every month
OPEN TO: General public

Lake County Zen Center

The Lake County Zen Center is operated by Rev. Suirin Witham, an ordained disciple of Kongo-Roshi of the Zen Buddhist Temple of Chicago. The Lake County Zen Center has no regular membership, but exists primarily for the dissemination of information. Zazen services, classes, and seminars are available upon request.
ADDRESS: 404 Shorewood Road, Round Lake Beach, IL 60073
PHONE: (312) 546-7496 (evenings only)
LINEAGE: Soto Zen (Japanese)
SPIRITUAL HEAD: Rev. Kongo Langlois
RESIDENT DIRECTOR: Rev. Suirin Witham
AFFILIATED WITH: Zen Buddhist Temple of Chicago
FACILITIES: See description
RETREATS OFFERED: Zazen services, classes, and seminars available by request
OPEN TO: General public

Chicago Meditation Center

The center provides a facility for weekly group sittings. We have sponsored retreats led by teachers from both the Vipassana and Zen schools, including teachers such as Ajahn Sobin Namto and Korean Zen Master Seung Sahn. Basic instructions are offered in insight (Vipassana) meditation and also in Zen Meditation as taught by Korean Zen Master Seung Sahn. Advanced instructions are offered at retreats and at solitary retreats arranged according to individual schedules and teacher availability.

ADDRESS: C/O D. Joshi, 1807 North Stoddard, Wheaton, IL 60187

PHONE: (312) 653-7388

LINEAGE: Theravada—Thai and Korean Zen, Chogye Order

SPIRITUAL HEAD: Achan Sobin Namto (Korean) and Master Seung Sahn (Korean)

RESIDENT DIRECTOR: Weekly meditation in the home of D. Joshi in Wheaton on Sundays and at Bultasa-Korean Temple, 4358 West Montrose. Fall and spring weekend Zen retreats are also held at Bultasa.

AFFILIATED WITH: Zen component: Kwan Um Zen School

ESTABLISHED: 1985

FACILITIES: Rented facilities; also Korean temple

RETREATS OFFERED: Week-long or weekend Vipassana and Zen retreats; occasional all day retreats

OPEN TO: General public

KANSAS

Kansas Zen Center

The Kansas Zen Center is a residential Zen community founded in 1983 in Lawrence, Kansas, by students of the Korean Zen Master Seung Sahn. Affiliated with the Kwan Um Zen School, we offer daily morning and evening practice and three or seven-day retreats several times a year. Talks by visiting teachers, classes for beginners, and other special events, such as

poetry readings, are offered. Ordained members are available to perform Buddhist weddings and funerals and to provide individual counselling. Zen practice at Kansas Zen Center derives from the Korean Chogye tradition as taught in the West by Zen Master Seung Sahn. The Chogye lineage is perhaps the world's closest living link to the classical Ch'an of Tang Dynasty China. Practice includes prostrations, sitting meditation, and chanting. Meditation techniques include breath awareness, mantra, use of a *kong-an*, and "just sitting." Students are encouraged to attend retreats and engage in private, face-to-face Dharma combat with visiting teachers.

ADDRESS: 1115 Ohio, Lawrence, KS 66044

PHONE: (913) 842-8909

LINEAGE: Chogye Zen

SPIRITUAL HEAD: Zen Master Seung Sahn (Korean)

RESIDENT DIRECTOR: None

AFFILIATED WITH: Kwan Um Zen School

ESTABLISHED: Sitting group 1979; Zen Center 1983

FACILITIES: Urban meditation center

RETREATS OFFERED: Three or seven-day Yong Maeng Jong Jin, four to six times a year.

OPEN TO: General public

KENTUCKY

Lexington Zen Center

A nonresidential Zen practice center affiliated with the Kwan Um Zen School, under the direction of Korean Zen Master Seung Sahn Soen Sa Nim. We offer daily meditation practice as well as bi-monthly teacher-supervised retreats. Practice includes sitting, bowing, and chanting meditation. We are in the process of developing a 110-acre country retreat facility in the Appalachian foothills, one hour from Lexington. Kwan Seum Sang Ji Sah, a name which means "perceive world sound high land temple," will be a Korean/American healing and spiritual retreat center.

ADDRESS: 345 Jesselin Drive, Lexington, KY 40503
PHONE: (606) 277-2438
LINEAGE: Korean Zen
SPIRITUAL HEAD: Seung Sahn Soen Sa Nim (Korean)
RESIDENT DIRECTOR: None
AFFILIATED WITH: Kwan Um Zen School
ESTABLISHED: 1984
FACILITIES: Urban meditation center developing a country retreat facility; solitary retreat facilities available.
RETREATS OFFERED: Supervised retreats and unsupervised retreats, on opposite months
OPEN TO: General public

MAINE

Kanzeon Zen Center

Kanzeon Center was established to propagate Soto Zen Buddhism in the lineage of Taizan Maezumi-Roshi through the practice of zazen. The center offers a daily schedule of sitting as well as regular *daisan* and classes, monthly workshops, three to seven day sesshins, and public lectures. Kanzeon is a residential center which maintains a library and other facilities and resources for the teaching and practice of Zen Buddhism. All activities are open to the public and are carried out under the teaching and supervision of Genpo Merzel-Sensei, Dharma successor to Taizan Maezumi-Roshi. Genpo-Sensei conducts annual one-month sesshins, and will begin two and three-month training

periods this year. The purposes of Kanzeon also include, but are not limited to, community service activities, educational programs, and the publication of a quarterly journal. "To sit zazen is to empty the self of the self."

—Genpo-Sensei

ADDRESS: 33 Ledgelawn Avenue, Bar Harbor, ME 04609
PHONE: (207) 288-3569
LINEAGE: Soto and Rinzai Zen (Japanese)
SPIRITUAL HEAD: Genpo Merzel-Sensei (American)
RESIDENT DIRECTOR: Same
AFFILIATED WITH: Zen Center of Los Angeles
ESTABLISHED: 1987
FACILITIES: Urban meditation center
RETREATS OFFERED: Three and seven-day sesshin and two and three-month training periods
OPEN TO: General public

Morgan Bay Zendo

The Morgan Bay Zendo was founded by Walter Nowick as the Moonspring Hermitage in 1969. The name of the organization was changed when Walter Nowick resigned in 1985. At present we have nineteen members. Our facilities consist of a Zendo, lecture hall, sanzen house, and a number of small retreat cabins, located in central coastal Maine. We offer a regular Zazen schedule and occasional lectures and retreats by visiting scholars and teachers of various Buddhist traditions.

ADDRESS: Morgan Bay Road, Surry, ME 04684
PHONE: (207) 667-5428
ESTABLISHED: 1969
FACILITIES: Country retreat facility with accommodations for solitary retreats
RETREATS OFFERED: See description
OPEN TO: General public

Dr. Gosung Shin, American Zen College, Germantown,
Maryland.

MARYLAND

American Zen College

Zen Master Gosung Shin, Ph.D., teaches
a Zen which is well suited to the needs of
the American practitioner and includes
both breathing and koan meditation. The
AZC offers the following weekly: a half
day meditation practice, a meditation instruction class, and a Dharma lecture by

Zen Master Shin. Monthly three and six-
day sesshin are also led·by Master Shin.
Activities are open to both members and
the general public. The American Zen
College is located twenty minutes Northwest of Washington, D.C. on a thoroughly converted dairy farm bordering a
350-acre state park in rural Maryland.
ADDRESS: 16815 Germantown Road,
Germantown, MD 20784

PHONE: (301) 428-0665
LINEAGE: Chogye Sect
SPIRITUAL HEAD: Zen Master Gosung Shin, Ph.D. (Korean)
RESIDENT DIRECTOR: None
AFFILIATED WITH: Autonomous
ESTABLISHED: 1976
FACILITIES: Urban meditation center and country retreat facility with accommodations for solitary retreats
RETREATS OFFERED: Combination Rinzai/Soto sesshin and weekend sittings offered once a month
OPEN TO: General public

MASSACHUSETTS

Living Dharma Center

The Living Dharma Center is a community of lay women and men from many backgrounds and walks of life, who support each other in this effort toward greater awareness and freedom. Together we seek to translate the ancient tradition of Zen into forms appropriate to our time and place. At our weekly meetings we share sitting and walking meditation, lectures, and discussions, or interviews with the teacher. We also hold frequent intensive meditation retreats (sesshins) and periodically offer introductory workshops on Zen practice.
ADDRESS: RFD 3, Pratt Corner Road, Amherst, MA 01002-9805
PHONE: (413) 259-1611
LINEAGE: American Soto and Rinzai Zen
SPIRITUAL HEAD: Richard Clarke (Canadian); for more information about Rev. Richard Clarke, please refer to Living Dharma Center, Bolton, Connecticut.
RESIDENT DIRECTOR: Same
AFFILIATED WITH: Headquarters
ESTABLISHED: 1972
FACILITIES: Urban meditation center and country retreat facility

RETREATS OFFERED: Three to seven-day sesshin
OPEN TO: Members only

American Buddhist Shim Gum Do Association

For centuries, martial arts have been practiced as a system of war. In China Buddhists learned martial arts so they could defend their monasteries from bands of thieves. The temples became powerful fortresses which could contend even with the state. As times changed and gun power increased, martial arts lost importance and deteriorated. In 1965 Founding Master Chang Sik Kim received enlightenment in martial arts and founded Shim Gum Do. This revitalization at a time when nuclear power reigns supreme is most interesting, for Shim Gum Do is like a valuable antique, a work of art crafted with techniques which have become obsolete and cannot be duplicated. Shim Gum Do is active meditation through martial art forms. Attention is fully focused, for if a thought intrudes, the form is lost. To master the art, one must practice martial arts mentally during sitting meditation. Shim Gum Do is an exercise which strengthens one's ability to cope with stress and adversity. Its spirit is that of the knight of medieval times, the Japanese Samurai, the Korean Hwarang warriors of Silla.
ADDRESS: 203 Chestnut Hill Avenue, Brighton, MA 02135
PHONE: (617) 787-1506
LINEAGE: Chogye Order (Korean Zen)
SPIRITUAL HEAD: Founding Master, Chang Sik Kim (Korean)
RESIDENT DIRECTOR: Maria Kim (American)
AFFILIATED WITH: Autonomous
ESTABLISHED: 1978
FACILITIES: Urban meditation center
RETREATS OFFERED: Three-month Kyol-che once per year, chanting re-

treats, prostration retreats; monthly retreats of one week duration offered the
first week of each month.
OPEN TO: Both general public and
members

Boston Zen Group

Boston Zen Group is a small, formal za-
zen group with morning and evening sit-
tings and occasional all-day and weekend
sittings. Formal activities include zazen,
kinhin, chanting, and *teisho* tapes from
the Zen Center of Rochester. The group
is open to anyone interested in serious,
guided zazen.
ADDRESS: 28 Shea Road, Cambridge,
MA 02140
PHONE: (617) 547-6586
LINEAGE: Integral Zen (Soto)
SPIRITUAL HEAD: Roshi Kapleau and
Bodhin Kjolhede-Sensei
RESIDENT DIRECTOR: James M.
Robicsek
AFFILIATED WITH: Informally affiliated
with the Zen Center, Rochester, New
York
ESTABLISHED: 1974
FACILITIES: Urban meditation center
using rented facilities
RETREATS OFFERED: Weekend sittings
each month or every two months
OPEN TO: Members only

Cambridge Buddhist Association

The Cambridge Buddhist Association was
founded in 1957 as a nonresidential, nonsectarian meditation and study center.
Maurine Stuart-Roshi, trained in the Rinzai tradition, leads monthly sesshins and
introductory classes at the center and elsewhere around the country. Members have
library privileges.
ADDRESS: 75 Sparks Street, Cambridge,
MA 02138
PHONE: (617) 491-8857
LINEAGE: Nonsectarian Buddhist Center

SPIRITUAL HEAD: Maurine Stuart-Roshi
RESIDENT DIRECTOR: Same
ESTABLISHED: 1957
FACILITIES: Urban meditation center
RETREATS OFFERED: Two, five, and
seven-day Zen sesshin
OPEN TO: General public

Cambridge Zen Center

The heart of the Kwan Um Zen School,
founded by Zen Master Seung Sahn, is
the consistent daily practice which goes
on in its Zen centers and affiliated groups.
Practicing and working together, we discover what it means to be human. As we
learn to let go of our illusions of separation, we are able to live our lives more
openly with increasing clarity and compassion. The Cambridge Zen Center offers a daily schedule of bowing, sitting,
and chanting, as well as monthly retreats
and bi-weekly interviews with a master
Dharma teacher. Public talks every Thursday evening are free and open to the community, as is daily practice.
ADDRESS: 199 Auburn Street, Cambridge, MA 02139
PHONE: (617) 576-3229
LINEAGE: Chogye Zen
SPIRITUAL HEAD: Ven. Seung Sahn
Soen Sa Nim (Korean)
RESIDENT DIRECTOR: Mu Deung
AFFILIATED WITH: Kwan Um Zen
School
ESTABLISHED: 1974
FACILITIES: Urban meditation center
with access to cabins for solitary retreats
RETREATS OFFERED: Three-month *Kyol-
che*, chanting retreats, a "Day of Mind-
fulness"; weekend sittings offered every
month.
OPEN TO: General public

Pioneer Valley Zendo

A small rural Zendo practicing Shikan-
taza in the tradition of Dogen Zenji,

Ven. Issho Fujita of the Pioneer Valley Zendo, Charlemont, Massachusetts.

Kodo Sawaki-Roshi, and Kosyo Uchi-yama-Roshi. Japanese monks from Antai-ji and American practitioners built the Zendo. We sit together daily with a one-day sesshin on Sunday and a five-day sesshin every month. Practitioners are always welcome to sit. Our practice, Shikan-taza, means "just sitting." In Shikan-taza we only aim at the correct posture with flesh and bones and leave everything up to it. So it is quite different from meditation. Just sitting itself is *satori*. It has no purpose such as gaining some sort of special enlightenment. Shikan-taza is to do myself with myself by myself and to be intimate with the reality of Self.

ADDRESS: 263 Warnerhill Road, Charlemont, MA 01339

PHONE: (413) 339-4000

LINEAGE: Soto Zen

SPIRITUAL HEAD: Koho Watanabe (Japanese)

RESIDENT DIRECTOR: Issho Fujita (Japanese)

AFFILIATED WITH: Autonomous

ESTABLISHED: 1971

FACILITIES: Country retreat facility
RETREATS OFFERED: Soto Zen sesshin;
five-day sesshin once a month; one-day
sesshin Sundays
OPEN TO: General public

MICHIGAN

Zen Lotus Society/Zen Buddhist Temple

The Zen Lotus Society—Zen Buddhist
Temple of Ann Arbor offers resident and
nonresident training in Zen meditation
under the direction of Ven. Samu Sunim.
A three to five-year priest and Dharma
teacher training program adapts traditional Zen training to the North American situation, with scripture studies emphasizing spiritual cultivation in daily life
and social concern. Meditation and/or
chanting practice is held daily, morning
and evening. Scriptural and doctrinal
studies are offered through Friday evening
sessions and during a two-month summer
training period. Retreats are conducted
five times a year, and a year-round visitor's
program accommodates short and medium term visitors. All training members
of the Zen Lotus Society are encouraged
to take active part in social issues that
concern us all. To this end Samu Sunim
founded Buddhists Concerned for Social
Justice and World Peace. The Zen Lotus
Society publishes *Spring Wind: Buddhist
Cultural Forum*, an international nonsec-
tarian Buddhist quarterly.
ADDRESS: 1241 Packard Road, Ann
Arbor, MI 48104
PHONE: (313) 761-6520
LINEAGE: Chogye
SPIRITUAL HEAD: Ven. Samu Sunim
(Korean)
RESIDENT DIRECTOR: Sukha Murray
(Canadian)
AFFILIATED WITH: Zen Lotus Society

ESTABLISHED: 1981
FACILITIES: Urban meditation center
RETREATS OFFERED: Weekend, five-day
retreats, two-month summer retreat,
and visitor's program year-round
OPEN TO: Members and general public

So Getsu-In

So Getsu-In is a Zendo in our home, established twelve years ago and dedicated
by my teacher Kobun Chino-Sensei.
There was at one time a regular group of
practitioners here, but most have since
moved to other parts of the country.
There are now a few local people who
come to sit occasionally, and we have
short sesshins. I also receive visits from
Kobun Chino and from other teachers
traveling in the area and from practition-
ers or nonpractitioners who wish to
come and sit. We do not have residence
facilities.
ADDRESS: Box 39, Fremont, MI 49412
PHONE: (616) 924-3464
LINEAGE: Soto Zen
SPIRITUAL HEAD: Kobun Chino-Sensei
RESIDENT DIRECTOR: Dan Gerber (Jo
Yo Gen Shin)
AFFILIATED WITH: Hokoji, Taos, New
Mexcio
ESTABLISHED: 1976
FACILITIES: Zendo in home
RETREATS OFFERED: One to three-day
sesshins

MINNESOTA

Hokyoji—Catching the Moon Zen Mountain Center

Hokyoji is the country practice center for
the Minnesota Zen Meditation Center.
MZMC is a Soto Zen practice community
under the spiritual direction of Dainin
Katagiri-Roshi, who has been a practicing

Zen monk for forty years. Hokyoji-CMZMC is situated in a remote valley in the scenic Mississippi River basin of southeastern Minnesota, a beautiful three-and-a-half hour drive south of Minneapolis along the Mississippi River, and within driving distance of the Milwaukee-Chicago area and the Plains states. It is open to the public for both private and public retreats. Retreat schedules are relaxed and spacious with opportunity to share silence with birds, trees, and sky. There is also a more extensive schedule of seven-day sesshins and an eight-week practice period, which are open to those with Zen practice experience.

ADDRESS: C/O 3343 East Calhoun Parkway, Minneapolis, MN 55408
PHONE: (612) 822-5313
LINEAGE: Soto Zen (Japanese)
SPIRITUAL HEAD: Dainin Katagiri-Roshi (Japanese)
RESIDENT DIRECTOR: Same
AFFILIATED WITH: Autonomous
ESTABLISHED: 1973
FACILITIES: Country retreat facility
RETREATS OFFERED: Soto Zen sesshins, writing workshop, Dogen workshop, women's retreats
OPEN TO: General public

Minnesota Zen Meditation Center

The Minnesota Zen Meditation Center is a center established for the practice of Soto Zen under the guidance of Dainin Katagiri-Roshi. The focus is on sitting meditation and daily life, and the center offers daily zazen, lectures, services, discussions, introductory workshops and zazen instruction, family service, a Buddhist studies program, retreats and practice periods, both in the city and country.

ADDRESS: 3343 East Calhoun Parkway, Minneapolis, MN 55408
PHONE: (612) 822-5313
LINEAGE: Soto Zen
SPIRITUAL HEAD: Dainin Katagiri (Japanese). Abbot of Minnesota Zen Meditation Center, Katagiri was born in Osaka, Japan, in 1928. At eighteen he became a monk with Daicho Hayashi-Roshi. He later practiced with Hashimoto-Roshi at Eiheiji Monastery in Japan. He came to the United States in 1963, first working with the Japanese Soto Zen congregation of Los Angeles, and then working for nine years with Suzuki-Roshi at Zen Center in San Francisco. In December 1972 he moved to Minneapolis to become the resident teacher of the Minnesota Zen Meditation Center. He continues to apply himself to the transmission of Zen Mind to the West by teaching in Minnesota and throughout the country.
RESIDENT DIRECTOR: Same
AFFILIATED WITH: Autonomous
ESTABLISHED: 1973
FACILITIES: Urban meditation center with country retreat facility and accommodations for solitary retreats
RETREATS OFFERED: Soto Zen sesshin, two-month training period, spring retreats for women, and spirituality workshop on Dogen Zenji; writing retreats with Natalie Goldberg.
OPEN TO: General public

St. Paul Zendo

Our little Sangha of six to eight members meets every Sunday night for two hours. After a fifteen-minute Hatha Yoga session, we have a discussion on some aspect of Zen practice. Following that there is a period of zazen in accordance with Soto Zen form. The members are committed to weekly attendance.

ADDRESS: 136 Amherst, St. Paul, MN 55705
PHONE: (612) 698-8933

LINEAGE: Soto Zen (USA)
RESIDENT DIRECTOR: Beverly White
AFFILIATED WITH: Autonomous
ESTABLISHED: 1981
FACILITIES: Urban meditation center
OPEN TO: General public

MISSOURI

Missouri Zen Center

Zazen is the only meditation system.
Shikan-taza is what is taught. We follow
closely the Fukanzazengi of Dogen. It all
comes down to sitting quietly, solidly—
no more.
ADDRESS: 220 Spring Avenue, St. Louis,
MO 63119
PHONE: (314) 961-6138
LINEAGE: Soto Zen
SPIRITUAL HEAD: Rosan Yoshida, Ph.D.
(Japanese)
RESIDENT DIRECTOR: Same
AFFILIATED WITH: Autonomous
FACILITIES: Urban meditation center
with partial use of member cabins for
retreats
RETREATS OFFERED: Soto Zen sesshin
offered bi-monthly
OPEN TO: General public

NEBRASKA

Kearney Zendo

Kearney Zendo emerged out of the Shuri-
ryu Karate and Kobudo Dojo, directed by
Dr. Dirk Mosig, Seventh Dan. Mosig-
Sensei is a student of Dainin Katagiri-
Roshi, who comes to Kearney once a year
to offer a sesshin. Kearney Zendo is affiliated with the Minnesota Zen Meditation
Center (MZMC) and follows the tradition of Soto Zen. Daily zazen practice is
scheduled for mornings, afternoons, and
evenings. The Zendo houses a Buddhist

library of over one thousand volumes, an
altar, and fourteen sets of Zafu/Zabuton.
Kearney Zendo combines traditional Soto
Zen sitting practice (Shikan-taza) with
the martial arts disciplines of Okinawan
Shuri-style Karate and Kobudo.
ADDRESS: 3715 Avenue F, Kearney, NB
68847
PHONE: (308) 236-5650
LINEAGE: Soto Zen
SPIRITUAL HEAD: Dainin Katagiri-
Roshi (Japanese)
RESIDENT DIRECTOR: Dirk Mosig
(German)
AFFILIATED WITH: Minnesota Zen
Meditation Center (MZMC)
ESTABLISHED: 1983
FACILITIES: Zendo uses the facilities of
Kearney's Shuri-Ryu Karate and
Kobudo Dojo.
RETREATS OFFERED: Soto Zen sesshin
once a year and daily sittings
OPEN TO: General public

Nebraska Zen Center

There is sitting seven days a week from
5:50 A.M. to 6:30 A.M. Chanting follows.
Every Sunday there is an 8:00 P.M. zazen,
and a "Sangha Supper Social" on the first
Sunday of every month.
ADDRESS: 816 South 67th Street,
Omaha, NB 68106
PHONE: (402) 551-4063
LINEAGE: Soto Zen
SPIRITUAL HEAD: Ven. Katagiri-Roshi
RESIDENT DIRECTOR: Gordon Becker
AFFILIATED WITH: Minnesota Zen
Center
ESTABLISHED: 1973
FACILITIES: Newly constructed urban
Zen meditation center
RETREATS OFFERED: Daily sitting and a
yearly three-day Soto Zen sesshin
OPEN TO: General public

NEVADA

Lian Hwa Temple

The Lian Hwa temple is a branch of Hsi-Lai Temple. There is daily *puja* and open meditation; many forms of meditation are taught. For more information, see description of Hsi-Lai Temple, Hacienda Heights, California.

ADDRESS: 905 North 21st Street, Las Vegas, NV 89101
LINEAGE: Nonsectarian
SPIRITUAL HEAD: Hon. Hsiang Yun (Chinese)
RESIDENT DIRECTOR: Revolving system assigned by Hsi-Lai Temple
AFFILIATED WITH: Hsi-Lai Temple
ESTABLISHED: 1981
FACILITIES: Urban meditation center
RETREATS OFFERED: Soto Zen sesshin, Rinzai Zen sesshin, chanting retreat, a "Day of Mindfulness," weekend sittings; offered monthly.
OPEN TO: General public

Silver Mountain Sangha

Silver Mountain Sangha holds Sunday evening group meditation and Zen chanting. Several one-day workshops on Rinzai Zen Buddhism with guest teachers are held each year. The Sangha follows the Rinzai Zen meditation system taught by Ven. Eido Tai Shimano-Roshi and is affiliated with his monastery, Dai Bo Satsu Zendo Kongo-ji, in Lew Beach, New York. Eido-Roshi comes to the Sangha in Reno once a year.

ADDRESS: 3060 Sagitarius, Reno, NV 89504
PHONE: (702) 786-1484
LINEAGE: Rinzai Zen
SPIRITUAL HEAD: Eido Tai Shimano-Roshi (Japanese)
RESIDENT DIRECTOR: John Burden (American)

AFFILIATED WITH: Dai Bo Satsu Zendo
FACILITIES: Suburban meditation center
RETREATS OFFERED: One workshop and weekly Sunday meditations
OPEN TO: General public

NEW JERSEY

Zen Temple of Cresskill

Today the arts in the Western world have been reduced to commodities, for sale in the market place of fashion and style. The depth and radiance of art inspired by the living awareness of a multi-dimensional reality have all but disappeared. However, we believe that the opportunity of our time is for people of all kinds—not just professional artists—to find the artist, singer, dancer, or writer within, and to use these forms as expressions of the sacred. Dr. Sun-ock Lee, one of Korea's foremost traditional and modern dancers and choreographers is the director of Zen Dance Center in New York, as well as of the Zen Temple of Cresskill, New Jersey. Her Zen Dance Workshop aims at a heightening of mind-body control and the development of focus and concentration. Beginning with the breathing exercises essential to the meditative state, and utilizing the vedic sounds of mantra, the course teaches both floor exercises and dance movements in space. The creative expression of a personal dance vocabulary is the natural outgrowth of Zen dance techniques.

ADDRESS: 185 6th Street, Cresskill, NJ 07626
PHONE: (201) 567-7468
LINEAGE: Korean Son (Zen)
SPIRITUAL HEAD: Zen Master Song Dahm at Inchun, Korea (Yong Hwa Son Won)
RESIDENT DIRECTOR: Dr. Sun-ock Lee

AFFILIATED WITH: Yong Hwa Son Won (Zen Temple) in Korea
ESTABLISHED: 1988
FACILITIES: Urban meditation center; country retreat facility
RETREATS OFFERED: Weekend Son sesshin (Yong Meng Jong Jin)
OPEN TO: General public

NEW MEXICO

Place of Peace

Place of Peace is a small sitting group with participants from both Rinzai and Soto Zen lineages, and a Tibetan lineage. We sit weekly, presently on Tuesday nights, with occasional discussions following sitting. Most participants are lesbian or gay.
ADDRESS: 1104 Stanford Northeast, Albuquerque, NM 87106 (Mailing address: P. O. Box 807, Albuquerque, NM 87103)
PHONE: (505) 842-9585
LINEAGE: Japanese Soto and Rinzai Zen
AFFILIATED WITH: Autonomous
ESTABLISHED: 1986
FACILITIES: Member's home
OPEN TO: Members only

Jemez Bodhi Mandala

Bodhi offers a daily schedule of zazen, chanting, and work practice drawn from the Rinzai Zen tradition. Each spring and fall there is a two to three-month period for intensive training in Zen. Throughout the year, zazen weekends and seven-day sesshins are offered for all levels of students. Each summer the Seminar on the Sutras explores Buddhism with various scholars and teachers of Buddhism.
ADDRESS: P. O. Box 8, Jemez Springs, NM 87025
PHONE: (505) 829-3854
LINEAGE: Rinzai Zen

SPIRITUAL HEAD: Rev. Joshu Sasaki-Roshi (Japanese)
RESIDENT DIRECTOR: Seishu
AFFILIATED WITH: Rinzai-Ji
ESTABLISHED: 1974
FACILITIES: Country retreat facility
RETREATS OFFERED: Rinzai Zen sesshin, weekend sittings, two to three-month training periods; offered spring and fall each year.
OPEN TO: General public

Zen Center of Las Cruces

Rev. Ken McGuire-Roshi and Rev Fern McGuire teach Soto Zen in the traditional manner imparted to them by Zen Master Matsuoka. The Las Cruces Center, both in discipline and doctrinal presentation, grounds each student in Shikan-taza with the practice of koan only for the more advanced student. While we maintain the backbone and the heart of Zen practice as taught by Dogen Zenji, we are modifying the formality where needed for the American practitioner. Three times a week formal meditation and chanting is conducted with private sessions provided for students with special needs. The advanced student is offered historical background and Sutra study and an extensive library of religious and philosophical works is open to all.
ADDRESS: 3810 Paradise Lane, Las Cruces, NM 88005
PHONE: (505) 525-2329
LINEAGE: Japanese Soto Zen
SPIRITUAL HEAD: Rev. Dr. Soyu Matsuoka (Japanese)
RESIDENT DIRECTOR: Rev. Ken McGuire-Roshi and Rev. Fern McGuire
AFFILIATED WITH: Long Beach Zen Center
ESTABLISHED: 1987
FACILITIES: Urban meditation center

RETREATS OFFERED: Soto Zen sesshin
OPEN TO: General public

Mountain Cloud Zen Center

The center offers a regular schedule of
meditation and chanting, as well as Beginner's Nights and extended sittings. We are
fortunate to have Roshi Philip Kapleau,
semi-retired founder of the Rochester
Center, give *teisho* and (to his formal students only) *dokusan* from time to time as
well. Practice at Mountain Cloud Zen
Center is in the tradition of Harada-Roshi
and Yasutani-Roshi (that is, an amalgam
of Japanese Soto and Rinzai practices),
adapted to American students by Roshi
Philip Kapleau, as described in his book
The Three Pillars of Zen.
ADDRESS: Rt. 7 (Old Santa Fe Trail)
Box 125MC, Santa Fe, NM 87505 (Mail-
ing address: P. O. Box 5768, Santa Fe,
NM 87502)
PHONE: (505) 988-4396
LINEAGE: Harada-Roshi, Yasutani-Roshi
lineage (amalgam of Soto and Rinzai
Zen)
SPIRITUAL HEAD: Ven. Philip Kapleau-
Roshi (American)
RESIDENT DIRECTOR: Same
AFFILIATED WITH: The Zen Center,
Rochester, New York
ESTABLISHED: 1984
FACILITIES: Semi-urban meditation
center
RETREATS OFFERED: Extended sittings,
sesshin (see lineage), of one, two and
four-days
OPEN TO: General public with restric-
tions. Please call ahead for information.

Hokoji

Hokoji is located fifteen minutes north of
Taos, New Mexico, in the southern Rocky
Mountains. We follow the tradition of
Soto Zen Buddhism. There is daily morn-
ing sitting and service, with periodic ses-
shin and instruction.
ADDRESS: C/O Watkins, P. O. Box 1837,
Taos, NM 87571
LINEAGE: Soto Zen (Japanese)
SPIRITUAL HEAD: Kobun Chino Oto-
gawa (Japanese)
RESIDENT DIRECTOR: Bob Watkins
(American)
AFFILIATED WITH: Autonomous
ESTABLISHED: 1984
FACILITIES: Country retreat facility
RETREATS OFFERED: Daily sittings and
sesshins
OPEN TO: General public

NEW YORK

Albany Affiliate Group

The Albany Affiliate Group, MRO is an
associate center of the Mountain and
River Order, an organization of associated
Zen Buddhist temples, practice centers,
and sitting groups in the United States
and abroad, founded by John Daido
Loori, its spiritual director. The headquarters of the MRO is Zen Mountain
Monastery in Mount Tremper, New York.
The group meets weekly for zazen ses-
sions on Tuesdays from 7:15–8:45 P.M. at
293 Hamilton Street in Albany. The group
also sponsors periodic public talks and
weekend retreats led by Rev. Loori. For
information contact Bruno Kyoshin Zupp
at (518) 271-0879 or Jules Shuzen Harris at
(518) 457-0296.
ADDRESS: 135 Lancaster Street, Albany,
NY 12210
PHONE: (518) 465-6228
LINEAGE: Soto/Rinzai combination
SPIRITUAL HEAD: John Daido Loori
(American)
AFFILIATED WITH: Mountain and River
Order

Handmade adobe Zendo of Hokoji, near Taos, New Mexico.

ESTABLISHED: 1982
FACILITIES: Urban meditation center
and also rented accommodations
RETREATS OFFERED: Weekend sesshins
and introductory Zen sessions offered
twice yearly
OPEN TO: General public

AFFILIATED WITH: Mount Baldy Zen
Center
ESTABLISHED: 1980
FACILITIES: Small town urban medita-
tion center
RETREATS OFFERED: One day retreats
OPEN TO: General public

Clear Mountain Zen Center

Rev. Sogen Rick Hart is the abbot of the
Clear Mountain Zen Center. Sogen has
been studying Zen for over eighteen
years, the past ten under Joshu Sasaki-
Roshi. He teaches at local colleges and has
lectured at Duke University, The New
School for Social Research, College of the
Redwoods, and the New York Medical
Society.
ADDRESS: 8 School Street, Chatham,
NY 12037
PHONE: (518) 392-3513
LINEAGE: Rinzai Zen (Japanese)
SPIRITUAL HEAD: Joshu Sasaki-Roshi
(Japanese)
RESIDENT DIRECTOR: Sogen Rick Hart
(American)

Institute of Chung-Hwa Buddhist Culture Meditation Center

Master Sheng-Yen has received transmission in the two major branches of Ch'an
(Zen) Buddhism, the Lin-Chi (Rinzai)
and the Ts'ao-tung (Soto). His teachings
and lectures provide a focus for those who
wish to explore the path of Ch'an and its
methods of practice. These include koan
and *hua-t'ou* methods. The center offers
four seven-day retreats, weekend sittings,
philosophy classes, beginners' and intermediate classes, as well as Sunday open
house.
ADDRESS: 90–56 Corona Avenue, Elmhurst, NY 11373

PHONE: (718) 592-6593
LINEAGE: Soto and Rinzai Zen
SPIRITUAL HEAD: Master Sheng-Yen Chang (Chinese)
RESIDENT DIRECTOR: None
AFFILIATED WITH: Autonomous
ESTABLISHED: 1979
FACILITIES: Urban meditation center
RETREATS OFFERED: Combination Rinzai/Soto sesshin (seven days) four times a year and weekend sittings twelve times a year
OPEN TO: General public

Zen Studies Society/Dai Bosatsu Zendo Kongo-Ji

Dai Bosatsu Zendo Kongo-ji, the Zen Studies Society's mountain monastery, was formally dedicated on July 4, 1976, America's Bicentennial. From the beginning it has been a lay monastery dedicated to the vital tradition of Rinzai Zen. Here monks and lay residents work with Eido Shimano-Roshi to sustain a place where anyone is welcome to discover in himself or herself the liberating spirit of Zen. In this clearing beside a mountain lake, the daily schedule of work and meditation provides a balancing perspective to the demands of a busy world. From the beginning, Dai Bosatsu Zendo Kongo-ji has been the site of continuous and dedicated Zen practice. Eido-Roshi has said, "The seed of Buddha Dharma is planted in this continent, and through the years it will sprout and flourish. Thus, may we extend this mind over the whole universe so that all beings together may attain maturity in Buddha's wisdom."

ADDRESS: HCR 1 Box 80, Lew Beach, NY 12753
PHONE: (914) 439-4566
LINEAGE: We uphold the Takuju tradition of Rinzai Zen, but in addition, because of Karmic connections with Nyogen Senzaki and Yasutani Hakuun-

Roshi, their influence has also been great. Eido-Roshi himself did Inzan practice as well, so the two traditions are combined in him.
SPIRITUAL HEAD: Ven. Eido Tai Shimano-Roshi (Japanese)
RESIDENT DIRECTOR: "Bugyo" David Schner (American)
AFFILIATED WITH: Autonomous
ESTABLISHED: 1976
FACILITIES: Country retreat facility with accommodations for solitary retreats
RETREATS OFFERED: Six Rinzai sesshin per year and two three-month training periods (Kessei).
OPEN TO: Members, as well as those of the general public who have some experience of Rinzai Zen sesshin

Zen Mountain Monastery

Zen Mountain Monastery is a nonprofit religious corporation which functions as both an American Zen Buddhist Monastery (headquarters of the Mountain and River Order) and a Training Center for monks, nuns, and lay Zen practitioners. Its central purpose is the realization and actualization of the Buddha Way through Zen meditation and practice. Located on a two hundred-acre site surrounded by thousands of acres of state forest wilderness preserve on Tremper Mountain in the Catskills, the Monastery provides a year-round daily Zen Mountain Training Program comprising Zen meditation, face-to-face teaching, Dharma discourses, liturgy, work practice, body practice, and art practice. Zen teacher John Daido Loori-Sensei, whose training is in both the rigorous school of koan Zen and the subtle Dharma of Dogen's Zen, is in full-time residence. Each month a silent Zen Meditation Retreat ("sesshin") is offered. The spring quarter of each training year is a ninety-day Zen Training Intensive, and during each summer and fall, the regular

schedule is supplemented with seminars and workshops in the Zen arts and Buddhist studies. The winter training period emphasizes study and introspection. Residencies are available for the full year, training quarter, monthly, or for shorter periods. A sample of the Monastery's quarterly journal, *Mountain Record*, will be sent on request. At Zen Mountain Monastery a comprehensive ten-stage training in zazen and six other specific areas of Zen practice (Zen study with the teacher, academic study, liturgy, work, art, and body practice) involve the trainee in an in-depth study of the self and its expression in all aspects of daily life. The first stages comprise what is designated the "ascending the mountain" training in which concentration is developed through work with the breath, and the search for the nature of the self is begun in earnest with preliminary koans. This is followed by stages which involve "realization," the personal and direct experience of the ground of being and a deepening and clarifying of that experience. Over seven hundred koans, as well as "Shikan-taza" (just sitting practice), are utilized in the formal training program, which culminates in "descending the mountain training," the expression and actualization of what's been realized in the world.
ADDRESS: Box 197, South Plank Road, Mount Tremper, NY 12457
PHONE: (914) 688-2228
LINEAGE: Soto and Rinzai Zen
SPIRITUAL HEAD: Sensei John Daido Loori (American)
RESIDENT DIRECTOR: Same
AFFILIATED WITH: Zen Mountain Monastery is the parent organization of Mountain and River Order.
ESTABLISHED: 1980
FACILITIES: Urban meditation center and country retreat facility
RETREATS OFFERED: Rinzai/Soto Zen sesshin, three-month Ango training,

Zen arts retreats, academic retreats, introduction to Zen retreat, and supervised solitary retreats. All retreats are held several times each year.
OPEN TO: General public

Chogye International Zen Center of New York

Chogye International Zen Center of New York offers daily meditation and chanting practice as well as weekly public talks. Once a month the center has an intensive one-day sitting of six hours or a weekend retreat. All activities are offered to both members and nonmembers. Richard Shrobe is the abbot and a Master Dharma teacher of the Kwan Um Zen School. Retreats are led by either Zen Master Seung Sahn, Richard Shrobe, or one of the other Master Dharma teachers of the Kwan Um Zen School. Practice includes sitting, chanting, bowing, *kong-an* study, and shared work.
ADDRESS: 400 East 14th Street, #2E, New York, NY 10009
PHONE: (212) 353-0461
LINEAGE: Chogye Zen (Korean)
SPIRITUAL HEAD: Seung Sahn Soen Sa Nim (Korean)
RESIDENT DIRECTOR: Richard Shrobe, Abbot (American)
AFFILIATED WITH: Kwan Um Zen School
ESTABLISHED: 1975
FACILITIES: Urban meditation center
RETREATS OFFERED: Weekend group Zen retreats called "Yong Meng Jong Jin"
OPEN TO: General public

First Zen Institute of America

The First Zen Institute of America was founded in 1930 by the Japanese Zen Master Sokei-an Sasaki-Roshi to bring the tradition and practice of Rinzai Zen Buddhism to the West. Every Wednesday throughout the year the institute is open to the public at 7:30 P.M. for meditation, sutra-chanting, and the reading of Sokei-an's lectures. Weekly morning zazen is from 6:30–7:30 A.M. One weekend of each month is set aside for a two-day sit; this is open to nonmembers by prior arrangement. Also since 1954 the institute has been publishing *Zen Notes* ten times a year.

ADDRESS: 113 East 30th Street, New York, NY 10016
PHONE: (212) 686-2520
LINEAGE: Rinzai Zen (Japanese)
SPIRITUAL HEAD: None
RESIDENT DIRECTOR: None
ESTABLISHED: 1930
FACILITIES: Urban meditation center
RETREATS OFFERED: Weekend sesshins
OPEN TO: Both general public and members

Grace Gratitude Buddhist Temple

There is no full-time translator available at the moment, so all instructions are currently given in Chinese. Rev. Fa Yun spent eight years as a young monk disciple of the famous Ch'an Master Hsu Yun. Rev. Fa Yun says that he will make Ch'an teachings available to serious Western students as they become available. Currently the students are all Chinese.

ADDRESS: 48 East Broadway, New York, NY 10002
PHONE: (212) 925-1335
LINEAGE: Yun-men Ch'an, Lin-chi Ch'an (Chinese)
SPIRITUAL HEAD: Grand Ch'an Master Hsu Yun (Void Cloud)
RESIDENT DIRECTOR: Rev. Chau-Fan and Rev. Fa Yun (Chinese)
AFFILIATED WITH: Autonomous
ESTABLISHED: 1981
FACILITIES: Urban meditation center and Buddhist temple with country re-

treat facility and accommodations for solitary retreats
RETREATS OFFERED: Intermittent Ch'an retreats of varying durations
OPEN TO: General public

New York City Extension

New York City Extension, MRO is an associate center of the Mountain and River Order, an organization of associated Zen Buddhist temples, practice centers, and sitting groups in the United States and abroad founded by John Daido Loori, its spiritual director. The headquarters of the MRO is Zen Mountain Monastery in Mount Tremper, New York. NYCE meets twice weekly for zazen on Mondays and Tuesdays from 6:00–7:45 P.M. Monthly all-day zazen retreats are held on Saturdays from 9:00 A.M. to 5:00 P.M. and include a video-taped Dharma Discourse by Rev. Loori. The group also sponsors periodic public talks, weekend "Introduction to Zen Training" retreats, and sesshins, all led by Rev. Loori. For information contact Pat Enkyo Quarles at (212) 674-0832.

ADDRESS: 15 Washington Place (4D), New York, NY 10003
PHONE: (212) 674-0832
LINEAGE: Soto/Rinzai combination
SPIRITUAL HEAD: John Daido Loori (American)
RESIDENT DIRECTOR: None
AFFILIATED WITH: Mountain and River Order
ESTABLISHED: 1985
FACILITIES: Urban meditation center using rented accommodations
RETREATS OFFERED: Monthly all-day sittings
OPEN TO: General public

Zen Studies Society/New York Zendo Shobo-Ji

Established in 1968, the New York Zendo Shobo-ji is the city branch of the Zen

Ven. Eido Tai Shimano-Roshi, New York Zendo Shoboji, Zen Studies Society. Photo by Gerard Murrell.

Studies Society, which also maintains a monastic retreat and training facility, Dai Bosatsu Zendo Kongo-ji in the Catskill Mountains. Under the direction of the Ven. Eido Tai Shimano-Roshi, the New York Zendo offers instruction in Rinzai Zen meditation which includes koan practice. In addition to an intensive schedule of daily zazen, frequent weekend sesshin are offered. A beginner's night is held each week. (Please phone for details.)

ADDRESS: 223 East 67th Street, New York, NY 10021
PHONE: (212) 861-3333
LINEAGE: Japanese Rinzai Zen (Takuju tradition)
SPIRITUAL HEAD: Ven. Eido Tai Shimano-Roshi (Japanese)
RESIDENT DIRECTOR: Genro, Lee Milton (American)
AFFILIATED WITH: Autonomous
ESTABLISHED: 1968

FACILITIES: Urban meditation center
RETREATS OFFERED: Weekend sesshin
five times each year and daily zazen
OPEN TO: Members only or experienced
members of the general public

Rochester Zen Center

Ven. Bodhin Kjolhede-Sensei teaches an integral Zen grounded in the doctrines and disciplines of both the Soto and Rinzai sects, which includes koan practice. The Rochester center offers a daily schedule of meditation and chanting with periodic four and seven-day sesshins, a full-time staff program, and training programs. Introductory workshops are also available.
ADDRESS: 7 Arnold Park, Rochester, NY 14607
PHONE: (716) 473-9180

LINEAGE: Integral Zen (Soto/Rinzai)
SPIRITUAL HEAD: Philip Kapleau-Roshi,
founder and advisor; Bodhin Kjolhede-
Sensei, abbot
RESIDENT DIRECTOR: Same
AFFILIATED WITH: Autonomous
ESTABLISHED: 1966
FACILITIES: Urban meditation center
RETREATS OFFERED: Combination
Rinzai/Soto sesshin, weekend sittings;
offered eight to ten times per year at
Rochester, fifteen to twenty times per
year (total) at affiliates.
OPEN TO: General public

Ocean Zendo

No description available.
ADDRESS: Bridge Lane, Sagaponack,
NY 11962
LINEAGE: American Soto Zen

Back gardens and outdoor meditation path at Rochester Zen Center, Rochester, New York. Photo by David Sachter.

SPIRITUAL HEAD: Tetsugen Glassman-
Sensei (American)
RESIDENT DIRECTOR: Peter Matthiessen
(American)
AFFILIATED WITH: Zen Center of New
York
ESTABLISHED: 1984
FACILITIES: Local zazen center
RETREATS OFFERED: None
OPEN TO: General public

Suffolk Institute for Eastern Studies

The Suffolk Institute for Eastern Studies
offers intensive training in the Japanese
martial art of Aikido. Eleven classes are
offered each week. Chief Instructor is
Howard Pashenz, Ph.D., Third Degree
Black Belt, and Zen Student of Joshu
Sasaki-Roshi. The institute is a member of
the United States Aikido Federation, and
Dr. Pashenz is a certified instructor. The
martial art of Aikido is viewed as a Buddhist art endeavoring to teach wisdom
and compassion while transcending the
duality of subject and object. Compassion
is evident in the physical form of the art
(self-defense techniques) in that an
attacker must not be seriously injured.
There is no kicking or punching, and
joints are only turned in the direction that
nature intended so they are never broken.
The Aikidoist learns to blend with an attacker's force, lead him to an unbalanced,
helpless position, and then either immobi-
lize him safely, or throw the attacker so
another may be engaged. All movements
are circular, and the Aikidoist learns to
maintain a straight, balanced posture as
the attacker is guided into a circular path
and controlled through centrifugal force
and basic principles of physics related to
anatomical structure. Wisdom is developed in pragmatically understanding the
laws of physics (direction of forces and
meeting them tangentially or blending

with them) and in understanding that
an attacker is essentially no different than
oneself; to counterattack destructively
would be to attack an aspect of oneself.
The dualism of subject and object (defender and attacker) is transcended by re-
peatedly attempting to join and flow with
an attacker's force—striving for one harmonious movement wherein attacker and
defender are moving as joined elements
on one continuous circular path. In Aikido there is a searching for the "absolute"
in the perfecting of the exactness of technique, which is then subjectively experienced as "effortless." The Aikidoist, after
learning the mechanics of technique, focuses on a point in his lower abdomen
and performs the self-defense movements
in a state of "no-mind," on an unconscious level of habit and reflex without
conceptualization.
ADDRESS: 330 Moriches Road, St.
James, NY 11780
PHONE: (516) 584-6085
SPIRITUAL HEAD: Howard Pashenz,
Ph.D.
AFFILIATED WITH: Autonomous
ESTABLISHED: 1986
FACILITIES: Dojo
RETREATS OFFERED: Half-day seminars
in Aikido, combined with zazen; of-
fered monthly.
OPEN TO: General public

Won Kak Sa Buddhist Temple

Rev. Young B. Oh (Bup An), Abbot of
Won Kak Sa Buddhist Temple, conducts
Zen study groups and Zen meditation retreats in the tradition of the Korean Chogye Order, which incorporates koan practice, mantra, breath control, Shikan-taza
(quiet mind), etc. There is daily meditation and chanting, with monthly weekend
Zen retreats. In addition, there is a lecture schedule in both Korean and English.
The Thursday evening English lecture and

Zen meditation practice (7:00–9:00 P.M.) is open to the public.
ADDRESS: 301 A Clove Road, Salisbury Mills, NY 12577
PHONE: (914) 496-4165
LINEAGE: Chogye Order (Korean)
SPIRITUAL HEAD: Rev. Young B. Oh (Rev. Bup An) (Korean)
RESIDENT DIRECTOR: Same
AFFILIATED WITH: Korean Buddhist Chogye Order
ESTABLISHED: 1976
FACILITIES: Country retreat facility with accommodations for solitary retreats
RETREATS OFFERED: Weekend Zen meditation, Zen study
OPEN TO: General public

Long Island Zen Center of Rinzai-Ji

We offer sittings open to the public twice weekly, as well as weekend sesshin and instruction for beginners.
ADDRESS: 6 Brewster Court, Setauket, NY 11733
PHONE: (516) 751-8408
LINEAGE: Rinzai Zen
SPIRITUAL HEAD: Joshu Sasaki-Roshi
RESIDENT DIRECTOR: Sogen Kann
AFFILIATED WITH: Rinzai-ji
ESTABLISHED: 1977
RETREATS OFFERED: Weekend sesshin
OPEN TO: General public

Lotus Flower Zendo

The Lotus Flower Affiliate Group, MRO, at Green Haven Correctional Facility, is an associated center of the Mountain and River Order, an organization of associated Zen Buddhist temples, practice centers, and sitting groups in the United States and abroad founded by John Daido Loori, its spiritual director. The headquarters of the MRO is Zen Mountain Monastery in Mount Tremper, New York.

The group meets twice weekly for zazen, services, and study sessions. It holds a yearly two-day Rohatsu Sesshin led by Rev. Loori, who, in addition, visits the group frequently to give talks and conduct *dokusan*. The group can be contacted through the Senior Chaplain, Dr. Davis, at Drawer B, Stormville, NY 12582. Similar groups are also in existence at both the Fishkill and the Napanoch Correctional Facilities, also in New York state.
ADDRESS: Drawer B, Green Haven Correctional Facility, Stormville, NY 12582
PHONE: (914) 221-2711
LINEAGE: Soto and Rinzai
SPIRITUAL HEAD: John Daido Loori (American)
RESIDENT DIRECTOR: None
AFFILIATED WITH: Mountain and River Order
ESTABLISHED: 1983
FACILITIES: Sitting group in maximum security prison
RETREATS OFFERED: One two-day sesshin each year
OPEN TO: Inmates only

Kanzeon Zendo

Kanzeon Zendo, in Water Mill, New York, was dedicated on August 12, 1968 by Yasutani-Roshi, Soen-Roshi, and Eido-Roshi (then the monk Tai-san). The Zendo is in the home of Jiryu Jill Bart. Zazen is usually on Thursdays at 1:30 P.M. Call or write to inquire.
ADDRESS: Box 761 Paul's Lane, Water Mill, NY 11976
PHONE: (516) 537-1163
LINEAGE: Rinzai Zen (Japanese)
SPIRITUAL HEAD: Ven Eido Tai Shimano-Roshi
RESIDENT DIRECTOR: Jiryu Jill Bart
ESTABLISHED: 1968
FACILITIES: Zendo in private home
OPEN TO: General public

Zen Community of New York

The Zen Community of New York, under the direction of Bernard Tetsugen Glassman-Sensei, is a nonprofit, interfaith, residential community committed to the realization of our spiritual potential and the actualization of that potential in our daily lives. There are five aspects of our lives that serve as focal points for the Zen practice of the community: meditation, study, work practice, social action, and interfaith expression. Our goal is to find a balanced expression of these five elements. The core practice of our community is meditation. We have a daily meditation schedule, and we offer free meditation instruction twice a month. Having grounded ourselves in this practice, the next step for our community was to establish a right livelihood. Right livelihood is one of the elements of the Buddha's Eightfold Noble Path, which expresses the content of his enlightenment experience. Zen monasteries have traditionally considered it of vital importance (both financially and spiritually) to find successful ways of achieving self-sufficiency. In 1982 we started the Greyston Bakery, and in four years we have built a nationwide reputation as a gourmet bakery of the highest quality and consistency. We now feel confident that our bakery is firmly established as a work practice for our trainees. The Greyston Bakery is now in the position of supporting the Zen Community. We have learned a lot from the bakery about "giving practice," as opposed to taking, not merely doing good for oneself, but rather doing good for others in a way which expresses the fundamental unity of all living and nonliving things. We are ready to bring another aspect of our practice into sharper focus, namely social action. Right action is another of the elements of the Buddha's Eightfold Noble Path which is essential to the full expression of our lives.

ADDRESS: 114 Woodworth Avenue, Yonkers, NY 10701
PHONE: (914) 375-1510
LINEAGE: Soto Zen (Japanese)
SPIRITUAL HEAD: Bernard Tetsugen Glassman-Sensei (Jewish, Zen priest)
RESIDENT DIRECTOR: Same
AFFILIATED WITH: Zen Center of Los Angeles
ESTABLISHED: 1980
FACILITIES: Urban meditation center
RETREATS OFFERED: Seven-day sesshin, weekend sesshin, ten-day seminary
OPEN TO: General public

NORTH CAROLINA

Chapel Hill Zen Group

Chapel Hill Zen Group is located near the University of North Carolina campus. Zazen is open to the public and occurs one night weekly, on Tuesdays. There are two sittings with walking meditation. Membership ranges from six to nine active participants. Backgrounds are diversified. We are not formally affiliated with any one center, although three members have been at San Francisco Zen Center. Katagiri-Roshi of the Minnesota Zen Center has led three retreats.

ADDRESS: 307 Cameron Avenue, Chapel Hill, NC 27516
PHONE: (919) 967-9256
LINEAGE: Zen
SPIRITUAL HEAD: None
RESIDENT DIRECTOR: None
AFFILIATED WITH: Autonomous
ESTABLISHED: 1982
RETREATS OFFERED: Annual weekend retreat each autumn
OPEN TO: General public

Squirrel Mountain Zendo

Squirrel Mountain Zendo stands in a hardwood forest about fifteen miles south

of Chapel Hill. The sitting schedule includes Sunday zazen, and Zen weekends in spring and fall. Please write for details. The practice follows the form of Rinzai-ji, founded by Joshu Sasaki-Roshi, and is led by his long-time students, Gentei Sandy and Susanna Stewart.
ADDRESS: High Dirt Court, Saralyn (Mailing address: Rt. 5, Box 114, Pittsboro, NC 27312)
PHONE: (919) 542-4379
LINEAGE: Rinzai Zen (Japanese)
SPIRITUAL HEAD: Joshu Sasaki-Roshi
RESIDENT DIRECTOR: G. S. Stewart (American)
AFFILIATED WITH: Rinzai-ji, Inc., Los Angeles, California
ESTABLISHED: 1975
FACILITIES: Backwoods Zendo
RETREATS OFFERED: Zen weekends spring and fall
OPEN TO: General public

Piedmont Zen Group

The Piedmont Zen Group is a small group offering an ongoing schedule of zazen (Zen meditation) several times a week. The Zendo (meditation room) is equipped with all necessary cushions. Anyone interested in zazen practice is welcome to participate.
ADDRESS: 3805 Greenleaf Street, Raleigh, NC 27606
PHONE: (919) 833-6200
LINEAGE: Soto and Rinzai (Japanese Zen)
SPIRITUAL HEAD: Sensei Bodhin Kjolhede—Head of Rochester Zen Center (American)
RESIDENT DIRECTOR: None
AFFILIATED WITH: Informally affiliated with the Zen Center in Rochester, New York
ESTABLISHED: 1985
FACILITIES: House owned by member

RETREATS OFFERED: Occasional half-day or one-day Zen sittings
OPEN TO: General public

OHIO

Cleveland Buddhist Temple

Rev. Koshin Ogui-Sensei, an eighteenth generation Buddhist priest from Japan, teaches an integral Zen grounded in the awareness and disciplines of both Jodo Shin Shu and Zen, including zazen, koan, and oneness in Amida Tathagata. The Zen Shin Sangha, organized under the sponsorship of the Cleveland Buddhist Temple, offers meditation practice every Tuesday for beginners and every Wednesday for advanced students. One-day sesshins are conducted monthly, and seminars featuring noted practitioners are held throughout the year. Students are taught "counting-breath *samadhi*," the practice of counting odd numbers on the inhalation and even numbers on the exhalation, and so on up to ten. Students are encouraged to let thoughts and sounds come and go as they will. *Kinhin* (walking meditation) is also practiced, as is chanting meditation. Classes in Shomyo chanting are offered to the public.
ADDRESS: 1573 East 214 Street, Euclid, OH 44117
PHONE: (216) 692-1509
LINEAGE: Jodo Shin Shu
SPIRITUAL HEAD: Sensei Koshin Ogui (Japanese)
RESIDENT DIRECTOR: None
AFFILIATED WITH: Buddhist Churches of America
ESTABLISHED: 1945
FACILITIES: Urban meditation center
RETREATS OFFERED: Combination Rinzai/Soto sesshin, a "Day of Mindfulness," weekend sittings; offered once every three months
OPEN TO: General public

Ohio Sitting Group

The Ohio Sitting Group, MRO is an associated center of the Mountain and River Order, an organization of associated Zen Buddhist temples, practice centers, and sitting groups in the United States and abroad founded by John Daido Loori, its spiritual director. The headquarters of the MRO is Zen Mountain Monastery in Mount Tremper, New York. The group meets weekly for zazen and conducts periodic one-day zazen retreats and videotaped Dharma Discourses given by Rev. Loori. For information contact Bob Rogers at (216) 467-2802.

ADDRESS: 61 Sandy Hill Drive, Sagamore Hills, OH 44067
PHONE: (216) 467-2802
LINEAGE: Soto/Rinzai
SPIRITUAL HEAD: John Daido Loori (American)
AFFILIATED WITH: Mountain and River Order
ESTABLISHED: 1985
FACILITIES: Urban meditation center using some rented facilities
RETREATS OFFERED: One-day zazen retreats three times a year
OPEN TO: General public

OREGON

Eugene Buddhist Priory

Eugene Buddhist Priory is a church dedicated to the practice of Serene Reflection Meditation (Chinese: Ts'ao Tung, Japanese: Soto) as taught by the Order of Buddhist Contemplatives at Shasta Abbey, Mount Shasta, California. The priory's meditation hall is open to the public on Tuesdays, Wednesdays, and Thursdays from 10:00 A.M. to 5:30 P.M. and on Saturdays from 10:30 A.M. to 3:30 P.M. Anyone is welcome to stop in and meditate during these hours; however, we ask that you receive meditation instruction

before attending scheduled meditation and services. The priory also maintains a Buddhist library and a meditation supplies and book shop.

ADDRESS: 2255 Hilyard Street, Eugene, OR 97405
PHONE: (503) 344-7377
LINEAGE: Soto Zen and Chinese Mahayana
SPIRITUAL HEAD: Rev. Roshi Jiyu-Kennett
RESIDENT DIRECTOR: All priories are staffed by a fully-qualified resident senior priest from the Order of Buddhist Contemplatives.
AFFILIATED WITH: Shasta Abbey, Mount Shasta, California
ESTABLISHED: 1973
FACILITIES: Urban meditation center, library, and bookstore
RETREATS OFFERED: Regularly scheduled full-day retreats
OPEN TO: General public

Oregon Zen Priory

The Oregon Zen Priory is an independent temple for lay practice, emphasizing the integration of traditional zazen meditation and Soto Zen training within daily life. Roshi Kyogen Carlson and Rev. Teacher Gyokuko Carlson teach regular classes in Soto Zen Dharma, following a liturgical calendar. Senior membership with advanced teaching is available to participants after a year of attendance and the taking of lay ordination, and senior members, in turn, may take lay discipleship, which involves a formal master-disciple relationship with a priest. Regular one-day and three-day retreats are held as well as ceremonies for Buddhist holidays, weddings, and funerals.

ADDRESS: 2539 Southeast Madison, Portland, OR 97214
PHONE: (503) 239-4846
LINEAGE: Soto Zen

SPIRITUAL HEAD: Roshi Kyogen Carlson and Rev. Teacher Gyokuko Carlson
RESIDENT DIRECTOR: None
AFFILIATED WITH: Autonomous
ESTABLISHED: 1973
FACILITIES: Urban meditation center using rented facilities; accommodations for solitary retreats.
RETREATS OFFERED: Soto Zen sesshin, supervised solitary retreats; one-day retreats—introductory Dharma intensive; two sesshins a year, one-day retreats once a month.
OPEN TO: General public

Zen Community of Oregon

Our group maintains a lay practice under the guidance of Jan Chozen Bays, a Dharma successor of Maezumi-Roshi. We are traditionally, but not officially, associated with Zen Center of Los Angeles. We gather for evening sitting twice a week with one-day sittings scheduled each month if possible. We meet in members' homes. Due to time and work schedules, we generally can only have personal interviews with Chozen during the one-day sitting each month. Thus, each person must rely in large part on his/her own daily practice. Anyone is welcome to join us for zazen. Please call for times and locations.
ADDRESS: 6323 Southeast 22nd, Portland, OR 97201
PHONE: (502) 235-8265
LINEAGE: Soto Zen (Japanese)
SPIRITUAL HEAD: None
RESIDENT DIRECTOR: Jan Chozen Bays-Sensei (American)
AFFILIATED WITH: Unofficially affiliated with Zen Center of Los Angeles
ESTABLISHED: 1978
FACILITIES: Member's home
RETREATS OFFERED: One-day sitting each month with three-day sesshins occasionally scheduled
OPEN TO: General public

PENNSYLVANIA

Philadelphia Buddhist Association

The Philadelphia Buddhist Association was founded in 1985 by American practitioners of several Buddhist traditions. It has about fifty active members and a mailing list of a hundred and fifty friends. The current teacher is Rev. Soho Machida, a senior Rinzai Zen monk from Daitokuji temple in Kyoto, Japan. Activities include twice-weekly evening sittings, monthly all-day sittings, introductory workshops, and ceremonies on Buddhist holidays. The house rented by the group has a first-floor meditation hall; two members live upstairs.
ADDRESS: 138 Gorgas Lane, Philadelphia, PA 19119
PHONE: (215) 247-3516
LINEAGE: Nonsectarian, Zen-style sitting
SPIRITUAL HEAD: None
RESIDENT DIRECTOR: Rev. Soho Machida (Japanese Rinzai Zen) teacher in residence.
AFFILIATED WITH: Autonomous
ESTABLISHED: 1985
FACILITIES: Urban meditation center
RETREATS OFFERED: Monthly all-day or weekend sittings
OPEN TO: General public

Zen Studies Society of Philadelphia

Ann Waginger writes: "In early spring of 1986, when I began looking for a house in Philadelphia, I knew there had to be room for a Zendo. . . . Three of us began sitting in the corner of the bedroom, using our own cushions, while the dog sat on the bed watching. Soon afterward, we cleaned up the large third floor of the house and . . . installed a small Buddha, a Soen-Roshi calligraphy, a candle, incense, and flowers

on a table at one end of the room. We
now have regular zazen meetings Tuesday
and Thursday evenings from 7:00–9:00
P.M. and will increase our schedule as
need and desire dictate. We have had three
one-day long workshops and have plans
for many more in the future."
ADDRESS: 214 Monroe Street, Philadel-
phia, PA 19147
PHONE: (215) 625-2601
LINEAGE: Rinzai Zen Chinese-Japanese
SPIRITUAL HEAD: Eido Tai Shimano-
Roshi (Japanese)
RESIDENT DIRECTOR: Rev. Genro Lee
Milton (American)
AFFILIATED WITH: Autonomous
ESTABLISHED: 1986
FACILITIES: Urban meditation center
RETREATS OFFERED: Weekend and
week-long sesshins
OPEN TO: General public

RHODE ISLAND

Providence Zen Center/
Diamond Hill Zen Monastery

The Providence Zen Center is a residential Zen meditation center established in
1972 with the teaching and guidance of
Zen Master Seung Sahn. It is now located
twenty minutes north of Providence,
Rhode Island, on fifty acres of beautiful
land. There is space for about twenty-five
residents. Daily practice of sitting, chanting, and bowing is offered as well as
monthly retreats of one to seven-days.
Meditation instruction and personal Zen
interviews with the resident teachers are
available weekly and by appointment. The
Diamond Hill Zen Monastery, which is
located on the grounds, is where the
twenty-one to ninety-day intensive retreats
take place, winter and summer. Introductory workshops, ceremonies, conferences,
rental facilities, guest space and solo retreat space are also offered. Daily practice

is open to the public and free of charge.
Our practice is Zen meditation: cultivating before-thinking mind—not knowing.
On the inhalation for about a count of
three: clear mind, clear mind, clear mind.
On the exhalation for about a count of
seven: Don't Know, Don't Know, Don't
Know. We emphasize following the breath
(abdominally). The tools of mantra,
kong-an (koan), and Hwato (What is
this? moment to moment) are also used.
We stress always coming back to an open
and alert body/mind after wandering and
slumping—without criticism, judgement,
or identification; we alternate thirty to
forty-minute sittings with ten minutes of
walking. (It is possible to stand during sittings if there is too much body pain or
sleepiness.)
ADDRESS: 528 Pound Road, Cumberland, RI 02864
PHONE: (401) 769-6464
LINEAGE: Chogye Korean Zen
SPIRITUAL HEAD: Zen Master Seung
Sahn (Korean)
RESIDENT DIRECTOR: Jacob Perl, Bobby
Rhodes, Lincoln Rhodes
AFFILIATED WITH: Kwan Um Zen
School
ESTABLISHED: 1972
FACILITIES: Country retreat facility with
accommodations for solitary retreats
RETREATS OFFERED: Combination Rin-
zai/Soto sesshin, three-month Kyol-che,
chanting retreats, weekend sittings, su-
pervised or unsupervised solitary re-
treats; generally offered once a month
(one to seven days).
OPEN TO: General public

Rhode Island Shim Gum Do

See American Buddhist Shim Gum Do
Association of Brighton, Massachusetts,
for description.
ADDRESS: 123 Farnum Avenue, North
Providence, RI 02911

PHONE: (401) 353-6638
LINEAGE: Chogye Korean Buddhist
SPIRITUAL HEAD: Founding Master,
Chang Sik Kim
RESIDENT DIRECTOR: Joan Overcash
AFFILIATED WITH: American Buddhist
Shim Gum Do Association of Brighton, Massachusetts
OPEN TO: General public and members

The Meditation Place

The Meditation Place offers meditation instruction and supportive sitting and discussion groups for meditators of all backgrounds. The schedule includes daily morning meditation, several evening sittings a week, and monthly one-day sittings on weekends. TMP is an affiliate of the Kwan Um Zen School and maintains close ties to the Providence Zen Center, but has dropped Zen ritual and robes in favor of a more relaxed atmosphere.
ADDRESS: 168 Fourth Street, Providence, RI 02906
PHONE: (401) 274-4026
LINEAGE: Korean Zen
SPIRITUAL HEAD: Zen Master Seung Sahn (Korean)
RESIDENT DIRECTOR: Ellen Sidor
AFFILIATED WITH: Kwan Um Zen School
ESTABLISHED: 1985
FACILITIES: Urban meditation center
RETREATS OFFERED: Weekend sittings and one-day sittings once a month
OPEN TO: General public

TEXAS

Dallas-Fort Worth Zen Center

DFW Zen Center is an affiliate center of Rinzai-Ji of America. Most of this city center's *sangha* are students of Kyozan Joshu Sasaki-Roshi. The center provides instruction in zazen, daily meditation, chanting, work practice, and intense zazen weekends for the *sangha*. There is living space for eight residents who wish to embrace a discipline that combines traditional Zen practice with urban work responsibilities. Our practice is Rinzai Zen from the Myoshin-Ji tradition of Japan: zazen meditation, chanting, work practice (*samu*), and communal living based upon the teachings of Joshu Sasaki-Roshi.
ADDRESS: 3602 Cole Avenue, Dallas, TX 75204
PHONE: (214) 521-9408
LINEAGE: Rinzai Zen (Japanese)
SPIRITUAL HEAD: Kyozan Joshu Sasaki-Roshi (Japanese)
RESIDENT DIRECTOR: Jokun Jeff Webb (American)
AFFILIATED WITH: Rinzai-Ji of America
ESTABLISHED: 1984
FACILITIES: Urban meditation center
RETREATS OFFERED: Zazen weekends
OPEN TO: General public

Austin Area Zazen Club

Students of Kyozan Sasaki-Roshi, Rinzai Zen Master, practice Zen and sit together Saturday mornings in Austin.
ADDRESS: 226 East Austin Street, Elgin, TX 78621
PHONE: (512) 285-3810
LINEAGE: Rinzai Zen
SPIRITUAL HEAD: Kyozan Joshu Sasaki-Roshi (Japanese)
RESIDENT DIRECTOR: None
AFFILIATED WITH: Rinzai-Ji
ESTABLISHED: 1976
FACILITIES: Urban meditation center using rented facilities with no accommodations for solitary retreats
RETREATS OFFERED: Weekend sittings every week
OPEN TO: General public

Texas Buddhist Association

The teaching of Dharma and a discussion of the sutras is scheduled every Saturday

and Sunday. Meditation is offered on
Thursdays and Saturdays. We meditate
forty-five minutes per session. Two meth-
ods are taught: 1) Count your breath from
one to ten and repeat: 2) Recite Buddha's
name in your mind.
ADDRESS: 13210 Land Road, Houston,
  TX 77047
PHONE: (713) 434-0211
LINEAGE: Zen and Pure Land
SPIRITUAL HEAD: Jan-Hai and Hung-I
  Shih
RESIDENT DIRECTOR: None
AFFILIATED WITH: Autonomous
ESTABLISHED: 1978
FACILITIES: Urban meditation center
RETREATS OFFERED: Chanting retreat,
  a "Day of Mindfulness," weekend sit-
  tings; offered monthly
OPEN TO: General public

Dallas Buddhist Association
No description available.
ADDRESS: 422 Apollo Road, Richard-
  son, TX 75081
PHONE: (214) 234-4401
LINEAGE: Chinese
SPIRITUAL HEAD: Rev. Chin Kung
  (Chinese-Taiwanese)
RESIDENT DIRECTOR: Rev. Wu Bun
  (Chinese-Taiwanese)
AFFILIATED WITH: Autonomous
ESTABLISHED: 1982
FACILITIES: Home converted into medi-
  tation center
RETREATS OFFERED: Lectures, retreat
  on reciting "Amita Buddha"
OPEN TO: General public

UTAH

Wasatch Zen Group
No description available.
ADDRESS: 11th East 7th South, Salt Lake
  City, UT 84108
PHONE: (501) 583-9308

LINEAGE: Japanese Soto Zen
SPIRITUAL HEAD: Taizan Maezumi-
  Roshi (Japanese)
RESIDENT DIRECTOR: None
AFFILIATED WITH: Zen Center of Los
  Angeles
ESTABLISHED: 1981
FACILITIES: Urban meditation center
RETREATS OFFERED: Three-day sesshins
OPEN TO: General public

VERMONT

Zen Center of Burlington, Vermont
Zen Center of Burlington, MRO is an associated center of the Mountain and River
Order, an organization of associated Zen
Buddhist temples, practice centers, and
sitting groups in the United States and
abroad founded by John Daido Loori, its
spiritual director. The headquarters of the
MRO is Zen Mountain Monastery in
Mount Tremper, New York. ZCB meets
weekly for zazen on Mondays from
5:00–6:00 P.M. at the First Unitarian
Universalist Church in Burlington. The
Group also meets periodically for one-day
zazen retreats and video-taped Dharma
Discourses given by Rev. Loori. For in-
formation contact Henry Chigen Finney
at (802) 862-2000 or Bob Tokushu Sen-
ghas at (802) 658-6466.
ADDRESS: First Unitarian Universalist
  Church (Mailing address: 54 River-
  mount Terr., Burlington, VT 05401)
PHONE: (802) 658-6466
LINEAGE: Soto/Rinzai
SPIRITUAL HEAD: John Daido Loori
  (American)
RESIDENT DIRECTOR: None
AFFILIATED WITH: Mountain and River
  Order
ESTABLISHED: 1981
FACILITIES: Urban meditation center
  using rented facilities

RETREATS OFFERED: Public talks and combination Rinzai/Soto sesshin and introduction to Zen retreats, offered twice yearly
OPEN TO: General public

VIRGINIA

Blue Ridge Zen Group

Our Zen group provides instruction for beginners and the opportunity for daily meditation with others at our Zendo in Charlottesville. We have periodic weekend retreats at our mountain Zendo.
ADDRESS: 214 Rugby Road, Charlottesville, VA 22901 (Mailing address: Rt. 1, Box 18, Earlysville, VA 22936)
PHONE: (804) 973-5435
LINEAGE: Rinzai Zen (Japanese)
SPIRITUAL HEAD: Joshu Sasaki-Roshi (Japanese)
RESIDENT DIRECTOR: William A. Stephens
AFFILIATED WITH: Rinzai-Ji
ESTABLISHED: 1975
FACILITIES: Urban meditation center with country retreat facility
RETREATS OFFERED: Zen weekends
OPEN TO: General public

Sai Sho An Zen Group

Sai Sho An Zen Group meets on Sundays at 7:30 A.M. in a rural location near Markham, Virginia. The group has been meeting regularly since 1970. We organize occasional weekend sittings and meet with other Zen practitioners in Charlottesville, Virginia. For intensive seven-day sesshin, we attend retreats conducted by other, larger Zen groups.
ADDRESS: Rt 1, Box 529, Delaplane, VA 22025
PHONE: (703) 592-3701
LINEAGE: Rinzai Zen
SPIRITUAL HEAD: Sasaki-Roshi

RESIDENT DIRECTOR: Tom Davenport and Arthur Dyago
AFFILIATED WITH: We study with Sasaki-Roshi from Mount Baldy Zen Center.
ESTABLISHED: 1971
FACILITIES: Sunday meeting in small Zen hut
RETREATS OFFERED: Irregular weekend sittings
OPEN TO: General public

WASHINGTON

North Cascades Buddhist Priory

Members and friends of North Cascades Buddhist Priory meet weekly in Seattle (Wednesday) and Olympia (Tuesday). Day retreats are held regularly in Seattle. The priory is building a place for retreats on the Nisqually River. There is instruction in meditation and private spiritual guidance (*sanzen*), and memorial and other services are available on request. The practice of North Cascades Buddhist Priory is Serene Reflection Meditation (Shikan-taza).
ADDRESS: Box 152, McKenna, WA 98558
PHONE: (206) 458-5075
LINEAGE: Soto Zen (Chinese and Japanese)
SPIRITUAL HEAD: Rev. Master Jiyu-Kennett, M.O.B.C. (British)
RESIDENT DIRECTOR: All priories are staffed by a fully qualified resident senior priest from the Order of Buddhist Contemplatives.
AFFILIATED WITH: Shasta Abbey (Order of Buddhist Contemplatives)
ESTABLISHED: 1986
FACILITIES: Urban meditation center with a building in the country (urban meditation held in rented facility); accommodations for solitary retreats.
RETREATS OFFERED: Short sesshin (Soto Zen); private retreats (Soto Zen)
OPEN TO: General public

Daigakuji

Daigakuji began under John Dennis
Govert-Roshi in 1979 and is currently un-
der the direction of Thomas Goldstein.
The center offers sitting meditation on
Sundays for members only. Prospective
students must first set up an interview
with the instructor.
ADDRESS: 10420 23rd Northeast, Seattle,
   WA 98125
PHONE: (206) 527-8563
LINEAGE: Soto Zen (Japanese)
SPIRITUAL HEAD: Matsuoka-Roshi
RESIDENT DIRECTOR: T. Goldstein
AFFILIATED WITH: Long Beach Zen
   Center
ESTABLISHED: 1929
FACILITIES: Urban meditation center

Dharma Friendship Foundation

Dharma Friendship Foundation is a nonprofit educational and religious organization. Its primary purpose is to provide
public talks, lecture series, retreats, and
seminars on Buddhist philosophy, psychology, ethics, meditation, and cognitive
sciences as presented by the most highly
qualified teachers able to come to the
Seattle area. Additionally, our efforts are
directed toward the preservation of the
written, oral, and meditative traditions
of Mahayana Buddhism. A variety of
Tibetan Buddhist practices are taught,
including Shamatha meditation ("Calm
Abiding") using breath-awareness or
visualization techniques; Lo Jong (Seven-
point Mind-Training); Lam Rim ("Graduated Path"); reflective, analytical meditation and meditations on loving-kindness.
ADDRESS: 3654 Dayton Avenue North,
   Seattle, WA 98103 (Mailing address:
   4945 145th Avenue Southeast, Bellevue,
   WA 98006)
PHONE: Bellevue (206) 641-5469; Seattle
   (206) 547-0053
LINEAGE: Tibetan Mahayana

SPIRITUAL HEAD: B. Alan Wallace
   (American)
RESIDENT DIRECTOR: Ven. Gen Lam-
   rimpa (Tibetan)
AFFILIATED WITH: Autonomous
ESTABLISHED: 1985
FACILITIES: Urban meditation center
   (see Dayton Street address above);
   country retreat facility. (We use Cloud
   Mountain retreat center near Castle
   Rock, Washington. Facilities for solitary
   retreats).
RETREATS OFFERED: Weekend, five-day,
   three-month, one-year meditation
   retreats
OPEN TO: General public

Gold Summit Monastery (Branch of Dharma Realm Buddhist Association)

Gold Summit Monastery has an ongoing
schedule of lectures and practices for
adults and children throughout the year.
There is a Sunday school available, which
offers Buddhist studies, Chinese studies,
and meditation. Lectures are given twice
a day at 1:00 P.M. and 7:30 P.M. On
weekends there are activities at the
monastery from 8:00 A.M. to 3:00
P.M., including bowing ceremonies, meditation, recitation of the Shurangama mantra, recitation of the chapter on Universal
Worthy's (Samantabhadra) Vows from the
Avatamsaka Sutra, and other sutra recitations. Orthodox Buddhism is taught and
practiced at the monastery every day. Like
all monasteries of the Dharma Realm
Buddhist Association, no smoking, meat,
or intoxicants are permitted in the monastery. Individuals at the Gold Summit
Monastery learn a vast variety of traditional Buddhist practices including: sitting in Ch'an meditation (not focused on
one lineage to the exclusion of others—all
five major lineages in Ch'an are studied

and practiced), Pure Land Recitation (reciting Amitabha Buddha's and Kuan Yin—Avalokiteshvara Bodhisattva's names), bowing repentances, and recitation of mantras according to the orthodox secret school. In sitting in meditation, whether reciting mantras, the Buddha's name, reciting scriptures from memory, or investigating a Ch'an "Hua t'o," sitting or working toward the ability to sit in full lotus posture is emphasized.

ADDRESS: 1431 Minor Avenue, Seattle, WA 98101
PHONE: (206) 340-0569
LINEAGE: We propagate all major lineages in Mahayana and even Theravada.
SPIRITUAL HEAD: Ven. Hsuan Hua (Chinese)
RESIDENT DIRECTOR: Several teachers, all Bhikshus
AFFILIATED WITH: Dharma Realm Buddhist Association
ESTABLISHED: 1975
FACILITIES: Urban meditation center with accommodations for solitary retreats.
RETREATS OFFERED: Chanting retreat, prostration retreat, weekend sittings; offered every couple of months and weekends.
OPEN TO: General public

Seattle Dharma Center

No description available.
ADDRESS: 1147 Northwest 57th Street, Seattle, WA 98107
PHONE: (206) 783-8484
LINEAGE: Korean Zen
SPIRITUAL HEAD: Seung Sahn Soen Sa Nim
RESIDENT DIRECTOR: None
AFFILIATED WITH: Kwan Um Zen School
ESTABLISHED: 1983
FACILITIES: Both an urban center and a retreat center on Vashon Island.

RETREATS OFFERED: Three-day retreat quarterly.
OPEN TO: General public

Three Treasures Sangha

The Three Treasures Sangha is a lay Zen meditation group studying under Joan Reich Jo-Un-Roshi. We offer daily zazen, monthly *Zazenkai*, and seven-day sesshin twice yearly. Joan Reich-Roshi received permission to teach from Yamada Ko-un-Roshi of the Sango-Kyodan lineage in Japan.
ADDRESS: 331 17th Avenue East, Seattle, WA 98112
PHONE: (206) 322-2447
LINEAGE: Japanese Sanbo Kyodan (Harada-Yasutani line)
SPIRITUAL HEAD: Yamada-Roshi
RESIDENT DIRECTOR: Joan Reich Jo-un-Roshi
AFFILIATED WITH: Autonomous
ESTABLISHED: 1978
FACILITIES: Urban meditation center.
RETREATS OFFERED: Seven-day sesshin, *Zazenkai* (weekend) retreats, and daily sittings.
OPEN TO: General public

WISCONSIN

Madison Zen Center

We are an affiliate of the Rochester Zen Center and follow its guidelines and traditions. Our members usually attend sesshin and ceremonies at the Rochester Center. In Madison we maintain a schedule of daily sitting, chanting, ceremonies, and retreats. We offer a brief introduction to beginners once a month and longer workshops once or twice a year. We practice according to the style of the Rochester Zen Center including zazen, chanting, ceremony, retreats, and work practice.
ADDRESS: 1820 Jefferson Street, Madison, WI 53711

Tozen Akiyama, Resident Priest, Milwaukee Zen Center.

PHONE: (608) 255-4488
LINEAGE: Soto/Rinzai
SPIRITUAL HEAD: Sensei Bodhin Kjolhede (Founded by Philip Kapleau-Roshi)
RESIDENT DIRECTOR: None
AFFILIATED WITH: Rochester Zen Center
ESTABLISHED: 1974
FACILITIES: Urban meditation center.
RETREATS OFFERED: Weekend sittings offered two or three times a year.
OPEN TO: Members only

Milwaukee Zen Center

Tozen Akiyama, resident priest, practices strict Soto Zen in the tradition of Eihei Dogen. Milwaukee Zen Center offers daily morning and evening Zen sitting, a weekend study class, and one-day sittings once a month. Introductory workshops are held every three or four months.
ADDRESS: 2825 North Stowell Avenue, Milwaukee, WI 53211
PHONE: (414) 963-0526
LINEAGE: Soto Zen
SPIRITUAL HEAD: Tozen Akiyama (Japanese)
RESIDENT DIRECTOR: Same
AFFILIATED WITH: Autonomous
ESTABLISHED: 1979
FACILITIES: Urban meditation center.
RETREATS OFFERED: Weekend sittings once a month.
OPEN TO: General public

Mahayana Centers—Canada

ALBERTA

Avatamsaka Monastery

Avatamsaka Monastery offers ceremonies and lectures seven days a week to the pub-lic from 12:30 to 3:00 P.M. and from 6:30 to 9:30 P.M. On Saturdays and Sundays ceremonies take place throughout the day from 7:30 A.M. to 9:30 P.M. Lectures are in English, Mandarin, and Vietnamese. Three and seven-day recitation sessions are given every few months. Pure Land recitation, Ch'an meditation, bowing repentances, and mantra recitation are all conducted every day, as is the case at all monasteries of the Dharma Realm Buddhist Association.
ADDRESS: 1152 10th Street, Southeast, Calgary, Alberta, Canada T2G 3E4
PHONE: (403) 269-2960
LINEAGE: All major Mahayana schools
SPIRITUAL HEAD: Ven. Hsuan Hua (Chinese)
RESIDENT DIRECTOR: Bhikshu Heng Chang (Vietnamese-American)
AFFILIATED WITH: Dharma Realm Buddhist Association
ESTABLISHED: 1985
FACILITIES: Urban meditation center
RETREATS OFFERED: Chanting retreat, prostration retreat, traditional Ch'an. Retreats are given every month.
OPEN TO: General public.

BRITISH COLUMBIA

Dharma Realm Buddhist Association (Canadian Headquarters)

Open 8:00 A.M. to 9:00 P.M. weekdays, Gold Buddha Monastery offers daily chanting of sutras and mantras, two trilingual Dharma lectures daily, daily meditation (at scheduled times only), and daily recitation of Amitabha Buddha's name. Weekend Dharma assemblies begin at 7:30 A.M., as do special recitation sessions. There are adult classes in Mandarin Chinese, and an all-day Sunday school for young students. The library and bookstore offer English translations of major Mahayana sutras and other Buddhist texts. The monastery's Dharma activities are administered by ordained Bhikshus or Bhikshunis (monks and nuns). Ch'an meditation practiced at Gold Buddha Monastery involves investigation of a meditation topic such as "Who is mindful of the Buddha?" with no attachment to the false thoughts that arise. Emphasis is on sitting in full lotus posture for sustained periods.

ADDRESS: 301 East Hastings Street, Vancouver, B.C., Canada V6A 1P3

PHONE: (604) 684-3754

LINEAGE: We propagate all major lineages in Mahayana and work closely with Theravada.

SPIRITUAL HEAD: Ven. Hsuan Hua (Chinese)

RESIDENT DIRECTOR: Several

AFFILIATED WITH: Dharma Realm Buddhist Association—City of 10,000 Buddhas, Talmadge, California (international headquarters).

ESTABLISHED: 1984

FACILITIES: Urban meditation center and monastery

RETREATS OFFERED: Ch'an meditations (scheduled); chanting retreat (approximately five seven-day sessions per year); prostration retreat (one session per year; 10,000 or more prostrations); two-day lectures on Sutras. Retreats are given approximately bi-monthly; trilingual and bilingual, one-month session reciting Earth Store Sutra; bowing Earth Store repentance daily.

OPEN TO: General public; however participants are expected to follow the rules and comply with the schedule.

Lions Gate Buddhist Priory

Lions Gate Buddhist Priory is a lay meditation and training center directly affiliated with Shasta Abbey, the Buddhist monastery of the Serene Reflection (Soto Zen) tradition in northern California. A program of regular meditation, services, and classes is scheduled, as well as introductory and advanced retreats and the celebration of Buddhist festivals. In addition, the priest conducts memorials, naming ceremonies for children, house blessings, and other religious services. Private spiritual counselling is available by appointment. Please contact the prior to make arrangements.

ADDRESS: 1745 West 16th Avenue, Vancouver, B.C., Canada V6J 2L9

PHONE: (604) 738-4453

LINEAGE: Japanese Soto Zen, the Serene Reflection School

SPIRITUAL HEAD: Rev. Roshi Jiyu-Kennet, M.O.B.C.

RESIDENT DIRECTOR: Rev. Roshi Koten Benson, M.O.B.C.

AFFILIATED WITH: Shasta Abbey, Mount Shasta, California

ESTABLISHED: The priory was formed in 1986 out of the Vancouver Soto Zen Meditation Group, which had been in existence since the mid-1970s.

FACILITIES: Urban meditation center

RETREATS OFFERED: Monthly Soto Zen sesshin

OPEN TO: General public; however persons new to the priory should receive introductory meditation instruction before attending any other activities.

Victoria Zen Centre

Our roshi is Joshu Sasaki of California and New Mexico. The monk Eshin Godfrey joins us once each month for our regular weekly sitting at the Victoria Buddhist Dharma Centre. People come, people go, but we have a core which is not soft and a little bit hard. During sum-

Zazenkai in Kendo Hunter's woods, proposed country retreat facility of the Victoria Zen Society.

mer we hold *Zazenkai* in Kendo Hunter's woods, where a Zendo is in the making.
ADDRESS: 203 Goward Road, Victoria, B.C., Canada V8X 3X3
PHONE: (604) 479-4937
LINEAGE: Rinzai Zen
SPIRITUAL HEAD: Roshi Joshu Sasaki (Japanese)
AFFILIATED WITH: Rinzai-Ji
ESTABLISHED: 1980
FACILITIES: Urban meditation center, country retreat facility (during the summer months we sit in the country for weekend retreats).

RETREATS OFFERED: Weekend sittings monthly (from May–September these weekend sittings are held at the country retreat property). Supervised solitary retreats (summer only at present).
OPEN TO: Memebers only

ONTARIO

Kingston Zen Group
We are a small group of Zen practitioners who sit together regularly. We are affiliated with the Montreal Zen Centre under the direction of Albert Low. For further

information contact the Montreal Zen
Centre.
ADDRESS: C/O Montreal Zen Centre,
824 Park Stanley, Montreal, Quebec,
Canada H2C 1A2
LINEAGE: Harada-Yasutani Line of Japa-
nese Zen.
SPIRITUAL HEAD: Albert Low
AFFILIATED WITH: Montreal Zen
Centre
FACILITIES: Member's home
RETREATS OFFERED: Regular group
sittings
OPEN TO: General public

London Zen Meditation Group

The London Meditation Group meets
Sunday afternoons at 3:00 P.M. in the
Taoist Tai Chi Centre, 203-179 King
Street, London, Ontario. The afternoon
session includes two half-hour sittings,
with walking meditation in between. A
verse is said before and after the medita-
tion. Group leader Peter Georgelos is a
student of Zen Master Samu Sunim of
Toronto, Ontario, and follows his instruc-
tions in a traditional Korean manner.
ADDRESS: 352 Princess Avenue, London,
Ontario, Canada
PHONE: (619) 433-4203
LINEAGE: Korean Zen
SPIRITUAL HEAD: Samu Sunim
RESIDENT DIRECTOR: Peter Georgelos
AFFILIATED WITH: Toronto Zen Bud-
dhist Temple
RETREATS OFFERED: Beginning and
advanced retreats are held at our
headquarters, Toronto Zen Buddhist
Temple.

Ottawa Zen Group

We sit twice a week, Thursday evenings
and Sunday mornings (of late, only on
Sunday mornings). We are not a large
group—perhaps ten or a dozen, of which

four or so sit regularly. Albert Low comes
down for infrequent one-day retreats.
Mostly we go to Montreal, only two and
a half hours away, for retreats at the Mon-
treal Zen Center.
ADDRESS: 330 Metcalfe Street #802,
Ottawa, Ontario, Canada K2P 1S4
LINEAGE: A gentle Rinzai Zen
SPIRITUAL HEAD: Mr. Albert Low
AFFILIATED WITH: Montreal Zen
Center
ESTABLISHED: 1970
FACILITIES: Member's home
RETREATS OFFERED: Occasional one-
day retreats

White Wind Zazenkai

Ven. Paul Anzan Lee-Sensei (Anzan
Hoshin) is a Dharma heir to Ven. Yasuda
Joshu-Roshi and a priest ordained in the
Soto Zen lineage. Sensei is accessible and
informal, working closely with all students. He teaches Shikan-taza as the root
practice along with such aids as koan
(questioning meditation), chi-kung, movement exercises, and so on. Daijozan is the
headquarters of a loosely organized international sangha which stresses intensive
personal practice. Daijozan has a daily
schedule of sitting, walking, and chanting
practice, three weekly group sittings for
members, frequent dokusan (interviews),
and monthly retreats. Occasional workshops on subjects such as the precepts and
individual instruction in shodo (Zen brush
practice) and Zen arts are also offered.
ADDRESS: Daijozan Zen Training Centre, 345 Somerset Street East, Ottawa,
Ontario, Canada K1N 6W6 (Mailing
address: P.O. Box 203, Street A, Ottawa, Ontario, Canada K1N 8V2)
PHONE: (613) 232-7851
LINEAGE: Soto Zen
SPIRITUAL HEAD: Ven. Paul Anzan Lee-
Sensei
RESIDENT DIRECTOR: Same

AFFILIATED WITH: We are the headquarters
ESTABLISHED: 1984
FACILITIES: Urban residential meditation center. We are in the process of renting facilities for solitary retreats.
RETREATS OFFERED: Soto Zen sesshin, weekend sittings, supervised solitary retreats, Dharma assemblies, household retreats.

Dharma Light Zen Center/Poep Kwang Dojang

Affiliated with the Kwan Un Zen School, we follow the Korean Son (Zen) tradition taught by Chogye Son Master Seung Sahn Soen Sa Nim. Sitting and walking Zen meditation is complemented with the vigorous chanting of *Sutra* and *Dharani* (also know as Ki-Do or "Energy Path"), bell sound meditation, yoga relaxation, *chikung* breathing, Tai Chi Chuan (moving meditation), and other awareness exercises. Dharma Talks and guidance are offered at every sitting.
ADDRESS: 265 Main Street, #606, Toronto, Ontario, Canada M4C 4X3
PHONE: (416) 691-0875
LINEAGE: Korean-Chogye-Son (Zen)
SPIRITUAL HEAD: Hal Bong Sunim (Uruguay)
RESIDENT DIRECTOR: Miguel Palavecino (Uruguay)
AFFILIATED WITH: Kwan Um Zen School
ESTABLISHED:1983
FACILITIES: Urban meditation center and country retreat facility
RETREATS OFFERED: One full-day retreat once a month
OPEN TO: General public

Ontario Zen Centre

The OZC teaches Zen practice in the Korean/North American tradition as established by Zen Master Seung Sahn. The OZC offers full practice for the public on Sunday evenings at 7:00 P.M. There are also six-hour sittings once a month and weekend retreats four times a year. The OZC is associated with the Kwan Um Zen school of North America. The OZC utilizes traditional breath meditation, *kong-an* (koan), and mantra practice. We also incorporate extensive chanting and bowing (full prostrations) into our full services or group practice.
ADDRESS: 515 Logan Avenue, Toronto, Ontario, Canada M4K 3B3
PHONE: (416) 482-9168
LINEAGE: Korean Zen
SPIRITUAL HEAD: Seung Sahn Soen Sa Nim (Korean)
AFFILIATED WITH: Kwan Um Zen School, Providence, Rhode Island
ESTABLISHED: 1978
FACILITIES: Urban meditation center
RETREATS OFFERED: Three-day Zen retreats
OPEN TO: General public

Toronto Zen Centre

The Toronto Zen Centre is an autonomous Zen training center under the direction of Ven. Zenson Gifford-Sensei, Dharma heir of Ven. Philip Kapleau-Roshi. The center offers a full schedule of introductory workshops, daily zazen with regular *teisho* (Dharma Talk) and *dokusan* (face to face interview), as well as periodic sesshin of four to seven days in length. We practice an integral Soto/Rinzai Zen with basic breathing practices and a major focus on koan training.
ADDRESS: 33 High Park Gardens, Toronto, Ontario, Canada M6R 1S8
PHONE: (416) 766-3400
LINEAGE: Rinzai Soto Zen (Diun Harada)
SPIRITUAL HEAD: Ven. Zenson Gifford-Sensei (American)

Ven. Zenson Gifford-Sensei, Zen Center, Toronto, Ontario.

RESIDENT DIRECTOR: Same
AFFILIATED WITH: Autonomous
ESTABLISHED: 1972
FACILITIES: Urban meditation center
RETREATS OFFERED: Combination Rinzai/Soto Sesshin, two, four, or seven days in length, given eight to ten times per year
OPEN TO: Members only or practicing members of other Zen centers

Zen Lotus Society/Zen Buddhist Temple

The Zen Lotus Society/Zen Buddhist Temple, Toronto, under the direction of Ven. Samu Sunim, offers residential and nonresidential training in Zen meditation and Buddhism. A three to five-year priest and Dharma teacher training program combines traditional Zen training adapted to the North American situation with scripture studies, emphasizing spiritual cultivation in daily life and social concern. Meditation and/or chanting practice is held daily, morning and evening. Spiritual and doctrinal studies are offered through the Buddhist Institute of Canada. Retreats are held five times per year, and a year-round visitors' program accommodates short and medium-term visitors. All training members of the Zen Lotus Society are encouraged to take active part in social issues that concern all. To this end Samu Sunim founded Buddhists Concerned For Social Justice and World Peace. The Zen Lotus Society publishes *Spring-Wind— Buddhist Cultural Forum*, an international nonsectarian Buddhist quarterly.
ADDRESS: 46 Gwynne Avenue, Toronto, Ontario, Canada M6K 2C3
PHONE: (416) 533-6911
LINEAGE: Chogye Order of Korean Zen
SPIRITUAL HEAD: Ven. Samu Sunim (Korean)

RESIDENT DIRECTOR: Sujata Linda Klevnick
AFFILIATED WITH: Autonomous
ESTABLISHED: 1968
FACILITIES: Urban meditation center
RETREATS OFFERED: Weekend retreats, five five-day retreats, a two-month summer retreat, and an ongoing visitors' program year-round.
OPEN TO: Members and the general public.

QUEBEC

Association Dojo Zen de Montreal

The Montreal Branch of Taisen Deshimaru-Roshi's Sangha teaches Soto Zen disciplines. The Montreal Dojo offers daily zazen meditation periods with three Zen sesshins (seasonal) a year plus a summer camp in June.
ADDRESS: 982 Gilford East, Montreal, Quebec, Canada H2J 1P4
PHONE:(514) 523-1534
LINEAGE: Soto Zen
SPIRITUAL HEAD: Taisen Deshimaru-Roshi died in 1981. Two years later, three of his French Disciples (Etienne Zeisler, Roland Reich, Stephane Thibault) received the transmission, "Shiho," from Niwa Zenji (the Zen Soto authority of Japan and chief of Eiheiji Temple). They are now working full time spreading the Dharma.
RESIDENT DIRECTOR: Richard Goulet, Raoul Lecourt, Richard Lacroix, Gilles Martin, and Roger Boucher.
AFFILIATED WITH: Association Zen International
ESTABLISHED: 1979
FACILITIES: Urban meditation center
RETREATS OFFERED: Soto Zen sesshin three times yearly
OPEN TO: General public

Taisen Deshimaru-Roshi (1914–1981). Kaikyokosokan, great missionary and Supreme Chief of the Transmission (Soto Zen) in the West. Founder of the Association Zen Internationale, which includes more than three hundred centers around the world.

Montreal Zen Dojo, in collaboration with the Association Zen Internationale, organizes sesshins three times a year.

Montreal Zen Centre

Albert Low teaches an integral Zen grounded in the doctrines and disciplines of both the Soto and Rinzai sects, which includes koan practice for experienced students. The Montreal center offers a daily schedule of meditation and chanting with periodic four and seven-day sesshins open to members. Introductory workshops are also available. The practice here is Shikan-taza and koan meditation as taught by Harada-Roshi and Yasutani-Roshi and learned from Philip Kapleau-Roshi. Thirty-five minutes rounds of sitting alternate with five-minute walking meditations.

ADDRESS: 824 Park Stanley, Montreal, Quebec, Canada H2C 1AZ

PHONE: (514) 388-4518

LINEAGE: Soto/Rinzai (Harada-Yasutani Line)

SPIRITUAL HEAD: Albert Low

RESIDENT DIRECTOR: Same

AFFILIATED WITH: Autonomous

ESTABLISHED: 1974 (became autonomous in 1986)

FACILITIES: Urban meditation center

RETREATS OFFERED: Combination Rinzai/Soto sesshin. Retreats are given once per month in Montreal, two times in Texas.

OPEN TO: General public

Centre Zen de Sillery

We are following the teaching of Taisen Deshimaru-Roshi, who died in 1982. We

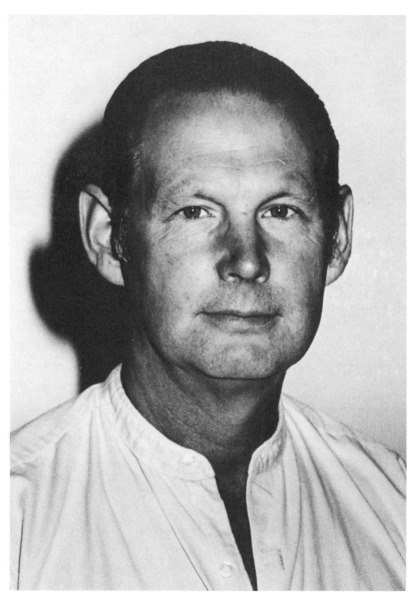

Albert Low-Sensei, Montreal Zen Center.

are Soto Zen, which means that we do Shikan-taza (just sitting) meditation facing the wall (no koans). We do zazen Thursday and Sundays.

ADDRESS: 2197 Boulevard, Laurier, Sillery, Quebec, Canda G1T 1B8

PHONE:(418) 688-9424

LINEAGES: Soto Zen

SPIRITUAL HEAD: Taisen Deshimaru-Roshi (deceased)

RESIDENT DIRECTOR: Guy Des Rochers

AFFILIATED WITH: Association Zen International, France

ESTABLISHED: 1981

FACILITIES: Urban meditation center

RETREATS OFFERED: Full Soto Zen sesshin four times a year and a one-day retreat each month.

OPEN TO: General public

PART III

Vajrayana

The Path of Devotion

Vajrayana: The Path of Devotion

BY ROBIN KORNMAN

If the devastating and irresistible techniques of Vajrayana Buddhism are used correctly, it can be "the quick path to Enlightenment". If misused, it can destroy the pracitioner.

When troops from the People's Republic of China entered Tibet in 1956, they catalyzed an exodus of Tibetan Buddhist religious practitioners, who fled across the Himalayas to India and little by little further west. Refugees of the Tibetan Diaspora—lamas (gurus) and scholars of Buddhist philosophy—reached the United States in less than ten years and rapidly spread the teachings of Buddhist Tantra throughout North America so that today their doctrines of creative visualization, mantra, yoga, and transmutation of neurosis into sanity are a dominant element in the North American practice of Oriental religions.

The tantric approach to Buddhist practice is called "Vajrayana," the indestructible vehicle. Actually the *vajra* is a kind of brass sceptre held by lamas and advanced tantric practitioners during ceremonies. Mythologically, however, the *vajra* was the weapon held by Indra, the king of the gods. It was forged from the bones of a *rishi*, one of the legendary Aryan super-meditators who in ancient times brought the practice of yoga to the Indian sub-continent. Because it is made of this magical material, the *vajra* is adamantine; that is, it is the hardest substance in existence, capable of cutting anything, though itself is uncuttable. Whenever Indra launched the *vajra* at an enemy, it was a law of nature that defense was impossible and that the enemy would be completely destroyed.

In the same way, Vajrayana Buddhism is supposed to be not merely psychologically but also *magically* effective, employing devastating and irresistible techniques to destroy ego. If it is used correctly, it can be "the quick path to Enlightenment." If misused, it can destroy the practitioner.

The principal distinction between Vajrayana and other forms of Mahayana is its emphasis on *transmutation*—as opposed to destruction—of neurosis. Where other approaches to Buddhist meditation seek to destroy passion, aggression, and ignorance so that the practitioner can be free from ego-clinging, Vajrayana seeks to transform the three poisons directly into wisdom, actually transmuting the constituents of ego directly into principles of Buddhahood.

For this reason Vajrayana is often compared to medieval Western alchemy, which seeks to transmute lead into gold as a symbol for magically turning the unspiritual in man's nature into the spiritual. The difference in the two systems is that Buddhist Tantra does not really believe in a fundamentally unspiritual element in reality. Lead can be transformed into gold because there is, in the end, no such thing as lead, but only gold.

The Buddhist understanding of why transmutation is possible involves this precise peculiarity in the tantric view. According to Buddhist Tantra, neurosis can be transformed into wisdom because, in essence, it is already wisdom in an unrecognized form. So in a sense no real change is necessary. All we have to do is recognize the basic nature of our problems, and the problems become in themselves solutions. Tantric meditation is thus primarily a method of developing confidence—confidence in the self-enlightened self-nature of mind and phenomena.

This philosophy is simple in expression but very complex in application. In expression it simply means that there is no difference between illusory cyclic existence (*samsara*) and *nirvana*. Enlightenment is not the destruction of *samsara*, but the realization of its inseparability from its supposed opposite, liberation. In application this means that almost any human activity can be turned into a method of gaining enlightenment. Thus, tantric teachers give their students an amazing variety of exercises. Each guru seems to have his own special path and tradition.

Consequently, students of different tantric teachers are typically incredulous of each other's paths when they compare notes.

A few things, however, are obvious and common to all lineages of Vajrayana Buddhism: secrecy, personal transmission and guru devotion, visualization practice and symbolic teachings, lengthy group and individual retreats, and a special emphasis upon profound, wordless meditation practice.

Secrecy

Vajrayana is sometimes called "Esoteric Buddhism" because the principal teachings are supposed to be secret—only given to the most sophisticated and devoted disciples. Traditionally, these disciples have already studied Hinayana and Mahayana Buddhism for many years before they receive real Vajrayana teachings, which are presented as long withheld secrets, finally revealed during elaborate occasions of ceremonial instruction. Actually, many of the so-called "secret" teachings can easily be found in popular translations of tantric texts—texts such as *The Life and Teachings of Naropa* and the various biographies of Padmasambhava. Still, even though they are widely available, the tantric teachings are considered "self-secret," because, unless they are given to the disciple in a personal, face-to-face oral transmission by a qualified guru, they will never be intuitively understood. The theory is that in the teacher-disciple relationship there is a special power of direct communication—a power that transcends words and ordinary experience.

In actual fact, even if the mysterious power of oral transmission were not necessary, the teachings would still be more or less secret because they are usually written down in symbolic form, almost as iconographic codes. Without personal instruction from a qualified teacher, most tantric books would be misunderstood because all of the symbolic sections would be misread. For example, an uninstructed student would take the deities to be actual supernatural entities instead of symbols of principles of enlightened human nature.

So the oral instructions are necessary. Typically a student will prepare for years to receive these special oral instructions. The preparation involves a variety of preliminary practices which aim to soften and open the mind. Equally important is the life of serious study and attendance upon a guru—a life of devotion and passionate discipleship which forges an almost telepathic link between the teacher and his or her student. In the end, if the two succeed in creating this special connection, then the guru should be able to communicate the experience of enlightenment to the disciple through words, esoteric symbols, and gestures in special teaching situations called "transmissions." Sometimes the transmissions are quite formal and occur in groups. But many also occur suddenly in the midst of casual communication.

As a result, Vajrayana is preeminently a devotional path. Disciples must love their gurus and worship them as higher beings. Tantric students take special vows of obedience and imitation called "*samaya* vows." The word "*samaya*" is very important. It literally means "commitment" or "promise." Some *samayas* are quite literal and involve promising to complete specific undertakings, such as the daily performance of a set number of mantras or the bi-monthly performance of ritual feasts in honor of tantric deities. Other *samayas* are very subtle and involve promises to regard the guru not as an ordinary human being, but as the Buddha himself.

The essence of the *samaya* vow is actually the concept of transmutation through recognition of the indestructible Buddha-nature of all things. A person who keeps the *samayas* will see the world as self-existing and sacred, beyond pure and impure. Such an attitude should make it easy to transmute neurosis into enlightenment, because the neurosis is fundamentally respected as a slightly twisted version of Buddha-nature.

If the *samaya* that links guru and disciple is unobstructed, the guru can transmit a temporary experience of the Goal or Fruition. This sudden glimpse is terribly important. It is the aim, for example, of most of the special ceremonies students go through as they study Tantra in weekend programs and retreats. It is also the reason that students experiment with numerous teachers until they find one to whom they can be devoted. It may take years to find somebody worthy of this trust, but the search is worth the trouble because an attitude of rapt, devoted attention makes the transmission of glimpses of awakened mind relatively easy.

If the student actually has a momentary glimpse of the nature of awakened mind, then the next step is to adjust his or her practice until it is in harmony with this special dispensation. Thus, Vajrayana is sometimes called the Vehicle of Fruition because one is supposed to see the journey in terms of fruition—to be drawn along by a memory of the goal, instead of merely being driven away from illusion.

In other vehicles the meditator practices in order to escape *samsara* (cyclic existence), and "revulsion for the Dharmas of *samsara*" is the primary motivation. In Tantra, on the other hand, one develops a kind of passionate yearning for the goal, which is actually nothing more than the state of mind of one's guru, and so instead of mere escape from illusion, there is a positive sense of the pursuit of awakening.

Symbolic Teachings

Another important characteristic of Tantra is the use of complex symbolism in the meditation practice. Vajrayana ritual texts use symbolic diagrams called *mandalas* to represent the phenomenal world from the point of view of fruition—that is, as seen by a Buddha. In such a world, all sounds are regarded as the sacred formulas known as *mantra*; every human being is one of the five Buddhas who reside in the *mandala*; and all thoughts are the naked mind of the Buddha—nondiscursive insight beyond distinctions. These are just three among literally thousands of other symbolic figures which are used to describe every aspect of daily reality. Through these myriad symbols, the practitioner sees the phenomenal world as a naturally occurring *mandala* and moves towards the world instead of away from it. This leads to a series of special practices called "meditation in action"—practices which use the symbolic element to transform ordinary activities into an enlightened path.

The aim of this sophisticated system is to enable Buddhist students to live in the world without sacrificing their spiritual principles or slow-ing their advancement. In theory, a Vajrayana practitioner should be able to transform every daily activity—livelihood, eating, social relations, even entertainment—into a sort of tantric yoga to speed him or her along the path. Ultimately domestic existence and the path become one so that the concept of spiritual advancement itself appears to be a primitive notion.

Retreats

In theory, through tantric practice one should be able to abandon ego without abandoning the world. In practice, however, there are times when a tremendous amount of meditation is appropriate, and students must perform lengthy retreats. These retreats may be as short as a weekend or a week, but often are months in length. Practical experience of the last thousand years in Tibet has developed a system that combines thorough engagement in worldly life with a series of carefully supervised meditation retreats—some in small groups, some in solitary cabins maintained by meditation centers throughout Canada and America. Every Tibetan meditation center has its own style of retreat practice. Some organizations only support the traditional solitary retreats in which a student performs whatever practices the guru specifies in his or her case.

Other organizations have developed standardized group retreats in which students meditate eight to twelve hours a day for a week or a month. Although such group practice sessions are very popular in North America, it should be noted that many of them have been developed recently in partial imitation of the famous Zen *sesshin*.

There are also intensive study retreats, usually taught by traveling gurus when they visit a specific meditation center. These programs are usually advertised in advance and will include specific instructions in a particular body of teachings. If the teachings involve a specific tantric practice, then initiation in that practice may be the last event of the program.

Initiation

Ceremonies of empowerment or initiation are an essential component of Esoteric Buddhism. Since the teachings are secret, students must receive in person from enlightened masters permission to practice them. In some cases this is not enough, and students must also receive special blessings and dispensations of spiritual energy before they can perform a specific practice. These ceremonies are called *wang* or *abhisheka*. There is actually an art to receiving such empowerments, an art that *Tantrikas* gradually learn as they journey from one meditation workshop to another.

Empowerment is particularly necessary in the case of the complex visualization practices which are a specialty of Vajrayana. In these practices students visualize mandalas. These mandalas are not just colored patterns people contemplate. They are matrices of symbolic entities or deities who stand for different aspects of enlightenment and the mind of the practitioner as a potentially enlightened being. Students who are committed to the tantric view of life and path meditate on different mandalas of deities, visualizing the symbolic beings in a prescribed manner.

Some of these practices are quite gentle and harmless and are given to beginners as tantric approaches to mindfulness and insight meditation. Other visualization practices are complex and psychologically dangerous for the untrained. Students who perform these advanced visualizations should have already been trained in Hinayana and Mahayana Buddhism by their gurus. They must also receive *abhisheka* from an authentic guru who knows them well and has agreed to undertake their education in exchange for obedience and loyalty.

Strangely enough, even a newcomer to a meditation center may be invited to attend an *abhisheka*. This does not mean that he or she is being offered empowerment in the difficult advanced practices. For the beginner *abhishekas* are often considered merely glorified blessings, healthy because they create a karmic situation where the student might one day find a genuine guru and truly receive the real empowerment and oral instructions.

Meditation

Interestingly enough, the most advanced of all tantric practices, formless meditation, is very similar to the insight practice of the modern
Theravadans, as well as to Soto Zen meditation. It is also very close to
the view of Rinzai practice, even though Rinzai uses koans (for an explanation of koan practice please refer to Part II of this book). In formless meditation a student sits in stillness and attends to a simple object
such as the breathing. This meditation is considered both the most advanced and the most fundamental practice. Beginners receive it and do
almost nothing else for years. Advanced meditators, after years of visualization and mantra practice, complex physical yogic exercises, control
of vital energies, and arcane magical contemplations, often return to
simply sitting without any goal or technique, remaining mutely aware
of their thoughts and perceptions. When beginners do it, it is called
vipashyana (Vipassana). When *Tantrikas* do it, it is called *Mahamudra*,
the Great Symbol, or *Maha Ati*, the Great Perfection. The precious oral
instructions which turn the beginner's formless sitting practice into the
most advanced practice are very difficult to attain and require a very
special relationship between guru and disciple.

The Path

There are several different ways in which the tantric teachings can be
ordered. Here are two examples:
   The Vajradhatu system of urban and rural meditation centers in
America and Canada is quite famous. Every student who attends a
Dharmadhatu or urban center follows the same pattern. First they
spend several years receiving Hinayana (Theravada) and Mahayana
teachings by attending classes once a week. They practice insight meditation and do occasional weekend workshops. Vajradhatu teachers call
the practice they transmit during this period *shamatha*, which means
tranquility. But actually it is a modified form of *shamatha*—a form designed to rapidly bring about *vipassana* or insight practice. Students at
Dharmadhatus periodically take week or month vacations during which

they attend Tibetan-style *sesshin* called *dathun*. A *dathun* lasts one month, but many students attend for shorter periods because of the demands of their livelihood and domestic life. Some *dathuns* even have a special child-care staff so that married couples and single parents can attend with their children.

After a few years most students have done at least one, perhaps two *dathuns*. They may also have done one or several solitary retreats in cabins at a mountain meditation center. Up to this point there is no real tantric practice. Students engage in the Vajradhatu system of training for their own benefit and ours (Mahayana altruism) but without making any special commitments to a particular guru.

The first serious commitment comes when a Vajradhatu student decides to take Refuge in the Three Jewels and formally become a Buddhist. Eventually most disciples undertake the Mahayana vow of compassion, promising to place the welfare of others before their own. Such students undertake a new set of meditation practices which aim to perform the Six Paramitas or Mahayana Perfections.

Actually tantric practice and commitment does not occur until after the special three-month group retreat called the Vajradhatu Seminary. This is led by Vajradhatu's highest teacher, the lineage holder of the Vidyadhara Chogyam Trungpa, Rinpoche. Students have studied conventional Buddhism for four or five years before they undertake the commitments of such an extensive educational program. During the seminary, tantric teachings are formally given for the first time. There is a large staff of experienced older students and visiting lamas. Many evenings Osel Tendzin himself, the lineage holder, gives a lecture to the entire assembly, which may number as many as four hundred.

After the seminary students receive some of the precious and much sought after oral instructions. They then begin to do the famous Vajrayana Preliminary Practices or *ngondro*. *Ngondro* includes especially rigorous and radical tantric rituals. One begins with the performance of one hundred thousand complete prostrations before a tantric shrine. On each prostration the student places the entire body face down on the floor and utters a prayer. There is also the repetition of a hundred-syllable mantra one hundred thousand times, the formal offering of one hundred thousand mandalas made out of colored rice, and the repetition of a short guru supplication one million times. The entire series can be done in two years. The average student will spend from two to five months of that time in solitary and group retreats. People with demanding jobs often take longer. However you look at it, *ngondro* is a supreme test—a terrible challenge that students must overcome in order to receive the powerful and remarkably effective *vajra* teachings.

Students who successfully complete *ngondro* are ready for the profound and subtle psychology of tantric visualization practice. They receive *abhisheka* (or empowerment) in an advanced deity practice and complete instruction in its performance. This practice is so complicated that it may take a year to learn all of its details. After that there are successions of visualization practices and special retreats stretching out across the years. Students develop the habit of using every vacation for intensive retreats. Periodically they arrange to take three months to work exclusively on their own education or to fulfill the next Vajrayana practice. Some students will quit their jobs and spend a year just meditating each day and taking care of their families. Other students move for several years into one of the Vajradhatu meditation centers to work as staff and teachers while enjoying the privilege of an extended daily meditation schedule.

The Very Venerable Kalu, Rinpoche, a great tantric master who specialized during his training in three-year ascetic retreats, also runs a system of Vajrayana training centers in North America. At these centers students study with monk disciples of Kalu, Rinpoche. Typically students begin with a simple visualization practice in which they identify with *Avalokiteshvara (Chenrezig)* the Bodhisattva of Compassion. Although this is technically a tantric practice, Kalu, Rinpoche, has explained that it develops insight and tranquility just like the formless Hinayana practice of the Vajradhatu centers. Eventually Kalu, Rinpoche's students also do *ngondro*, although unlike Vajradhatu it is not automatically required of every student.

But the real ultimate goal of Kalu centers seems to be the Three-Year Retreat. Here the most committed and trained students take monastic vows and then practice day and night for three years, three months, and three days. Graduates of the Three-Year Retreat usually speak fluent Tibetan and are outstanding experts in tantric liturgical practice. They also have received the special sixfold exercises of physical yoga—the Six Dharmas of Naropa or Niguma. These very advanced practices are rarely given outside of the most intensive retreats. A number of Kalu, Rinpoche's students have done two Three-Year Retreats and are now considering their third set. When they have completed their training, they will be great masters and leaders in the Western Buddhist community. Most of them will probably also be monks or nuns rather than laymen.

Some Tibetan teachers have no single system by which they transmit Tantra. Using the special richness, flexibility, and variety of Vajrayana disciplines, they tailor their teachings to fit the students at hand. A single group of students might receive ten or twenty different *abhishekas* and transmissions. Then the guru would recommend to each student which practices should be his or her specialty. A student for whom passion is the salient neurosis might meditate upon deities related to that principle. One for whom the *klesa* of aggression is strongest might concentrate on a whole different set of disciplines. Some students do not work with iconography at all, but simply meditate on the nature of their own minds without any technique. Since the deities are purely symbolic, either approach will work. It simply depends on the personal psychology of the guru and disciple.

Many Tibetan meditation centers in America and Canada have developed sophisticated programs of graded instruction in Mahayana Buddhism. This is particularly true of Gelugpa and Sakyapa Centers, which are generally famous for their clear outlines of the Buddhist path. These systems tend to concentrate a great deal of energy on teaching the philosophy of emptiness known as *Madhyamaka* or "The Middle Way." While a disciple is studying the nature of emptiness and the arguments which establish the phenomenal world as illusory, he or she is also doing simple and extremely safe tantric practices. When philosophical understanding of the view has become good, then more complex and challenging Vajrayana meditation is introduced.

Ultimately all the teachings of the *Vajra Vehicle* agree at one point—in their faith and respect for an authentic *Vajra* guru. It is said that there are many charlatans in the world and that students always run a terrible risk in entering the Vajrayana. But if a Buddhist meditator can find a genuine tantric Master who has realized the essence of mind as Buddha and the essence of the phenomenal world as self-existing sacredness, then success is possible. If such a teacher has a karmic link with the meditator, so that the two can come to love and trust each other, then the mind of teacher and disciple can become one and enlightenment can be realized in one lifetime.

Robin Kornman is a senior student of the Vidyadhara, the Ven. Chogyam Trungpa, Rinpoche, and a founding member of the Nalanda Tibetan Translating Committee. He is presently a graduate student in the Comparative Literature Department at Princeton University, specializing in Chinese and epic literature, East and West.

One Hundred and Eight Thousand Prostrations*

BY DAVID LEWIS

After a while the force of falling became the force of rising and the prostrations entered an effortless and blissful space.

Prostration practice is an important feature of *ngondro* (preliminary) practice in the Vajrayana system. The *ngondro* in its simplest form has five main sections of one hundred thousand repetitions each. They are *refuge, bodhicitta, mandala, Vajrasattva* (purification), and *guru yoga*. Prostrations are generally related to taking refuge, but they can be used in the other four sections as well. The foundation practices (*ngondro*) are important because they prepare the body, speech, and mind of the student for the more profound subtleties of the higher tantric practices. Without *ngondro* it is almost impossible to correctly progress along the path.

Therefore, in the beginning everyone in this tradition is required to do the prostrations, and in my case I did them slowly over many years. When I had completed them, my teacher, His Eminence Shenphen Dawa, asked me to do them over again, but this time within a shorter period of two or three months. This came as quite a shock, since I had assumed that this hurdle had been jumped. Not so.

I arranged a period for prostration retreat, scheduling it for the next two months. Khenpo Palden Sherab, our resident abbot, suggested that I try to accomplish three thousand prostrations a day. I was able, in the beginning, to do two hundred a day and, after a week, was eking out

---

*Ngondro Practice at Urgyen Cho Dzong, Greenville, New York

around seven hundred. My body was out of shape, and my muscles and bones felt utterly bruised. I ached to the core. If I rested in any position for longer than five minutes, it required all of my effort to withstand the pain of even the simplest move.

By the following week, things had begun to smooth out somewhat. By this time I was able to do two thousand a day, and the exercise had put me in shape. I established a routine of getting up at 4:00 A.M., doing a session of seven hundred, then after breakfast another session of the same, and finally completing the balance just before supper.

During the prostration sessions I visualized as well as possible the lineage tree surrounded by the Buddhas and their families looking down upon me and blessing the practice. After the first fifteen minutes, the acrid sweat would pour out of me; each time my folded hands were raised above my head in salutation it would drip into my eyes and leave them burning.

I was using a polished hardwood board for the prostrations, along with two cloth pot holders to expedite the sliding of my hands along the wood. In order to perform a proper prostration, one first raises the hands over the head, palm to palm, in salutation and then lays out completely so that the forehead, chest, hands, and knees are touching the ground. How to go down quickly without sustaining injury is important, simply because after doing a hundred thousand one still wants to enjoy the use of one's body. Quite a few practitioners are unable to complete the practice because of improper technique, and they have been known to sustain serious knee and back injuries. I placed a pad for my knees on the board and would slide down like a falling tree, not letting the knees touch until my chest had taken the brunt of the impact. Consequently, my knees rarely hurt, and the stale airs were shocked from my body.

After a while the force of falling became the force of rising, and the prostrations entered an effortless and blissful space.

After completing the first twenty-five thousand, I worked my way up to three thousand prostrations a day. I could only continue at this pace for three days at a time because some obstacle would always manifest— an illness or infection, an unexpected visitor who could not be ignored, or a sudden family emergency. I realized that this was my limit and that the activity of purification was influencing my whole environment. I was beginning to comprehend how the prostrations were affecting me and how subtle and inborn the obstacles to purification were. How great are those practitioners who have gained the compassion necessary to work for others on this level of penetration! I had touched the very fiber of *bodhisattva beingness* and though it was not mine to keep at that point, through raw effort a kind of self-initiation had allowed access to this truth. My image of teachers changed from from one of idealism to one of recognition, and I felt a deep satisfaction in belonging to the *sangha*.

By the time I had accomplished one hundred thousand prostrations, I had lost twenty pounds, my sweat had become sweet instead of salty, and I felt ready for the next one hundred thousand.

David Lewis has been studying Nyingmapa Vajrayana since 1971. He works as the coordinator of Urgyen Cho Dzong and restores antiques for a living. He has done retreat in India, Africa, and the Pacific Northwest.

All-Night Vigil to Yumka*

BY WEST ABRASHKIN

Things were getting sort of twilight, and in such an atmosphere it was OK to bother this deity above me with my revolving chant. He looked at me with compassion and, just like it is supposed to happen, a rain of nectar began to fall on me . . .

Valentine's Day, 1988. A giant snowstorm dumped two feet on our little temple. I had been living next door in a small retreat cabin, and when I got up that day I was worried that people couldn't get through, especially since the plow had gotten stuck four times just trying to clear the parking lot. I called Tulku, our Tibetan lama. He didn't seem at all concerned.

When we started this group—the Mahasiddha Nyingmapa Center in Hawley—back in 1973, we used to joke about how we were "flounders," floundering and flopping in spiritual naivete. Well, people were really floundering that afternoon, but in snow, not Dharma! Bundled up, carrying sleeping bags and provisions, they crawled up the hill with the wind howling and snow blowing horizontally.

Once inside, people fell into the routine of retreats. Some scurried to the kitchen downstairs to start dinner, while the rest of the twenty or so participants started the main practice in the shrine room. Since it was the twenty-fifth day of the lunar month, it was Dakini day and our practice was a *tsok* (feast) to the Queen of the Vajra Dakinis, the consort of Guru Padmasambhava, Yeshe Tsogyal.

For an hour we chanted the *Sadhana*, everybody settling into it

*Mahasiddha Nyingmapa Center, Hawley, Massachusetts

nicely, and when we came to the root mantra, to *Yumka* (Yeshe Tsog-yal)—OM PADMO YOGINI JNANA VARAHI HUNG—we divided into three groups, each continuing the chant for four hours so that it would go on all night.

I was in the first group with Tulku. We recorded ourselves for a while, playing the tape back and chanting with it, going a bit too fast for my taste, but I figured you needed energy to keep going and so screwed myself up to speed.

I usually sit in the back, the better to hide (though I'm the oldest student), but this time I found myself near the front. Being lazy, I never bothered to learn to visualize (our main practice), hoping that some-time the visions would spontaneously appear (as our chief teacher has said). But this time I was impressed by Tulku's description of the visu-alization, and because he made it seem so simple, I resolved to try.

In this visualization, we transformed into the sparkling light body of the Goddess, red and transparent, holding drum and skinning knife (to skin the ego), dancing in an advancing posture, sexually magnetic, with a great haughty demeanor, disciplining the beings. In the past a big problem for me had been imagining myself as a female. But this time—maybe because the Goddess seemed so powerful—I succeeded! Glancing up with my single eye, I saw the Guru above me, and he was Rinpoche. I began to spin the root mantra in my heart.

Things were getting sort of twilight, and in such an atmosphere it was OK to bother this deity above me with my revolving chant. He looked at me with compassion and, just like it is supposed to happen, a rain of nectar began to fall on me. Once before I had had the experience of a veil of blessings, drifting down like desert dust or TV snow. The air tingled, and my back crawled, but I was determined to concentrate.

Suddenly I was transfixed—I mean really lifted. The profound final mantra of all the Buddhas poured forth like thunder: OM GUHYAJ-NANA BODHISITTA MAHA SUKHA RULU RULU HUNG JHO HUNG! Joy flooded my heart, and I could hardly hold back my tears.

I staggered back to my cabin but couldn't drop off to sleep. Waves of blissful energy, like fast-moving clouds, kept scudding past my eyelids. I finally knew how other disciples, who are more proficient at visualization than I, must feel and why their faith is so strong. I wanted to be back in that light body with my lama pouring down the sweet elixir that makes my troubles and stupid ego dissolve.

The next morning, after a call from my mother who has a brain tumor near her ear, we completed the *Sadhana* and ate the food offerings. I felt that I had succeeded in the practice to some degree, but I was sad that I couldn't sustain the vision in a post-meditative state.

> May you all accomplish your virtuous practices,
>   you great Beings!

An artist, West Abrashkin has been a member of the Mahasiddha Nyingmapa Temple in Hawley, Massachusetts, since 1973.

The Three-Year Retreat

BY KEN M^CLEOD

I said goodbye to my wife. . . . Then we proceeded in formal procession behind Rinpoche, our retreat director, and other lamas to the gates of the men's retreat. The sealing ceremonies were done outside in a cold rain, where liturgies were read by a car's headlights . . . we entered the retreat one by one, and the door closed. We would not see the outside world for three years and three months.

Intimations

Toronto, Canada, autumn 1974. Kalu, Rinpoche, had just arrived for his second visit to North America, and I had come to interpret for him. Every day there were interviews and every evening a public talk. Amidst all this activity, a friend who had been with Rinpoche in Europe said that a three-year retreat was being planned for Westerners. A three-year retreat for Westerners? At that point, such an idea was barely conceivable. But the thought . . .

Confirmation

A month later we were in Vancouver. Things were returning to normal after the magical visit of His Holiness Karmapa on his first visit to Vancouver, and we were preparing for Rinpoche's visit to the United States. A few students had taken ordination with His Holiness. Several people had also heard the rumors about the three-year retreat, and we could now bring the subject up with Rinpoche. Yes, he was planning a retreat for Westerners. It would be in France. Could we be part of it? Yes, but there were certain requirements.

Pre-Requisites

In the Kagyu tradition of Buddhism in Tibet, the Three-Year Retreat is a systematic training in advanced meditation techniques. Selected monks and re-incarnated teachers enter a retreat center and spend approximately three years and three months practicing meditation at least sixteen hours a day. The retreat center is totally isolated from the world, no exits are permitted, and only very high lamas or teachers are allowed to visit to give additional instruction. And seven or eight of us from Vancouver were intending to follow this tradition? Most of us had never dared to dream of such an opportunity—the chance to receive instruction and to practice the legendary methods of such teachers as Naropa, Marpa, and Milarepa. What were these requirements?

Foundations

"For fundamental change to take place, motivation must change." Our training from Kalu, Rinpoche, up to this point had certainly shown that he was familiar with this maxim. Rinpoche had consistently emphasized the general foundations. Human existence provides a precious, rare, and fragile opportunity to practice Buddhism. Death may come at any moment; a moral and ethical way of life is necessary in view of the workings of karma. And *samsaric*, or ego-based, existence is inherently unsatisfying. However, these basic motivating principles, while necessary for the three-year retreat, are not sufficient. The special foundations of the *mahamudra* tradition must also be completed. These involve five simple acts: prostration, refuge prayer, a long purification mantra, a symbolic offering of the universe, and a prayer for union of one's mind with the teacher's. Each is repeated one hundred thousand times. For most of us, this was not a problem, since we had all done this set of practices at least once already.

Tibetan

The next requirement was language. Everything would be in Tibetan, the teaching, the texts, the meditation manuals, the rituals. Everything!

Without fluency in Tibetan, it would be like attending a school in a country whose language one doesn't know. Rinpoche made it clear that the language was very important. We would be dealing with ideas and concepts which could not be formulated in English. We would be studying texts written by great masters, and it was important to be able to study them directly. We would be performing rituals composed in Tibetan verse, and we should understand the sense of what we were doing and not just repeat words. And our retreat director would only be able to instruct us in Tibetan!

Finances

The third requirement was money—enough for food and minimal personal expenses for the period of the retreat. Rinpoche said that he would send word when it was time to come to France. After Rinpoche's departure, we set out to earn what we would need. Some went to work in copper mines in northern British Columbia; I worked as a teaching assistant at the university and helped as a house parent for children who were government wards.

Preparation

Eventually, we received word to come to France. We arrived at Kagyu Ling in June. At that time Kagyu Ling consisted of a mock chateau built around the turn of the century, along with associated buildings. It was situated on fifteen acres of meadows and woods, in rolling hills about midway between Paris and Lyons. At that time there was a bad drought in the whole region; water was in short supply, and the weather was generally hot. When we asked where the retreat facilities were, we were told that we were going to build them. We laughed.

Construction

A few days later, Rinpoche arrived and we soon found out that, yes, we *were* going to build our own retreat structures. And while we were doing that, we were also to learn the regular ceremonies, how to prepare shrines, how to play the various musical instruments, and how to lead chanting. It looked like a full summer.

As it turned out, it was really quite a wonderful time. Every morning we would get up, chant the Tara ritual, have breakfast, and work and study all day until Mahakala ritual in the evening. As time went on, we even worked nights. We learned how to mix concrete, lay bricks, put in windows, lay floors, and plaster walls. We were also taught how to make *tormas* and how to play cymbals, beat drums, and blow instruments while inhaling the breath, without missing a note. A nice trick!

After a few months, our retreat structures had begun to take shape. There were two separate, but identical, enclosures, one for men and one for women. Each contained eight rooms, one temple, a kitchen, a communal washroom, and an area for yoga practice. Hundreds of people had come to help with construction; dry wall experts, architects, and carpenters appeared out of thin air just when they were needed. All the construction work was directed and supervised by a young Englishman, whose ability to teach people to work effectively, and to overcome every problem encountered, soon won our respect and appreciation.

At a certain point, Rinpoche began giving the thirty or forty empowerments which form the basis of the practices we would be doing in retreat. Our work schedule became even more intense. Rinpoche had set December 5, 1976 as the date of entry. At least one additional month of work seemed necessary. We worked harder and longer, sloshing around in the freezing November rains, digging drainage ditches, installing shelves, building individual shrines, and often working late into the night. All this time our anxiety about the next step, complete isolation from the world and the engagement of very intensive practice, began to weigh on us.

Entry

The last of the empowerments was completed. Out of appreciation, all the retreatants offered a long-life ceremony to Rinpoche. In this ceremony, an effigy is offered to all the forces which might normally shorten or threaten the teacher's life. The weather and general atmosphere—the winds, the clouds and storm which developed in the course of the ceremony—left us with a very powerful sense of magic and wonder. A few days later, we gathered in the main temple, where we were served tea, presented with offerings, and then said goodbye to all the people with whom we had worked so closely over the last six months building the retreat. I said goodbye to my wife, who was entering the women's retreat. Though sad, it didn't feel like an actual parting or separation. Then we proceeded in formal procession behind Rinpoche, our retreat director, and other lamas to the gates of the men's retreat. The sealing ceremonies were done outside in a cold rain, where liturgies were read by a car's headlights. Rinpoche was magnificently arrayed in his ceremonial brocade. At the conclusion of the ceremony, we entered the retreat one by one, and the door closed. We would not see the outside world for three years and three months.

Leaving the World

The first reaction was one of relief. After the frantic pressure of the last few days, the effort to complete as many necessary tasks as possible, suddenly we were free just to sit and practice. However, there were a few things to adjust to.

Our rooms were approximately ten feet square and contained a shrine, shelves for texts and clothes, and a meditation box, which at various times served as a couch, a meditation platform, a writing desk, or an eating table. At night it became my bed. Learning to sleep sitting up was just one adjustment, one that was not always successfully made. I'd heard much about how strenuously meditators in Tibet apply themselves, never lying down, putting lighted candles on their heads, fighting off sleep in every conceivable way. Rinpoche told me that he had prevented himself from drifting off to sleep by balancing on a window ledge. Whenever he fell asleep, he fell off! Now it was my turn to follow in the footsteps of these great masters, but certainly not without difficulties. Going to sleep sitting up was not so difficult after a couple of days of three to four thousand prostrations and no sleep. However, *staying* sitting up was another matter. Every morning, and sometimes in the middle of the night, I'd find myself in some strange position, curled up like a dog at the bottom of the box, legs up in the air at some impossible angle—stiff, cramped, and sore. Some of my fellow retreatants adjusted with only a little trouble and found that sleeping sitting up brought about a lighter sleep and clearer dreams. Others had as much difficulty as I. They tied strings to the ceiling and to their hair, tried to jam extra blocks into the box to keep the body upright—ingenious, but ultimately ineffective. Sometimes I was so exhausted I would even dream that I was falling asleep. Then I would have to wake up twice, once during the dream, and once again into "real life." After a couple of these episodes, I began to question seriously the conventional distinctions between reality and dreams.

Yet despite all these "inconveniences" we were all very happy to be in retreat. Through our teacher, through a lot of hard work, and through the kindness of innumerable people who helped in so many ways, our dream of entering the retreat had been realized. That feeling of gratitude would stay with us for the whole retreat, a constant encouragement to make full use of the precious opportunity we had been given.

Retreat

The first meditation session began at four o'clock in the morning and continued till six. Half an hour later, we met in the temple to do Tara ritual, a series of prayers to Tara, a female Bodhisattva who embodies the principle of awakened compassion and protection. At eight o'clock we went to the kitchen to fetch our breakfast (which was prepared by our cook/attendant) to eat in our rooms. The second session began at nine and was two and a half hours long. Lunch was followed by a period for rest, study, or whatever. We began sitting again at two. At five, we met once more to do the evening protector rituals, took supper to our rooms at six, and sat again from seven to nine.

We soon discovered that there was more to learn about our daily routine. There were a number of supplementary practices to fit into this schedule: a couple of morning meditations, followed by prostrations, water offerings, and chanting of mantras between the end of the first session and Tara ritual; our own daily practices whenever we could; and two additional meditations in the evening after the final session, one for protection and one for developing compassion. In addition, we studied the commentaries which explained the various meditation practices, both how to do them and what they meant. We met with our retreat director every few days to go over new material and resolve questions or difficulties; and those who were weak in Tibetan endeavored to improve their comprehension and skills. In short, this was no holiday!

Several times a month we did major rituals together in the temple, instead of in our regular individual sessions. Full moon days were marked by special prayers to the lineage of teachers. The tenth day of both the waxing and waning moon was celebrated with *yidam* (meditation deity) ceremonies of self-empowerment. On the twenty-ninth day, we did extensive protector rituals, and on both full moon and new moon days a ceremony for the renewal of vows.

Subject Matter

While this was our basic schedule, our actual meditation practice during the four daily sessions was constantly changing. Over the course of the retreat, we practiced most of the key meditation techniques of both the Shangpa Kagyu and Karma Kagyu traditions, as well as a number of other associated practices.

The First Year

The first year was spent establishing a proper foundation for spiritual development. At the beginning, a full week was devoted to reflecting on the unique opportunity human existence affords for realization, another week on death and impermanence, and a week each on Dharma and the nature of suffering in existence. These reflective meditations were difficult. While we were all familiar with this material, spending more than eight hours a day contemplating these themes had a profound effect on outlook and motivation. One began to see life, the world, and existence itself in a very different light and to appreciate, on a much deeper level, the importance of spiritual understanding as an essential part of life and being.

During the next four months we concentrated on the special foundations. Although we had all completed them before coming into the retreat, emphasis on these practices was particularly important for generating a sound basis for further development and removing obstacles through purification. Practicing them with this kind of intensity was a new experience.

We were still becoming accustomed to the strenuous routine of the retreat. It was mid-winter and for many of us, it was the first time we had lived without heat, depending only on warm blankets to keep out the cold. Yet our enthusiasm and energy carried us through, exhausted though we might be from doing over three thousand prostrations a day.

With this as our basis, we turned to meditations and practices whose focus was the guru, in order to bring the mind of the guru and the mind of the student together through the power of faith and devotion. Despite the fact that we had virtually no contact with Rinpoche for much of the retreat, these practices made us very aware of his presence and blessing in the retreat.

After these meditations, we turned to techniques for developing love, compassion, and *bodhicitta*—the intention to realize awakening in order to help others. For me, this was one of the most wonderful and powerful periods of retreat. Eight to ten hours of intensive reflection on the needs, pain, and yearnings of others in contrast to one's own made me realize how self-centered we really are. Anger, I realized, is based solely on a sense of personal territory—physical, emotional, or intellectual. Through the technique of "taking and sending," one gradually discovers that it is not necessary to maintain rigid territorial boundaries. The freedom and joy that come from that realization left me with a deep appreciation for the profundity and power of compassion.

The final practice in the first year of retreat was Shamatha/Vipassana, tranquility and insight. In the Kagyu tradition, there are two special features of these practices. First, because they lead directly into the sutra tradition of *Mahamudra* (meditation on what is ultimately real), the method of meditation remains basically the same through all the stages of experience and understanding. Secondly, as it is said, the Kagyu tradition specializes in faith and devotion towards the guru, so each period of meditation starts with prayers to the guru for blessing. In the retreat environment, one clearly appreciates the kindness and love of one's teacher, the role his or her inspiration has played in leading one forward on the spiritual path, and the amazing depth and richness of their concise instructions on this kind of meditation.

Yidams

Virtually the entire second year was taken up with *yidam* practice, deity meditation. Here I had to assimilate ideas and approaches to the world which have no counterpart in modern Western culture. Identification with a particular symbolic expression of awakened mind, day after day, gradually leads one to see the world very differently. No longer does it seem solid and rigid; everything takes on a magical, sacred quality and increasingly appears as a reflection or echo of one's own mind.

It is worth mentioning again at this juncture that life in retreat is not easy. Seven men, each with strong ideas about "how things should be" make for an interesting environment. As time went on, however, we found that we were not seven separate minds. The state or attitude of one person affected everyone else, and we learned, sometimes painfully, that what we experienced was directly related to our outlook. In other words the retreat environment provided a very clear mirror of one's state of mind. We were confronted as individuals with the decision of whether to ignore the mirror or to face ourselves, however difficult or painful that might be.

As we continued working with *yidam* practice, we came to appreciate the tremendous power and support that ritual provides in meditation and spiritual development. Ritual becomes an enactment, virtually a drama, of the unfolding, acknowledgement, and honoring of enlightened mind in oneself. In both the daily and monthly rituals, the expression of one's awakened nature is nourished, refined, and made manifest in actual experience. The dream-like nature of experience is brought out clearly. Gradually, this view colors and transforms one's experience of ordinary reality.

Advanced Practices

The final year of the retreat was filled with advanced practices such as the Six Teachings of Naropa. These practices dissolve still more subtle kinds of clinging, to enable the mind to rest naturally without contrivance, wandering, or reference. Generally, we only had time to become familiar with the meditations, but that was enough to convince us of the real possibility of understanding the nature of the mind through them.

Towards the end of the third year, there was a month's practice of *Cho* (cutting through), during which we practiced together all day in the main temple. A celebration of thanks to all who had helped us through the retreat, much of the ceremony was concerned with *dakinis*, female personifications of dance, joy, openness, and the mischievousness of awakened mind. The word *dakini* means "sky-traveler," one who dances in the space of awakened mind.

One day during these ceremonies we heard a strange roar. We stopped and listened . . . nothing. We resumed, and the strange roar came again. We finished the chant and waited. Again and again, the roar sounded—intermittently, unpredictably. We looked around. Had someone left the gas on? It was checked—no. The roar seemed to come from outside, so we went to investigate. Nobody could see anything, until someone happened to look up in the sky. And what a sight! A large, brightly-colored hot air balloon was flying overhead, and the roar had been the sound of the gas burners heating the air in the balloon to slow its descent. Vacationers on a balloon tour of France!

What It Is

The three-year retreat, then, is primarily a program of training in meditation. It is virtually a college of contemplative techniques. There is a considerable amount of material to assimilate, both theoretical and practical. And it is an important step into a contemplative life, a life of retreat and practice. In many ways, it is the essence of monasticism—a group of people who are occupied totally with spiritual or mystical practice and have little contact or interest in the world at large.

In addition, it is a chance to practice, and practice very intensively. All the difficulties, struggles with physical discomfort, and interactions with other retreatants all become part of one's path. One finishes the retreat with the feeling that one has done something very significant which, at the same time, is just the smallest beginning on the path.

What It Is Not

When I originally went into the retreat, at some level I had the idea that it was a solution to all problems, that, at last, I would receive the most profound instructions, be able to practice them without distraction, and, if not actually attain awakening, at least make some healthy progress along the path. Needless to say, my expectations, both conscious and unconscious, were not fulfilled, at least not in the way I expected. Oh yes, the profound instructions were given, and it was possible to practice them, but there was one big catch and that was "I."

Firstly, I didn't find the retreat easy nor meditation particularly blissful. It was hard work from start to finish. The schedule is demanding, even if one is in good health both physically and mentally. However, the intensity of practice and the general conditions bring up a lot of "stuff." Physical difficulty, whether it is simply sore knees from prostrations or sitting, or actual illness, has to be faced directly. There is no escape, though one tends to spend a lot of effort trying to find one. In the end, however, one sees more and more clearly how everything begins and ends with oneself—how one creates one's own experience of the world—and finally accepts things for what they are. The truly wonderful consequence of that acceptance is that one finds a totally unsuspected freedom and joy independent of any set of conditions or circumstances.

Secondly, the retreat certainly isn't a guarantee of enlightenment. I gained a much better understanding of how deeply emotional and ego-based patterns are imbedded in us. While I reluctantly came to realize that the ignorance and confusion of aeons were not going to be removed in a few months, I also saw clearly that the methods of Buddhist practice will, without doubt, clear them away. The only requisite is to work with constant enthusiasm. In short, my confidence and trust in the Dharma were firmly established in experience.

Finally, retreat isn't a vacation from *samsara*, from ordinary egocentric experience. In fact, the retreat was more like a super-*samsara*; everything was intensified and magnified to such an extent that I couldn't avoid the chaos created by my own confusion and ignorance.

Exit

Time passes in retreat at an extraordinary pace. Sometimes I felt that the seasons were scenes from a movie—spring changing into summer, then fall, then winter, day by day. The time soon came for us to exit. Since this was the first retreat for Westerners, a large crowd had gathered outside the gates. We stepped out straight into the lens of a movie camera and paraded past literally hundreds of cameras clicking and flashing. But the overriding impression was one of spaciousness. I felt that I was walking in the sky! After forty months of a view confined to half an acre, the meadows, sky, clouds, and woods were infinite vistas, brilliantly clear and vivid. It all seemed like a dream, not really real, yet very much there. This feeling endured and was easily recalled many months later. People's faces seemed different. It was possible to see peace, anxiety, fear, or love written clearly in the set of a mouth or chin, in the glance of an eye. And riding in a car, for some reason, sent me immediately to sleep.

As time went on, I became aware of less obvious effects of the retreat. It was much easier for me simply to listen to people than it had been before, and it was easier to understand what was motivating certain types of behavior. My general outlook on the world had changed, too. The impermanence of situations was accepted with much less resistance. I was always aware that how I felt in a situation determined how I experienced it (rather than the opposite).

The most important effect, however, was a solid confidence and trust in the teachings of Buddha and Rinpoche. There was no doubt left in my mind that these teachings could and would lead one to realization and that the obstacle to that was simply one's own habitual patterns.

Finding a Place in or out of the World

After the retreat, each of us had to decide what to do. Some (including myself) elected to return and do a second three-year retreat. The overriding reason for this choice was the desire to continue to practice, to try to take another small step on the path. Others were asked to teach in centers in Europe and North America. After the second retreat, Rinpoche asked me also to assume responsibility for teaching at his center in Los Angeles, a position I took in May 1985. In this position, one is faced with the challenge of communicating the training and experience of the Dharma in a very different environment from retreat. Yet the retreat experience constantly guides one in focusing on the core of the Buddha's teachings, the clear and open mind, compassionate, unconfused by the turbulence of emotions, and responsive to the needs of others.

The retreat itself is really training for a contemplative life, not a training for future teachers. Many of the retreatants take and maintain monastic ordination in order to preserve a simple life style and concentrate on practice. Others, like myself, find themselves teaching in centers. And still others return to a more normal life with family and profession. At this point, there is very little support for people who have completed this kind of training. The readjustment to life has been difficult. As one retreatant warned me after I left the second retreat, "It takes two to three years to adjust." She was right! Or maybe one never "adjusts" completely, and the understanding and experience of retreat remains always.

Ken McLeod is a senior student of the Very Ven. Kalu, Rinpoche. A Buddhist for over fifteen years, he has completed two traditional three-year retreats and is currently the resident teacher at Kagyu Do-Nga Chuling in West Los Angeles, California. In addition to his accomplishments as an interpreter for Tibetan teachers, and as a translator of Tibetan texts, he is the spiritual consultant for the Buddhist AIDS Project.

The Vajrayana Centers of North America

Centers are listed alphabetically first by state, then by city and, should there be more than one within a given city, by the names of the centers themselves.

ARIZONA

Karma Thegsum Choling

The main purposes of the center are to encourage the practice of meditation, to apply the principles of mindful awareness to everyday life, to develop intuition, and to provide a teaching center for visiting Tibetan Buddhist lamas. The weekly schedule at the center includes sitting practice at 6:30 P.M. on Monday and Thursday evenings and at 6:00 A.M. on Wednesday mornings; study, discussion, and oral teachings on the Buddhist path at 7:30 P.M. on Monday evenings; group meetings linking Buddhist philosophy to other paths and to our Western way of life; and monthly seminars on weekends.
ADDRESS: 6231 East Exeter Boulevard, Scottsdale, AZ 85251
PHONE: (602) 264-2930
LINEAGE: Karma Kagyu
SPIRITUAL HEAD: Gyalwa Karmapa (Tibetan)
RESIDENT DIRECTOR: Erma Pounds (American)
AFFILIATED WITH: Karma Triyana Dharmachakra, Woodstock, New York
ESTABLISHED: 1981
FACILITIES: Urban meditation center

Phoenix Dharma Study Group

Students of the Vidyadhara, the Ven. Chogyam Trungpa, Rinpoche, practice Shamatha/Vipassana meditation. Study of Trungpa, Rinpoche's writings and tapes on Hinayana (Theravada) and Mahayana practice, as well as other Buddhist material, takes place weekly in a residence partly supported by the group. Monthly *nyinthuns* (all-day sittings), occasional rural weekend retreats, and bi-annual hosted programs comprise the larger schedule. Shamatha (tranquility) meditation instruction is available.
ADDRESS: C/O Evans, 1049 West 10th Street, Tempe, AZ 85281
PHONE: (602) 829-8255
LINEAGE: Karma Kagyu
SPIRITUAL HEAD: Vajra Regent Osel Tendzin. Founded by the Vidyadhara, the Ven. Chogyam Trungpa, Rinpoche.
RESIDENT DIRECTOR: William L. Evans
AFFILIATED WITH: Vajradhatu International/USA
ESTABLISHED: 1979
FACILITIES: Urban meditation center
RETREATS OFFERED: Weekly evening meditation; monthly *nyinthun*.
OPEN TO: General public. Membership is optional.

Tucson Dharma Study Group

TDSG meets Tuesday evenings at 7:15 P.M. for meditation, followed by study, tapes, and discussion. Meditation instruction is available. Information is also available on current activities of Vajradhatu-USA/Canada and the major practice and

retreat centers of the Tibetan Kagyu Lineage.
ADDRESS: 739 East 5th Street, Tucson, AZ 85702 (Mailing address: P.O. Box 1174, Tucson, AZ 85702)
PHONE: (602) 792-9235 (after 5:00 P.M.)
LINEAGE: Karma Kagyu
SPIRITUAL HEAD: Vajra Regent Osel Tendzin. Founded by the Vidyadhara, the Ven. Chogyam Trungpa, Rinpoche.
RESIDENT DIRECTOR: William Streit
AFFILIATED WITH: Vajradhatu International/USA
ESTABLISHED: 1975
FACILITIES: Rented facility owned by Quakers
RETREATS OFFERED: A retreat center in Arivaca, Arizona, is currently being developed by G. Keegan, P.O. Box 56221, Tucson, AZ 85703-6221.
OPEN TO: General public

CALIFORNIA

Bakersfield Forming Dharma Study Group
Refer to Vajradhatu/USA, Boulder, Colorado, for a description.
ADDRESS: 2318 20th Street, Bakersfield, CA 93301
PHONE: (805) 327-0507
LINEAGE: Karma Kagyu
SPIRITUAL HEAD: Vajra Regent Osel Tendzin. Founded by the Vidyadhara, the Ven. Chogyam Trungpa, Rinpoche.
RESIDENT DIRECTOR: Susan Stone
AFFILIATED WITH: Vajradhatu International/USA
OPEN TO: General public

Berkeley Dharmadhatu
Refer to Vajradhatu/USA, Boulder, Colorado, for a description.

ADDRESS: 2288 Fulton Street, Berkeley, CA 94704
PHONE: (415) 841-3242; 841-3245
LINEAGE: Karma Kagyu
SPIRITUAL HEAD: Vajra Regent Osel Tendzin. Founded by the Vidyadhara, the Ven. Chogyam Trungpa, Rinpoche.
AFFILIATED WITH: Vajradhatu International/USA
OPEN TO: General public

Chagdud Gonpa Foundation, Inc.
Chagdud Tulku, Rinpoche, an incarnate lama, is a master of Buddhist meditation, a Tibetan physician, an accomplished artist, and a world traveler. He instructs both new and advanced students, offering teachings, meditation practice, and empowerments. Activities include introductory meetings, weekly group meditation practice, weekend workshops, and month-long and more extensive longer retreats.
ADDRESS: 1933-D Delaware, Berkeley, CA 94709
PHONE: (415) 849-3300
LINEAGE: Nyingma
SPIRITUAL HEAD: Chagdud Tulku, Rinpoche
RESIDENT DIRECTOR: Linda Richmoon
AFFILIATED WITH: Autonomous
ESTABLISHED: 1980
FACILITIES: Urban meditation center
RETREATS OFFERED: Four, six, and twelve-week retreats
OPEN TO: General public

Nyingma Institute
Situtated in the Berkeley hills, the Nyingma Institute overlooks the San Francisco Bay and the Golden Gate Bridge. For over fourteen years people from throughout the United States and abroad have come here to study and practice the teachings of Tarthang Tulku. The

meditation rooms, library, bookstore, and meditation garden, with its prayer wheels and prayer flags, support an atmosphere for study and practice. Offering classes, seminars, and long-term retreats, the institute is also a residential setting for Nyingma community volunteers. To visit the institute, please make arrangements or come to specially scheduled events. There are public events every Sunday from 5:00–7:00 P.M.

ADDRESS: 1815 Highland Place, Berkeley, CA 94709
PHONE: (415) 843-6812
LINEAGE: Nyingma
SPIRITUAL HEAD: Founded by Tarthang Tulku, Rinpoche
RESIDENT DIRECTOR: Western staff
ESTABLISHED: 1973
FACILITIES: Meditation rooms, library, bookstore, and meditation garden. Residential setting.
RETREATS OFFERED: Kum Nye, Nyingma meditation, and training programs.

Vajrapani Institute
ADDRESS: P.O. Box I, Boulder Creek, CA 95006
SPIRITUAL HEAD: Lama Thubten Zopa, Rinpoche
AFFILIATED WITH: Foundation for the Preservation of the Mahayana Tradition
ESTABLISHED: 1977
FACILITIES: Country retreat facility for solitary retreats
RETREATS OFFERED: Weekend courses in the summer. Solitary retreat facilities.
OPEN TO: General public

Santa Cruz Karma Thegsum Choling
Please refer to Karma Triyana Dharmachakra, Woodstock, New York, for a description of Karma Thegsum Choling.

ADDRESS: 122 Central Avenue, Capitola, CA 95010
PHONE: (408) 462-3955
LINEAGE: Karma Kagyu
SPIRITUAL HEAD: His Holiness the Gyalwa Karmapa
RESIDENT DIRECTOR: Zeinob Burnham
AFFILIATED WITH: Karma Triyana Dharmachakra, Woodstock, New York
OPEN TO: General public

San Diego Karma Thegsum Choling
Please refer to Karma Triyana Dharmachakra, Woodstock, New York, for a description of Karma Thegsum Choling.
ADDRESS: 904 Edwina Way, Cardiff, CA 92007
PHONE: (619) 942-2963
LINEAGE: Karma Kagyu
SPIRITUAL HEAD: His Holiness the Gyalwa Karmapa
RESIDENT DIRECTOR: Bill Bradshaw
AFFILIATED WITH: Karma Triyana Dharmachakra
OPEN TO: General public

Davis Dharma Study Group
Davis Dharma Study Group is a small urban center offering weekly sessions of sitting meditation practice and periodic classes. Instruction is provided by resident senior students of Chogyam Trungpa, Rinpoche, or by visiting teachers.
ADDRESS: 129 E Street, Suite D-3, Davis, CA 95616 (Mailing address: 1108 Cypress Lane, Davis, CA 95616)
PHONE: (916) 758-1440; 758-3576
LINEAGE: Karma Kagyu
SPIRITUAL HEAD: Vajra Regent Osel Tendzin. Founded by the Vidyadhara, the Ven. Chogyam Trungpa, Rinpoche.
RESIDENT DIRECTOR: Manuel Medeiros
AFFILIATED WITH: Vajradhatu International/USA

ESTABLISHED: 1987
FACILITIES: Urban meditation center
OPEN TO: General public

Chakpori Ling Foundation

Chakpori Ling Foundation was established in the United States in 1970 in Houston, Texas, by its founder the Venerable Norbu L. Chan, O.M.D., Ph.D., C.A., a Tibetan-Nepali-Italian trained lama. In 1974 Chakpori Ling Foundation moved to Northern California where it currently occupies a forty-five acre facility. The monastery has services two or three times daily for the residents and is open Sundays at 10:00 A.M. to the general public.

ADDRESS: 10400 Highway 116, Forestville, CA 95432 (Mailing address: P.O. Box 370, Forestville, CA 95432)
PHONE: (707) 887-7859; 869-3111
LINEAGE: Nyingma
SPIRITUAL HEAD: Lama Gonpo Tsultim, Rinpoche
RESIDENT DIRECTOR: Yabgen, Rinpoche and Tulku Orgyen Jigme Dorje, Rinpoche
AFFILIATED WITH: Buddhist Vajrayana churches
ESTABLISHED: 1959
FACILITIES: Country retreat facility
RETREATS OFFERED: Supervised solitary retreats, three-year Vajrayana retreat.
OPEN TO: Members only

Garberville Dharma Study Group

Refer to Vajradhatu/USA, Boulder, Colorado, for a description.
ADDRESS: 434 Maple Lane, Garberville, CA 95440
PHONE: (707) 923-3891
LINEAGE: Karma Kagyu
SPIRITUAL HEAD: Vajra Regent Osel Tendzin. Founded by the Vidyadhara, the Ven. Chogyam Trungpa, Rinpoche.

RESIDENT DIRECTOR: Timothy Clark
AFFILIATED WITH: Vajradhatu International/USA
OPEN TO: General public

Chagdud Gonpa of Los Angeles

Chagdud Gonpa of Los Angeles is a traditional urban Tibetan Buddhist meditation center with a regular schedule of teachings, practice, and retreats on three evenings and on weekends. Chagdud Tulku, Rinpoche, visits twice a year for ten days to give teachings, empowerments, and medical consultations. Nubpa Chodak Gyatso Lama, Rinpoche, will become resident lama of Chagdud Gonpa of Los Angeles in 1988. He speaks excellent English.

ADDRESS: 2503 West 117th, Inglewood, CA 90303
PHONE: (213) 754-0466; 877-7331
LINEAGE: Nyingmapa
SPIRITUAL HEAD: Chagdud Tulku, Rinpoche
RESIDENT DIRECTOR: Nubpachodak Gyatso Lama, Rinpoche
AFFILIATED WITH: Chagdud Gonpa, Cottage Grove, Oregon
FACILITIES: Urban meditation center. Solitary retreat facilities.
RETREATS OFFERED: Regular meditation retreats on weekends and holidays.
OPEN TO: General public

Ewam Choden Tibetan Buddhist Center

Ewam Choden ("integration of method and wisdom, compassion and voidness," and "possessing the Dharma") was established to provide an opportunity for the practice and study of Tibetan religion and culture. The center is especially interested in maintaining close relations with the Tibetan community in India by sending students to study there with the few remain-

ing great teachers, and through lending
sorely needed aid to refugees.
ADDRESS: 254 Cambridge Avenue, Kensington, CA 94708
PHONE: (415) 527-7363
LINEAGE: Sakya Tradition (Tibetan Buddhism)
SPIRITUAL HEAD: Lama Kunga Thrartse, Rinpoche. Trained at Ngor Monastery in western Tibet, Rinpoche is a reincarnated lama, his line of succession originating in Sevan Repa, a heart disciple of the illustrious Mila Repa.
RESIDENT DIRECTOR: Lama Kunga, Rinpoche
ESTABLISHED: 1971
FACILITIES: Urban meditation center; solitary retreat facility.
RETREATS OFFERED: Solitary retreats and weekend *nyinthuns*
OPEN TO: General public

Palo Alto Dharmadhatu

The Palo Alto Dharmadhatu (which, due to rising rentals, is now in Los Altos) presents an oasis for quiet practice in the middle of Silicon Valley. Located on the campus of a former elementary school, surrounded by a park and open space, we are a relatively small group of strong, long-term practitioners, and are able to give new practitioners considerable individual attention. We offer a wide range of classes and group practice situations.
ADDRESS: 201 Covington Road, Los Altos, CA 94022
PHONE: (415) 949-3082
LINEAGE: Karma Kagyu
SPIRITUAL HEAD: Vajra Regent Osel Tendzin. Founded by the Vidyadhara, the Ven. Chogyam Trungpa, Rinpoche.
RESIDENT DIRECTOR: Charlotte Linde
AFFILIATED WITH: Vajradhatu International/USA
ESTABLISHED: 1972

FACILITIES: Urban meditation center
RETREATS OFFERED: *Nyinthun* (daylong sitting), weekend sittings, and Shambhala training.
OPEN TO: General public

Dharmadhatu of Los Angeles

Refer to Vajradhatu/USA, Boulder, Colorado, for a description.
ADDRESS: 8218 West 3rd, Los Angeles, CA 90004
PHONE: (213) 653-9342
LINEAGE: Karma Kagyu
SPIRITUAL HEAD: Vajra Regent Osel Tendzin. Founded by the Vidyadhara, the Ven. Chogyam Trungpa, Rinpoche.
RESIDENT DIRECTOR: Nina Toumanoff-Tyson
AFFILIATED WITH: Vajradhatu International/USA
ESTABLISHED: 1973
FACILITIES: Urban meditation center
RETREATS OFFERED: Weekend sittings, *nyinthun*/Shambhala training.
OPEN TO: General public

Kagyu Do-Nga Chuling

Ken McLeod teaches meditation methods of the Kagyu tradition of Buddhism from Tibet. Introductory and in-depth courses, workshops, retreats, and seminars are given regularly to provide a strong background for personal practice. Ken McLeod is available for counselling in practice, meditation, and the issues they raise in personal life. At KDC, three meditation techniques form the basis of practice. The first is Shamatha/Vipassana (quieting the mind and understanding its nature). The second is training in compassion through the methods of Mahayana mind training. The third is the Vajrayana practice of mantra and visualization meditation on Avalokiteshvara, the embodiment of awakened compassion. Advanced

training in motivation, the foundations of Mahamudra practice, and other practices of the Tibetan tradition are available to individuals who wish to practice intensively.
ADDRESS: 12021 Wilshire Boulevard, Suite 667, West Los Angeles, CA 90025
PHONE: (213) 820-0046
LINEAGE: Kagyu
SPIRITUAL HEAD: Kalu, Rinpoche (Tibetan)
RESIDENT DIRECTOR: Ken McLeod (Western Teacher)
AFFILIATED WITH: Kagyu Dharma
ESTABLISHED: 1985
FACILITIES: No physical center at present. Using rental facilities as needed.
RETREATS OFFERED: *Nyinthun*, weekend sittings; monthly.
OPEN TO: General public. Some retreats require previous practice.

Los Angeles Karma Thegsum Choling

Shamatha meditation and Chenresig practice in Tibetan are held weekly. L.A. KTC also sponsors teachings by resident and visiting lamas and rinpoches.
ADDRESS: 3586 Tacoma Avenue, Los Angeles, CA 90065
PHONE: (213) 222-8269
LINEAGE: Karma Kagyu
SPIRITUAL HEAD: The Gyalwa Karmapa and Ven. Khenpo Karthar, Rinpoche (Tibetan)
RESIDENT DIRECTOR: Ven. Lama Ganga (Tibetan)
AFFILIATED WITH: Karma Triyana Dharmachakra, Woodstock, New York
ESTABLISHED: 1978
FACILITIES: Urban meditation center

Los Angeles Yeshe Nyngpo

Los Angeles Yeshe Nyngpo, under the direction of Gyatrul, Rinpoche, exists first as a practice center for people interested

in Vajrayana Buddhism as taught by the Nyingma lineage, and second to bring lamas of the lineage to the Los Angeles area to teach directly. Group practice sessions are conducted weekly in a member's home.
ADDRESS: 12021 Wilshire Boulevard, #708, Los Angeles, CA 90025
PHONE: (213) 452-3511
LINEAGE: Nyingma
SPIRITUAL HEAD: Gyatrul, Rinpoche
AFFILIATED WITH: Yeshe Nyngpo, Inc., P.O. Box 124, Ashland, Oregon 97520
ESTABLISHED: 1982
FACILITIES: Member's house
RETREATS OFFERED: Weekend sittings and Dharma intensives with the Lama when he is in town.
OPEN TO: General public

Thubten Dhargye Ling

Founded in 1979 by Geshe Tsultrim Gyeltsen, TDL offers beginning and advanced studies in Sutra and Tantra. His Holiness the Dalai Lama gave the center its name; Thubten Dhargye Ling means Land of Increasing Buddha's Teachings. TDL is affiliated with other Tibetan centers in the United States and Canada. TDL conducts classes in meditation, religious debate, and Tibetan language, as well as classes in Tantra for advanced students with the proper initiations. Retreats are frequently held at the center. Special arrangements can be made to assist those wishing to conduct a retreat in their own homes. Private interviews with Geshe Gyeltsen are available upon request.
ADDRESS: 2658 La Cienaga Avenue, Los Angeles, CA 90034
PHONE: (213) 838-1232
LINEAGE: Gelupga
SPIRITUAL HEAD: Geshe Tsultrim Gyeltsen
RESIDENT DIRECTOR: Same
ESTABLISHED: 1978

FACILITIES: Urban meditation center
RETREATS OFFERED: Vipassana courses,
chanting retreats, prostration retreats,
weekend sittings, supervised solitary retreats. Retreats given approximately
four times a year.
OPEN TO: General public. Some retreats
for members only.

Karma Thegsum Choling of Palo Alto

ADDRESS: P.O. Box 11793-A, Palo Alto,
CA 94306
PHONE: (415) 941-7968
LINEAGE: Tibetan
AFFILIATED WITH: Formerly Karma
Tengay Ling
ESTABLISHED: 1973

Sonoma County Dharma Study Group

The Sonoma County Dharma Study
Group offers regular meditation periods,
open house talks on Buddhism and mod-
ern living, and meditation instruction, as
well as special seminars and family social
events.
ADDRESS: 24 Western Avenue, Room 5,
Petaluma, CA 94952 (Mailing address:
P.O. Box 2004, Petaluma, CA 94953)
PHONE: (707) 762-0195
LINEAGE: Karma Kagyu
SPIRITUAL HEAD: Vajra Regent Osel
Tendzin. Founded by the Vidyadhara,
the Ven. Chogyam Trungpa, Rinpoche.
RESIDENT DIRECTOR: Doug McCanne
AFFILIATED WITH: Vajradhatu Interna-
tional/USA
ESTABLISHED: 1981
FACILITIES: Urban meditation center,
public shrine room
RETREATS OFFERED: None
OPEN TO: General public

Drikung Dharmamati Center

Lilo St. Lorant writes: "The Ven. K. C.
Ayang, Rinpoche, established my residence as a Drikung Dharma center in
January 1985, after having given *Phowa*
("transference of consciousness") teach-
ings here on several previous occasions.
The center basically serves as a residence
for Rinpoche and other Drikung lamas
when they visit the area. There are no for-
mal practice sessions other than the teach-
ings which are given by the lamas when
they are in residence."
ADDRESS: 981 La Mesa, Portola Valley,
CA 94025
PHONE: (415) 854-3537
SPIRITUAL HEAD: Ven. K. C. Ayang,
Rinpoche (Tibetan)
RESIDENT DIRECTOR: Lilo St. Lorant
ESTABLISHED: 1985
FACILITIES: Member's home

Thubten Rimay Chuday

ADDRESS: 706 North Eucalyptus, Rialto,
CA 92376

San Diego Dharma Study Group

Senior students of Vidyadhara, the Venerable Chogyam Trungpa, Rinpoche, give
instruction in Shamatha/Vipassana, and
teach introductory Dharma through
weekly talks and occasional courses. Students are guided along a path presented
by the Vidyadhara. Local group practice
consists of weekly sitting, monthly half-
day sitting and walking meditation, and
chanting. Kagyu *ngondro* and *Sadhana*
practices are privately scheduled among
authorized students. The group is growing and expects to offer a more complete
schedule for practice and study.
ADDRESS: 3521 Adams Avenue, San Diego, CA (Mailing address: C/O Dan
Gregory, 2030 Teton Pass Street, El Ca-
jon, CA 92020)

PHONE: (619) 447-7596 (Dan)
LINEAGE: Karma Kagyu
SPIRITUAL HEAD: Vajra Regent Osel Tendzin. Founded by the Vidyadhara, the Ven. Chogyam Trungpa, Rinpoche.
RESIDENT DIRECTOR: Dr. Nancy Porter-Steele
AFFILIATED WITH: Vajradhatu International/USA
ESTABLISHED: 1982
FACILITIES: Facilities rented for one evening per week, one morning per month, and for special programs.
RETREATS OFFERED: Half-day *nyinthun*, sitting and walking practice; second Sunday most months.
OPEN TO: General public

Kagyu Droden Kunchab

KDK is a center for the study and practice of Tibetan Mahayana and Vajrayana Buddhism, founded by the Very Venerable Kalu, Rinpoche. Our senior spiritual teacher and resident director, Ven. Lama Lodo, is also the director of Kalu, Rinpoche's centers in the United States and Canada. Lama Lodo leads meditation sessions and answers questions weekly at various affiliate centers in the Bay Area. Each full moon he guides a two-day *Nyung Nes* retreat of meditation and fasting at the San Francisco center. KDK maintains a country property in Oregon for use as a three-year retreat facility. In order to qualify for such a retreat, a student must have studied with Lama Lodo for at least five years and have permission from parents or spouse.
ADDRESS: 1892 Fell Street, San Francisco, CA 94117
PHONE: (415) 752-5454
LINEAGE: Kagyu
SPIRITUAL HEAD: Lama Lodo
FACILITIES: Urban meditation center
RETREATS OFFERED: *Nyung Nes* (two-day) retreat; monthly.

Maitreya Institute

Maitreya Institute is a nonprofit, ecumenical educational and cultural organization founded by H. E. Tai Situ, Rinpoche, one of the four incarnate Regents of the Kagyu Lineage. One month each year His Eminence offers teachings and ceremonies through the institute. Besides Tibetan Buddhism, the institute offers cross-cultural programs in psychology, spirituality, geomancy, health and healing, economics, art, and music.
ADDRESS: 3315 Sacramento Street, Suite 622, San Francisco, CA 94118
LINEAGE: Sufi, Christian, etc.; ecumenical, with Kagyu teaching.
SPIRITUAL HEAD: H. E. Tai Situ, Rinpoche
RESIDENT DIRECTOR: Many multicultural teachers
AFFILIATED WITH: Autonomous
ESTABLISHED: 1985
FACILITIES: Urban center

San Francisco Dharmadhatu

Like most Dharmadhatu centers under the direction of Vajradhatu, San Francisco Dharmadhatu offers an ongoing program of meditation instruction, group and individual practice, and graduated studies in basic Buddhist views. The emphasis is on integrating the essential wisdom and sanity of Buddhist teachings into the life styles of lay practitioners from all walks of life. Additionally, a series of weekend intensives organized to teach meditation within the context of Shambhala are hosted by San Francisco Dharmadhatu. Opportunities to study with visiting teachers are periodically offered to members, as are group and individual retreat programs at other contemplative centers.
ADDRESS: 2017 Mission Street, 3rd Floor, San Francisco, CA 94110
PHONE: (415) 626-0852
LINEAGE: Karma Kagyu

SPIRITUAL HEAD: Vajra Regent Osel Tendzin. Founded by the Vidyadhara, the Ven. Chogyam Trungpa, Rinpoche. RESIDENT DIRECTOR: Alan Schwartz AFFILIATED WITH: Vajradhatu International/USA ESTABLISHED: 1972 FACILITIES: Urban meditation center RETREATS OFFERED: *Nyinthun*, weekend sittings OPEN TO: General public, depending on retreat

The Source

The Source was recently founded to present Tibetan Buddhism from an experiential viewpoint. Weekly talks and meditation integrate the stages of the path of Vajrayana Buddhism into vital principles of being and becoming. The basic meditation practice of The Source resides in the conscious actualization of the relationship between experiencer and experienced. The awareness, explorations, enhancement, and fulfillment of this relationship lead one through the stages of renunciation, *bodhicitta*, emptiness, and Tantra. ADDRESS: 785 6th Avenue, San Francisco, CA 94118 PHONE: (415) 387-6044 LINEAGE: Gelugpa SPIRITUAL HEAD: David Berger RESIDENT DIRECTOR: David Berger AFFILIATED WITH: Autonomous ESTABLISHED: 1986 FACILITIES: Urban meditation center

Yeshe Nyingpo

Since our branch center is an urban center, we do not have retreat facilities here, but we do sponsor many events for our own lamas, as well as for other lamas in both the Nyingma and Kagyu lineages. Ongoing group practices are open to the public.

ADDRESS: 5224 Riverside Avenue, #1, San Pablo, CA 94806 PHONE: (415) 524-7913; 237-8534 LINEAGE: Nyingma SPIRITUAL HEAD: His Eminence Shenphen Dawa, Rinpoche RESIDENT DIRECTOR: Venerable Gyatrul, Rinpoche AFFILIATED WITH: Tashi Choling, Ashland, Oregon; Yeshe Nyingpo, New York, and O.C.D. FACILITIES: Urban center RETREATS OFFERED: Ongoing group practice. We sponsor Dharma teachings for our own and visiting lamas. OPEN TO: General public

Marin Study Group

Please refer to Karma Triyana Dharmachakra, Woodstock, New York, for a description. ADDRESS: 304 Devon Drive, San Rafael, CA 94903 PHONE: (415) 499-1778 LINEAGE: Karma Kagyu SPIRITUAL HEAD: His Holiness the Gyalwa Karmapa RESIDENT DIRECTOR: Kahn AFFILIATED WITH: Karma Triyana Dharmachakra OPEN TO: General public

Drikung Dharma Center

ADDRESS: 1515 State Street, #4B, Santa Barbara, CA 93101 LINEAGE: Drikung Kagyu SPIRITUAL HEAD: Drikung Chetsang, Rinpoche ESTABLISHED: 1980 FACILITIES: Urban meditation center RETREATS OFFERED: Fourteen-day *Phowa* (transmission of consciousness at the time of death). OPEN TO: Members only

Karma Thegsum Choling (KTC)

KTC of Santa Barbara was founded at the request of H. H. Gyalwa Karmapa in the late 1970s. Members gather for group practice every Sunday morning in a member's home. From time to time KTC hosts visiting lamas, who give teachings in the Santa Barbara area.

ADDRESS: 841 Mission Canyon Road, Santa Barbara, CA 93101
PHONE: (805) 682-4169
LINEAGE: Karma Kagyu
SPIRITUAL HEAD: His Holiness The Gyalwa Karmapa
RESIDENT DIRECTOR: Janice Chase
AFFILIATED WITH: Karma Triyana Dharmachakra, Woodstock, New York
ESTABLISHED: 1978
FACILITIES: Private home
RETREATS OFFERED: Our chapter has not given a retreat yet.
OPEN TO: General public

Santa Barbara Dharma Study Group

Refer to Vajradhatu/USA, Boulder, Colorado, for a description.
ADDRESS: 1129 B. State Street, #25, Santa Barbara, CA 93101
PHONE: (805) 962-7076
LINEAGE: Karma Kagyu
SPIRITUAL HEAD: Vajra Regent Osel Tendzin. Founded by the Vidyadhara, the Ven. Chogyam Trungpa, Rinpoche.
RESIDENT DIRECTOR: Roderick McGavock
AFFILIATED WITH: Vajradhatu International/USA
OPEN TO: General public

Rigpa Fellowship

Rigpa is an association of people who study under the guidance of Ven. Lama Sogyal, Rinpoche, an incarnate lama and meditation master from Tibet. Each year

Rinpoche gives talks, weekend teachings, and retreats in the United States, Europe, Australia, and New Zealand. Rigpa is currently establishing a meditation center in the San Francisco Bay Area. Ongoing practice groups also meet in Santa Cruz, San Diego, Seattle, Boston, New York, and Washington, D.C.

ADDRESS: P.O. Box 7326, Santa Cruz, CA 95061
PHONE: (415) 482-3585
LINEAGE: Nyingma
SPIRITUAL HEAD: Ven. Lama Sogyal, Rinpoche (Tibetan)
AFFILIATED WITH: Sister organizations of Rigpa, London, and Rigpa, Paris
ESTABLISHED: 1980
FACILITIES: Urban meditation center (in process)
RETREATS OFFERED: Weekend, and two-week retreats on various topics such as Dzog Chen (Ati Yoga), death and dying, and healing.
OPEN TO: General public

Santa Cruz Forming Dharma Study Group

Refer to Vajradhatu/USA, Boulder, Colorado, for a description.
ADDRESS: 112 Kennan, Santa Cruz, CA 95060
PHONE: (408) 476-3248
LINEAGE: Karma Kagyu
SPIRITUAL HEAD: Vajra Regent Osel Tendzin. Founded by the Vidyadhara, the Ven. Chogyam Trungpa, Rinpoche.
RESIDENT DIRECTOR: Rosalyn Riversong
AFFILIATED WITH: Vajradhatu International/USA
OPEN TO: General public

Ukiah Dharma Group

Our group was founded by two students who took refuge with His Eminence Tai

Situ, Rinpoche. At his direction, the focus is on the Lord Buddha. Thus, in the Rimay Tradition, all disciplines and levels of practice are honored. Our members are from the Vajrayana, Zen, and Vipassana traditions. We share two weekly silent meditation practices in a rented space. We hope to have many visiting Dharma instructors. To date, Ven. Lama Dudjom Dorje and Ven. Lama Lodo have both given teachings.
ADDRESS: 152 Standley, Ukiah, CA 95482 (Mailing address: 866 South Dora, Ukiah, CA 95482)
PHONE: (707) 468-8061
LINEAGE: Karma Kagyu
SPIRITUAL HEAD: His Eminence Tai Situ, Rinpoche
RESIDENT DIRECTOR: Lama Dudjom, Rinpoche; Lama Lodo
ESTABLISHED: 1987
FACILITIES: Rented facilities
RETREATS OFFERED: None yet
OPEN TO: General public

Drikung Shenphen Kunchab Ling
In 1985 Ayang, Rinpoche, conducted a retreat in Southern California in which he presented *Phowa* teachings (the transmission of consciousness at the time of death). At the request of the participants at this retreat, Ayang, Rinpoche, founded Drikung Shenphen Kunchab Ling as a center for the practice of the *Phowa* teachings, as well as a forum for visiting lamas of the Drikung Kagyu Lineage. A frequent visiting teacher is the Ven. Khenpo Konchog Gyaltsen, Rinpoche, of Washington, D.C. Khenpo is the translator of *The Garland of Mahamudra Practices*, (Ithaca: Snow Lion Publications, 1986). At this time the group practices in members' homes and uses rented facilities to conduct retreats, when lamas are available.
ADDRESS: 17 Horizon Avenue, Venice, CA 90291

PHONE: (213) 396-6541; 859-6996
LINEAGE: Drikung Kagyu
SPIRITUAL HEAD: H. H. Chetsang, Rinpoche, Patron; Ayang, Rinpoche, Founder; Ven. Khenpo Konchog Gyaltsen, Rinpoche, of Washington, D.C., principal visiting teacher.
RESIDENT DIRECTOR: None
AFFILIATED WITH: Autonomous
ESTABLISHED: 1985
FACILITIES: Members' homes
RETREATS OFFERED: Various Vajrayana retreats whenever lamas are available
OPEN TO: General public

COLORADO

Dechen Yonten Dzo Meditation Center
The Ven. Jetsun Pema, Rinpoche, and her assistants teach the *Dzogpa Chenpo Logchen Nyingthig* cycle of graduate Vajrayana *sadhanas* or spiritual exercises, culminating in *Dzog Chen*, or the Great Perfection. Members each receive their own individual *sadhanas* and participate in group practice three times a week.
ADDRESS: 1775 Linden Avenue, Boulder, CO 80302
PHONE: (303) 442-0796
LINEAGE: Longchen Nyingthig Nyingma
SPIRITUAL HEAD: Ven. Jetsun Pema Chodzin Sangugak Wangmo, Rinpoche (Sikkimese)
RESIDENT DIRECTOR: Ven. Tsedzin Dechen Lhamo (Tibetan) and Loppon Pema Chophel (American)
AFFILIATED WITH: Dzog Chen Choling in Philadelphia, Pennsylvania, and Longchen Nyingthig Buddhist Society in New York and New Jersey, but these are not parent organizations.
ESTABLISHED: 1982
FACILITIES: Urban meditation center with a country retreat facility. Facilities for solitary retreats.

RETREATS OFFERED: Chanting retreats
and supervised solitary retreats; three
annual group retreats.
OPEN TO: Members only

Karma Dzong

Karma Dzong, Boulder, is the largest
Vajradhatu practice center. At the present
time we have 750 members and offer
meditation programs and ongoing classes
covering the three *yanas*. Karma Dzong
was founded in 1971 by The Venerable
Chogyam Trungpa, Rinpoche. It occupies
a 12,000-square-foot building in Boulder,
Colorado, and has hosted the major
tulkus of both the Nyingma and Kagyu
schools of Tibetan Buddhism.
ADDRESS: 1345 Spruce Street, Boulder,
   CO 80302
PHONE: (303) 444-0190
LINEAGE: Karma Kagyu
SPIRITUAL HEAD: Vajra Regent Osel
Tendzin. Founded by the Vidyadhara,
the Ven. Chogyam Trungpa, Rinpoche.
RESIDENT DIRECTOR: Robert Scully and
Diane Spearly
AFFILIATED WITH: Vajradhatu Interna-
tional/USA
ESTABLISHED: 1971
FACILITIES: Urban meditation center
RETREATS OFFERED: *Nyinthuns* once
each week; all *Abishekas*.
OPEN TO: General public

Marpa House

Marpa House was founded in 1973 to
house students of Buddhism interested in
meditation and is under the direction of
The Vidyadhara Chogyam Trungpa, Rinpoche. It offers communal living and a
strong practice environment of daily
meditation and weekend programs. Four
shrine rooms accommodate all levels of
practitioners.
ADDRESS: 891 12th Street, Boulder, CO
   80302

PHONE: (303) 442-9980
LINEAGE: Karma Kagyu
SPIRITUAL HEAD: Vajra Regent Osel
Tendzin. Founded by the Vidyadhara,
the Ven. Chogyam Trungpa, Rinpoche.
RESIDENT DIRECTOR: Jeffrey R. Herrick
and Betsy de Castro
AFFILIATED WITH: Vajradhatu Interna-
tional/USA
ESTABLISHED: 1973
FACILITIES: Four shrine rooms, dorm,
and kitchen.
RETREATS OFFERED: Weekend sittings,
daily meditations, weekend programs
OPEN TO: General public

The Naropa Institute

Naropa Institute is a fully accredited, private, nonsectarian, upper-division college
offering undergraduate and graduate programs in the arts, social sciences, and
humanities. Buddhist and Western Psychology and Buddhist Studies are among
several Bachelor of Arts degree programs
and one-year Certificate programs offered
by the institute. Master's Degree programs are currently offered in Contemplative Psychotherapy, Buddhist Studies, and
Dance Therapy. The institute is located on
two-and-one-half acres in the center of
Boulder, Colorado. The three-building
campus, with surrounding grounds,
houses the Performing Arts Center, a
meditation hall, classrooms, faculty and
administrative offices, and the school
library.
ADDRESS: 2130 Arapahoe Avenue, Boulder, CO 80302
PHONE: (303) 444-0202
LINEAGE: Karma Kagyu
SPIRITUAL HEAD: Vajra Regent Osel
Tendzin. Founded by the Vidyadhara,
the Ven. Chogyam Trungpa, Rinpoche.
RESIDENT DIRECTOR: Chancellor, Barbara Dilley
ESTABLISHED: 1974

FACILITIES: The institute houses two meditation halls, one of which is always open during building hours for sitting meditation. In addition, five custom-built *Maitri* rooms are available for use by participants in the *Maitri* Space Awareness courses offered through the M.A. Dance Therapy and B.A. Psychology programs.

RETREATS OFFERED: To foster a sense of community among students, faculty, and administration, and to help articulate the educational vision on which the Naropoa community is based, one all-community practice day is scheduled during each quarter. Classes are suspended for this day, and the entire community is invited to participate in group practice, talks, and discussion. Housed in the same building as The Naropa Institute, Shambhala Training offers an intensive meditation program to the general public. Shambhala Training is based on an ancient tradition of enlightened warriorship, originating in Central Asia, in which qualities of gentleness and fearlessness are cultivated through meditation.

OPEN TO: General public

Nyingma Institute of Colorado

The Nyingma teachings of Tharthang Tulku give a comprehensive model for human development. Transmitted with care and dedication, the Nyingma teachings offer keys for living a meaningful life in a contemporary world. Learning to relax within the reality of our situation, we find opportunities for growth within difficulties, and we establish a foundation for making a genuine contribution to life.

ADDRESS: 1441 Broadway, Boulder, CO 80302

PHONE: (303) 443-5550

LINEAGE: Nyingma

SPIRITUAL HEAD: Tharthang Tulku, Rinpoche

RESIDENT DIRECTOR: Robert Pasternak, J.D., Michael Zimmerman, M.A.

AFFILIATED WITH: Nyingma Institute of Berkeley, California

ESTABLISHED: 1977

FACILITIES: Urban meditation center with solitary retreat facilities

RETREATS OFFERED: Regularly scheduled weekly meditation and year-round capacity for solitary retreats

OPEN TO: General public

Vajradhatu International/USA

Vajradhatu International is a world-wide organization of meditation and study centers based in Halifax, Nova Scotia. Its headquarters in the United States is in Boulder, Colorado. It was founded in 1970 by the Vidyadhara, the Venerable Chogyam Trungpa, Rinpoche.

ADDRESS: 1345 Spruce Street, Boulder, CO 80302

PHONE: (303) 444-0190

LINEAGE: Kagyu-Nyingma

SPIRITUAL HEAD: The Vidyadhara passed away at the age of 47 on April 4, 1987. He was the former abbot of the Surmang monasteries in Tibet and a meditation master of the Kagyu and Nyingma lineages. He held the degree of Khenpo, the equivalent of a Doctor of Divinity degree, and studied at Oxford University as a Spaulding Fellow. At the present time Vajradhatu International is directed by the Vidyadhara's Dharma heir, the Vajra Regent Osel Tendzin, and by the Vajradhatu Board of Directors, who also direct the Nalanda Foundation, a nonsectarian educational organization founded by the Vidyadhara.

RESIDENT DIRECTOR: David Sanford

AFFILIATED WITH: This is organizational headquarters

ESTABLISHED: 1970

FACILITIES: Vajradhatu has more than one hundred centers, called Dharmadhatus or Dharma Study Groups, throughout the United States, Canada, and Europe, offering programs in the study of Buddhist philosophy and psychology and the practice of meditation. Three rural centers, Karme-Choling in Vermont, Rocky Mountain Dharma Center in northern Colorado, and Gampo Abbey in Cape Breton, Nova Scotia, provide the opportunity to study and practice in a more contemplative environment.

OPEN TO: General public and members

Dharmadhatus
Dharma Study Groups (DSG)
Forming Dharma Study Groups (FDSG)
Under the Auspices of Vajradhatu International/USA

Generally, whenever you see one of these names, it indicates a center associated with Vajradhatu, although to add to the merry confusion, a few groups aligned with Karma Triyana Dharmachakra (see Woodstock, New York) are also called Study Group, or Dharma Study Group.

A Dharmadhatu is a center *legally* affiliated with Vajradhatu. In order to be designated as such, a group must consist of twenty-five or more dues-paying members, have been in existence for more than two years, and maintain separate space for its activities. Dharmadhatus offer classes, hold open houses for beginners, and conduct regularly scheduled periods of meditation.

Dharma Study Groups are similar to Dharmadhatus, although they do not yet enjoy legal affiliate status. In order to be designated a DSG, a group must have been in existence for from one to two years and have ten or more members from whom dues are being collected.

Forming Dharma Study Groups might be considered the first step in the long journey toward full-fledged Dharmadhatuhood. A FDSG is simply an aggregation of up to ten members who have been meeting to study and practice together for from one to two years. It's not officially an affiliate, but it is nonetheless a part of the Vajradhatu mandala. Bear in mind that none of the foregoing is written in stone. The Vajradhatu affiliate structure is a fairly loose and fluid one, and the ground rules, like all else in the phenomenal world, are subject to change. —Editor

Denver Dharmadhatu

Denver Dharmadhatu is a branch of Vajradhatu/USA. Regular sitting meditation hours are Wednesday evening (7:00–9:00 P.M.) and Sunday all day (9:00–12:00 A.M. and 2:00–5:00 P.M.). Meditation instruction is available but usually must be arranged. Denver Dharmadhatu's present location is quite close to downtown Denver. This Dharmadhatu is somewhat different than others since Boulder (national headquarters) and the retreat facilities of Rocky Mountain Dharma Center and Dorje Khyung Dzong are so close.

ADDRESS: 718 East 18th Avenue, Suite 222, Denver, CO 80203
PHONE: (303) 863-8366
LINEAGE: Karma Kagyu
SPIRITUAL HEAD: Vajra Regent Osel Tendzin. Founded by the Vidyadhara, the Ven. Chogyam Trungpa, Rinpoche.
RESIDENT DIRECTOR: Bill Shean
AFFILIATED WITH: Vajradhatu International/USA
ESTABLISHED: 1975
FACILITIES: Urban meditation center
RETREATS OFFERED: *Nyinthun* (all-day) and weekend sittings, evening practice, programs including practice for one or two days. Practice sessions every Wednesday and Sunday are open to the public. Vajrayana feasts are also held.
OPEN TO: General public

Drikung Kagyu Meditation Center

Drikung Kagyu Tibetan Meditation Center, under the direction of H. H. Kabyon Chetsang, Rinpoche, is located in a 6,200-square-foot renovated community center within walking distance of downtown Denver. In addition to traditional Vajrayana teachings, the center encourages meditation masters of other Buddhist lineages to conduct retreats. The center has established connections with American Indian medicine men and also offers courses in Tai Chi Chuan. The group maintains a country retreat facility in the nearby Rocky Mountains.
ADDRESS: 801 West 5th Avenue, Denver, CO 80203
PHONE: (303) 623-1507
LINEAGE: Drikung Kagyu
SPIRITUAL HEAD: H. H. Kabyon Chetsang, Rinpoche
RESIDENT DIRECTOR: Khenpo Konchog Gyaltshen, Rinpoche
AFFILIATED WITH: Autonomous
ESTABLISHED: 1987
FACILITIES: Urban meditation center with country retreat facilities.
RETREATS OFFERED: Chanting retreats, prostration retreats, *dathun* (thirty-day), *nyinthun* (one-day sitting), weekend sittings, supervised solitary retreats. Three-year retreats are planned. We hold a retreat at least once a month.
OPEN TO: Most retreats are open to the general public.

Dzog Chen Community of the Rockies

Dzog Chen Community of the Rockies is a group of students of Namkai Norbu, Rinpoche, who meet every two weeks to do group practice, including Chod, Ganapuja, Guruyoga, and Mantra Yoga. Focus is on supporting individuals who have received transmissions from Namkai Norbu in the Semde Longde and Upadesha series of teachings.
ADDRESS: 2220 East Colfax, Denver, CO 80206
PHONE: (303) 388-5171; 722-4039
LINEAGE: Dzog Chen
SPIRITUAL HEAD: Namkai Norbu (Tibetan)
RESIDENT DIRECTOR: None
AFFILIATED WITH: Autonomous
ESTABLISHED: 1987
FACILITIES: Member's home
RETREATS OFFERED: Seven to ten-day teaching and sitting retreat, once a year, when the teacher is here.
OPEN TO: General public

Udiyan Maitreya Kosha

Udiyan Maitreya Kosha was founded in 1979 by Lucille Schaible and her students. An American original, Ms. Schaible was a self-taught Vajra master. Recognized in her later years by the principals of the Nyingma lineage, she initiated the formation of Udiyan Maitreya Kosha and two of its projects, the Denver Center for Buddhist Studies and Mary's Lake Lodge, a center for spiritual renewal. The Denver Center is a residential community where classes in meditation, philosophy, psychology, self-healing, and related topics are offered. Mary's Lake Lodge is a mountain retreat and community of supporters near Estes Park, Colorado. All Udiyan Maitreya Kosha projects and teachings are oriented toward fostering the understanding and practice of Tibetan Buddhism of the Nyingma lineage and its appropriate Western presentation.
ADDRESS: 1440 High Street, Denver, CO 80218
PHONE: (303) 377-1592
LINEAGE: Nyingmapa
SPIRITUAL HEAD: Lucille Schaible (deceased)

RESIDENT DIRECTOR: Khenpo Palden Sherab, Rinpoche; Khenpo Tsewang Dongyal, Rinpoche.

ESTABLISHED: 1979

FACILITIES: Urban meditation center with country retreat

RETREATS OFFERED: Chanting retreats, weekend sittings, unsupervised solitary retreats, and, in the summer, a week-long retreat. Topic of the week-long retreat varies. Retreats are held two to five times per year.

OPEN TO: General public

Marys Lake Lodge/Udiyan Maitreya Kosha

Formerly a summer hotel in Estes Park, Colorado, Marys Lake Lodge was partially destroyed by fire in 1978. It has been purchased by Udiyan Maitreya Kosha and is currently being restored by members of the group, who hope to make of it "a cooperative residential and retreat center for the preservation of Tibetan Buddhism and the managed adaptation of this precious body of teachings as it roots itself in the human soil and psyche. . . . It is anticipated that Marys Lake Lodge will become a focus of Vajrayana training, a site for conferences, seminars, and meetings, not only for Buddhists but for all religions."

ADDRESS: Long's Peak Route, Estes Park, CO 80517

PHONE: (303) 586-5237

LINEAGE: Nyingmapa

SPIRITUAL HEAD: Lucille Schaible (deceased)

RESIDENT DIRECTOR: Kenpo Palden Sherab, Rinpoche; Khenpo Tsewang Dongyal, Rinpoche.

AFFILIATED WITH: Udiyan Maitreya Kosha of Denver, Colorado

ESTABLISHED: 1983

Marys Lake Lodge in Estes Park, Colorado, country retreat facility of Udiyan Maitreya Kosha.

FACILITIES: Country retreat facility and cooperative residence. Projected uses include year-round residences, religious ceremonies, educational classes, and public accommodations with supporting retail and convenience outlets, cottage industries, a greenhouse, professional offices, and day care facilities.
RETREATS OFFERED: Week-long summer retreats two to five times per year
OPEN TO: General public

Dorje Kyung Dzong

Located in southern Colorado on 400 acres of alpine meadows and woods, 8,500 feet up the slopes of Mount Greenhorn, DKD is a center for solitary retreat. There are six comfortable, well-equipped cabins. Retreatants bring their own food.
ADDRESS: 288 County Road, Farisita, CO 81037 (Mailing address: P.O. Box 35, Farisita, CO 81037)
PHONE: (No phone)
LINEAGE: Karma Kagyu
SPIRITUAL HEAD: Vajra Regent Osel Tendzin. Founded by the Vidyadhara, the Ven. Chogyam Trungpa, Rinpoche.
RESIDENT DIRECTOR: Donna McIntyre, retreat coordinator
AFFILIATED WITH: Vajradhatu International
FACILITIES: Six retreat cabins
RETREATS OFFERED: DKD is open year round for supervised solitary retreats
OPEN TO: Retreats are available to anyone in the general public who has a meditation practice of some kind, be it Zen, Vajrayana, Vipassana, etc. The center is for practitioners only.

Rocky Mountain Dharma Center

Rocky Mountain Dharma Center is a year-round contemplative center founded by the Vidyadhara, the Venerable Chogyam Trungpa, Rinpoche. Situated on 350 secluded acres of highland meadows and pine and aspen forests in the northern Colorado Rockies, RMDC provides an ideal setting for programs and retreats devoted to the study and practice of meditation. The mindfulness/awareness meditation taught at RMDC is a natural, intrinsic process of allowing the mind to discover the nature of thought, emotion, and physical sensation, thereby revealing the mind's inherent purity and profundity. With such a practice of uncovering one's inherent nature, the spiritual path of Buddhist training is based on real experience, rather than on belief alone. Programs throughout the year encompass practice of all three *yanas*.
ADDRESS: 4921 County Road 68C, Red Feather Lakes, CO 80545
PHONE: (303) 881-2530
LINEAGE: Karma Kagyu
SPIRITUAL HEAD: Vajra Regent Osel Tendzin. Founded by the Vidyadhara, the Ven. Chogyam Trungpa, Rinpoche.
RESIDENT DIRECTOR: Dan Hessey and Mary Ann Flood
AFFILIATED WITH: Vajradhatu International
ESTABLISHED: 1971
FACILITIES: A country retreat facility
RETREATS OFFERED: Prostration retreat, *dathun* (thirty-day sitting), supervised solitary retreats. Open year round.
OPEN TO: Members, as well as the general public, depending on the nature of the program.

CONNECTICUT

New Haven Dharma Study Group

The Dharma Study Group of New Haven offers ongoing classes for beginning, intermediate, and senior students, and monthly *nyinthuns* (full days of meditation). We host periodic weekend programs of practice and study, including

View of Marpa Point at the Rocky Mountain Dharma Center, Red Feather Lakes, Colorado.

Shambhala training. Our fundamental practice is Shamatha/Vipassana meditation, or mindfulness and awareness, as presented by Chogyam Trungpa, Rinpoche.
ADDRESS: 42 Hubinger Street, New Haven, CT 06516
PHONE: (203) 397-8528
LINEAGE: Karma Kagyu
SPIRITUAL HEAD: Vajra Regent Osel Tendzin. Founded by the Vidyadhara, the Ven. Chogyam Trungpa, Rinpoche.
RESIDENT DIRECTOR: Judy Robison
AFFILIATED WITH: Vajradhatu International/USA
ESTABLISHED: 1978
FACILITIES: Practice center based in coordinator's home
RETREATS OFFERED: Nyinthun (all-day sitting)
OPEN TO: General public

DISTRICT OF COLUMBIA

Tibetan Meditation Center

The Ven. Khenpo Konchog Gyaltshen is the spiritual director of the Washington Tibetan Meditation Center. He travels widely throughout North and South America, as well as Europe, giving teachings in the Drikung Kagyu lineage. Our center welcomes practitioners of all types, whether novice or beginner; we have daily practices, lectures, weekend retreats, and a wide range of activities. Specialties of the Drikung lineage are the *Phowa* (transmission of consciousness at the time of death), the *ngondro* (destroying the ego), and the Medicine Buddha (purifying body and mind). These practices are done via guided visualizations with a fully qualified lama.

ADDRESS: 5603 16th Street, Northwest, Washington, DC 20011
PHONE: (202) 829-0005
LINEAGE: Drikung Kagyudpa
SPIRITUAL HEAD: Khenpo Konchog Gyaltshen
RESIDENT DIRECTOR: Khenpo Konchog Gyaltshen
ESTABLISHED: 1982
FACILITIES: Urban meditation center
RETREATS OFFERED: Weekend retreat (monthly) and seven to nine-day retreats six times a year.
OPEN TO: Most retreats are open to the public. Some require empowerment.

Washington Dharmadhatu

Refer to Vajradhatu/USA, Boulder, Colorado, for a description.
ADDRESS: 4321 Van Ness Street, Northwest, Washington, DC 20016
PHONE: (202) 244-5740
LINEAGE: Karma Kagyu
SPIRITUAL HEAD: Vajra Regent Osel Tendzin. Founded by the Vidyadhara, the Ven. Chogyam Trungpa, Rinpoche.
AFFILIATED WITH: Vajradhatu International/USA
OPEN TO: General public

FLORIDA

Atlantic Beach Forming Study Group

Refer to Vajradhatu/USA, Boulder, Colorado, for description.
ADDRESS: 10 10th Street, Atlantic Beach, FL 32233
PHONE: (904) 249-8419
LINEAGE: Karma Kagyu
SPIRITUAL HEAD: Vajra Regent Osel Tendzin. Founded by the Vidyadhara, the Ven. Chogyam Trungpa, Rinpoche.
RESIDENT DIRECTOR: Donna and Ed Hanczaryk

AFFILIATED WITH: Vajradhatu International/USA
OPEN TO: General public

Jacksonville Dharma Study Group

The Jacksonville Dharma Study Group is a KTC affiliate under the direction of the Venerable Khenpo Karthar, Rinpoche. Group meditation practice, as well as the study of Karma Kagyu teachings, takes place at the center twice weekly. Shamatha (tranquility) meditation classes are taught periodically, and group practice is open to anyone interested. Introduction to Buddhism and Introduction to Meditation are two classes currently available through the center. These classes are offered several times a year.
ADDRESS: 7405 Arlington Expressway, Jacksonville, FL 32211 (Mailing address: 3319 Pine Street #7, Jacksonville, FL 32205)
PHONE: (904) 387-4925
LINEAGE: Karma Kagyu
SPIRITUAL HEAD: Gyalwa Karmapa
RESIDENT DIRECTOR: Ven. Khenpo Karthar, Rinpoche
AFFILIATED WITH: Karma Triyana Dharmachakra
ESTABLISHED: 1986
FACILITIES: Urban meditation center
RETREATS OFFERED: None currently
OPEN TO: General public

Tampa Karma Triyana Dharmachakra (KTC)

Tampa KTC was founded in 1985 as an affiliate center of the Karma Triyana Dharmachakra monastery center in Woodstock, New York. By the recognition of Khenpo Karthar, Rinpoche, and under his strict guidance, the practitioners of Tampa KTC are committed to bringing the teachings of Tibetan Buddhism to anyone who is interested in learning more about the true

teachings of the Buddha and how these teachings can be applied to modern life and contemporary society. The center members meet weekly throughout the year and sponsor major teachers, such as Khenpo Karthar, Thrangu, Rinpoche, and Khenpo Gyaltshen. We invite interested members of the community to participate in these activities by calling the center prior to visiting.
ADDRESS: 820 South MacDill, Tampa, FL 33609.
PHONE: (813) 870-2904
LINEAGE: Karma Kagyu
SPIRITUAL HEAD: His Holiness The Gyalwa Karmapa
RESIDENT DIRECTOR: Khenpo Karthar, Rinpoche
AFFILIATED WITH: Karma Triyana Dharmachakra
ESTABLISHED: 1985
FACILITIES: Urban meditation center
RETREATS OFFERED: Weekend and *dathun* (thirty-day) retreats.
OPEN TO: General public

GEORGIA

Dharmadhatu of Atlanta

This center offers Shamatha (tranquility) meditation instruction by trained instructors and classes in Hinayana (Theravada) and Mahayana Buddhism. Classes for students who have completed the Vajradhatu seminary are offered in Vajrayana Buddhism. Dharmadhatu has regularly scheduled Shamatha meditation periods on Wednesdays and Sundays.
ADDRESS: 1458 Highland Road, Atlanta, GA 30306 (Mailing address: C/O Williams, 645 Elmwood Drive, Atlanta, GA 30306)
PHONE: (404) 885-9637; 876-3733
LINEAGE: Karma Kagyu
SPIRITUAL HEAD: Vajra Regent Osel Tendzin. Founded by the Vidyadhara, the Ven. Chogyam Trungpa, Rinpoche.

RESIDENT DIRECTOR: Carol Williams and Logan Patterson
AFFILIATED WITH: Vajradhatu International/USA
FACILITIES: Urban meditation center
RETREATS OFFERED: *Nyinthun* (one-day) retreats, weekend sittings, and supervised solitary retreats. Retreats available on request.
OPEN TO: Members only

HAWAII

Honolulu Forming Dharma Study Group

Refer to Vajradhatu/USA, Boulder, Colorado for description.
ADDRESS: 2721 Kapiolani Boulevard, Apt. B, Honolulu, HI 96826
PHONE: (808) 944-1796
LINEAGE: Karma Kagyu
SPIRITUAL HEAD: Vajra Regent Osel Tendzin. Founded by the Vidyadhara, the Ven. Chogyam Trungpa, Rinpoche.
RESIDENT DIRECTOR: Phil Bralich
AFFILIATED WITH: Vajradhatu International/USA
OPEN TO: General public

Kagyu Thegchen Ling

Founded by the Very Venerable Kalu, Rinpoche, in 1974 as a venue for the study and practice of the Karma Kagyu tradition of Tibetan Buddhism, KTCL was the first such center in Hawaii. Since 1976 the Venerable Lama Karma Rinchen has been resident lama, overseeing instruction and practice on an individual and group basis for novices and experienced practitioners alike. Organized teaching schedules are maintained, and frequent special programs by visiting teachers, as well as a daily *puja* schedule are outlined in the newsletter *Empty Mirror*. There is a residential center in Honolulu and a retreat facility in the countryside. As one of the

four main branches of Tibetan Buddhism, the Karma Kagyu tradition emphasizes exploring the pure nature of mind through individual meditation practice. Many methods of meditation are therefore taught and practiced daily—each chosen by the lama according to the individual student's ability, predisposition, and experience.
ADDRESS: 2327 Liloa Rise, Honolulu, HI 96822
PHONE: (808) 941-8561
LINEAGE: Karma Kagyu
SPIRITUAL HEAD: Very Venerable Kalu, Rinpoche (Tibetan)
RESIDENT DIRECTOR: Lama Karma Rinchen (Tibetan)
AFFILIATED WITH: Autonomous
ESTABLISHED: 1974
FACILITIES: Urban meditation center. Country retreat facility.
RETREATS OFFERED: Chanting and prostration retreats, weekend sittings, supervised and unsupervised solitary retreats, *Vajrasattva* (purification) retreats, *Nyung Nes* (fasting) retreats, and Shamatha/Vipassana (tranquility and insight meditation) retreats.
OPEN TO: General public

Kagyu Thubten Choling

Kagyu Thubten Choling is a country retreat center that is presently a small group of practitioners and a support group sponsoring guest teachers for classes, meditation, and short retreats. Our long-range vision is to offer retreat space to individuals and groups who wish to follow up their instructions from teachers with concentrated practice, supported by the *sangha* here on Kauai. We are looking for a good permanent location, funds, and energy to create the retreat facilities, and a larger structure for group retreats and teaching. We are primarily Vajrayana practitioners with a special interest in Dzog

Chen. Any interested persons wishing to help create and expand the potential for our vision, should contact us and come to visit. Kauai is a beautiful, open space to develop your personal practice and offers supreme opportunity to integrate practice with a closeness to nature. Aloha!
ADDRESS: Ko'olau Road, Beach Access, Ko'olau, Kilauea, HI 96754 (Mailing address: P.O. Box 639, Kilauea, HI 96754)
PHONE: (808) 828-1324
LINEAGE: Tibetan Vajrayana / Dzog Chen
SPIRITUAL HEAD: Ven. Kalu, Rinpoche and Namkai Norbu
RESIDENT DIRECTOR: Visiting teachers only, at this time.
AFFILIATED WITH: Karma Thegchen Ling, Namkai Norbu Dzog Chen
ESTABLISHED: 1982
FACILITIES: Country retreat facility developing, meetings in member's home. Solitary retreats available soon.
RETREATS OFFERED: Retreats tailored to participant and teacher
OPEN TO: General public

Nechung Drayang Ling / Wood Valley Meditation Center

Nechung Drayang Ling is a nonsectarian Buddhist temple and retreat center in Wood Valley on the island of Hawaii. The temple and retreat established by the Ven. Nechung, Rinpoche, frequently host visits by high lamas of all lineages of Tibetan Buddhism. Weekend seminars and longer retreats focusing on specific areas of Buddhist practice are held here and are open to the public. Wood Valley Temple is a renovated Japanese temple, built at the turn of the century, in a plantation community five miles above the town of Pahala on the island of Hawaii. It is surrounded by forest and sugar cane fields and is at an elevation of 2,000 feet with a

cool, temperate climate. The retreat center, dedicated to Tara, is also a renovated Japanese temple which has been moved from the town of Pahala. When not in use for temple activities, facilities are available for other groups or individuals, at a nominal fee. There is also a small book and gift store.
ADDRESS: P.O. Box 250, Pahala, HI 96777
PHONE: (808) 928-8539
LINEAGE: Tibetan Buddhist (nonsectarian)
SPIRITUAL HEAD: Nechung, Rinpoche (Tibetan)
RESIDENT DIRECTOR: Marya Schwabe, administrative director
AFFILIATED WITH: Nechung Monastery, Dharamsala, India
ESTABLISHED: 1973
FACILITIES: Country retreat and temple
RETREATS OFFERED: Vipassana courses, supervised solitary retreats, teaching, and short-term guided retreats on specific practices. Schedule depends on when lamas are visiting or in residence.
OPEN TO: General public

Karma Rimay O Sal Ling

The Venerable Lama Tenzin teaches Buddhist philosophy and practice in the Tibetan tradition. His teachings are well versed in the three vehicles of the Buddha's teachings. The Maui Dharma Center has a daily practice of meditation and chanting the sutras in Tibetan and English. The city center is large enough to accommodate live-in students and overnight guests. The country retreat is strictly for individual and small group retreats. Vajrayana practice is introduced and taught at Lama Tenzin's discretion. Weekly teaching on Sundays is an ongoing tradition. The center publishes a monthly newsletter.

ADDRESS: P.O. Box 1029, Paia, HI 96779-1029
PHONE: (808) 579-8076
LINEAGE: Kagyu
SPIRITUAL HEAD: Ven. Kalu, Rinpoche
RESIDENT DIRECTOR: Ven. Lama Tenzin
ESTABLISHED: 1974
FACILITIES: Urban meditation center. Country retreat.
RETREATS OFFERED: Shamatha/Vipassana (tranquility and insight) and Nyung Nes (fasting) retreats of varying lengths of time.
OPEN TO: General public

IDAHO

The Open Path

The Open Path is a center for Eastern and Western Studies which sponsors study groups, workshops, and meditation led by local members and visiting teachers. In addition to meditation and other group activities, the center has limited accommodations for those seeking an environment conducive to unfoldment. The Open Path is also a publisher and world-wide distributor of fine Dharma books. While members of The Open Path recognize the efficacy of many methods, Holistic Clearing Meditation (a technique developed by the Ven. Namgyal, Rinpoche) is the center's main course of instruction. Designed specifically for this modern age, Holistic Clearing Meditation is a distillation of the best methods of Eastern meditation and Western psychology.

ADDRESS: 703 North 18th Street, Boise, ID 83702
PHONE: (208) 342-0208
LINEAGE: Karma Kagyu
SPIRITUAL HEAD: Ven. Namgyal, Rinpoche
AFFILIATED WITH: Autonomous
ESTABLISHED: 1976

FACILITIES: Urban meditation center.
Country retreat center. Solitary retreat
facilities.
RETREATS OFFERED: Intermittently,
with courses
OPEN TO: General public

ILLINOIS

Chicago Dharmadhatu

Public programs offered here include:
Open House Evenings, which are offered
weekly and consist of sitting meditation,
talks, and discussion; One Day Seminars;
and *nyinthuns*, or practice periods, during
which free meditation instruction is available. The current *nyinthun* schedule is
7:00–9:00 P.M. Thursdays and 9:00
A.M. until noon Sundays. We invite you to
practice with us at these times. Our book-
store carries all of Chogyam Trungpa,
Rinpoche's books and other Dharma and
Dharma-inspired books. It is open during
these same hours.
ADDRESS: 3340 North Clark Street, Chi-
cago, IL 60657
PHONE: (312) 472-7771
LINEAGE: Karma Kagyu
SPIRITUAL HEAD: Vajra Regent Osel
Tendzin. Founded by the Vidyadhara,
the Ven. Chogyam Trungpa, Rinpoche.
RESIDENT DIRECTOR: Marita
McLaughlin
AFFILIATED WITH: Vajradhatu Interna-
tional/USA
ESTABLISHED: 1973
OPEN TO: General public

Chicago Karma Thegsum Choling

Please refer to Karma Triyana Dharmachakra, Woodstock, New York, for a description of Karma Thegsum Choling.
ADDRESS: 1311 West Arthur, Chicago, IL
60626
PHONE: (312) 743-5134

LINEAGE: Karma Kagyu
SPIRITUAL HEAD: His Holiness The
Gyalwa Karmapa
RESIDENT DIRECTOR: Bob Bryant
AFFILIATED WITH: Karma Triyana
Dharmachakra, Woodstock, New York
OPEN TO: General public

INDIANA

Elkhart Forming Dharma Study Group

Refer to Vajradhatu/USA, Boulder, Colo-
rado, for a description.
ADDRESS: 13698 County Road 8, Mid-
dlebury, IN 46540
PHONE: (219) 825-2853
LINEAGE: Karma Kagyu
SPIRITUAL HEAD: Vajra Regent Osel
Tendzin. Founded by the Vidyadhara,
the Ven. Chogyam Trungpa, Rinpoche.
RESIDENT DIRECTOR: Catherine Mandt
AFFILIATED WITH: Vajradhatu Interna-
tional/USA
OPEN TO: General public

KENTUCKY

Lexington Dharmadhatu

Please refer to Vajradhatu/USA, Boulder,
Colorado, for a description.
ADDRESS: 208 Catalpa Road, Lexington,
KY 40502
PHONE: (606) 266-9714
LINEAGE: Karma Kagyu
SPIRITUAL HEAD: Vajra Regent Osel
Tendzin. Founded by the Vidyadhara,
the Ven. Chogyam Trungpa, Rinpoche
RESIDENT DIRECTOR: Bill Gordon and
S. Anelin-Wagner
AFFILIATED WITH: Vajradhatu Interna-
tional/USA
OPEN TO: General public

LOUISIANA

Baton Rouge Dharma Study Group

Please refer to Vajradhatu/USA, Boulder, Colorado, for a description.
ADDRESS: 442 Albert Hart, Baton Rouge, LA 70808
PHONE: (504) 766-3126
LINEAGE: Karma Kagyu
SPIRITUAL HEAD: Vajra Regent Osel Tendzin. Founded by the Vidyadhara, the Ven. Chogyam Trungpa, Rinpoche
RESIDENT DIRECTOR: Mary Derouen
AFFILIATED WITH: Vajradhatu International/USA
OPEN TO: General public

MAINE

Dharma Study Group

Dharma Study Group of Brunswick, Maine, is the Vajradhatu meditation center for southern Maine, serving the Portland-Augusta area. The center offers a regular schedule of group practice and weekly classes on the Kagyu Dharma.
ADDRESS: 98 Maine Street, Brunswick, ME 04011
PHONE: (207) 729-4204
LINEAGE: Kagyu
SPIRITUAL HEAD: Vajra Regent Osel Tendzin. Founded by the Vidyadhara, the Ven. Chogyam Trungpa, Rinpoche
RESIDENT DIRECTOR: Richard and Debbie Genz
AFFILIATED WITH: Vajradhatu
ESTABLISHED: 1984
FACILITIES: Urban meditation center
RETREATS OFFERED: Nyinthun and weekend sittings
OPEN TO: General public

Camden Forming Dharma Study Group

Please refer to Vajradhatu/USA, Boulder, Colorado, for a description.
ADDRESS: P. O. Box 884, Camden, ME 04843
LINEAGE: Karma Kagyu
SPIRITUAL HEAD: Vajra Regent Osel Tendzin. Founded by the Vidyadhara, the Ven. Chogyam Trungpa, Rinpoche
RESIDENT DIRECTOR: Nancy Hodson
AFFILIATED WITH: Vajradhatu International/USA
OPEN TO: General public

MARYLAND

Baltimore Dharma Study Group

Please refer to Vajradhatu/USA, Boulder, Colorado, for a description.
ADDRESS: 2125 Maryland Avenue, Baltimore, MD 21218
PHONE: (301) 233-5317
LINEAGE: Karma Kagyu
SPIRITUAL HEAD: Vajra Regent Osel Tendzin. Founded by the Vidyadhara, the Ven. Chogyam Trungpa, Rinpoche.
RESIDENT DIRECTOR: Mark Beckstrom
AFFILIATED WITH: Vajradhatu International
OPEN TO: General public

Kunzang Odsal Palyul Changchub Choeling/ The World Prayer Center

Palyul Choeling is a Vajrayana center practicing in the Nyingma tradition. In addition to a schedule of bi-weekly classes and monthly retreats, the center maintains a twenty-four-hour-a-day vigil of continuous prayer and practice for the earth in its shrine room, which also houses the largest private collection of quartz crystals in the country. Palyul Choeling practices accord-

Tulku Ahkon Norbu Lhamo, founder and director of Kunzang Odsal Palyal Changchub Choeling, and H. H. Penn, Rinpoche, Supreme Head of the Palyal Lineage of Nyingmapa Buddhism.

ing to the Nyingma sect of Vajrayana, emphasizing the Nam Cho revelations of Terton Migyur Dorje. Accumulation retreats for the preliminary practices of *ngundro* are frequently done, as well as other retreats.

ADDRESS: 18400 River Road, Poolesville, MD 20837
PHONE: (301) 428-8116
LINEAGE: Nyingma-Palyul
SPIRITUAL HEAD: H. H. Pedma Norbu, Rinpoche—Supreme Head of Palyul Lineage of Nyingmapa Sect (Tibetan)
RESIDENT DIRECTOR: Tulku Ahkon Norbu Lhamo (American)
AFFILIATED WITH: Autonomous
ESTABLISHED: 1983
FACILITIES: Urban meditation center with country retreat facility.

RETREATS OFFERED: Chanting retreat, prostration retreat, supervised solitary retreats offered at least once a month.
OPEN TO: General public as well as members

Sakya Phuntsok Ling Center for Tibetan Buddhist Studies and Meditation

The Sakya Center for Tibetan Buddhist Studies and Meditation provides a varied weekly schedule of classes in Buddhist philosophy, meditation, and Tibetan language, led by the Ven. Lama Kalsang Gyaltsen. In keeping with the Sakya lineage's traditional emphasis on both philosophical study and meditation, the center's teaching program integrates the study of classical Buddhist texts and their associated meditations. Both group and individual meditation and study are encouraged. Monthly weekend retreats are held. The Sakya Center offers a weekly class in Shamatha and Vipassana meditation; however, the main practice of the center focuses on traditional meditations and techniques of mind-training designed to develop altruism and compassion. These are based on both the Mahayana and Vajrayana traditions. For more advanced students, the Ven. Lama Kalsang provides instruction in Vajrayana meditation, including the foundation practices and various deity yogas with creation, completion, and recitations.

ADDRESS: 8715 First Avenue, #1501D, Silver Springs, MD 20910
PHONE: (301) 589-3115
LINEAGE: Sakya
SPIRITUAL HEAD: H. H. Sakya Trizen (Tibetan residing in India)
RESIDENT DIRECTOR: The Ven. Kalsang Gyaltsen (Tibetan)
AFFILIATED WITH: Palden Sakya
ESTABLISHED: 1986
FACILITIES: Urban meditation center using rented facilities for retreats
RETREATS OFFERED: Chanting retreat, weekend sittings, supervised solitary retreats once per month.
OPEN TO: Some retreats for members only; retreats in each style open to general public.

MASSACHUSETTS

Sakya Center for Buddhist Studies and Meditation

The Sakya Center for Buddhist Studies and Meditation sponsors teaching programs in Cambridge in Mahayana and Vajrayana studies by various teachers of the Sakya Order, including His Holiness Sakya Trizin, His Eminence Ludhing Khen, Rinpoche, His Eminence Chogye Trichen, Rinpoche, Jetsun Kusho La, and Jamyang Khyentse, Rinpoche. Lama Pema Wangdak, from New York City's Jetsun Sakya Center, visits on a monthly basis to lead group study and meditation. Founded by the late Deshung, Rinpoche, in 1980, the Sakya Center was encouraged by him to purchase a retreat center in Barre, Massachusetts, in 1985. We expect to have a full-time resident teacher in 1989 after the visit of His Holiness Sakya Trizin. Our practice includes training in concentration and insight meditation using various methods found in the Mahayana tradition. Also Vajrayana empowerments by qualified teachers enable practice of deity yoga. Group meditation includes Chenrezig, the Bodhisattva of Great Compassion, and the Ritual of Four Mandalas offered to Tara. The main practice of the Sakya tradition is the Lam-Dre or Path-Result teaching originated with the Mahasidda Birwapa. For more information contact Susan Fairclough at the Cambridge address, or David Rich (617) 876-1160 at the Barre, Massachusetts, address.

ADDRESS: Sakya Cholchor Yangtse Retreat Center, Barre, MA 01005 (Mailing address: P. O. Box 606, Porter Square Station, Cambridge, MA 02140)
PHONE: Cambridge (617) 492-5370; Barre (617) 355-2092
LINEAGE: Sakya Tibetan
SPIRITUAL HEAD: H. H. Sakya Trizin (Indian)
AFFILIATED WITH: Autonomous
ESTABLISHED: 1980
FACILITIES: Country retreat facility; rental in city for teaching programs
RETREATS OFFERED: Weekend study and meditation when announced
OPEN TO: Retreats for members only; teaching programs for general public.

Boston Drikung Dharma Meditation Center

Boston Drikung Dharma Meditation Center is an affiliate of the main center in Washington, D.C., under the auspices of H. H. Chetsang, Rinpoche. A group meets once a week to do the Tibetan meditation practices of *Vajrasattva, Chenrezig, Chud,* or *Phowa.* We have introductory tapes and videos by our lamas on the practices of *bodhicitta* (Loving Kindness) and on introductory Tibetan practices such as the Four Foundations. We also bring the lamas to Boston once or twice a year to give *Phowa* retreat or *Mahamudra* retreat and to give different Tibetan Buddhist teachings. Please write if you wish to be on our mailing list.

ADDRESS: 1709 Commonwealth Avenue, Brighton, MA 02135
PHONE: (617) 254-9029
LINEAGE: Drikung Kagyu (Tibetan Buddhist)
SPIRITUAL HEAD: The Drikung Gyabgyon—H. H. Chetsang, Rinpoche
RESIDENT DIRECTOR: Khampo Gyaltsang, Rinpoche
AFFILIATED WITH: Trikung Kagyu Meditation Center of Washington DC
ESTABLISHED: 1984
FACILITIES: Shrine Room in an apartment and rented facilities for retreats.
RETREATS OFFERED: Once a year a seven-day *Mahamudra* or *Phowa* retreat
OPEN TO: General public during nonrestricted events

Kagyu Tinley Kunchab

Kagyu Tinley Kunchab was founded by the Ven. Kalu, Rinpoche, in 1975, and since 1977 has been under the guidance of Lama Norlha, Kalu, Rinpoche's personal representative in the eastern United States. The foundation practices and the *Sadhanas* for Chenrezig, Tara, and Ma-

hakala are regularly performed at the center, which has been visited by H. H. the Gyalwa Karmapa, Jamgon Kontrul, Rinpoche, and other eminent lamas. Lama Norlha teaches at the center, and during his visits personal interviews with him can be arranged.

ADDRESS: 7 Athens Street, Cambridge, MA 02138
PHONE: (617) 868-5248
LINEAGE: Tibetan Buddhism
SPIRITUAL HEAD: Ven. Kalu, Rinpoche (Kagyu Shangpa Tibetan)
RESIDENT DIRECTOR: Lama Norlha often visits from Kagyu Thubten Choling, New York.
AFFILIATED WITH: Kagyu Thubten Choling, Wappingers Falls, New York
ESTABLISHED: 1975
FACILITIES: Member's home (urban)
OPEN TO: General public

Tsegyalgar Dzog Chen Community of America

Our organization is an international community of individuals of varied backgrounds, who come together to take teachings from the Master Namkhai Norbu, Rinpoche, approximately once a year. We have a house in Conway, Massachusetts, where we have small gatherings for practices throughout the year. Anyone who has read or heard of Norbu and is interested is welcome to participate in the community. We also try to host other lamas whose teachings might be helpful to us as students on the Dzog Chen path.

ADDRESS: Parson's Street (Mailing address: Box 221, RFD 1, Conway, MA 01341)
PHONE: (413) 369-4435
LINEAGE: Dzog Chen (Tibetan Buddhist)
SPIRITUAL HEAD: Namkhai Norbu, Rinpoche (Tibetan)

RESIDENT DIRECTOR: None
AFFILIATED WITH: Autonomous
ESTABLISHED: 1982 as a Dzog Chen center
FACILITIES: Country retreat facility; housing for members.
RETREATS OFFERED: Three to four-month long retreats or two-week retreats with master, when available.
OPEN TO: General public

Falmouth Dharma Study Group

Please refer to Vajradhatu/USA, Boulder, Colorado, for a description.
ADDRESS: 7 Firetower Road, Falmouth, MA 02540
LINEAGE: Karma Kagyu
SPIRITUAL HEAD: Vajra Regent Osel Tendzin. Founded by the Vidyadhara, the Ven. Chogyam Trungpa, Rinpoche
RESIDENT DIRECTOR: James and Meredith Luyten
AFFILIATED WITH: Vajradhatu International/USA
OPEN TO: General public

Mahasiddha Nyingmapa Center

We belong to the Nyingmapa Sect of Tibetan Buddhism. The emphasis is on individual daily practice and retreats. The traditional *ngondro* or preliminary practice is common to everyone. Individuals may receive additional instruction and practice according to their nature and capacity. We meet on an irregular basis for receiving teaching or practicing together as opportunities arise.
ADDRESS: East Mt. Road, Hawley, MA 01339
PHONE: (413) 339-8339
LINEAGE: Tibetan Nyingma Buddhist
SPIRITUAL HEAD: Dodrup-Chen, Rinpoche (Tibetan)
RESIDENT DIRECTOR: Tulku Thondup, Rinpoche

AFFILIATED WITH: Autonomous
ESTABLISHED: 1975
FACILITIES: Country retreat facility with accommodations for solitary retreats.
RETREATS OFFERED: Solitary and Tsok on the 10th and 25th
OPEN TO: Retreats open to members only; facilities open to general public.

The Institute for Mindfulness

Thubten Kalsang, Rinpoche, was recognized at the age of three as the fourth incarnation of the founding Abbot of Rahaur Monastery in eastern Tibet. After early study with scholars and tantric lamas in his own region, he travelled to Lhasa at the age of twelve to complete his education at Drepung Monastic University. In 1959, warned by a countryman of the danger from the Chinese, he escaped over the Himalayas on foot and by horseback to safety in Nepal. From there he joined the Dalai Lama and began further work at Sanskrit University and with the senior tutors of the Dalai Lama. In 1964 he travelled to Thailand as representative of the Dalai Lama and spent nearly ten years studying Thai Buddhism and preparing translations and papers. From Thailand he went to Japan, where he lived for seven years studying Zen and Shingon (Japanese Tantric) Buddhism, working as a scholar at Schuchin and Kyoto Universities. In 1979 he came to the United States and has held academic positions at the University of Massachusetts, Amherst College, and Tufts University. In 1982 he established the Institute for Mindfulness to promote the study of Buddhism and comparative philosophical practice. He is the only Tibetan lama teaching regularly in the Boston area, where he now makes his home. He is currently offering classes in Tibetan language and meditation.
ADDRESS: 161 Clifton Street, Malden, MA 02148

PHONE: (617) 324-3421
LINEAGE: Gelug and Nyingma sects
(Tibetan)
SPIRITUAL HEAD: Thubten Kalsang
(Tibetan)
RESIDENT DIRECTOR: Same
AFFILIATED WITH: Autonomous
ESTABLISHED: 1982
FACILITIES: Teacher's house
RETREATS OFFERED: Sunday meetings
and classes.
OPEN TO: General public

Boston Dharmadhatu

Please refer to Vajradhatu/USA, Boulder,
Colorado, for a description.
ADDRESS: 515 Centre Street, Newton
Corner, MA 02158
PHONE: (617) 965-2827
LINEAGE: Karma Kagyu
SPIRITUAL HEAD: Vajra Regent Osel
Tendzin. Founded by the Vidyadhara,
the Ven. Chogyam Trungpa, Rinpoche.
RESIDENT DIRECTOR: None
AFFILIATED WITH: Vajradhatu Interna-
tional/USA
OPEN TO: General public

Dharmadhatu

Dharmadhatu offers residents of the Pioneer Valley a place to practice and study
the Buddhadharma. We have regularly
scheduled introductory classes, and meditation instruction is free of charge. Dharmadhatu is located in downtown Northampton. Come sit with us.
ADDRESS: 25 Main Street, Northampton,
MA 01060
PHONE: (413) 584-6415
LINEAGE: Kagyu (Tibetan)
SPIRITUAL HEAD: Vajra Regent Osel
Tendzin. Founded by the Vidyadhara,
the Ven. Chogyam Trungpa, Rinpoche.
RESIDENT DIRECTOR: Arthur Jennings

AFFILIATED WITH: Vajradhatu Interna-
tional/USA
ESTABLISHED: 1976
FACILITIES: Urban meditation center
RETREATS OFFERED: Nyinthun (all-day
sitting)
OPEN TO: General public

MICHIGAN

Ann Arbor Karma Thegsum Choling

Ann Arbor KTC is a practice center for
those interested in the Karma Kagyu tradition of Tibetan Buddhism. We offer
courses to the public and a regular meditation schedule. Lamas from the lineage
visit on a regular basis. We practice the
Kagyu system of meditation as taught by
the Ven. Khenpo Karthar, Rinpoche. The
most basic practice is sitting meditation
(Shamatha). Those with the appropriate
empowerment practice Chenrezig (Bodhisattva of Compassion) meditation and
several other traditional Tibetan chanting
practices. More advanced students are
practicing the ngondro (foundation) meditations on an individual basis. On a group
basis, we offer traditional Tibetan prayers
for the benefit of all beings, as well as for
the long life of the lineage lamas, and for
the swift reappearance of H. H. Gyalwa
Karmapa.
ADDRESS: 734 Fountain, Ann Arbor, MI
48103
PHONE: (313) 761-7495
LINEAGE: Karma Kagyu (Tibetan)
SPIRITUAL HEAD: Ven. Khenpo Karthar, Rinpoche (Tibetan)
RESIDENT DIRECTOR: None
AFFILIATED WITH: Karma Triyana
Dharmachakra
ESTABLISHED: 1978
FACILITIES: Urban meditation center;
the center owns a house in Ann Arbor.

RETREATS OFFERED: All-day sitting meditation once a month
OPEN TO: General public

Jewel Heart Temple

No description available.
ADDRESS: 508 Cherry Street, Ann Arbor, MI 48103
PHONE: (313) 994-3387
LINEAGE: Tibetan lineage (other lineages are also represented).
SPIRITUAL HEAD: Gelek, Rinpoche, an incarnate lama from Tibet
RESIDENT DIRECTOR: Same
AFFILIATED WITH: Autonomous
ESTABLISHED: 1987
FACILITIES: Temple space; urban meditation center.
RETREATS OFFERED: Ongoing weekly teachings; weekend sittings in which teachings are presented.
OPEN TO: General public

Battle Creek Dharma Study Group

"The whole practice of meditation is based upon the present moment, here and now, and means working with this situation, this present state of mind. Every act of our lives can contain simplicity and precision and thus can have tremendous beauty and dignity" (Chogyam Trungpa, Rinpoche, *The Myth of Freedom*) We are a very small group that gathers once a week in a member's home for group sitting and study.
ADDRESS: 139 Jericho, Battle Creek, MI 49017
PHONE: (616) 965-6150
SPIRITUAL HEAD: Vajra Regent Osel Tendzin. Founded by the Vidyadhara, the Ven. Chogyam Trungpa, Rinpoche.
RESIDENT DIRECTOR: Robert Brown

AFFILIATED WITH: Vajradhatu, Halifax, Nova Scotia
ESTABLISHED: 1975
FACILITIES: Member's home
RETREATS OFFERED: One day a week sitting and study

Heart Center KTC

Under the direction of Ven. Khenpo Karthar, Rinpoche, abbot of Karma Triyana Dharmachakra Monastery in Woodstock, New York, the center offers instruction and weekly practice sessions in basic sitting meditation. Teachings by visiting lamas are presented on a regular basis. *Shinay* (Shamatha) sitting meditation according to the methods of the Karma Kagyu lineage of Tibetan Buddhism is presently emphasized at the center.
ADDRESS: 315 Marion Avenue, Big Rapids, MI 49307
PHONE: (616) 796-2398
LINEAGE: Kagyu
SPIRITUAL HEAD: H. H. Gyalwa Karmapa
RESIDENT DIRECTOR: None
AFFILIATED WITH: Karma Triyana Dharmachakra, Woodstock, New York
ESTABLISHED: 1985
FACILITIES: Urban meditation center with country retreat facility; accommodations for solitary retreats.
RETREATS OFFERED: Unsupervised solitary retreats, family Dharma weekend; scheduling of retreats varies.
OPEN TO: Members as well as the general public

Ann Arbor Dharma Study Group

Please refer to Vajradhatu/USA, Boulder, Colorado, for a description.
ADDRESS: 126 West Harrison, Royal Oak, MI 48067
LINEAGE: Karma Kagyu

SPIRITUAL HEAD: Vajra Regent Osel
Tendzin. Founded by the Vidyadhara,
the Ven. Chogyam Trungpa, Rinpoche
RESIDENT DIRECTOR: Clive Smolana
AFFILIATED WITH: Vajradhatu International/USA
OPEN TO: General public

MINNESOTA

Twin Cities Dharma Study Group

The Twin Cities Dharma Study Group is
under the auspices of the Ven. Chogyam
Trungpa, Rinpoche, who is now deceased. His Dharma Heir, Osel Tendzin,
an American-born teacher, now resides
in Nova Scotia and remains our teacher.
The teachings are of the Tibetan Vajrayana
style. Meditation practice is basic Shamatha/Vipassana, which involves posture, attitude, and watching the breath. We also
offer Shambhala Training every couple of
months, which is instruction in meditation as it relates to our life from a nonsectarian point of view.
ADDRESS: 3314 Emerson South, Minneapolis, MN 55408
PHONE: (612) 825-4703
LINEAGE: Kagyu
SPIRITUAL HEAD: Vajra Regent Osel
Tendzin. Founded by the Vidyadhara,
the Ven. Chogyam Trungpa, Rinpoche
RESIDENT DIRECTOR: Tom and Viki
Adducci
AFFILIATED WITH: Autonomous
ESTABLISHED: 1984
FACILITIES: One evening per week
meditation practice and study
OPEN TO: General public

Sakya Thupton Dargye Ling

Sakya Thupten Dargye Ling is a Tibetan
Buddhist meditation center established in
1978 upon the encouragement of H. H.
Sakya Trizin, who visited briefly in the
Twin Cities earlier that year. His Eminence, the late Deshung, Rinpoche, became the Abbot of the center and provided guidance until his death in 1987.
Activities sponsored by this center have
included group meditation, teachings, and
empowerments by visiting lamas. Due to
a very small membership, the center is
currently rather inactive, its members
gathering only occasionally for group
meditation.
ADDRESS: 1615 Bruce Avenue, Roseville,
MN 55113
PHONE: (612) 633-0019
LINEAGE: Sakya Sect (Tibetan)
SPIRITUAL HEAD: H. H. Sakya Trizin
(Tibetan Head of the Sakya Sect)
RESIDENT DIRECTOR: None
AFFILIATED WITH: Autonomous
ESTABLISHED: 1979
FACILITIES: Urban meditation center
OPEN TO: General public

MISSOURI

Kongosatta-In, Tendai Buddhist Mission

Kongosatta-In, Tendai Buddhist Mission
teaches the study and practice of Japanese
Vajrayana Buddhism as found within the
Tendai denomination. Personal instruction and initiation in Tendai Mikkyo is offered to members only. Public instruction
and seminars are periodically offered.
There is practice of the "Esoteric Nembutsu," involving recitation of the Sacred
Name of Amida Buddha, while visualizing
the image and characteristics of Amida for
periods of several hours. We also offer
practice of the Esoteric Ritual Meditations, involving the use of *mudra*, mantra,
and visualization, including the Vajradhatu Mandala and the Garbhakosadhatu
Mandala.
ADDRESS: P. O. Box 212, Cape Girardeau, MO 63702-0212
PHONE: (314) 334-1492

LINEAGE: Tendai
SPIRITUAL HEAD: Archbishop Jion
Haba (Japanese)
RESIDENT DIRECTOR: Reverend Jikai
(American-born)
AFFILIATED WITH: Rei'Sho'In Temple,
Tokyo, Japan
ESTABLISHED: 1976
FACILITIES: Small urban center for
group meditation
RETREATS OFFERED: Chanting retreat,
prostration retreat, a "Day of Mindful-
ness," weekend sittings, seminars; of-
fered on request.
OPEN TO: Members only

Dharma Study Group
KCDSG conducts an open house on the
last Friday of each month, which includes
a presentation on the practice of meditation in daily life, followed by a discussion
period and an informal gathering with
members of the Dharma Study Group.
Refreshments are served, and the public is
invited. Meditation is Thursdays at 7:00
P.M. and Sundays from 9:00 A.M. to
noon and 1:30 to 4:30 P.M.
ADDRESS: 1701-1/2 Westport Road (Mail-
ing address: 5309 Northwest 59 Terr.,
Kansas City, MO 64111)
PHONE: (816) 587-8260
LINEAGE: Nyingma/Kagyu (Tibetan)
SPIRITUAL HEAD: Vajra Regent Osel
Tendzin. Founded by the Vidyadhara,
the Ven. Chogyam Trungpa, Rinpoche
AFFILIATED WITH: Vajradhatu
ESTABLISHED: 1977
FACILITIES: Urban meditation center
RETREATS OFFERED: Working person's
evening and weekend meditation
OPEN TO: General public

St. Louis Dharma Study Group
Please refer to Vajradhatu/USA, Boulder,
Colorado, for a description.

ADDRESS: 1167 B Appleseed Lane, Oliv-
ette, MO 63132
PHONE: (314) 997-0014
LINEAGE: Karma Kagyu
SPIRITUAL HEAD: Vajra Regent Osel
Tendzin. Founded by the Vidyadhara,
the Ven. Chogyam Trungpa, Rinpoche
RESIDENT DIRECTOR: Jeffrey Wilson
AFFILIATED WITH: Vajradhatu Interna-
tional/USA
OPEN TO: General public

MCFP Dharma Study Group
Please refer to Vajradhatu/USA, Boulder,
Colorado, for a description.
ADDRESS: Chaplain's Office, P. O. Box
4000, Springfield, MO 65808
LINEAGE: Karma Kagyu
SPIRITUAL HEAD: Vajra Regent Osel
Tendzin. Founded by the Vidyadhara,
the Ven. Chogyam Trungpa, Rinpoche
AFFILIATED WITH: Vajradhatu Interna-
tional/USA
FACILITIES: Prison Dharma center
OPEN TO: General public

MONTANA

Osel Shen Phen Ling
We hold two weekly meditation sessions,
video showings, and weekend meditation
retreats.
ADDRESS: P. O. Box 7604, Missoula,
MT 59807
PHONE: (406) 542-2110
LINEAGE: Gelugpa/Vajrayana (Tibetan)
SPIRITUAL HEAD: Lama Thubten Yeshe
and Lama Thubten Zopa, Rinpoche
RESIDENT DIRECTOR: Carleen Gonder
FACILITIES: Meditation building, li-
brary, dorm, kitchen.
RETREATS OFFERED: Weekend medita-
tion retreats
OPEN TO: General public

New Jersey

Mahayana Sutra and Tantra Center

The Mahayana Sutra and Tantra Centers of Howell, New Jersey, and Washington, D.C., were founded by Sermey Geshe Lobsang Tharchin, a graduate of Sermey Sutra (1929–1953) and Gyumey Tantric (1953–1959) monastic universities of Lhasa, Tibet. Geshe Tharchin teaches daily, in English, from the traditional classics of Buddhism. Classes are free of charge and open to all. Summer retreat is held yearly, usually concentrating on tantric practice (permission required). Tibetan language practice is stressed. Washington Center features intensive weekends with Geshe Tharchin once monthly. Monks' "Sojong" and bi-weekly Vajra Yogini rituals held on a regular basis. There is ongoing translation activity, a center press for publications, and an active program for support of Sera Mey Monastery in India. Meditation is taught directly from the original Buddhist texts and is practiced from both the sutra and tantra points of view. Main emphasis is on students learning to meditate at the center and then practicing at home on their own.
ADDRESS: 216A West Second Street, Howell, NJ 07731
PHONE: (201) 364-1824
LINEAGE: Mainly Gelukpa, but many of our teachings come from other traditions.
SPIRITUAL HEAD: Sermey Geshe Lobsang Tharchin (Tibetan)
RESIDENT DIRECTOR: None
AFFILIATED WITH: We are the headquarters, but we also have a branch center: Mahayana Sutra and Tantra Center of Washington, 1917 Rookwood Road, Silver Springs, MD 20910; (301) 585-4575.

ESTABLISHED: 1975
FACILITIES: Traditional Buddhist temple in Mongolian-American community.
RETREATS OFFERED: Annual group summer retreat and individual supervised retreats at request of student.
OPEN TO: General public

Tashe Lhunpo

Rev. T. Dakpa leads joined prayers or chantings in the organization. He will answer all questions about Buddhism.
ADDRESS: 12 Kalmuk Road, Howell, NJ 07731
PHONE: (201) 363-6012
LINEAGE: Gelug (the Yellow Hat)
SPIRITUAL HEAD: Rev. Tenzing Dakpa (Tibetan)
RESIDENT DIRECTOR: Same
AFFILIATED WITH: Autonomous
ESTABLISHED: 1955
FACILITIES: Facilities for solitary retreat
RETREATS OFFERED: Chanting retreats
OPEN TO: General public

Tibetan Buddhist Learning Center

The Tibetan Buddhist Learning Center was founded by Geshe Wangyal in 1958. The TBLC's approach is to convey to its students a basic knowledge of the many facets of Tibetan Buddhism. The classes are taught in English by both the resident Tibetan monk-scholars and associated American scholars. The primary aim is to develop a Buddhism that is culturally American and, at its heart, not different from the Buddhism that travelled from India throughout Asia, going in the eigth century to Tibet and from there in the twentieth century to America.
ADDRESS: Box 306A R.D. 1, Angen Road, Washington, NJ 07882-9767
PHONE: (201) 689-6080 (9:00 A.M. to 7:00 P.M.)

LINEAGE: Buddhist
SPIRITUAL HEAD: H. H. the Dalai Lama
RESIDENT DIRECTOR: We have four resident Geshes (monk-scholars) who teach in conjunction with our American scholars.
AFFILIATED WITH: Autonomous
ESTABLISHED: 1958
FACILITIES: Country retreat facility
RETREATS OFFERED: No retreats given; only classes and seminars.

NEW MEXICO

Albuquerque Forming Dharma Study Group

Please refer to Vajradhatu/USA, Boulder, Colorado, for a description.
ADDRESS: 10617 Cielo Vista Del Norte Northwest, Albuquerque, NM 87048
LINEAGE: Karma Kagyu
SPIRITUAL HEAD: Vajra Regent Osel Tendzin. Founded by the Vidyadhara, the Ven. Chogyam Trungpa, Rinpoche
RESIDENT DIRECTOR: Carol Hoy
AFFILIATED WITH: Vajradhatu International/USA
OPEN TO: General public

Karma Thegsum Choling, Albuquerque

Karma Thegsum Choling is a Tibetan Buddhist meditation center under the direction of Khenpo Karthar, Rinpoche, representative of H. H. the 16th Gyalwa Karmapa, Supreme Head of the Kagyu Lineage. We own our meditation center, with room enough for forty or more meditators at one time. We have regular evening practice every Tuesday and Sunday, as well as every new and full moon. We also offer children's classes on Sunday mornings. A three-week class in Shamatha (sitting) meditation is offered beginning the first Tuesday of every month at 6:30

P.M. This class is geared both toward those with an interest in continuing in Buddhism and those interested in learning the technique only. We also offer Sadhana practices involving visualization and mantra. Several lamas visit in the course of the year to give deeper instruction in meditation.
ADDRESS: 139 La Plata Northwest, Albuquerque, NM 87107
PHONE: (505) 344-7611; 299-0275
LINEAGE: Karma Kagyu
SPIRITUAL HEAD: Khenpo Karthar, Rinpoche (Tibetan)
RESIDENT DIRECTOR: None
AFFILIATED WITH: Karma Triyana Dharmachakra
ESTABLISHED: 1982
FACILITIES: Country retreat facility. There is an affiliated retreat center less than one hour away.
RETREATS OFFERED: Weekend sittings once or twice a year
OPEN TO: General public

Cerrillos Karma Thegsum Choling Retreat Center

Please refer to Karma Triyana Dharmachakra, Woodstock, New York, for a description of Karma Thegsum Choling.
ADDRESS: Box 31, Cerrillos, NM 87010
LINEAGE: Karma Kagyu
SPIRITUAL HEAD: H. H. the Gyalwa Karmapa
RESIDENT DIRECTOR: Kintzinger and Bailey
AFFILIATED WITH: Karma Triyana Dharmachakra
OPEN TO: General public

Kagyu Shenpen Kunchab

Kagyu Shenpen Kunchab is a residential Dharma center with three houses and a sixty-five-foot stupa containing a shrine room, located on two acres of land on the

outskirts of Santa Fe. There are regular daily meditations inside the stupa led by Lama Karma Dorje, as well as frequent teachings by visiting lamas.
ADDRESS: 751 Airport Road, Santa Fe, NM 87501
PHONE: (505) 471-1152
LINEAGE: Kagyu
SPIRITUAL HEAD: Kalu, Rinpoche
RESIDENT DIRECTOR: Lama Karma Dorje
AFFILIATED WITH: Kagyu Dharma
ESTABLISHED: 1978
FACILITIES: Urban meditation center
OPEN TO: General public

NEW YORK

Albany Dharma Study Group
Our group presently consists of senior students of the Ven. Chogyam Trungpa, Rinpoche. Hinayana, Mahayana, and Vajrayana group practices are available on a bi-monthly basis. Meditation instruction and classes are available for new students.
ADDRESS: 98 McKown Road, Albany, NY 12203
PHONE: (518) 459-4942
LINEAGE: Kagyu
SPIRITUAL HEAD: Vajra Regent Osel Tendzin. Founded by the Vidyadhara, the Ven. Chogyam Trungpa, Rinpoche.
RESIDENT DIRECTOR: Linda Kaufman and Bob Temple
AFFILIATED WITH: Vajradhatu International/USA
FACILITIES: Center in student's home

Albany Karma Thegsum Choling
Albany KTC is an affiliate of Karma Triyana Dharmachakra, the seat of H. H. Gyalwa Karmapa in North America. The Albany center offers Chenrezig, Sadhana, and Shamatha meditation every Monday evening. On Wednesdays the center offers

Shamatha meditation followed by group discussion or taped teachings. Seminars are given by visiting lamas several times a year. Meditation instruction is also available.
ADDRESS: 637 Washington Avenue, Albany, NY 12206
PHONE: (518) 489-2151
LINEAGE: Karma Kagyu (Tibetan)
SPIRITUAL HEAD: Khenpo Karthar, Rinpoche (Tibetan)
RESIDENT DIRECTOR: Laura M. Roth
AFFILIATED WITH: Karma Triyana Dharmachakra
ESTABLISHED: 1979
FACILITIES: Urban meditation center
RETREATS OFFERED: All-day sitting once a month
OPEN TO: General public

Syracuse Forming Dharma Study Group
Anyone interested in Vajrayana Buddhism and specifically the teachings of Chogyam Trungpa, Rinpoche, is more than welcome to help us develop the Dharma Study Group.
ADDRESS: 8818 Wandering Way, Baldwinsville, NY 13027
PHONE: (315) 635-7154
LINEAGE: Kagyu Nyingma (Tibetan)
SPIRITUAL HEAD: Vajra Regent Osel Tendzin. Founded by the Vidyadhara, the Ven. Chogyam Trungpa, Rinpoche
RESIDENT DIRECTOR: Madalyn Smith
AFFILIATED WITH: Vajradhatu
ESTABLISHED: 1977
FACILITIES: Private homes
RETREATS OFFERED: Sitting, when there is interest.
OPEN TO: General public

Dharma Study Group of Buffalo
Dharma Study Group is a Buddhist meditation center affiliated with Vajradhatu, an

international association of meditation centers founded by the Ven. Chogyam Trungpa, Rinpoche. Dharma Study Group offers sitting meditation, meditation instruction, open houses, and meditation intensives at no charge, as well as public classes and tape series on the study of Buddhist philosophy, psychology, and the practice of meditation.

ADDRESS: 50 Greenfield Street, Buffalo, NY 14214 (Mailing address: 299 Clearfield, Williamsville, NY 14221)
PHONE: (716) 837-0804; 688-1924
LINEAGE: Karma Kagyu
SPIRITUAL HEAD: Vajra Regent Osel Tendzin. Founded by the Vidyadhara, the Ven. Chogyam Trungpa, Rinpoche.
RESIDENT DIRECTOR: Ellen Rook and Philip Richman
AFFILIATED WITH: Vajradhatu
ESTABLISHED: 1984
FACILITIES: Urban meditation center. Karme Choling is the nearest Vajradhatu retreat facility.
RETREATS OFFERED: *Nyinthuns* once a month
OPEN TO: General public

Urgyen Cho Dzong

Located in the northern Catskill Mountains near Greenville, New York, Urgyen Cho Dzong is a traditional Nyingmapa practice center. Nyingma teachers are now in residence to instruct and assist practitioners. Seminars and retreats, under the guidance of H. E. Shenphen Dawa are attended by students from North America, Europe, and Asia. There are comfortable accommodations for one hundred people. The center maintains facilities for private retreat. While most of our activities are open to the general public, occasional seminars are reserved for initiates only. Practices: Dzog Chen, Tibetan teaching of "great perfection," effortless realization of the absolute nature approached through

the direct transmission of the Guru's Mind. Preliminary practice is required, consisting of the 500,000 practices (refuge, Bodhicitta, Prostrations, Vajrasattva, Mandala, and Guru Yoga). Emphasis on visualization and breathing practices.
ADDRESS: Box 555, Greenville, NY 12083
PHONE: (518) 966-4727
LINEAGE: Nyingmapa
SPIRITUAL HEAD: H. E. Shenphen Dawa (Tibetan)
RESIDENT DIRECTOR: Khenpo Palden Sherab (Tibetan)
AFFILIATED WITH: Yeshe Nyingpo, New York, New York
ESTABLISHED: 1980
FACILITIES: Urban meditation center with country retreat facility offering accommodations for solitary retreats.
RETREATS OFFERED: Weekend sittings, supervised solitary retreats, retreat seminars of Anu and Ati Yoga offered six to ten times a year.
OPEN TO: Both members and general public

Gaden Tenzin Ling
No description available.
ADDRESS: 120 West State Street, Ithaca, NY 14850
PHONE: (607) 273-4859
LINEAGE: Gelugpa
SPIRITUAL HEAD: H. H. Kyabje Ling, Rinpoche, H. H. Kyabje Trijang, Rinpoche, H. H. Kyabje Song, Rinpoche
RESIDENT DIRECTOR: President, Chip Aiello

Ithaca Dharma Study Group
Please refer to Vajradhatu/USA, Boulder, Colorado, for a description.
ADDRESS: 602 Mitchell Street, Ithaca, NY 14850
PHONE: (607) 272-0534
LINEAGE: Karma Kagyu

SPIRITUAL HEAD: Vajra Regent Osel
Tendzin. Founded by the Vidyadhara,
the Ven. Chogyam Trungpa, Rinpoche
RESIDENT DIRECTOR: L. Warner
AFFILIATED WITH: Vajradhatu Interna-
tional/USA
OPEN TO: General public

Dharmadhatu of New York

Dharmadhatu is a Buddhist meditation
center founded by the Vidyadhara the
Ven. Chogyam Trungpa, Rinpoche, and
currently under the direction of his
Dharma heir, and the President of Vajradhatu, the Vajra Regent Osel Tendzin.
Dharmadhatu offers free instruction in
meditation, is open for practice six days a
week, and provides a full range of classes
and seminars for the study and experience
of the Buddhist path. The basic meditation practice at Dharmadhatu is Shamatha-
Vipassana as transmitted through the Mahamudra and Maha Ati lineages of the
Kagyu and Nyingma traditions. Advanced
students move on to the *ngondro* and *Sadhana* after further training at the Vajradhatu seminary and approval by the Vajra
Regent Osel Tendzin. The discipline of
Shamatha, or sitting meditation, involves
specific points of posture with regard to
the body, attention to the out-breath,
and directions for how to relate to one's
thoughts, emotions, and perceptions. In-
struction on how to actually practice is
given free each Tuesday night at 6:30 P.M.
ADDRESS: 49 East 21st Street, New York,
NY 10010
PHONE: (212) 673-7340
LINEAGE: Karma Kagyu
SPIRITUAL HEAD: Vajra Regent Osel
Tendzin. Founded by the Vidyadhara,
the Ven. Chogyam Trungpa, Rinpoche
RESIDENT DIRECTOR: Randall B.
Sunday
AFFILIATED WITH: Vajradhatu Interna-
tional/USA
ESTABLISHED: 1970

FACILITIES: Urban meditation center
with country retreat facility
RETREATS OFFERED: All types of group
and individual retreats
OPEN TO: Primarily members only (with
exceptions)

Karma Thegsum Choling

Karma Thegsum Choling is a Tibetan
Buddhist meditation and study center established in 1976 by H. H. the 16th
Gyalwa Karmapa, head of the Karma Kagyu Lineage. The Ven. Khenpo Karthar,
Rinpoche, who resides in Woodstock,
New York, at Karma Triyana Dharma-
chakra, was appointed by His Holiness to
direct the Karma Thegsum Choling cen-
ters in North and South America. Tibetan
Buddhism is a disciplined practice of men-
tal development designed to awaken our
inherent wisdom of the true nature of re-
ality and our compassion for all sentient
beings.
ADDRESS: 412 West End Avenue, #5N,
New York, NY 10024
PHONE: (212) 580-9282
LINEAGE: Karma Kagyu (Tibetan)
SPIRITUAL HEAD: H. H. the Gyalwa
Karmapa and Ven. Khenpo Karthar,
Rinpoche (Tibetan)
RESIDENT DIRECTOR: None
AFFILIATED WITH: Karma Triyana
Dharmachakra
ESTABLISHED: 1976
FACILITIES: Urban meditation center
using rented facilities
RETREATS OFFERED: All-day sitting
meditation; schedule will vary.
OPEN TO: General public

Yeshe Nyingpo

H. E. Shenphen Dawa teaches the Nyingmapa Tantric path of realization according
to the instruction given him by his father,
H. H. Dudjom, Rinpoche (deceased),
founder of Yeshe Nyingpo and past su-

Khenpo Karthar, Rinpoche, currently the principal teacher at Karma Triyana Dharma Chakra, Woodstock, New York, as well as the spiritual head of all Karma Thegsum Choling Affiliate Centers.

preme head of the Nyingmapa tradition. This incorporates the yogas of breathing and visualization and the meditation practice of Dzog Chen (Great Perfection). These practices lead directly to the accom-plishment of Rainbow Body in this life-time. The basic meditation foundation practice is called *Shi-nye* (Shamatha), and it is practiced in many styles to achieve the calm detachment that leads to awareness of one's own thoughts and their inherent insubstantiality. The practice may require open or closed eyes, concentration on the breath, or on an object such as a seed syllable or colored dot or nothing at all. Another practice is the prostration, similar to the sun exercise. One is able to physically offer the body, speech, and mind to the Triple Gem. While doing the physical prostration saluting *samsara* and Nirvana, one recites a special prayer and maintains a specific visualization. This brings body, speech, and mind into a single focus of devotion.

ADDRESS: 19 West 16th Street, New York, NY 10011
PHONE: (212) 691-8523
LINEAGE: Nyingmapa
SPIRITUAL HEAD: H. E. Shenphen Dawa (Tibetan)
RESIDENT DIRECTOR: Khenpo Palden Sherab and Khenpo Tsewang Dongyal (Tibetan brothers)
AFFILIATED WITH: Autonomous
ESTABLISHED: 1976
FACILITIES: Urban meditation center with country retreat facility and accommodations for solitary retreats.
RETREATS OFFERED: Solitary retreats and retreat seminars year-round on all aspects of practice—offered at least once a month.
OPEN TO: Members only or general public with permission

Rochester Study Group

Please refer to Karma Triyana Dharmachakra, Woodstock, New York, for a description of Karma Thegsum Choling.
ADDRESS: 315 Gregory Street, Rochester, NY 14620
PHONE: (716) 461-0130
LINEAGE: Karma Kagyu
SPIRITUAL HEAD: H. H. the Gyalwa Karmapa
RESIDENT DIRECTOR: MacKenzie Stuart

AFFILIATED WITH: Karma Triyana Dharmachakra
OPEN TO: General public

Woodstock Karma Thegsum Choling

Please refer to Karma Triyana Dharmachakra, Woodstock, New York, for a description of Karma Thegsum Choling.
ADDRESS: 9A Pine Grove Street, Woodstock, NY 12498
PHONE: (914) 679-6211
LINEAGE: Karma Kagyu
SPIRITUAL HEAD: H. H. the Gyalwa Karmapa
RESIDENT DIRECTOR: None
AFFILIATED WITH: Karma Triyana Dharmachakra
OPEN TO: General public

Karma Triyana Dharmachakra

Karma Triyana Dharmachakra is the North American seat of H. H. the Gyalwa Karmapa, head of the Karma Kagyu school of Tibetan Buddhism. Founded in 1978, it offers traditional teachings as transmitted by the Kagyu lineage meditation masters since the tenth century. The center is located on a twenty-acre site in the Catskill Mountains above Woodstock, New York, surrounded by forests, meadows, and streams. Ven. Khenpo Karthar, Rinpoche, Abbot of Karma Triyana Dharmachakra, and the Ven. Bardor Tulku, Rinpoche, are the distinguished resident lamas appointed by H. H. Karmapa. Seminars on Buddhist philosophy, psychology, and meditation practice are offered by resident and guest teachers throughout the year. All are welcome to take advantage of the rare opportunity to study and practice Buddhism in a traditional environment. We are building a traditional Tibetan-style monastery, including a library.

ADDRESS: 352 Meads Mtn. Road, Wood-
stock, NY 12498
PHONE: (914) 679-5906
LINEAGE: Karma Kagyu
SPIRITUAL HEAD: H. H. Gyalwa Kar-
mapa XVIth. Karmapa passed away in
1981; we are awaiting announcement of
rebirth of the XVIIth Karmapa.
RESIDENT DIRECTOR: Ven.
Khenpo
Karthar, Rinpoche (Tibetan)
AFFILIATED WITH: Autonomous
ESTABLISHED: 1978
FACILITIES: Country retreat facility with
some accommodations for solitary
retreats
RETREATS OFFERED: Prostration re-
treats, weekend sittings, supervised soli-
tary retreats; offered occasionally.
OPEN TO: General public

Karma Thegsum Choling (KTC) Centers: Affiliates of Karma Triyana Dharmachakra of Woodstock, New York

"The Sanskrit word 'karma' means activity, and the Tibetan phrase 'Thegsum
Choling' means literally 'where the wheel
is turned.' These two combined give us a
sense for the true meaning of a Buddhist
Center: 'where the teachings of the Buddha flourish.'" All Karma Thegsum Choling (KTC) centers are affiliated with
Karma Triyana Dharmachakra (KTD) as
their main headquarters, and as such they
belong to the Karma Kagyu lineages of Tibetan Buddhism, which is headed by His
Holiness the Gyalwa Karmapa. In general,
except for the retreat center in Cerrillos,
New Mexico, they do not offer retreat facilities. Most centers have weekly meditation sessions, discussion groups, and/or
performance of the ritual practices of Avalokiteshvara, Amitabha, Green Tara, or
Medicine Buddha.

NORTH CAROLINA

Dharma Study Group of Durham, North Carolina

Comprised of students of the Vidyadhara,
the Ven. Chogyam Trungpa, Rinpoche,
and affiliated with Vajradhatu, which is
under the direction of the Vajra Regent,
Osel Tendzin, the Dharma Study Group
of Durham, North Carolina, provides for
the study and practice of Tibetan Vajrayana Buddhism. Programs in the practice of meditation and the study of Buddhist philosophy and psychology, ongoing
classes, open house discussion, and individual meditation instruction are offered
by senior students. The practice of sitting
meditation (Shamatha—resting the mind
in non-struggle) is taught, with the out-
breath as a minimal reference point.
Mindfulness is further cultivated through
walking meditation practice and *oryoki*, a
style of eating adapted from the Zen Buddhist monastic tradition.
ADDRESS: 1200 West Markham Avenue,
Durham, NC 27701
PHONE: (919) 286-1487
LINEAGE: Kagyu
SPIRITUAL HEAD: Vajra Regent Osel
Tendzin. Founded by the Vidyadhara,
the Ven. Chogyam Trungpa, Rinpoche
RESIDENT DIRECTOR: Steve Fisher
AFFILIATED WITH: Vajradhatu
ESTABLISHED: 1978
FACILITIES: Urban meditation center
RETREATS OFFERED: Monthly *nyinthuns*
OPEN TO: General public

North Carolina Triangle Area Karma Thegsum Choling

Please refer to Karma Triyana Dharmachakra, Woodstock, New York, for a description of Karma Thegsum Choling.
ADDRESS: 218 Landsbury Drive, Durham, NC 27707

PHONE: (919) 489-3759
LINEAGE: Karma Kagyu
SPIRITUAL HEAD: H. H. the Gyalwa
Karmapa
RESIDENT DIRECTOR: None
AFFILIATED WITH: Karma Triyana
Dharmachakra
OPEN TO: General public

Greenville Karma Thegsum Choling

Please refer to Karma Triyana Dharma-
chakra, Woodstock, New York, for a de-
scription of Karma Thegsum Choling.
ADDRESS: Box 4243, Greenville, NC
27836
PHONE: (919) 756-8750
LINEAGE: Karma Kagyu
SPIRITUAL HEAD: H. H. the Gyalwa
Karmapa
RESIDENT DIRECTOR: Byron Coulter
AFFILIATED WITH: Karma Triyana
Dharmachakra
OPEN TO: General public

OHIO

Dharma Study Group

Dharma Study Group is under the aus-
pices of Vajradhatu, the international Ti-
betan Buddhist organization founded by
Ven. Chogyam Trungpa, Rinpoche.
Weekly classes and meditation are held.
ADDRESS: 2330 Euclid Hts. Boulevard,
#104, Cleveland Heights, OH 44106
PHONE: (216) 791-7658; 381-6393
LINEAGE: Kagyu (Tibetan)
SPIRITUAL HEAD: Vajra Regent Osel
Tendzin. Founded by the Vidyadhara,
the Ven. Chogyam Trungpa, Rinpoche.
RESIDENT DIRECTOR: Richard L.
Weiner
AFFILIATED WITH: Vajradhatu Interna-
tional/USA
ESTABLISHED: 1985

FACILITIES: Urban meditation center
OPEN TO: General public

Columbus Dharma Study Group

Please refer to Vajradhatu/USA, Boulder,
Colorado, for a description.
ADDRESS: 46 Glenmont Avenue, Co-
lumbus, OH 43214
PHONE: (614) 263-7472
LINEAGE: Karma Kagyu
SPIRITUAL HEAD: Vajra Regent Osel
Tendzin. Founded by the Vidyadhara,
the Ven. Chogyam Trungpa, Rinpoche
RESIDENT DIRECTOR: Peter and Mary
Goodman
AFFILIATED WITH: Vajradhatu Interna-
tional/USA
OPEN TO: General public

Columbus Karma Thegsum Choling

The Columbus KTC was founded in September 1977 by the Ven. Khenpo Karthar,
Rinpoche, a Tibetan Buddhist lama of the
Kagyu tradition. The center provides a
regular schedule of sitting and chanting
meditation, as well as educational programs and celebrations of major Buddhist
holidays. Most programs are open to the
public, and one need not become a Buddhist to participate in the weekly meditation and teaching sessions. Currently the
center is located in the Loft One studio
space at 2663½ North High Street, on the
southwest corner of Dodridge and High
Streets. The center features a large shrine
room with a five-tiered traditional Tibetan
shrine designed by Khenpo Karthar, Rinpoche, and decorated with many beautiful
religious paintings and statues.
ADDRESS: 2663½ North High Street
(Mailing address: P. O. Box 02160, Columbus, OH 43202)
PHONE: (614) 457-5113
LINEAGE: Karma Kagyu

SPIRITUAL HEAD: H. H. the Gyalwa
Karmapa
RESIDENT DIRECTOR: Ven. Khenpo
Karthar, Rinpoche (Tibetan Kagyu
Lama)
AFFILIATED WITH: Karma Triyana
Dharmachakra
ESTABLISHED: 1977
FACILITIES: Urban meditation center
RETREATS OFFERED: *Ngondro* retreat
Saturday mornings (second Saturday of
each month)
OPEN TO: General public

OKLAHOMA

Tulsa Forming Dharma Study Group

Please refer to Vajradhatu/USA, Boulder,
Colorado, for a description.
ADDRESS: 4026 East 26th Avenue, Tulsa,
OK 74114
PHONE: (918) 583-6718
LINEAGE: Karma Kagyu
SPIRITUAL HEAD: Vajra Regent Osel
Tendzin. Founded by the Vidyadhara,
the Ven. Chogyam Trungpa, Rinpoche.
RESIDENT DIRECTOR: Paul Moore
AFFILIATED WITH: Vajradhatu Interna-
tional/USA
OPEN TO: General public

OREGON

Yeshe Nyingpo (Tashi Choling Retreat Center for Yeshe Nyingpo)

Yeshe Nyingpo Centers, established by
H. H. Dudjom, Rinpoche, supreme head
of the Nyingmapa tradition of Tibetan
Buddhism, exist in Los Angeles and Berkeley, California; and Ashland, Eugene—
Cottage Grove, and Portland, Oregon.
The retreat center, Tashi Choling, is located south of Ashland (Hilt, California
exit) and is the seat of the Ven. Gyatrul,

Rinpoche. Tashi Choling is the site of the
large Vajrasattva statue and the temple
which has been under construction for a
number of years. There are retreats that
occur during the warmer months, and
Vajrayana students are welcome. Costs
and length of retreats vary. For schedules
and information it is best to send your
name and address to be placed on the
mailing list. The practices done at Tashi
Choling are primarily those of the Dudjom Tersar Nyingma lineage and of the
Nam Cho of the Palyul Nyingma lineage.
The same is true of the Yeshe Nyingpo
Pacific centers. With the passing of H. H.
Dudjom, Rinpoche in 1987, the Tersar
lineage is under the guidance of H. E.
Shenphen Dawa, Rinpoche, who conducted a retreat at Tashi Choling in No-
vember 1987. Shenphen, Rinpoche, will be
returning in 1988 to Tashi Choling, as well
as visiting individual centers.
ADDRESS: 2001 Colestine Road, Ash-
land, OR 97520 (Mailing address: P. O.
Box 124, Ashland, OR 97520)
PHONE: (503) 488-0477
LINEAGE: Nyingmapa (Dudjom Tersar
and Palyul practices)
SPIRITUAL HEAD: H. H. Dudjom, Rin-
poche; H. E. Shenphen Dawa, Rin-
poche (Tibetan)
RESIDENT DIRECTOR: Ven. Gyatrul,
Rinpoche (Tibetan)
AFFILIATED WITH: Yeshe Nyingpo-
Pacific
ESTABLISHED: 1980
FACILITIES: Country retreat facility; stu-
dents must provide living space (trail-
ers, etc.)
RETREATS OFFERED: Retreats are when
visiting lamas or Gyatrul, Rinpoche,
provide them.
OPEN TO: Retreats are usually limited to
Vajrayana students, not necessarily
Tashi Choling.

Kagyu Yonten Gyatso

Founded by H. E. Kalu, Rinpoche, as a country seminar and retreat facility for groups in any Buddhist tradition, Kagyu Yonten Gyatso is located on 161 acres of conifer forests, meadows, creeks, and ponds. It is "remote, secluded, picturesque, and peaceful." Accommodations include a large log lodge, kitchen, sanitary and meeting facilities, hiking trails, horses, swimming, and camping for groups of up to 500 persons.
ADDRESS: 108 Milarepa Road, Azalea, OR 97410
PHONE: (503) 837-3636
LINEAGE: Kagyu Vajrayana (Tibetan)
SPIRITUAL HEAD: H. E. Kalu, Rinpoche (Tibetan)
AFFILIATED WITH: Pal Karmapai Chos, S.D.E.
ESTABLISHED: 1986
FACILITIES: Country retreat facility with accommodations for solitary retreats
RETREATS OFFERED: Buddhist retreats, seminars, and workshops
OPEN TO: General public

Corvallis Dharma Study Group

Weekly group meditation practice and quarterly group meditation retreats.
ADDRESS: 3256 Northwest Harrison, Corvallis, OR 97333 (Mailing address: P. O. Box 1965, Corvallis, OR 97339)
PHONE: (503) 758-4649
LINEAGE: Tibetan Kagyu
SPIRITUAL HEAD: Vajra Regent Osel Tendzin. Founded by the Vidyadhara, the Ven. Chogyam Trungpa, Rinpoche
RESIDENT DIRECTOR: Randy Chakerian
AFFILIATED WITH: Vajradhatu International/USA
ESTABLISHED: 1981
FACILITIES: Urban meditation center
RETREATS OFFERED: One-day and weekend sitting meditation retreats in a country retreat facility
OPEN TO: General public

Chagdud Gonpa Foundation

Ven. Chagdud Tulku, Rinpoche, teaches initiates the meditation techniques and Buddhist philosophy represented by the Vajrayana-Dzog Chen traditions of the Tibetan Nyingmapa lineage. The Cottage Grove Center offers a daily schedule of group meditation in accordance with these traditions, interspersed with seasonally scheduled three to five-day extended practice sessions. The meditation practices followed by Rinpoche's students are done with the intent of taming the mind. In addition to a series of practices done by all of the students, there are the *ngondro* (foundation) practices and, ultimately, more advanced material, which is available as *ngondro* is completed.
ADDRESS: 198 North River Road, Cottage Grove, OR 97424
PHONE: (503) 942-8619 (between noon and 6 : 00 P.M.
LINEAGE: Nyingmapa (Tibetan)
SPIRITUAL HEAD: Chagdud Tulku, Rinpoche
RESIDENT DIRECTOR: Lama Sonam Tsering (Tibetan)
AFFILIATED WITH: Autonomous
FACILITIES: Both urban and country retreat facilities
RETREATS OFFERED: Summer *ngondro* retreats for beginning students; winter retreats for advanced students.
OPEN TO: General public

Marcola Retreat Land

Marcola Retreat Land is a country retreat facililty under the auspices of Kagyu Droden Kunchab (Ven. Lama Lodo) of San Francisco, California. A strict three-year retreat is currently underway. The retreatants therefore ask that any requests for information be directed to the San Francisco center.
ADDRESS: Marcola, OR (Mailing address: Direct all requests for informa-

tion to Kagyu Droden Kunchab, 1892
Fell Street, San Francisco, CA 94117)
PHONE: (415) 752-5424
LINEAGE: Kagyu
SPIRITUAL HEAD: H. E. Kalu, Rinpoche
AFFILIATED WITH: Kagyu Droden Kun-
chab, San Francisco, California
FACILITIES: Country retreat facility
RETREATS OFFERED: Three-year Vajra-
yana retreats
OPEN TO: Please see description under
Kagyu Droden Kunchab, San Fran-
cisco, California, for prerequisites for
three-year retreats.

Kagyu Changchub Chuling
Lama Tinley Drupa is the resident teacher
of this center, under the direction of the
Very Ven. Kalu, Rinpoche. The center
maintains a daily schedule of meditation
practices in the Kagyu tradition of Vajrayana Buddhism. Special events include
day-long and weekend retreats, full moon
offering ceremonies, and Tibetan language
and art classes. The center hosts visiting
lamas, often for several consecutive days
of public teachings and ceremonies. It
owns a house occupied by resident students and a Dharma bookstore. There are
traditional Vajrayana (Tibetan) Buddhist
practices of deity yoga and *shi nye*
(Shamatha)/*Lhatong* (Vipassana). Deity
practices of Bodhisattva of Compassion,
Medicine Buddha, and others include
prayer, deity visualization, mantra recitation, and emptiness meditation. There is
chanting in the Tibetan language, at times
accompanied by traditional instruments.
A variety of techniques to develop concentration and insight during silent meditation are also taught.
ADDRESS: 73 Northeast Monroe, Portland, OR 97212
PHONE: (503) 284-6697
LINEAGE: Kagyu
SPIRITUAL HEAD: Ven. Kalu, Rinpoche
(Tibetan)

RESIDENT DIRECTOR: Lama Tinley
Drupa (Bhutanese)
AFFILIATED WITH: Kagyu Dharma
ESTABLISHED: 1976
FACILITIES: Urban meditation center
using rented facilities for retreats
RETREATS OFFERED: *Nyinthun*, week-
end sittings; approximately four retreats
per year.
OPEN TO: Most open to general public,
but not all.

Portland Dharma Study Group
For description please refer to Vajradhatu/
USA, Boulder, Colorado.
ADDRESS: 2221 Northeast 53rd., Port-
land, OR 97213
PHONE: (503) 281-4993
LINEAGE: Kagyu
SPIRITUAL HEAD: Vajra Regent Osel
Tendzin. Founded by the Vidyadhara,
the Ven. Chogyam Trungpa, Rinpoche.
RESIDENT DIRECTOR: Elizabeth A.
Goldblatt
AFFILIATED WITH: Vajradhatu Interna-
tional/USA
ESTABLISHED: 1978
FACILITIES: Urban meditation center
RETREATS OFFERED: Weekend sittings
OPEN TO: Members and the general
public.

Newport Yeshe Nyingpo
We are a small branch group of Chagdud
Gompa. Chagdud, Rinpoche (one hun-
dred miles away), is our lama, and he
functions under Yeshe Nyingpo.
ADDRESS: P. O. Box 405, Waldport, OR
97394
PHONE: (503) 563-2817; 265-9648
LINEAGE: Nyingmapa (Tibetan)
SPIRITUAL HEAD: H. H. Shepen Dawa
(Tibetan)
RESIDENT DIRECTOR: Chagdud Tulku,
Rinpoche (Tibetan)
AFFILIATED WITH: Yeshe Nyingpo

ESTABLISHED: 1981
FACILITIES: Individual houses

Chagdud Gonpa—Williams Retreat Center

The Williams Center is primarily a retreat center. The winter retreats for advanced students and some summer retreats (as scheduled) are held here. For a description of practices, please see paragraph included with description of Cottage Grove Center.

ADDRESS: Jamie Kalfas, C/O General Delivery, Williams, OR 97544
PHONE: (503) 846-6942 (between noon and 6:00 P.M.)
LINEAGE: Nyingmapa (Tibetan)
SPIRITUAL HEAD: Chagdud Tulku, Rinpoche (Tibetan)
AFFILIATED WITH: Chagdud Gonpa, Cottage Grove Center
FACILITIES: Country retreat facility
RETREATS OFFERED: Winter retreats for advanced students; other retreats as scheduled.
OPEN TO: General public

PENNSYLVANIA

Philadelphia Dharmadhatu

Please refer to Vajradhatu/USA, Boulder, Colorado, for a description.

ADDRESS: 2030 Sansom Street, Philadelphia, PA 19103
PHONE: (215) 568-6070
LINEAGE: Karma Kagyu
SPIRITUAL HEAD: Vajra Regent Osel Tendzin. Founded by the Vidyadhara, the Ven. Chogyam Trungpa, Rinpoche
RESIDENT DIRECTOR: Adrian Sopher
AFFILIATED WITH: Vajradhatu International/USA
OPEN TO: General public

SOUTH CAROLINA

Columbia Dharmadhatu

Dharmadhatu is an affiliate of Vajradhatu. Dharmadhatu offers meditation instruction by authorized teachers, extended meditation sessions on weekends, classes for the study of Buddhism, intensive meditation and study weekends, and Shambhala Training programs. The meditation instructors have received authorization from the founder of Vajradhatu, Vidyadhara, the Ven. Chogyam Trungpa, Rinpoche, to teach according to the tradition of the Kagyu and Nyingma lineages of Tibetan Buddhism. This meditation practice is based on our present state of mind and the present moment. By relating to the present with simplicity and precision, life contains tremendous beauty and dignity. Meditation is not a technique used to withdraw from the world. It is a way to open ourselves through discipline and see the world as it is, in a fresh way.

ADDRESS: 3301 River Drive, Columbia, SC 29201
PHONE: (803) 254-9048
LINEAGE: Kagyu and Nyingma (Tibetan)
SPIRITUAL HEAD: Vajra Regent Osel Tendzin. Founded by the Vidyadhara, the Ven. Chogyam Trungpa, Rinpoche.
RESIDENT DIRECTOR: Nancy Chesnutt (American)
AFFILIATED WITH: Vajradhatu International/USA
ESTABLISHED: 1978
FACILITIES: Urban meditation center
OPEN TO: General public

TEXAS

Austin Dharmadhatu

Please refer to Vajradhatu/USA, Boulder, Colorado, for a description.

ADDRESS: 1702 South 5th Street, Austin, TX 78704

PHONE: (512) 433-3263
LINEAGE: Karma Kagyu
SPIRITUAL HEAD: Vajra Regent Osel
Tendzin. Founded by the Vidyadhara,
the Ven. Chogyam Trungpa, Rinpoche.
RESIDENT DIRECTOR: Joe Inskeep and
Simon Luna
AFFILIATED WITH: Vajradhatu Interna-
tional/USA
OPEN TO: General public

Karma Thegsum Choling
The Dallas Karma Thegsum Choling is a
Tibetan Vajrayana Buddhist group affili-
ated with Karma Triyana Dharmachakra
in Woodstock, New York. Under the
guidance of Khenpo Karthar, Rinpoche,
the Dallas Center offers Shamatha medita-
tion; Vajrayana practices of Chenrezig,
Green Tara, and Medicine Buddha; week-
end *nyinthuns*; and *ngondro* intensives.
Meditation instruction and introductory
workshops are available.
ADDRESS: 522 Roundtop, Duncanville,
TX 75116
PHONE: (214) 780-9036
LINEAGE: Kagyu (Tibetan)
SPIRITUAL HEAD: Gwalya Karmapa
(Tibetan)
RESIDENT DIRECTOR: Khenpo Karthar,
Rinpoche
AFFILIATED WITH: Karma Triyana
Dharmachakra, Woodstock, New York
ESTABLISHED: 1984
FACILITIES: Urban meditation center
with country retreat facility offering ac-
commodations for solitary retreats.
RETREATS OFFERED: Weekend seminars,
month-long retreats, *ngondro* retreats.
OPEN TO: Most open to general public;
some require initiations into specific
practices.

Houston Dharma Study Group
Please refer to Vajradhatu/USA, Boulder,
Colorado, for a description.

ADDRESS: 2102 Dunstan, Houston, TX
77005
PHONE: (713) 520-1778
LINEAGE: Karma Kagyu
SPIRITUAL HEAD: Vajra Regent Osel
Tendzin. Founded by the Vidyadhara,
the Ven. Chogyam Trungpa, Rinpoche.
RESIDENT DIRECTOR: Pat Barrodale
AFFILIATED WITH: Vajradhatu Interna-
tional/USA
OPEN TO: General public

San Antonio Forming Dharma Study Group
Please refer to Vajradhatu/USA, Boulder,
Colorado, for a description.
ADDRESS: 406 Olney Drive, San Anto-
nio, TX 78209
PHONE: (215) 696-6861
LINEAGE: Karma Kagyu
SPIRITUAL HEAD: Vajra Regent Osel
Tendzin. Founded by the Vidyadhara,
the Ven. Chogyam Trungpa, Rinpoche.
RESIDENT DIRECTOR: Elisa Gonzalez
AFFILIATED WITH: Vajradhatu Interna-
tional/USA
OPEN TO: General public

UTAH

Salt Lake Dharma Study Group
The Salt Lake City Dharma Study Group
is a chapter of Vajradhatu, founded by
Chogyam Trungpa, a Kagyu Tibetan Bud-
dhist. Bi-weekly meditation and study ses-
sions are held. Intensive meditation work-
shops are held periodically.
ADDRESS: 1167 East 2nd S, Salt Lake
City, UT 84102
PHONE: (801) 583-1272
LINEAGE: Kagyu
SPIRITUAL HEAD: Vajra Regent Osel
Tendzin. Founded by the Vidyadhara,
the Ven. Chogyam Trungpa, Rinpoche
RESIDENT DIRECTOR: Justin Dituri

AFFILIATED WITH: Vajradhatu Interna-
tional/USA
ESTABLISHED: 1976
FACILITIES: Urban meditation center

VERMONT

Karme-Choling Buddhist Meditation Center

Karme-Choling, located in northern Vermont, offers programs in the practice of
meditation and the study of Buddhist philosophy and psychology. All programs
provide an integrated schedule of meditation, study, and work in which the Buddhist teachings can be applied to daily life
situations. All programs include meals and
informal accommodations. Meditation according to Buddhist tradition is a means
of relating with life directly and simply.
Through sitting meditation—the basic
practice of Buddhists for over twenty-five
hundred years—the practitioner is able to
see through confusion and struggle and
awaken clarity, precision, and gentleness
toward himself and others.
ADDRESS: Star Route, Barnet, VT 05821
PHONE: (802) 633-2384
LINEAGE: Kagyu (Tibetan)
SPIRITUAL HEAD: Vajra Regent Osel
Tendzin. Founded by the Vidyadhara,
the Ven. Chogyam Trungpa, Rinpoche
AFFILIATED WITH: Vajradhatu Interna-
tional/USA
FACILITIES: Country retreat facilities
with accommodations for solitary
retreats.
RETREATS OFFERED: Dathun and
"weekthun," in house retreats, Shambhala Training, advanced programs for
authorized students
OPEN TO: Most open to general public;
some to members only

Milarepa Center

Located in Vermont's scenic Northeast
Kingdom, 270-acre Milarepa Center is one

of thirty Buddhist centers of the world-
wide Foundation for the Preservation of
the Mahayana Tradition (FPMT), and
comes under the spiritual guidance of
Thubten Zopa, Rinpoche, teacher of
Buddhist philosophy and meditation for
thousands of students. Milarepa Center
hosts qualified Buddhist teachers, who
provide instruction in meditation and philosophy, and offers facilities for individual
and group retreats. An integrated schedule
of meditation, study, and work enables
residents to apply the Buddha's teachings
to daily life and yields a degree of self-
sufficiency that permits program attendance on a "by donation" basis. Facilities
include a twelve-room house, garage-
shop, barn, and a Dharma book-audio/
video tape library. Visitors are welcome
any time, except during winter retreats
(December to March). Camping is
permitted.
ADDRESS: Barnet Mountain, Barnet, VT
05821
PHONE: (802) 633-4136
LINEAGE: Gelug
SPIRITUAL HEAD: Thubten Zopa, Rinpoche (Tibetan Sherpa)
RESIDENT DIRECTOR: Geshe Lobsang
Jampa (Tibetan)
AFFILIATED WITH: Foundation for the
Preservation of the Mahayana Tradition
(FPMT)
ESTABLISHED: 1981
FACILITIES: Country retreat facility with
accommodations for solitary retreats
RETREATS OFFERED: Supervised solitary
retreats, tantric Sadhana retreats of
varying duration (one week to three
months); offered three to four times per
year.
OPEN TO: General public

Hanover Dharma Study Group

Please refer to Vajradhatu/USA, Boulder,
Colorado, for a description.

American monk Thubten Pelgye crossing the road at Milarepa Center, Barnet, Vermont. Photo courtesy of Peter Baker.

ADDRESS: R.R. 1, Box 171, Bradford, VT 05033
PHONE: (802) 222-9330
LINEAGE: Karma Kagyu
SPIRITUAL HEAD: Vajra Regent Osel Tendzin. Founded by the Vidyadhara, the Ven. Chogyam Trungpa, Rinpoche
RESIDENT DIRECTOR: Ken Ketchum
AFFILIATED WITH: Vajradhatu International/USA
OPEN TO: General public

Brattleboro Dharma Study Group

Please refer to Vajradhatu/USA, Boulder, Colorado, for a description.
ADDRESS: C/O Vinyard/Latches, Latches Hotel, Corner Flat and Main Streets, Brattleboro, VT 05301
LINEAGE: Karma Kagyu
SPIRITUAL HEAD: Vajra Regent Osel Tendzin. Founded by the Vidyadhara, the Ven. Chogyam Trungpa, Rinpoche

AFFILIATED WITH: Vajradhatu International/USA
OPEN TO: General public

Mandala Buddhist Center

Among the major sects of Japanese Buddhism, Shingon-shu, often referred to as Mikkyo (Esoteric Buddhism), maintains the closest affinity with Hinduism and with the Lamaist Buddhism of Tibet and the Himalayan countries. Founded by Kodo Daishi Kukai in the ninth century, this tradition was transmitted from India via China to Japan. Japanese Shingon (True Word) Buddhism is a Mahayana school of Tantric Buddhism, which bases its practice on the recitation of mantra, formation of *mudra* (symbolic hand gestures), visualizations, and silent meditation. The focus of Shingon-shu is on living with a spirit of great compassion.

Rev. Jomyo N. Tanaka, spiritual head of Mandala Buddhist Center, Bristol, Vermont, teaches a Japanese form of Vajrayana Buddhism.

ADDRESS: RD 1, Box 2380, Bristol, VT
  05443
PHONE: (802) 453-5038
LINEAGE: Shingon School
SPIRITUAL HEAD: Rev. Jomyo N.
  Tanaka (Japanese)
RESIDENT DIRECTOR: Rev. Susan Eko
  Tanaka (American)
AFFILIATED WITH: Singon Sect
  Daikakuji
ESTABLISHED: 1982
FACILITIES: Country retreat facility with
  accommodations for solitary retreats
RETREATS OFFERED: Chanting retreats,
  prostration retreats, weekend sittings,
  three-year Vajrayana retreat, six-year
  retreat.
OPEN TO: Members only

Sunray Meditation Society

Sunray Meditation Society is an international spiritual society dedicated to planetary peace. Its purpose is to manifest the Native American ideal of Caretaker Mind, so that we may create a world of beauty upon earth and throughout the family of life. Since 1983 Sunray is blessed as a Tibetan Buddhist Dharma Center of the Nyingma School, through the kindness of His Holiness Dudjom, Rinpoche, and in 1986 His Holiness the Drikung Kyabgon Chetsang, Rinpoche, acknowledged the meeting of the Drikung Kagyu and Sunray teachings as the fulfillment of prophecy. The Sunray teachings and practice are thus a beauteous lake receiving the streams of three ancient and intact spiritual lineages, which teach us practical methods to realize Caretaker Mind and Bodhisattva action.

Medicine Wheel Mandala
Mirrors Clear Mind
ADDRESS: P. O. Box 398, Bristol, VT
  05443

Ven. Dhyani Ywahoo, Sunray Meditation Society, Bristol, Vermont. Photo courtesy of Pamela Cabell-Whiting.

PHONE: (802) 453-4610
LINEAGE: Ywahoo lineage (Cherokee); Nyingma, through His Holiness Dudjom, Rinpoche; Drikung Kagyu, through His Holiness the Drikung Kyabgon Chetsang, Rinpoche

SPIRITUAL HEAD: Ven. Dhyani Ywahoo is a member of the traditional Etowah Band of the Eastern Tsalagi (Cherokee) Nation. Trained by her grandparents, she is the twenty-seventh generation to carry the ancestral wisdom of the Ywahoo lineage and is a guide to all who walk the Beauty road.

RESIDENT DIRECTOR: Barbara Du Bois, Ph.D., Education Program Coordinator AFFILIATED WITH: Sunray Meditation Society, Bristol, Vermont, is the international headquarters of the Society, which has regional communities, meditation circles, and training sites throughout the United States and Canada, and in Europe. The Society itself is affiliated with the Etowah Cherokee Nation and the Igidotsoiye Tsalagi Gadugi.

ESTABLISHED: 1968

FACILITIES: Sunray Peace Village Encampment (summer only) in the Green Mountains of Vermont—serene and beautiful setting for practice, study, and retreat. Accommodations include camping (tents, some RV sites) and outdoor cooking; showers and toilets available. Sunray Meditation Society also maintains a network of twenty regional communities and meditation circles throughout the United States and Canada. For information about activities in your area, please contact the Sunray office.

RETREATS OFFERED: The Peacekeeper Mission, yearly foundation training, is offered regionally in the United States, Canada, and Europe. Summer teachings in Native American and Buddhist studies at Sunray Peace Village Encampment, Vermont. Individual retreats for practitioners.

OPEN TO: The Peacekeeper Mission and summer programs are open to the general public.

Dharmadhatu of Burlington

Located on Elmwood Avenue in downtown Burlington, Dharmadhatu offers a regular schedule of daily meditation, which is open to the public, and also provides meditation instruction and a variety of classes and workshops. Dharmadhatu is a nonprofit organization supported entirely by membership dues, course fees, and donations. Mindfulness/awareness or Shamatha/Vipassana sitting practice is the essential formless meditation taught at Burlington Dharmadhatu. Classes involving Hinayana, Mahayana, and Vajrayana level teachings are available as students proceed along the path of practice, study, and work.

ADDRESS: 31 Elmwood Avenue, Burlington, VT 05401

PHONE: (802) 658-6795

LINEAGE: Karma Kagyu

SPIRITUAL HEAD: Vajra Regent Osel Tendzin. Founded by the Vidyadhara, the Ven. Chogyam Trungpa, Rinpoche

RESIDENT DIRECTOR: Richard Does

AFFILIATED WITH: Vajradhatu International/USA

ESTABLISHED: 1973

FACILITIES: Urban meditation center

OPEN TO: General public

Manchester Dharma Study Group

As an affiliate of Vajradhatu, the Manchester Dharma Study Group offers meditation practice and teaching in the tradition of Three Yana Buddhism of the Kagyu and Nyingma lineages of Tibet. Meetings are held weekly and one all-day period of meditation occurs each month. Individual meditation instruction is available.

ADDRESS: P. O. Box 436, Manchester, VT 05254

PHONE: (802) 325-3180

LINEAGE: Kagyu (Tibetan)

SPIRITUAL HEAD: Vajra Regent Osel Tendzin. Founded by the Vidyadhara, the Ven. Chogyam Trungpa, Rinpoche

RESIDENT DIRECTOR: Tom Melcher

AFFILIATED WITH: Vajradhatu International/USA

ESTABLISHED: 1980

FACILITIES: Meetings in house of a member; plans to rent soon.
RETREATS OFFERED: One *nyinthun* (all-day sitting) each month
OPEN TO: General public

Rutland Dharma Study Group

Please refer to Vajradhatu/USA, Boulder, Colorado, for a description.
ADDRESS: Hitzel Terrace, Rutland, VT 05701
PHONE: (802) 773-0909
LINEAGE:. Karma Kagyu
SPIRITUAL HEAD: Vajra Regent Osel Tendzin. Founded by the Vidyadhara, the Ven. Chogyam Trungpa, Rinpoche
RESIDENT DIRECTOR: Kate Woods
AFFILIATED WITH: Vajradhatu International/USA
OPEN TO: General public

WASHINGTON

Dharma Study Group of Bellingham, Washington

We meet once a week for sitting meditation and study. Meditation instruction is available. We also serve as a source of information about Tibetan Buddhist and Shambhala Training events taking place in nearby Seattle and Vancouver, B.C.
ADDRESS: 2405 Henry, Bellingham, WA 98225 (Mailing address: P. O. Box 5862, Bellingham, WA 98227-5862)
PHONE: (206) 676-0315
LINEAGE: Karma Kagyu
SPIRITUAL HEAD: Vajra Regent Osel Tendzin. Founded by the Vidyadhara, the Ven. Chogyam Trungpa, Rinpoche
RESIDENT DIRECTOR: Melanie Williams
AFFILIATED WITH: Vajradhatu International/USA
ESTABLISHED: 1973
FACILITIES: Member's home
OPEN TO: Members only; classes occasionally for general public.

Dharmadhatu

Dharmadhatu is one of over sixty-five affiliated centers founded by the Tibetan meditation master Chogyam Trungpa, Rinpoche, to present the Buddhist path, following the traditions of the Kagyu and Nyingma schools of Tibetan Buddhism. We offer a weekly schedule of classes and meditation, open to the public. Individual instruction is given by meditation instructors, who then establish a relationship with each student. It is considered essential that study and meditation practice, like two wings of a bird, be joined together.
ADDRESS: 7109 Woodlawn Avenue, Northeast, Seattle, WA 98115
PHONE: (206) 522-2199
LINEAGE: Kagyu
SPIRITUAL HEAD: Vajra Regent Osel Tendzin. Founded by the Vidyadhara, the Ven. Chogyam Trungpa, Rinpoche
RESIDENT DIRECTOR: Alan Ness, Practice Coordinator
AFFILIATED WITH: Vajradhatu International/USA
FACILITIES: Urban meditation center
RETREATS OFFERED: *Nyinthun*, weekend sittings offered weekly
OPEN TO: General public

Rigpa Fellowship

Rigpa is an association of people who study under the guidance of Ven. Lama Sogyal, Rinpoche, an incarnate lama and meditation master from Tibet. Each year, Rinpoche gives talks, weekend teachings, and retreats in the United States, Europe, Australia, and New Zealand. In addition to the Seattle center, ongoing practice groups meet in Santa Cruz, San Diego, Boston, New York and Washington, D.C. Rigpa is currently establishing a center in the San Francisco Bay Area.
ADDRESS: 5023 44th Avenue Northeast, Seattle, WA 98105

PHONE: (206) 522-2615
LINEAGE: Tibetan Nyingma
SPIRITUAL HEAD: Sogyal, Rinpoche
AFFILIATED WITH: Rigpa (Santa Cruz California)
ESTABLISHED: 1981
FACILITIES: Study group
RETREATS OFFERED: Contact Rigpa Santa Cruz, California, P. O. Box 7326, Santa Cruz, CA 95061 for retreat information.
OPEN TO: General public

Sakya Monastery of Tibetan Buddhism

H. H. Jigdal Dagchen Sakya and Associate Head Lama H. H. Trinly N. Sakyapa direct the wide variety of activities at Sakya monastery. Located in Seattle since 1974, the monastery is an international seat of the nonsectarian teachings of Tibetan Buddhism. There is a weekly schedule of meditations open to the public. Tsog Kor ceremonies are held twice a month in conjunction with the Tibetan lunar calendar, and Mahakala Puja is at the end of each month. Some of the monastery's traditional activities are the bestowing of refuge, initiations, personal audiences and instruction, translation and publication of texts, Tibetan language and religious music classes, and ethnic craft festivals. There are resident ordained and lay practitioners and a room for retreats. Sakya Monastery also includes the Pacific Northwest branch of the Library of Tibetan Works and Archives, of Dharamsala, India. Through the resources of Sakya Monastery and the guest lamas who come

Sakya Monastery is an international seat of nonsectarian Tibetan Buddhist teachings.

to teach, the whole diverse spectrum of Mahayana and Vajrayana Buddhist meditation techniques is available. The central practice of Sakya Monastery is the generation of love and compassion through meditation on Chenrezi (Avalokiteshvara), a tenth level Bodhisattva who is the emanation of compassion. Lord Buddha taught that love is the wish for all beings to experience happiness and that compassion is the aspiration that they be liberated from all suffering. The Chenrezi meditations practiced at the center have two main parts. The first part is the generation stage, during which one visualizes oneself as Chenrezi. The second part is the completion stage, which comprises an examination of the nature of one's own mind. The practice of these two aspects of meditation gradually awakens a deep sense of love and kindness toward other beings, as well as a keener awareness of the limitless and vast nature of one's own mind. In conclusion, the merit generated by the practice is dedicated to the benefit of all sentient beings.

ADDRESS: 108 Northwest 83rd Street, Seattle, WA 98117
PHONE: (206) 789-2573
LINEAGE: Sakya
SPIRITUAL HEAD: H. H. J. D. Sakya and Associate Head Lama H. H. Trinly Sakyapa (Tibetan)
RESIDENT DIRECTOR: Adrienne Chan, assistant to H. H. J. D. Sakya
AFFILIATED WITH: Autonomous
ESTABLISHED: 1974
FACILITIES: Urban meditation center with accommodations for solitary retreats
RETREATS OFFERED: "Days of Mindfulness"; supervised and unsupervised solitary retreats offered whenever necessary.
OPEN TO: General public

Seattle Karma Thegsum Choling

Seattle KTC was founded and is maintained for the study and practice of the three-vehicle approach of Shakyamuni Buddha, which has been transmitted uninterruptedly to the present day through the Karma Kagyu tradition. Meditation and discussion groups meet weekly, and any interested person is welcome to attend. Our practice is based on the emergence and growth of the Mahayana attitude during the study and application of mental training as set forth, for example, in the Seven Slogans of Atisha. As one's practice continues, both relative and ultimate aspects of *bodhicitta* (enlightened mind) are actualized, thereby accomplishing meaningful and beneficial activities for oneself and others.

ADDRESS: 939 25th Avenue South, Seattle, WA 98144
PHONE: (206) 324-4992
LINEAGE: Kagyu
SPIRITUAL HEAD: H. H. Karmapa (Tibetan)
RESIDENT DIRECTOR: Richard Baldwin, President
AFFILIATED WITH: Autonomous
ESTABLISHED: 1981
FACILITIES: Urban meditation center

Padma Amrita Buddhist Meditation Center

Padma Amrita Buddhist Meditation Center is associated with, but not an affiliate of, Chagdud Gonpa Foundation. Lama Tarchin is the senior lama. Chagdud Tulku, Rinpoche, has offered Lama Inge Sandvoss as an assistant to Lama Tarchin in the guidance of this group. Teachings are offered and a daily meditation schedule is maintained.

ADDRESS: Lama Inge Sandvoss, West 1019 6th Avenue, Spokane, WA 99204

PHONE: (509) 747-1559
LINEAGE: Nyingmapa (Tibetan)
SPIRITUAL HEAD: Chagdud Tulku, Rinpoche, and Lama Tarchin (both Tibetan)
RESIDENT DIRECTOR: Lama Inge Sandvoss (German)
AFFILIATED WITH: Autonomous
ESTABLISHED: 1984
FACILITIES: Urban meditation center
RETREATS OFFERED: There is land near Tom Tom, Washington, which has a stupa built on it. Plans are being made to make retreats available there.
OPEN TO: General public

Tsechen Kunkhab Choling

Sakya Tsechen Kunkhab Choling is a Tibetan Buddhist Center affiliated with Sakya Monastery of Seattle, Washington. H. H. Jigdal Dagchen Sakya is the Head Lama. Through this center a retreat facility is presently under construction and will include a shrine room, a branch of the Library of Tibetan Works and Archives of the Pacific Northwest, a kitchen and dining area, separate bathrooms, and four sleeping cubicles. Currently members of Sakya Tsechen Kunkhab Choling practice meditation on Chenrezi, the Bodhisattva of Compassion, every Thursday and Sunday. Inquiries may be made to Bill Kingery, Bob Saunders, Michael White, or Brian Demaris.
ADDRESS: 3809 Hoadley Street, Tumwater, WA 98502
PHONE: (206) 786-9357; 754-7841
LINEAGE: Sakya
SPIRITUAL HEAD: H. H. Jigdal Dagchen Sakya and Associate Head Lama H. H. Trinly Sakyapa (Tibetan)
RESIDENT DIRECTOR: Bob Saunders, President
AFFILIATED WITH: Sakya Monastery
FACILITIES: Urban meditation center. Currently building a country retreat fa-

cility. Private rooms will be available for solitary retreats after construction.
RETREATS OFFERED: Three-month Vipassana retreat, a "Day of Mindfulness," weekend sittings, supervised solitary retreats.
OPEN TO: General public

WISCONSIN

Eau Claire Dharma Study Group

Please refer to Vajradhatu/USA, Boulder, Colorado, for a description.
ADDRESS: 126 Gilbert Avenue, Eau Claire, WI 54701
PHONE: (715) 834-9612
LINEAGE: Karma Kagyu
SPIRITUAL HEAD: Vajra Regent Osel Tendzin. Founded by the Vidyadhara, the Ven. Chogyam Trungpa, Rinpoche.
RESIDENT DIRECTOR: Rita Gross
AFFILIATED WITH: Vajradhatu International/USA
OPEN TO: General public

Madison Forming Dharma Study Group

Please refer to Vajradhatu/USA, Boulder, Colorado, for a description.
ADDRESS: 221 West Lakeside Street, Madison, WI 53704
PHONE: (608) 257-1081
LINEAGE: Karma Kagyu
SPIRITUAL HEAD: Vajra Regent Osel Tendzin. Founded by the Vidyadhara, the Ven. Chogyam Trungpa, Rinpoche
RESIDENT DIRECTOR: Patricia Lloyd
AFFILIATED WITH: Vajradhatu International/USA
OPEN TO: General public

Milwaukee Dharmadhatu

Please see Vajradhatu International/USA, Boulder, Colorado, for description

H. H. Jigdal Dagchen Sakya, Head Lama of the Sakya Order of Tibetan Buddhism.

ADDRESS: 2615 North Hackett, Milwaukee, WI 53211
PHONE: (414) 332-4540
LINEAGE: Kagyu (Tibetan)
SPIRITUAL HEAD: Vajra Regent Osel Tendzin. Founded by the Vidyadhara, the Ven. Chogyam Trungpa, Rinpoche

RESIDENT DIRECTOR: David Shapiro
AFFILIATED WITH: Vajradhatu International/USA
ESTABLISHED: 1977
FACILITIES: Urban meditation center
OPEN TO: General public

Vajrayana Centers—Canada

ALBERTA

Marpa Gompa Meditation Society

A small meditation center offering weekly meditations (Shamatha/Vipassana and Vajrayana practice), taped lectures, and visiting lamas.
ADDRESS: 1346 Frontenac Avenue Southwest, Calgary, Alberta, Canada T2T 1B8
PHONE: (403) 244-2382
LINEAGE: Karma Kagyu (Tibetan)
SPIRITUAL HEAD: Ven. Karma Thinley, Rinpoche
ESTABLISHED: 1979
FACILITIES: Member's home
OPEN TO: General public

Edmonton Dharmadhatu

Dharmadhatu is an urban center for the practice and study of the Buddha's teachings. It is an affiliate of Vajradhatu, an association of Buddhist meditation and study centers organized under the guidance of the late Chogyam Trungpa, Rinpoche. Dharmadhatu offers a regular schedule of meditation practice sessions, with extended sessions the second and fourth Sunday of each month. Dharmadhatu also offers public classes at regular intervals.
ADDRESS: 301, 10442 82nd Avenue, Edmonton, Alberta, Canada T6G 2A2
PHONE: (403) 432-1788
LINEAGE: Karma Kagyu
SPIRITUAL HEAD: Vajra Regent Osel Tendzin. Founded by the Vidyadhara, the Ven. Chogyam Trungpa, Rinpoche.
RESIDENT DIRECTOR: Elaine Phillips
AFFILIATED WITH: Vajradhatu International/Canada
ESTABLISHED: 1975
FACILITIES: Urban meditation center, solitary retreat facilities

RETREATS OFFERED: Yearly nyinthun, Labor Day weekend
OPEN TO: General public

BRITISH COLUMBIA

Kagyu Kunkhyab Chuling

KKC was established in 1972 by the Ven. Kalu, Rinpoche, to provide Westerners an opportunity to study and practice Vajrayana teachings from the Kagyu lineage. The center in Burnaby offers daily sitting, nightly pujas, and occasional weekend seminars. The Clear Light Retreat Centre in Saltspring Island accommodates the traditional Tibetan three-year-three-month-three-day retreat. The prerequisite Four Foundational Practices are taught by Lama Tsenjur at the Burnaby Centre. Also taught are courses in basic sitting practice. In addition, KKC sponsors public talks by visiting lamas.
ADDRESS: 4941 Sidley Street, Burnaby, B.C., Canada V5J 1T6
PHONE: (604) 434-4920
LINEAGE: Kagyu (Tibetan)
SPIRITUAL HEAD: Ven. Kalu, Rinpoche (Tibetan)
RESIDENT DIRECTOR: Lama Tsenjun, Rinpoche (Tibetan)
AFFILIATED WITH: Autonomous
FACILITIES: Urban meditation center, country retreat facility, facilities for solitary retreat.
RETREATS OFFERED: Three-year-three-month-three-day traditional major Kagyu retreats.
OPEN TO: General public

Buddhist Association Supporting Interfaith Service

Ven. Jhampa Shaneman lived in India for fourteen years studying with Tibetan masters. This included completing a three-year solitary retreat within the Gelugpa

tradition. The Buddhist Association offers weekly classes and opportunities for private instruction in Vajrayana. Introductory workshops are offered at the local college. Longer retreats have to be organized privately at present, but retreat facilities are planned for the near future.
ADDRESS: P.O. Box 5, Duncan, B.C., Canada V9L 3X1
PHONE: (604) 748-6028
LINEAGE: Gelugpa
SPIRITUAL HEAD: His Holiness The Dalai Lama (Tibetan)
RESIDENT DIRECTOR: Jhampa Shaneman (Canadian)
AFFILIATED WITH: Autonomous
ESTABLISHED: 1984
FACILITIES: Urban meditation center. Developing a country retreat facility. Solitary retreat center planned.
RETREATS OFFERED: Prostration retreat, weekend sittings, supervised and unsupervised solitary retreats, three-year Vajrayana retreat.
OPEN TO: General public

Kootenay Dharmadhatu

We offer two week night public sittings and a three-hour sitting on Sunday mornings. Buddhist intensive weekends and Shambhala training are offered periodically. Week night classes range from beginning Shamatha to Vajrayana.
ADDRESS: 444 Baker Street, Nelson, B.C., Canada (Mailing address: Box 136, Nelson, B.C., Canada V1L 4W9)
PHONE: (604) 352-6559
LINEAGE: Karma Kagyu
SPIRITUAL HEAD: Vajra Regent Osel Tendzin; founded by the Vidyadhara, the Ven. Chogyam Trungpa, Rinpoche.
RESIDENT DIRECTOR: Russell Rodgers, Richard Cima, Kathy Cima, Fallo Ings, Margaret McKeown, Tim and Sally Albert

AFFILIATED WITH: Vajradhatu International/Canada
ESTABLISHED: 1975
FACILITIES: Urban meditation center, cabins for solitary retreats
RETREATS OFFERED: Nyinthun, weekend sittings, supervised and unsupervised solitary retreats. Evening sittings on Tuesdays and Thursdays, and on Sundays from 9:00–12:00 A.M.
OPEN TO: General public

Tashi Choling

ADDRESS: P.O. Box 4, Nelson, B.C., Canada V1L 4W9
PHONE: (604) 352-2579
LINEAGE: Gelugpa
SPIRITUAL HEAD: H. H. Kyabje Ling, Rinpoche, H. H. Kyabje Trijang, Rinpoche, H. H. Kyabje Song, Rinpoche.
RESIDENT DIRECTOR: President Mousi Tchir

Dharmadhatu Vancouver

We have open house every Monday evening at 7:30 P.M., which includes a public talk and discussion, as well as meditation instruction from qualified instructors. This program is offered free of charge and is designed to give individuals an opportunity to explore their personal interest in the Buddhist path. In addition, both newer and older practitioners are encouraged to come to the longer meditation sessions on Thursday nights and Saturday mornings. These nyinthuns are two and a half hour sessions that combine sitting and walking meditation. A series of graduated classes that introduce students to the full Buddhist path are offered every quarter. Contact Dharmadhatu for a current schedule.
ADDRESS: 3275 Heather Street, Vancouver, B.C., Canada V6N 4A2
PHONE: (604) 874-8420

LINEAGE: Karma Kagyu
SPIRITUAL HEAD: Vajra Regent Osel
Tendzin. Founded by the Vidyadhara,
the Ven. Chogyam Trungpa, Rinpoche.
RESIDENT DIRECTOR: Frank and Susan
Ryan
AFFILIATED WITH: Vajradhatu International/Canada
ESTABLISHED: 1974
FACILITIES: Urban meditation center
OPEN TO: General public

Zuru Ling Center

Zasep Tulku, Rinpoche, is our spiritual
advisor and visits the center at least once a
year to give teachings and initiations. The
center meanwhile provides meditation instruction and Dharma teachings for beginners one night a week given by local
experienced Dharma teachers as well as a
Sadhana evening for experienced students. Day retreats are held from time to
time as well as visits, usually every three
months, by Tibetan lamas and monks.
Practices at Zuru Ling include Anapanasati (mindfulness of breathing) and Sadhana (chanting) practice. We focus mainly
on the purification practice of Vajrasattva.
Occasionally we do a form of Guru Yoga
called the Guru Puja Tsog, which is a bimonthly ritual feast offering with chanting. From time to time we do a healing
practice called Medicine Buddha and the
meditation of the wisdom deity, Green
Tara.
ADDRESS: 2577 Willow St, Vancouver,
B.C., Canada (Mailing address: P.O.
Box 15283, Vancouver, B.C., Canada
V6B 5B1)
PHONE: (604) 261-4143; 251-3651;
291-2426; 255-1699
LINEAGE: Gelugpa
SPIRITUAL HEAD: Zasep Tulku,
Rinpoche
AFFILIATED WITH: Autonomous
ESTABLISHED: 1982

FACILITIES: Urban meditation center
RETREATS OFFERED: One-day and
weekend sittings, one-week retreats
with visiting teachers. Retreats are
given every three to six months, and
some are held in the country.
OPEN TO: General public. Members only
for high initiation retreats.

Dharma Study Group, Victoria

Refer to Vajradhatu/Canada, Halifax,
Nova Scotia, for description.
ADDRESS: 608 Toronto Street, Victoria,
B.C., Canada V8V 1P6
LINEAGE: Karma Kagyu
SPIRITUAL HEAD: Vajra Regent Osel
Tendzin. Founded by the Vidyadhara,
the Ven. Chogyam Trungpa, Rinpoche.
AFFILIATED WITH: Vajradhatu/Canada
OPEN TO: General public

Kagyu Kunkhyab Chuling (KKC) Victoria

Until 1987 the Kagyu Kunkhyab Chuling
(KKC) in Victoria was a study group offshoot of the KKC Vancouver Center.
However, in 1987 officers were appointed
for our own Victoria center, and we are
encouraging people to become members.
The cost is $120 per year. We have been
meeting each Monday night at the home
of one of our members for course presentation or for meditation practice. The two
courses offered so far have been Foundations of Buddhist Meditation and Basic
Buddhist Concepts. Also, in conjunction
with KKC in Vancouver and on Saltspring Island, visits by several lamas have
been sponsored. We have been fortunate
to have visits from their Eminences Tai
Situ, Rinpoche, and Jamgon Kongtrul,
Rinpoche. Our aim is to acquire a permanent center and to support a resident
lama, Lama Tsering Lhamo.

ADDRESS: C/O 2942 Leigh Road, Victoria, B.C., Canada V9B 4G3
PHONE: (604) 474-3728
LINEAGE: Tibetan Kagyu
SPIRITUAL HEAD: Kalu, Rinpoche (Tibetan)
AFFILIATED WITH: Kagyu Kunkhyab Chuling (Vancouver)
ESTABLISHED: 1987
FACILITIES: Member's home, at present.

Sakya Thubten Kunga Choling / Victoria Buddhist Dharma Society

The salient feature of this center is the presence of the resident *geshe*, Sakya Lama Tashi Namgyal, whose regular teachings and accessible guidance provide a rare opportunity to study all aspects of Mahayana and Vajrayana, while experiencing the subtle pressures of personal involvement through contact with this jovial, extremely good natured, witty, and insightful teacher. His efforts are made possible largely by the long-standing devotion of Avi Dechen Drolma, who has aided and supported him in every way for many years. Lama's translated teachings, and his own English teachings, provide complementary detail and motivation for comprehensive study. Emphasis is on integration of the teachings in everyday life: how to transcend unwholesome mentation; to practice stabilizing and insight meditation; to study *madyamika* philosophy; and how to use the experiences so gained for the betterment of work-related and personal activities. Emphasis is on the need for ongoing study and practice at whatever level permits the student to maintain interest and enthusiasm. There are daily ceremonies and meditation. Tibetan language study and a tape library are also available.

ADDRESS: 1149 Leonard Street, Victoria, B.C., Canada V8V 2S3
PHONE: (604) 385-4828
LINEAGE: Sakya
SPIRITUAL HEAD: Geshe Tashi Namgyal (Tibetan)
AFFILIATED WITH: Sakya Centre, Dehra Dun (India)
ESTABLISHED: 1974
FACILITIES: Urban meditation center, private rooms available for solitary retreats.
RETREATS OFFERED: Weekend retreats, solitary retreats (study with the lama).
OPEN TO: Members only

MANITOBA

Dharma Study Group, Winnipeg

Refer to Vajradhatu/Canada, Halifax, Nova Scotia, for description.
ADDRESS: #1–118 Grove Street, Winnipeg, Manitoba, Canada R2W 3K8
LINEAGE: Karma Kagyu
SPIRITUAL HEAD: Vajra Regent Osel Tendzin. Founded by the Vidyadhara, the Ven. Chogyam Trungpa, Rinpoche.
RESIDENT DIRECTOR: Robyn Traill
AFFILIATED WITH: Vajradhatu International/Canada
OPEN TO: General public

NOVA SCOTIA

Karma Dzong, Halifax

Karma Dzong/Halifax is an urban meditation center in the Kagyu-Nyingma tradition of Tibetan Buddhism. It was founded by the Vidyadhara, the Ven. Chogyam Trungpa, Rinpoche. An affiliate of Vajradhatu/Canada, its activities are coordinated with Vajradhatu/USA, a sister organization. The center offers regular periods of Shamatha/Vipassana meditation and instruction in this basic technique. Classes are also offered for all levels of experience

and knowledge of Buddhism. Seminars
are given by the Vajra Regent Osel Tend-
zin, Dharma heir to the Ven. Trungpa,
Rinpoche, and also by other teachers of
the Kagyu and Nyingma lineages. Lim-
ited retreat facilities are available through
Karma Dzong.
ADDRESS: 1084 Tower Road, Halifax,
Nova Scotia, Canada B3H 2Y5
PHONE: (902)420-1118
LINEAGE: Karma Kagyu
SPIRITUAL HEAD: Vajra Regent Osel
Tendzin. Founded by the Vidyadhara,
the Ven. Chogyam Trungpa, Rinpoche.
RESIDENT DIRECTOR: Osel Tendzin
AFFILIATED WITH: Vajradhatu Interna-
tional/Canada
ESTABLISHED: 1979
FACILITIES: An urban meditation cen-
ter, we also offer some facilities for soli-
tary retreats.
RETREATS OFFERED: Solitary retreat fa-
cilities are available.
OPEN TO: General public

Vajradhatu, Canada

Vajradhatu/Canada is the sister organiza-
tion of Vajradhatu/USA. It oversees and
coordinates the activities of a number of
affiliate centers in the major cities of
Canada. These local Dharmadhatus and
Dharma Study Groups offer regular pe-
riods of sitting meditation, classes for all
levels of experience and practice, and a va-
riety of seminars, special programs, and
intensive practice sessions.
ADDRESS: 1084 Tower Road, Halifax,
Nova Scotia, Canada B3H 2Y5
PHONE: (902) 420-1118
LINEAGE: Karma Kagyu
SPIRITUAL HEAD: Vajra Regent Osel
Tendzin. Founded by the Vidyadhara,
the Ven. Chogyam Trungpa, Rinpoche.
RESIDENT DIRECTOR: Vajra Regent
Osel Tendzin (American)

AFFILIATED WITH: Vajradhatu
International
ESTABLISHED: 1975
FACILITIES: Urban meditation center
with some retreat facilities available.
RETREATS OFFERED: Solitary retreats of
varying lengths
OPEN TO: General public

Dharmadhatus
Dharma Study Groups (DSG)
Forming Dharma Study Groups
(FDSG)
Under the Auspices of Vajradhatu
International/Canada

Generally speaking, whenever you see one
of these names, it indicates a center associated with Vajradhatu, although, to add to
the merry confusion, a few groups aligned
with Karma Triyana Dharmachakra (see
Woodstock, N.Y.) are also called Study
Group, or Dharma Study Group.

Technically speaking, a Dharmadhatu is
a center *legally* affiliated with Vajradhatu.
In order to be designated as such, a group
must consist of twenty-five or more dues-
paying members, have been in existence
for more than two years, and maintain
separate space for its activities. Dharmadhatus offer classes, hold open houses for
beginners, and conduct regularly scheduled periods of meditation.

Dharma Study Groups are similar to
Dharmadhatus, although they do not yet
enjoy legal affiliate status. In order to be
designated a DSG, a group must have
been in existence for from one to two
years and have ten or more members from
whom dues are being collected.

Forming Dharma Study Groups might
be considered the first step in the long
journey toward full-fledged Dharmadhatuhood. A FDSG is simply an aggregation
of up to ten members who have been

meeting to study and practice together for from one to two years. It's not officially an affiliate, but it is nonetheless a part of— the Vajradhatu mandala. Bear in mind that none of the foregoing is written in stone. The Vajradhatu affiliate structure is a fairly loose and fluid one, and the ground rules, like all else in the phenomenal world, are subject to change. —Editor

Gampo Abbey (Monastic Center for Vajradhatu)

Gampo Abbey is a Tibetan-style monastary for Western monks and nuns and for "candidates" for ordination. The year is divided into four parts: Winter Retreat (December–March), during which time practice and study are pursued intensively; the schedule differs from year to year. Spring/Summer Work Period (April– August), during which time there is a minimum of four hours of meditation. Construction, gardening, and so forth are stressed; this is open to all. Rain's Retreat (August–September or October—date changes from year to year), which is closed to anyone except monks, nuns, and serious candidates; and Fall Work Period, which follows the same schedule as the Spring Work Period. Although various Vajrayana practices are used here, the basic meditation technique is Shamatha/ Vipassana:

Taking a good upright posture, with eyes open and hands resting open, palms down on the thighs, one feels the breath as it goes out. There is a pause, and then one feels the next breath as it goes out. When thoughts take one away, they are noted without judgement, using the label 'thinking' . . . then one simply returns again to the outbreath.

ADDRESS: Pleasant Bay, Nova Scotia, Canada B0E 2P0
PHONE: (902) 224-2752
LINEAGE: Karma Kagyu
SPIRITUAL HEAD: Founder: Vidyadhara, the Ven. Chogyam Trungpa, Rinpoche. Current Abbot: Ven. Thrangu, Rinpoche
RESIDENT DIRECTOR: Bhikshuni Pema Chodron (American)
AFFILIATED WITH: Vajradhatu International
ESTABLISHED: 1983
FACILITIES: A country retreat facility. We are primarily here to train monks, nuns, and candidates; so we are not really "public" in the usual sense. Cabins for solitary retreats.
RETREATS OFFERED: Rain's Retreat for ordained Sangha and candidates only. Winter Retreat is the same, but open on some occasions to others. See notes above for year-round programs.
OPEN TO: Monks, nuns, monastic candidates, and some lay people

ONTARIO

Urgyan Osal Cho Dzong

The Ven. Lama Karma Jampa Rabjam, our resident teacher, and his senior students teach Shamatha and Vipassana meditation for beginners. For more advanced students, the teachings and practices of the Karma Kagyu and Nyingma orders of Tibetan Buddhism are available. We have a daily schedule of meditation and pujas with several annual retreats of ten to fifteen days each. Introductory classes are available, taught by senior students of Ven. Lama Jampa.
ADDRESS: P.O. Box 68, R. R. 3, Madoc, Ontario, Canada K0K 2K0
PHONE: (613) 478-2568

LINEAGE: Karma Kagyu/Nyingma,
Long Chen Nying Thig, and Nam Cho
SPIRITUAL HEAD: H. H. Karmapa and
H. H. Penor, Rinpoche (Tibetan)
RESIDENT DIRECTOR: Ven. Lama Karma
Jampa Rabjam (Spanish-German)
ESTABLISHED: 1979
FACILITIES: Urban meditation center,
country retreat facility, facilities for soli-
tary retreats
RETREATS OFFERED: Mahamudra and
Dzog Chen, as well as Shamatha and
Vipassana for beginners.
OPEN TO: Members and the general
public

Gaden Phen De Ling
ADDRESS: P.O. Box 414, Orleans,
Ontario, Canada K1C 1S8
PHONE: (613) 744-7330
LINEAGE: Gelugpa
SPIRITUAL HEAD: H. H. Kyabje Ling,
Rinpoche, H. H. Kyabje Trijang, Rin-
poche, H. H. Kaybje Song, Rinpoche
RESIDENT DIRECTOR: Bob Kapitany

Dharmadhatu of Ottawa
For description look under Vajradhatu/
Canada, Halifax, Nova Scotia.
ADDRESS: McLennan, #4–115 Daly Ave-
nue, Ottawa, Ontario, Canada K1N
6E6
LINEAGE: Karma Kagyu
SPIRITUAL HEAD: Vajra Regent Osel
Tendzin. Founded by the Vidyadhara,
the Ven. Chogyam Trungpa, Rinpoche.
RESIDENT DIRECTOR: Palden and Val-
erie McLennan
AFFILIATED WITH: Vajradhatu Interna-
tional/ Canada
ESTABLISHED: 1978
FACILITIES: Urban meditation center
RETREATS OFFERED: Nyinthun (one-
day) and weekend sittings.
OPEN TO: General public

St. Catherines Karma Kargyu Centre
For description, see Toronto Karma Kar-
gyu Centre.
ADDRESS: 23 Gromley Crescent, St.
Catherines, Ontario, Canada L2M 5Y3
PHONE: (416) 934-4145
LINEAGE: Karma-Kargyu
SPIRITUAL HEAD: Cho Je Lama Namse,
Rinpoche.
AFFILIATED WITH: Karma Kargyu Soci-
ety of Canada
ESTABLISHED: 1983
FACILITIES: See Toronto Karma Kargyu
RETREATS OFFERED: See Toronto
Karma Kargyu
OPEN TO: General public

Potala Tibetan Meditation Centre (Thunder Bay)
Zasep Tulku, Rinpoche, teaches Gaden
Tibetan Buddhism two to three times a
year in Thunder Bay. Potala Centre mem-
bers meet every Tuesday evening in a
member's home and offer occasional in-
troductory weekend workshops and initia-
tions through visiting Buddhist teachers.
ADDRESS: 453 Darwin Cresent, Thunder
Bay, Ontario, Canada P7B 5W5
PHONE: (807) 345-3077
LINEAGE: Gelugpa
SPIRITUAL HEAD: Zazep Tulku,
Rinpoche.
RESIDENT DIRECTOR: See Gaden Chol-
ing Mahayana Buddhist Meditation
Centre, Toronto.
AFFILIATED WITH: Gaden Choling
Mahayana Buddhist Meditation Centre,
Toronto
ESTABLISHED: 1981
FACILITIES: Member's home
RETREATS OFFERED: Weekend sittings
and workshops, weekend teachings, re-
treats three to four times a year.
OPEN TO: General public

Dharmadhatu Buddhist Meditation Centre of Toronto

Dharmadhatu is an urban center for the practice and study of Buddhist teachings, founded by the Vidyadhara, the Venerable Chogyam Trungpa, Rinpoche. Dharmadhatu offers a regular schedule of meditation practice, as well as regular all-day practice sessions known as *nyinthuns*. Public classes offer a further introduction to Buddhist teachings and provide a way to examine and understand the personal experience of meditation practice.

The whole practice of meditation is based upon the present moment, here and now, and means working with this situation, this present state of mind. Every act of our lives can contain simplicity and precision and thus can have tremendous beauty and dignity. (From *Myth of Freedom* by Chogyam Trungpa, Rinpoche.)

ADDRESS: 670 Bloor Street West, 3rd Floor, Toronto, Ontario, Canada M6G 1L2
PHONE: (416) 588-6465
LINEAGE: Karma Kagyu
SPIRITUAL HEAD: Vajra Regent Osel Tendzin. Founded by the Vidyadhara, the Ven. Chogyam Trungpa, Rinpoche.
RESIDENT DIRECTOR: James Colosi (American)
AFFILIATED WITH: Vajradhatu International/Canada
ESTABLISHED: 1972
FACILITIES: Urban meditation center

Gaden Choling Mahayana Buddhist Meditation Centre

Gaden Choling was founded in 1980 with the arrival of our resident teacher, Ven. Lama Zasep Tulku, Rinpoche. He was asked to fulfill this by His Holiness Ling, Rinpoche, Senior Tutor to His Holiness the Dalai Lama of Tibet. Rinpoche gives regular teachings on Buddhist philosophy and practice as well as initiations and private interviews. There are also weekly meditation sessions and occasional teachings by his senior students and members of the house. Gaden Choling wishes to serve as many people as possible. We are here to create an oasis of serenity amidst the busy confusion of big city life and to offer refuge, resources, and the teachings of the Gelugpa tradition.

ADDRESS: 637 Christie Street, Toronto, Ontario, Canada M6C 3E6
PHONE: (416) 651-3849
LINEAGE: Gelugpa
SPIRITUAL HEAD: H. H. Kyabje Ling, Rinpoche, H. H. Kyabje Trijang, Rinpoche, H. Y. Kyabje Song, Rinpoche
RESIDENT DIRECTOR: Ven. Zasep Tulku, Rinpoche
AFFILIATED WITH: Autonomous
ESTABLISHED: 1980
FACILITIES: Urban meditation center. We use the sister center in Ithaca, New York, for retreats.
RETREATS OFFERED: Shorter Vipassana courses, day-long and weekend sittings, and various retreats as the need arises (tantric, etc.).
OPEN TO: General public

Toronto Karma Kargyu Center

A schedule of daily and weekly teachings and *pujas* are conducted by Ven. Lama Namse, Rinpoche, visiting lamas, and senior students. Rituals (*Chenrezig*, Green Tara, and Mahakala) involve chanting and silent sitting in the Kargyu tradition of Tibetan Buddhism.

ADDRESS: 503 Huron Street, Toronto, Ontario, Canada M5R 2R6
PHONE: (416) 323-0282
LINEAGE: Tibetan Kargyu

Ven. Zasep Tulku, Rinpoche, of Gaden Choling Mahayana Buddhist Meditation Centre, Toronto.

SPIRITUAL HEAD: Cho Je Lama Namse, Rinpoche
RESIDENT DIRECTOR: Same
AFFILIATED WITH: Karma Kargyu Society of Canada
ESTABLISHED: 1976
FACILITIES: Urban meditation center
RETREATS OFFERED: Short Vipassana courses, chanting retreats, weekend sittings, *Nyung Nye*, empowerments, *pujas*.
OPEN TO: General public

QUEBEC

Dharmadhatu Montreal

Senior students teach Shamatha/Vipassana meditation and give six-week classes on the teachings of the Buddha, both Hinayana and Mahayana. Dharmadhatu is open three evenings a week for meditation and all day on Sundays. Instructions and teachings are given in both French and English. We also offer complete Shambhala training in both languages.

ADDRESS: 5311 Park Avenue #200, Montreal, Quebec, Canada H2V 4G9
PHONE: (514) 279-9115
LINEAGE: Kagyu
SPIRITUAL HEAD: Vajra Regent Osel Tendzin. Founded by the Vidyadhara, the Ven. Chogyam Trungpa, Rinpoche.
RESIDENT DIRECTOR: Several senior students

AFFILIATED WITH: Vajradhatu International/Canada
ESTABLISHED: 1976
FACILITIES: Urban meditation center, rented facilities
RETREATS OFFERED: *Nyinthun* (daylong) and weekend sittings, and Shambhala training.
OPEN TO: General public

PART IV

Nonsectarian Buddhism and Other New Directions

Friends of the Western Buddhist Order*

BY MANJUVAJRA

This is not simply a rag bag of Buddhist practices, but a developing Western tradition that owes its allegiance to the Three Jewels, and not to any particular school of Buddhism. It is not, therefore, Theravada, Mahayana, or Vajrayana, but simply Buddhayana.

 At Aryaloka the morning bell rings at six o'clock, calling between ten and twenty-five retreatants from their sleep. In the silence they rise. Some take a walk outside, circumambulating the twin geodesic domes that form the main building; some stroll through the trees to the river bank and watch the insects scoot across the surface of the water. Others, like myself, take a cup of tea in the large, circular, dome-roofed sitting room. A second bell rings in the quiet dawn, and we gather in the third floor shrine room. In silence we take our seats, sitting in lines perpendicular to the shrine, facing into the room. Before the leader enters, some sit thoughtfully, others look around the room taking in the other meditators, others watch the rising incense smoke, or, on rainy days, listen to the sound of the rain on the roof. The leader enters, and together we chant the threefold salutation before the shrine: *"Namo Buddaya, Namo Dharmakaya, Namo Sanghaya, Namo Nama, Om, Ah, Hum."* We chant the refuges and precepts in Pali and then enter into a period of meditation practice.

The Buddhist tradition has a wide range of meditation practices. The Friends of the Western Buddhist Order (FWBO) makes use of a number of them. Everyone is taught Mindfulness of Breathing, *Metta Bhav-*

*Aryaloka Community, New Market, New Hampshire

ana (meditation on loving kindness), and "just sitting." But those who have been ordained into the Western Buddhist Order also practice other Theravada meditations and visualization practices. Over the years the community of Vajraloka, a FWBO meditation center in Wales, United Kingdom, has developed a systematic program of instruction in meditation. This approach is being adopted by most FWBO Centers throughout the world and even meditators with twenty years of experience claim that it has revolutionized their practice.

The bell rings, signaling the beginning of a session of Mindfulness of Breathing. First I run through PIPER: *P*osture, *I*ntrospection, *P*urpose, *E*nthusiasm, *R*esolve.

Posture: first the legs and height of my seat, then the angle of my pelvis, straightened back well-balanced, the hands at the right height, without strain on the arms, supported by the lap or a small cushion, check chest, neck, shoulders, and the angle of the head.

Introspection: How am I feeling at this moment? What is on my mind? What are likely to be the distractions and hindrances to my meditation?

Purpose: What is the purpose of the practice? To be mindful of the breath and to develop concentration.

Enthusiasm: It is raised for this purpose by considering the value of mindfulness and awareness, by remembering the experiences of meditation in the past, and by many other methods.

Resolve: Finally after resolving to stick with the practice, and to keep trying even though it may become difficult, I set out on the practice itself.

For the first period of ten minutes, I count my breaths at the end of each exhalation, for the second I count at the beginning of each inhalation, for the third I simply follow my breath, and finally I follow the sensation of my breath as it passes through my nostrils. Every now and again I may run through PIPER, or work consciously on one of the five hindrances, or try to balance the factors of *dhyana* (meditation) as they appear in "access" concentration. Meditation is work, and I use the tools of the trade. I work without will, without forcing, as an artist will work on a poem or on a wood carving. By taking the raw material, the contents of my ordinary mind, and by shaping and directing it, I see emerging the creative mind—steadied, perfectly purified, translucent, untainted, supple and pliable, fit for wielding, established and immovable. At times I experience a deep tranquility; at times a ripple of delight runs through my body; on some occasions a torrent of ecstasy lifts me out of myself. At other times it seems as if I will never gain even a little mindfulness; at times meditation is painful. On retreats, however, even if there are no powerful meditation experiences, I still experience the gradual development of a more positive state that is clearer, brighter, friendlier, and more energetic than the one which I normally experience.

The bell marks the end of this phase of practice and the beginning of a period of walking meditation. Slowly we leave our seats, form a circle, and walk around the circular shrine room, maintaining awareness of the body and the input of the senses: the perfume of the incense, the sound of creaking floorboards and swishing clothing, the taste of tea still lingering, the brush of air against the skin, the sight of knots in the pine floor, the back of the person in front of me, and the shrine as I pass by. In this way, the awareness developed in the sitting meditation is carried into an activity that is closer to everyday life. After ten or fifteen minutes, the bell rings again, and we take our seats for a second period of meditation.

Once again I run through PIPER and then enter *Metta Bhavana* practice, the development of Universal Loving Kindness. I develop warmth and friendliness towards myself, towards a near and dear friend, a neutral person, and an enemy. Finally, in the fifth section, that loving kindness is directed outward ever further until all beings in the universe are included in its sphere. As the retreat progresses, my feelings of friendliness toward the other people with me increases noticeably. Even the irritation that I feel with some of them gradually subsides as I turn my attention to their more positive qualities, and I come to accept their irritating ones. I even start to feel a genuine affection for their foibles.

After meditation we eat breakfast at a long, broad table beneath the spacious dome, and although the period of silence is now officially over, many people sit quietly. At another table people start to talk. We normally observe silence over night, between the end of the *puja* and the beginning of breakfast. Often there are longer periods. When the retreat began, the silence was awkward for some, but gradually, as the retreat took hold, people happily slipped into a quieter mode of communication.

Ben and I decide to take a walk before the study group starts. We had not met before the retreat started two days ago. Even so we feel as if we have known each other for a long time. There is already a feeling of trust and friendliness that is partly a result of the communication exercises that we did together yesterday afternoon. Although the three simple exercises seemed a little silly to start with, we entered into them with a light spirit, and at the end of an hour we found that they had indeed improved our ability to communicate, to empathize, and to appreciate each other. As we walk, we talk of the usual things, of relationships, jobs, plans, and our difficulties. We both show concern about how to live our lives—more like we live them on retreat. We discuss how we could make concrete changes that would enable us to live in this brighter, simpler, more loving state.

Retreats organized by the FWBO are of many types. Some are entirely devoted to meditation, some emphasize study, although meditation is always part of the program. On this retreat there is an equal amount of meditation and study.

The Buddhist tradition is often described as a treasure chest of jewels. One of the characteristics of a jewel is that it is attractive to look at. As one looks more deeply into the play of color and light, it becomes ever more delightful. Study means to pick up one aspect of Buddhism and look at it, to explore all its facets and gaze deeply into its core. Only in this way do the teachings on ethics, psychology, and philosophy reveal their delightful nature. Without exception, all aspects of the Buddhist tradition are practical. Study serves to strengthen the basis on which we practice, but it also opens the mind to a wider vision and deeper

Aryaloka Community—a study group in session.

understanding. It challenges our preconceived notions. It clarifies our
thoughts and the way in which they influence how we live our lives.
And it provides an opportunity to communicate with other people on
a higher level than usual.

On retreat we study in three ways. Firstly, people make use of the
library to explore the richness of the Buddhist literary tradition. Secondly, talks are given "live," by a member of the Western Buddhist Order, or from a tape by the Ven. Sangharakshita. His talks, given to
Western students (in England) over the past twenty years, are informative, erudite, and inspiring. Thirdly, we investigate traditional texts in
detail in our study groups. Over the past fifteen years, Sangharakshita
has led study on over fifty texts or sections of texts from all the major
Buddhist traditions—from the *Dhammapada* to the *Life and Liberation
of Padmasambhava*, from the *Abhidharma* to the *Songs of Milarepa*. His

method of study and his commentary are passed on by his students. Study groups are always led by qualified members of the Western Buddhist Order.

In the atmosphere of a retreat, it is delightful to sit with others, to clear aside misunderstandings, and to open oneself to the vision that the text is attempting to communicate. To glimpse, however imperfectly, the purified mind of the Buddha is a powerful force of inspiration, which clears away a mass of confusion. The study session lasts about two hours, during which about ten of us sit in a circle and go through the text, paragraph by paragraph. It is surprising to discover that the Buddha's communication to a disciple in the forests of northern India twenty-five hundred years ago is still relevant to us today. I also find that I am building a strong connection with the monks in the ancient texts, many of whom had characteristics that are instantly recognizable. In fact, there are people exactly like them in this very study group, and it is here, in the study group, that the Dharma—the Buddha's teaching—comes alive. His presence is felt as the material sinks deeper and fires the imagination.

After a light lunch I take a walk with a man who has visited many different Buddhist groups. He is concerned about what particular Buddhist tradition the FWBO belongs to. I explain to him that it is eclectic. There are meditation practices, chanting, and the study of the Pali texts—activities associated with the Theravada. Yet there is also *puja* in which the Bodhisattvas are mentioned and during which the *Prajnaparamita* texts are recited. The study and lectures are frequently based on one of the great Mahayana scriptures or on what is clearly a Mahayana doctrine. But we also make use of *Milarepa, Padamsambhava, dakinis* (feminine deities), gurus, and the foundation practices of the Vajrayana. Chinese meditation texts, Japanese poems, a modified tea ceremony, and Zen stories—all may appear during the course of a retreat. As we discuss the matter, however, it soon becomes clear that this is not simply a rag bag of Buddhist practices, but a developing Western tradition that owes its allegiance to the Three Jewels, and not to any particular school of Buddhism. It is not, therefore, Theravada, Mahayana, or Vajrayana, but simply *Buddhayana*.

Western cultural conditioning has presented particular problems for

Western Buddhists. It has been necessary to search the whole of the Buddhist tradition to find those practices and texts that really are of practical use. Once a text or practice is found to be useful, it becomes incorporated into the new tradition; it becomes part of the FWBO. Without trying to be different from, or the same as, any Eastern school, the FWBO exhibits a strong connection with the Buddhist tradition by devoting itself to discovering the best way to practice Buddhism in a modern industrialized world.

At three o'clock we return again to the shrine room to practice meditation. I find myself sleepy, but following the instructions for sloth and torpor, I open my eyes and look at a bright spot on the floor. Still I doze. I continually run through PIPER. I try to think of the times that I have been clear and bright in meditation, but still the world swims in confusion. Then I recall the image of the Buddha. I imagine the Buddha to be in the room, sitting on the shrine, but still I cannot keep my eyes open. The Buddha, as it were, leaps from the shrine, transformed into a wild, red *dakini*, flying and swirling about the room, her black hair flying in all directions, her naked, red body radiating energy. I sit bolt upright as a jet of energy shoots through my body, followed by another, and yet another. Then silence descends, and I feel tranquil but perfectly alert. My drowsiness has vanished completely, and I spend the rest of the afternoon in delightful concentration, keenly aware of my breathing and of radiating warmth to all those around me.

After dinner, which like all meals is vegetarian, we listen to a lecture by Sangharakshita—one of a series on aspects of the Bodhisattva—that outlines the major doctrinal basis of this sublime spiritual ideal. As with the earlier study group, this lecture provides many practical insights, as well as the inspiration for working toward that ideal.

At nine o'clock we gather once again in the shrine room for the final meditation and *puja*. A *puja* is a devotional practice in seven parts, consisting of recitation, chanting, and readings from Buddhist texts, usually of the more poetic and inspirational type. Each part of the *puja* is associated with one of the seven emotional states necessary for the experience of *bodhicitta*—committing oneself to the attainment of enlightenment for the sake of all sentient beings. The recitation and chanting with other people stimulates and gives expression to these emotional states and thus opens the door of the heart to a vision of enlightened mind. Enlightenment, or any level of insight (*vipassana*), is not simply a cold intellectual understanding, but an emotionally charged realization that affects the whole being. Too easily we understand sublime spiritual truths with our intellect and assume that to be the end of the matter. It is but a first step. Rational understanding is important, but it must be allowed to penetrate the whole of our being; the emotions must also be engaged and transformed by understanding, so that insight may arise. The *puja* works directly on the emotions. With recitation, chanting, and mantras we open the heart and feel the emotions respond to the Buddha, the Dharma, the Bodhisattvas, and the whole *sangha*. As the final bell of the *puja* reverberates around the shrine room, and we sit in silence before the shrine. I watch the soft candlelight illuminate the gentle face of the Buddha figure and the smoke of the incense rising in wisps and clouds. A thought passes through my mind. For hundreds of years, for over a hundred generations, followers of the *Buddhadharma* have had this same experience. In the tropical heat of India, the cold vastness of Tibet, the mountain temples of China, and the stark Zendos of Japan, many millions of people have experienced this same tranquility and deep sense of satisfaction. They have watched the same swirling incense smoke, the same lights. What a marvel, what a delight! Tears of joy swell in my eyes and roll slowly over my cheek.

Just sitting. Silence. Perfection.

An Englishman, Manjuvajra became interested in Buddhism after reading Jack Kerouac's The Dharma Bums. *He encountered Ven. Sangharakshita in 1970 and was ordained by the Friends of the Western Buddhist Order three years later. After a ten thousand-mile motorcycle tour of American Dharma centers in 1984, he established Aryaloka, a men's spiritual community and retreat center in New Hampshire where he currently lives and works.*

Graduating from Buddhism*

BY CHRISTOPHER REED

To practice Buddhism, or to practice anything, we must go back to our roots. There are many aspects of the Judaeo-Christian tradition which reflect nondualistic understanding. If we come in touch with them, with the joy of our own traditions, standing firmly in our own roots, we can be vehicles for Buddha-Dharma as it comes to the West.

We cannot do anything for peace without ourselves being peace. If you cannot smile, you cannot help other people smile. If you are not peaceful, then you cannot contribute to the peace movement. If one person is a real person, living happily, smiling, then all of us, all the world, will benefit from that person. A person doesn't have to do a lot to save the world. A person has to be a person. That is the basis of peace.

—Thich Nhat Hanh

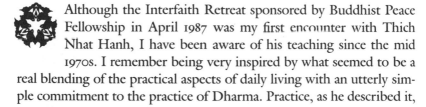 Although the Interfaith Retreat sponsored by Buddhist Peace Fellowship in April 1987 was my first encounter with Thich Nhat Hanh, I have been aware of his teaching since the mid 1970s. I remember being very inspired by what seemed to be a real blending of the practical aspects of daily living with an utterly simple commitment to the practice of Dharma. Practice, as he described it, seemed to be completely "practical."

Recently I had been feeling stale in my own practice. For several

*An interfaith retreat with Thich Nhat Hanh sponsored by the Buddhist Peace Fellowship

months I had been feeling disconnected, both from my surroundings and from what I sensed had become just a habit of practice. My sadness about the unlikely survival of our society, our planet, left me hopeless, angry, disgusted, and hollow. I came to this retreat with a feeling that perhaps I needed to graduate from "Buddhism," at least what I presently understood as Buddhism, to become a human being again—to return to some point of simplicity, to what is "practical."

Thich Nhat Hanh began by telling us that instead of having international conferences on religion, it might be better to have an International Conference on Cooking, where participants could prepare and share food together, or an International Conference on Looking at Trees! In a conference on cooking, no one would discuss the "truth" of one cuisine or another; they would just enjoy the food. He suggested that the sharing of our traditions in this Interfaith Retreat could be done in the same spirit, not observing the various menus from the outside, but participating in each in order to enjoy it. It was the nearest I've ever come to attending an International Conference on Looking at Trees.

The first thing I noticed was the complete absence of any hint of hierarchy, authority, forced structure, or rigidity. Perhaps I had simply become tired of imposing those stereotypes on myself, or maybe it had something to do with being around Thich Nhat Hanh. It was something I sensed rather than something tangible, and it made me realize how often I have approached practice as an obligation, a chore by which I might gain something. Looking back, retreats and *sesshins* have usually been arduous endeavors for me—a kind of quest. However much I may have consciously understood otherwise, I usually found myself struggling very hard to do, to become . . . to become mindful, and to deepen my practice—instead of simply appreciating what I might already be. Thich Nhat Hanh spoke a lot about *apranahita* (aimlessness), walking without a destination. I found his teaching a complete joy. Perhaps I'd come with some intuition that now I might move into some new mode that could express itself without much of a struggle.

Walking meditation under the enormous trees at La Casa de Maria, a very beautiful Catholic retreat center near Santa Barbara, was wonderful. Simply being under those trees, hearing the birds sing in the clear air, was "interbeing," emptiness, coming to mean that there is room for perceptions to shift and open, to simply be.

At first it wasn't clear what this retreat was going to be. An Interfaith Retreat? Each of us was invited to say something about the religion of our birth. I remembered how, while traveling as a Westerner in India, strangers would come up and ask my name and country. Often there was a third question, "What religion are you?" By that they meant not your assumed religion but the religion of your parents. The understanding is that your roots are undeniable, like a tree's; they are the means through which all nourishment reaches you.

A large majority of the participants were practicing Buddhists— ex-Catholics, ex-Protestants, or Jews by birth, rather than by faith. There were also a number of practicing Catholics and two Quakers. How were we going to make an Interfaith Retreat out of this group of mainly Buddhist converts?

But spontaneously the retreat began to take on a form of its own. On the second day we were invited to join in Quaker worship—sitting in silence, mindfulness, sharing the spirit when it moved into words. Later we participated in a formal Quaker dialogue, each answering the question, "Give an example of how some nonviolent action has expressed itself in your life." The act of sharing some difficult memories became, in itself, an act of peace, of opening to others. Questions led to other questions, revealing assumptions we make about peace and conflict and responsibility. The fear and determination by which we express our convictions about peace seem to be the very source of conflict. Buddhists are supposed to know all about this. It seems that Quakers do, too.

On the evening of the third day, we celebrated the Eucharist, a service improvised by the one priest and several Catholics on the retreat. We participated in eating the body and drinking the blood of Christ, our feet washed as Christ washed the feet of his disciples at the last supper. I remembered the words, "Be still, and know that I am God."

On the fourth day it was the Protestants' turn, myself among them. We turned out to be a mixed group of very ex-Protestants. (Those Catholics always had been a hard act to follow!) I wondered how I had got myself into volunteering to be part of a Protestant service, and how to express all the mixed feelings I had about my upbringing in the Anglican Church. In secret, we painted forty eggs and placed them along the path where we did walking meditation every day, a symbol of the seed of continuing life. I recalled that the cross from which Jesus was hung is the same cross that, in other traditions, represents the completion of things—the mandala, the vertical ascent through the horizontal worlds and heavens; and that the Christmas evergreen is also the emblem of continuing life—the May-pole, fertility and regeneration. It was clear to me that my roots extend way beyond the specific beliefs of the schoolmaster ministers of my English childhood. How exquisite is Handel's *Messiah* and the language of the King James *Bible*—experiences that go much deeper than simply being born into a particular religion, or than the arbitrary selection of some chosen belief-system.

Later that morning we learned a Cherokee Dance of Power, or was it a Dance of Life, or Dance of Peace? The same dance was repeated in the dawn of the following day. Then finally, on the last evening, we shared a Passover dinner, with wine, matzoh, and a wealth of readings and chants from the *Hagadah*, all expressing the richness of Jewish spirit and understanding. "In this day and age," said Rabbi Moshe, "the greater devotion, greater than learning and praying, consists in accepting the world exactly as it happens to be."

Twice during the course of the retreat, under the guidance of Thich Nhat Hanh and Sister Phuong, we practiced a formal tea meditation, something like the Buddhist equivalent of a Quaker worship, where words, poems, and songs can be shared as the spirit moves. We made a picture, unrolling a scroll of paper like a river around the room; as the brush passed from hand to hand, we painted images along its bank. Like water in different rivers, we came together in an ocean that makes no distinctions. I recall that my fantasy of California, during the sixties, before I even thought of coming here, was something along the lines of this retreat. Something more than eclecticism—a deep sharing, moving past forms to something rich beyond.

I don't know why this retreat was so powerful for me. Perhaps it was just being around Thich Nhat Hanh and Sister Phuong. We seldom sat in meditation, as talking was practiced as often as silence. This showed me how much I have, in the past, hidden behind silence and conventional forms of practice—for no reason except I assumed that more was always better. As we were reminded, "It is the quality, not the quantity of meditation that matters."

Finally, this retreat was a chance to acknowledge my own roots and to appreciate that it is truly our roots which either nourish us or poison us. Maybe they need trimming from time to time; maybe parts of them need to be cut right off. Sometimes we may establish new roots in some altogether different direction. Perhaps it shows that Buddhism in the West will have to be Jewish-Buddhism, Catholic-Buddhism, and Protestant-Buddhism. Perhaps it might help in making peace with ourselves if we first come to a reconciliation with roots that have been denied—and nourish them. Just as leaves fall to the ground and give nourishment to the tree that produced them, so our origins might also be our destination.

Christopher Reed is the head teacher at Ordinary Dharma, *a Vipassana center in Venice, California, and the coordinator for the Los Angeles chapter of BPF.*

Lotus in the Fire: Prison, Practice, and Freedom*

BY JOHN DAIDO LOORI-SENSEI

---

*The fire burns
    and the lotus
blooms.
It is because the fire
burns
    that the lotus
blooms.*

A few years ago I received a letter from an inmate of the Greenhaven Correctional Facility in upstate New York. The inmate had been a Zen Buddhist practitioner for a number of years and was instrumental in starting practice groups in at least three of New York's maximum security prisons. He was new at Greenhaven prison and requested that I help him start a Zen practice group there. The state maximum security prison regulations require that religious practice groups be sponsored by a bona fide member of the clergy affiliated with an outside temple or church.

The letter took me back thirty-five years to my own past karma. While serving in the United States Navy, I received a captain's mast for a minor infraction: refusing to peel potatoes under direct orders from an officer. As a result, the captain awarded me ten days solitary confinement on bread and water at the Marine prison in the harbor. I was young, and the experience terrified me. The solitary cells were tiny.

*Lotus Flower Zendo, Greenhaven Correctional Facility, Stormville, New York

Three times a day the guard would bring three slices of bread, a bowl of water, and a little bit of salt. Bedding was removed at dawn and returned in the evening. There was nothing to do, nothing to read, no one to communicate with, nothing to watch—except for a guard in the distance. It was an incredibly claustrophobic experience that kept the edges of my being raw. By the time the ten days were up I had learned my lesson very well. I would avoid that kind of confinement at all costs.

As the years passed, that experience remained in my memory. There was always the fear that somehow, by accident, I might end up in a prison cell for a long period of time, or perhaps for life, and not be able to tolerate it. That fear remained with me for many years until, one day in the middle of a *sesshin*, after a number of years of practice, I realized that I could do it if I had to; I realized that I could live a solitary life, that *zazen* was the doorway to the strength and the power necessary to do it, and that, clearly, *zazen* is a practice every prisoner should be aware of. I felt the need to do something about bringing Zen practice into prisons, but somehow I didn't quite know where to start. So I kept postponing what I knew would be a very difficult task. I didn't seek it out, but eventually it came to me through this very special prisoner, whom I shall call Brother E. I immediately made an appointment to see him and the chief minister of the prison.

When I went to the prison, there were many gates, security checks, and complications. It took about an hour to get to where we were going after we entered the first gate of the prison. During that time, I passed other inmates visiting with family and relatives, trying to touch each other through the visitor's gate. It was terribly depressing to see and feel what was going on there. That was our first visit.

We made plans to create the sitting group and started doing all the paper work to make it happen. Almost from beginning we encountered difficulties because the guards didn't know us. They knew the Protestant minister. They knew the Catholic priest. They knew the Rabbi. They knew the Muslims. But they had no idea who the Zen Buddhists were. All they knew was that we were somehow vaguely connected with Kung Fu, and they did not want martial arts being taught to prisoners. Consequently, the guards made it difficult to gain entry and there was always some kind of red tape. A two or three-hour journey to the prison

John Daido Loori-Sensei. Portrait by Kerry Jikishin Dugan.

would result in having to spend most of our time in the waiting room and never getting to see the inmates.

Now, Brother E. was no ordinary prisoner. He was the one that had initiated the whole thing from the beginning. Although he probably has no more than a grade school education, when we began to encounter difficulties he immediately went to the prison library to research the laws on establishing a new religious group in a state prison. He then wrote a legal brief and sent it to a justice of the federal court, who found it worthy of a court case. Keep in mind that a federal court justice sees many complaints of this kind. This was one of, perhaps, two hundred which he considered having enough merit to warrant the attention of the federal courts. Next an attorney was appointed, and we went to the federal district court for a settlement. That battle continued for about a year. When the case was settled, Zen Buddhism was officially recognized by the state as a bona fide religion to be practiced at the state prisons. This precedent-making decision was the result of the effort and determination of this one Bodhisattva prisoner.

We then arranged for our first meeting with the prisoners. The Protestant chaplain gave us a room to use as a Zendo. Of course we had nothing. We had no money, no Zendo equipment. I assumed we'd be sitting on the hard wooden floors, without *zafus* (cushions) or *zabutons* (mats), until we figured out how to get what we needed. As I approached the room, escorted by a guard, I was met by prisoners wearing sitting robes. What followed was incredible to see. The students bowed in *gassho* (hands palm to palm) as I walked into a room that had become a Zendo. There were eighty prisoners sitting on *seiza* benches (small wooden benches that enable the meditator to sit in a kneeling position), which they had made. When I entered, someone struck the clappers, and they all jumped to their feet. I looked and there was an altar complete with a Buddha and *butsudan* (shrine), a *mokugyo* (a carved, hollow wooden fish used for keeping time during chanting ceremonies), and a *han* (a large block of wood, suspended from the ceiling, struck with a wooden mallet to signal the beginning of a period of meditation)—all of which they themselves had made. They had researched it in the prison library, and having examined pictures, they created everything necessary to make a functioning Zendo. Brother E. evidently had been training them because, when I went to the altar, there was a *jisha* (Zendo officer) ready to hand me a stick of incense. When I prepared to do three bows, someone started striking an *inkin* (a small bell used to signal the beginning and end of a round of *zazen*, or to cue students to bow during ceremonies), and they all did the bows with me. At that moment, I knew we had a *sangha*.

As I became familiar with what they wanted, what their needs were, I was struck by the fact that I was dealing with a kind of monastic environment. Poverty, chastity, and obedience were clearly functioning.

They even call each other "brother," as Catholic monks do. It is a life commitment: whether voluntary or not, most of the inmates are in for life. There is an incredible personal discipline going on. But, most importantly, their questions were real questions. Questions regarding the "Ground of Being," the meaning of life and death, what reality is, what truth is, what freedom is. Many had clearly raised the Bodhi mind. I was grateful to have encountered such an extraordinary group of students.

I told them at the first meeting that they should come up with a name for the group. I would then take it to our Board of Directors and request that they become an official affiliate of our monastery. As such, they could be governed by the bylaws and the monastic rules, and have all the benefits that any other affiliate had, including nonprofit status; and they would each have all the benefits that any other practicing student would have. They chose the name Lotus Flower Zendo.

For obvious reasons, the question of freedom was very important to them. Indeed, our practice is concerned with freedom. Zen practice is a way of using your mind, living your life, and living among people. But we do not provide a rule book to follow, so each one of us has to go very deeply into ourselves to find the foundations of our practice and our life. Our practice is concerned with freedom. There are all kinds of "freedoms." Needless to say, I am not talking about the freedom of license, of "I do what I want." This is not real freedom. In fact, it is exactly the opposite: another kind of cage. It soon became clear that there are many prisoners inside Greenhaven who are really free, just as there are many so-called free people outside the prison who are really prisoners.

The kind of prison that we talked about in those first days at Greenhaven was the imprisonment in the "bag of skin," the imprisonment in the illusion of a self that is separate and distinct from everything else. That prison is something we create with our minds because, in fact, the self doesn't exist. The self is an idea, a thought, something we are taught, something we learn, something we believe. In actual fact, the skin-bag doesn't define the boundaries of who we are. Our life is much more than that.

Attachment propagates the illusion of a separate self. Our attachment to things, ideas, and positions constantly reinforces the idea that there is a self. The bonds that restrict us, the cage that confines us, the limits and boundaries that we find in our life, are all self-created. Each and every one of us is free and unhindered, right from the very beginning. But until we realize this inherent freedom through our own experience, it can not begin to function in our lives. Once having realized it, there are no boundaries, no limits, no hindrances.

So we focused on the question of what freedom is. We considered karma, cause and effect. "Wondrous cause and effect," as Dogen Zenji calls it. He says, "Cause is not before and effect is not after. Cause is perfect and effect is perfect. Cause is non-dual; Dharma is non-dual. Effect is non-dual; Dharma is non-dual. Though effect is occasioned by the cause, they are not before or after, because the before and the after are non-dual in the Way." "Wondrous cause and effect," he called it.

What you do and what happens to you are the same thing. What you do is what you do with your body, with your words, and with your thoughts. Most of us can understand that we create karma by what we do with our body. It is also easy to appreciate that we create karma by what we say. But we do not as easily understand that we create karma by what we think. Punching somebody in the nose obviously creates some kind of cause and effect. Saying, "I would like to punch you in the nose," creates some kind of cause and effect. Just as certainly, thinking "I would like to punch you in the nose," equally creates some kind of cause and effect. This, in particular, became a topic for much discussion with these students.

The cause of their incarceration was violating the precept "Do not kill." The effect was lifetime imprisonment, a lifetime of being separated from their loved ones, some from their children and families. What do you do about that? What you do and what happens to you are the same thing—"cause and effect are one." When you really realize what that means, you begin to understand responsibility. Responsibility comes from the realization of no-separation: no separation from the actions that we create.

There are all kinds of acts. Those same prisoners that create despair through killing can create compassion through practice. There is a sense of responsibility: I am responsible for the whole thing. This responsibility, when you truly realize it—not when you understand you are responsible, not when you believe you are responsible, but when you realize that there is no separation between yourself and the ten thousand things—is, in itself, freedom. This is an extraordinary thing. It means you are responsible for everything. You are responsible for the past, for the future and, of course, for this moment that contains the past and the future.

It sounds like a tremendous burden. You are responsible for what is going on in Africa; you are responsible for what is going on in the whole universe. But when you really look at that responsibility, you come to realize that this is really freedom. This is freedom because when you are responsible you can no longer blame. Blaming becomes an absurdity. Saying "he made me angry" no longer makes sense. You know that only you can make you angry; you can no longer be a victim. You realize that you are the master of your own life, that what you do and what happens to you are the same thing. This means that there is something you can do, that you are not a helpless victim of circumstance.

The Lotus Flower Zendo needs continuous commitment. We, therefore, established a group of senior students from Zen Mountain Monastery to help share the responsibilities. We trained them to go into the prison to work with the prisoners. These students sit with the inmates, give talks, and help train them in service positions. We call them lay Buddhist ministers because they need to have an official title to satisfy the prison authorities.

One thing we needed to realize right from the outset was that we weren't bringing anything into the prison. Everything needed was already there. Wisdom and compassion were already there. Where does wisdom come from? Each one of those inmates in his *zazen* was manifesting the enlightened life just as we were at the monastery. The practice-and-enlightenment of those prisoners is one thing. Cause-and-effect is one thing. Wisdom is the realization of this truth of the self. To realize the nature of the self is to realize the nature of the universe. Compassion is the manifestation of that wisdom in action.

There has always been a mystique among prisoners concerning the outside world. There is a kind of magic about the outside; everything they want is outside. The "cage" is their special world, their special universe. Everything they need and want comes in, somehow, from outside. Suddenly, here was something that did not come from the outside. Something that can't come from the outside because there is no inside or outside, because there is nothing to be given, and nothing to be received—because each one of them right from the very beginning is perfect and complete, lacking nothing, just like each one of us. Of course, we can lecture about that; but to someone who is being pushed around by guards and locked up in a little room at the end of the day, it takes much sitting and emptying out to begin to realize what the truth of that really is. No matter how effectively someone talks about this, it just never "cuts it" until you manifest this in your own practice. The words and ideas that describe a reality are not the reality itself, but an abstraction. The truth is the direct, intimate, and personal experience itself. Only that direct intimacy can make us free.

Most of the prisoners in the group sit on a regular basis. They sit alone every morning and evening, but not really alone because they have begun to understand what the Three Treasures (the Buddha, Dharma, and *sangha*) is about. They have begun to understand the *sangha* treasure and its manifestation in the ten directions. So even separated by the courtyards, all of them sit as one in their separate cells, just the way they sit in the Zendo. Most of them are following the same schedule that we follow at the monastery: sitting an hour and a half in the morning and evening. They are not allowed to burn incense and candles in their cells. That is only permitted in the Zendo. But they do sit. Once a week we get together for service, interview, and Dharma Talk, in addition to *zazen*.

Wisdom and compassion begin to manifest right there in the prison. It is almost like a different civilization with its own language. An incredible hierarchy exists, for example. There are not enough guards to take care of several thousand prisoners so they depend upon the prisoners themselves to keep the peace. Some inmates in their late sixties have been at Greenhaven since they were seventeen or eighteen years old. These elder statesmen of the prison are the men that really keep the peace; for the prisoners who are in for life, this is their home. They do not want anybody disturbing the peace and tranquility of their home. So the environment stays peaceful and controlled because of the prisoners themselves.

Racial and ethnic mixing within the prison is rare. The Zen Buddhist group, however, is the only racially mixed religious group. There are caucasians, blacks, and hispanics in close to equal proportions. I have no idea why or how any of these inmates came to practice, but when you walk into the Zendo it becomes obvious that there is an incredible strength to their practice. They are the most determined group of people I have ever encountered. This group, among the several affiliates we have along the East Coast, is by far the most powerful and the most rewarding to work with.

That depressing feeling we experienced during those first few days soon ended because the brothers are so appreciative of our presence. I have never felt so appreciated in my life. When the sitting is over, we have only ten to fifteen minutes of informal relationship, because the guards immediately start sending them back to their cells for a head count. The prisoners just want to touch, they want to shake hands; they want to touch people from the outside. They want to communicate. It is obvious that our presence is appreciated, and that makes the whole thing extremely worthwhile. They repay us a hundredfold for our smallest efforts. I am convinced that what I and our lay ministers are learning from them is far more that what the prisoners are learning from us.

Compassion is the manifestation of the life of Kannon Bodhisattva. Remember the koan "The hands and Eyes of Great Compassion?" Ungan asked Dogo, "What does Kannon Bodhisattva do with those thousand hands and eyes?" Dogo replied, "It is like a person in the middle of the night reaching back for his pillow." Ungan said, "Oh, I understand." Dogo asked, "What do you understand?" Ungan said, "The whole body is hands and eyes." Dogo remarked, "That is only eighty percent." Ungan asked, "How would you say it, teacher?" Dogo answered, "Throughout the body are hands and eyes."

How, indeed, does Kannon Bodhisattva, the Bodhisattva of compassion, manifest her life within the walls of that prison? Every time an inmate helps another prisoner, the life of Kannon Bodhisattva is manifested right there inside those walls. Compassion arises from wisdom, and wisdom is the realization of no-separation. Compassion is the activity of that no-separation. It means that when someone falls you pick them up. There is no sense of doer, nor of act being done. There is no sense of reward, no sense of separation. You do it the way you grow your hair: no-effort. It grows. As the days and months go by at the prison, the presence of wisdom and compassion seem evident.

We don't have much contact with these prisoners. Where are they learning these incredibly subtle teachings that are beginning to materialize in their relationships with each other? It has got to come out of their sitting. Now we are almost two and a half years into our prison practice. The fire burns, and the lotus blooms.

We now celebrate the Buddhist holidays. The holidays have been recognized by the prison authorities, which means that the prisoners' family and friends can actually come into the prison and have direct contact with them to celebrate those days. We just recently celebrated Buddha's birthday. There were almost two hundred people there. We used the gymnasium and the courtyard and had a beautiful altar with the baby Buddha. At least twenty children carried candles to participate in the ceremony. Sure, the whole thing was encircled by guards, but what was really happening was inside that circle of practitioners. The parents, the wives, and the children all participated. What is going on at the Lotus Flower Zendo has extended beyond the walls of the prison.

We are now planning a *sesshin* which, as you can imagine, is a little more complicated. Everything we do seems very strange to the people who are not practicing. In spite of the fact that I have made all kinds of literature available to the other ministers and the prison officials, it still has taken a while for them to get used to us. They are beginning to trust us now, and they are beginning to see that we are just as normal as they are. So time has come for *sesshin*. We are going to start with a one-day *sesshin*. If that is successful, we will work our way toward a short *rohatsu* (a retreat which commemorates the Buddha's Enlightenment—said to be the most arduous of Zen *sesshins*) around New Year's time, and then *jukai* (precept ceremony). I have been leading a study group on the precepts with four of the senior students. They will be receiving *jukai* sometime this winter.

It all really points to Ummon's "medicine and sickness curing each other." Ummon, speaking to his assembly, said, "Medicine and sickness heal each other. All the world is medicine, where do you find the self?" The sickness is to violate the precept, "Do not kill." What is the medicine? It is at-one-ment, atonement, no separation, taking responsibility for our actions, for our karma. When the cause is *zazen*, what is the effect? Cause-and-effect is one. When the first thought comes from delusion, all subsequent thoughts are deluded. When the first thought springs from enlightenment, all subsequent thoughts are enlightened. A few of these inmates are looking forward to the possibility of a parole and to continuing their training at the monastery.

There are thousands of prisoners at Greenhaven. Sometimes when you walk in there, the air is electric with tension. The atmosphere fills with fear, anger, and hostility as I walk through the halls. It can be felt among the guards and among the prisoners—the fire burns. Then I reach the small *sangha* of Zen Buddhists, who are sitting in a small room at the Protestant ministry, sitting and emptying themselves. That sitting, that stillness radiates beyond the Zendo. It radiates beyond the walls of the prison itself. **The lotus blooms.** Medicine and sickness heal each other. All the world is medicine; where do you find yourself? **It is because the fire burns that the lotus can bloom.**

What we are doing at that prison started with my teacher, and he with his teacher, and so on back through the generations. Seeing it happen in a place like Greenhaven is a very special experience in my life. It is impossible not to be grateful for the fact that this incredible Dharma is alive and well in this country. The amazing thing is that it has always been here, just as we did not bring the Dharma to Greenhaven prison, it was always there. It doesn't come from Asia or India. Each of us carries it with us. Underneath the layers of conditioning is hidden a Buddha. Our responsibility is to let go of all the debris that is covering it and give life to that Buddha. I am truly grateful for this practice. The only way I can repay that gratitude is by giving my life to the practice.

John Daido Loori is the Vice-Abbot of Zen Mountain Monastery. Rev. Loori has been a student of Maezumi-Roshi since 1976. Zen Mountain Monastery is an American Zen Buddhist monastery for monks, nuns, and lay practitioners. Located on a two-hundred-acre site surrounded by state forest wilderness on Tremper Mountain in the Catskills, the monastery provides a year-round daily Zen training program. This article is derived from a talk given at Zen Center of Los Angeles, July 1986.

Karate-Do and the Actualization of Enlightenment*

BY DIRK MOSIG-SENSEI

We do not train to conquer our enemies. The only true adversary worth conquering is our own self.

Karate-do is a way to actualize the innate enlightenment of the individual practitioner. And yet, it is not a way to acquire enlightenment. Neither is it merely a method to achieve mastery over one's adversaries. It is the failure to understand this truth which lies at the root of the chaos and confusion that prevail in the martial arts world today. Not only are the arts misunderstood by the general public, but also by the majority of their contemporary practitioners in the Western world.

In general it can be said that the Western assimilation of Eastern disciplines has consisted of a wholesale, and more or less indiscriminate, ingestion of their content with little or no comprehension of the function of their form. Meditation, *karate-do* (and other forms of *budo*), the tea ceremony (*chado*), and the art of calligraphy (*shodo*), to mention only a few examples, have been recast in the dualistic mentality of the West with catastrophic consequences. Meditation became a game to strive for the prize of enlightenment; the martial arts were turned into a toy to enhance the ego and ward off external assailants for fun and profit; the tea ceremony was used as a dilettante's tool to chase after tranquility and peace of mind; and even the way of the brush was twisted into a technique to imitate masterpieces for personal glorifica-

*Kearney Zendo, Kearney, Nebraska

tion and social reinforcement. All of these usages completely miss the real essence of the Eastern practices involved.

The most fundamental and indispensable practice of all the patriarchs and men of enlightenment in the past has always been *zazen*. For thousands of years, *zazen* has been the basic practice, and the practice of *zazen* is just as necessary today as it was in past millenia. No one can hope to truly master the martial arts or any of the other Eastern disciplines without practicing *zazen*; to think otherwise is to be thoroughly deluded.

Although *zazen* is often defined as "sitting meditation," it is an error to assume that only sitting in meditation can be *zazen*. Standing, walking, eating, breathing, bathing, and even using the toilet can be *zazen*, too. Conversely, a person could sit in a meditative pose for countless hours every day and not have practiced a moment of *zazen*. Every experience in a person's life can be *zazen*, if it involves mindfulness, a total commitment to the full awareness of the present moment, devoid of attachment and aversion. Endless sitting with legs crossed in the appearance of meditation, while the undisciplined mind scurries around and cavorts about in discriminative thought, is no meditation at all.

To be truly *zazen*, sitting in *zazen* must be done *shikan-taza*: the sitting should be "just sitting," and nothing more. Not sitting and thinking. Not meditating about something. Not even sitting and thinking about not thinking. Not trying to empty the mind. Not striving to reach enlightenment. Just sitting. Fully awake, alert, aware. Total mindfulness. But without thinking about it or about anything else. Like a mirror that reflects what is in front of it, the mind is totally aware. Without reaching for what is not yet in front of it, and without trying to hold onto what is passing by, the without-thinking mind is devoid of discriminations, free of attachments and aversions. What is, is as it is, with nothing lacking and no excess. This is the experience of the absolute reality of the moment. The mind is not separate from its momentary contents, but is identical with such contents. Nothing is outside or inside of the mind, which is the entire universe in the eternal *now*. All dualisms, all dichotomies, all discriminations have melted away. There is nothing to be attained, no goal to be pursued. The practice is *mushotokko*—performed with no thought of profit. *Zazen* is not a tool to chase after enlightenment. *Zazen is* enlightenment.

Everything in the universe, including each and every one of us, has the Buddha-mind, the capacity for enlightenment. It is fundamental to realize that enlightenment is not gained or acquired from outside, but is instead actualized from within. It is something that we always had, that we never lost. Do not seek for it outside. Actualize your Buddha-nature through your practice, but do not practice in order to achieve Buddha-nature. Practice in order to practice. You must develop the conviction, the faith even, that your chosen way is worthy of your practice. Then throw away all thoughts of profit and just practice. The way will open before you, as you transform every aspect of your life into your practice. Become your practice, and all of your life will become *zazen*.

The great patriarch Bodhidharma, who brought the teaching of Zen to China in A.D. 520, taught for nine years by sitting *zazen* in a cave by the Shaolin Temple (*Shorin-ji*). He is also credited with teaching the original exercises of the *I–Chin-Ching*, which are at the root of the martial arts that have been transmitted to us, including karate-do. His exercises involved the cultivation of *samadhi* (one-pointedness) by using the breath. Mindfulness of breathing (*anapanasati*) is an essential method taught over twenty-five hundred years ago by Shakyamuni Buddha. This mindfulness can be extended to encompass everything that the individual experiences, and then everything becomes *zazen*. It is foolish only to practice an hour of meditation in the morning, followed by twenty-three hours of nonmeditative life. It is wise to make one's entire life a meditative experience.

There is a famous saying, "When you eat, just eat; when you sit , just sit." Once a Zen master was asked whether he could perform miracles. He replied in the affirmative, and when questioned as to the nature of his miracles, he responded: "When I am hungry, I eat; when I am tired, I sleep." These are splendid miracles, indeed. Unlike most of us, this master just ate when hungry and rested when tired. He was able to fully experience his food with total mindfulness, undistracted by discriminative thought and free of attachment and aversion. He did not crave the food before eating it, nor did he long to prolong the experience once it was finished. But while eating, his eating was truly *zazen*. When tired, he was able to sleep fully and completely, undisturbed by the brooding and the worrying that cause most of us to toss around in bed half awake and to wake up only half-rested in the morning. When he slept, he just slept. In the same manner, we must learn to "just sit" when we sit in *zazen*, to "just eat" when eating, and to "just rest" when resting. Then, and only then, will our sitting, our eating, and even our resting become *zazen*; then *zazen* will be the fundamental experience of our life.

The same principle must be applied to the practice of karate-do. When you punch, you must just punch. When you kick, just kick. When you block, just block. The primary training method in karate-do consists of the traditional formal exercises known as *kata*. *Kata* is karate. Without *kata*, there is no karate. But *kata* is truly karate only when it is practiced as moving meditation, as an exercise in mindfulness. Then *kata* is *zazen*, and only then is *kata* truly *kata*. When *kata* is *zazen*, then there are karate-do, enlightenment, and the nondualistic experience of the universe in its suchness.

In order for *kata* to be *zazen*, the sequence of movements must first be practiced over and over, tens of thousands of times, until the movements just "happen," with no planning and no thinking. Without thinking about it, become the movement as it occurs. Do not cling to it, do not become attached to your skill of execution nor upset over your imperfections. Do not dwell on the past movement nor anticipate the next one. Each movement has its own time, has its own past, present, and future, but as you become the action you should experience no attachment and no aversion. More than that, there is no longer a doer and a deed. You are not performing the movement, but are performed by it. You are not executing the *kata*, but you are being executed by it. You now *are* the *kata*, fully and absolutely, and experience the great emptiness that is identical with its form and that is the essence of your own being. "Form is exactly the same as emptiness; emptiness is exactly the same as form." The *kata* is "*kata*-ing," and its full experience is *zazen*. This is the actualization of enlightenment. This is what karate-do is all about.

The practice of karate-do is not restricted to the hours spent in the

Dojo (training hall). With the correct understanding, all of one's life becomes karate-do. Karate grandmaster Robert A. Trias once gave this maxim to his students: "Whatever you do, be the best at it." This does not mean that only the person who is the best at a particular activity is living up to the grandmaster's maxim. Instead, it means that everyone should engage in every activity endeavoring to become the best at it he or she can become. It means to perform each and every action with one's full being, in total mindfulness, with undivided attention, completely committed to the experience of the moment. When every action is performed with full concentration and one hundred percent of one's being, every action becomes the practice of karate-do, every movement becomes *zazen*. Karate-do is not just kicking and punching. It is not limited to the performance of *kata* in the Dojo, just as the practice of *zazen* is not restricted to sitting meditation in the Zendo. Instead, the mental discipline of *zazen* practice and karate-do training applied to everyday life transmutes all activities into karate-do and transforms the life experiences of the individual into *zazen*.

It is of utmost importance that the foregoing not be misunderstood. Although walking, sitting, eating, and the practice of karate-do, when undertaken in full mindfulness, represent an extension of meditative practice, it does not follow that they are in any way a replacement for the actual practice of *zazen* in the form of sitting meditation, *shikantaza*. Sitting in *zazen* remains always the fundamental and indispensable practice, for novice and expert alike, for the beginner as well as for the man of enlightenment. As Dogen Zenji put it, "What is the beginner's mind? Where is not the beginner's mind? Where should the beginner's mind be placed?" May we always keep our beginner's minds and never assume that we have progressed beyond the need to practice. Some argue that since any activity can involve the practice of Zen, sitting in *zazen* is not really necessary. This is a grave error, resulting most often from conscious or unconscious attempts to justify living in a slothful style. All other forms of practice serve only to extend the mental training of *zazen* to everyday life, but in no way represent a substitute for the actual practice of sitting in meditation (*zazen*). It is as if we asked someone to prepare a cake for us. If all we got on our plate were a spoonful of icing, this would hardly be satisfactory. Know that the external aspects of karate and of other "ways" are analogous to the icing—we cannot have the real cake without sitting in *zazen*. Karate-do, as a way of life, must emphasize the practice of *zazen* and the disciplining of the mind.

Armed with this understanding, we do not train to conquer our enemies. The only true adversary worth conquering is our own self. He who conquers himself is better than one who defeats a thousand men. This self-discipline is the essence of karate-do. The practice of this art is not for victory or defeat, nor to win a trophy. If you have chosen karate-do, practice it because it is your way, with no thought of profit, and the enlightenment which is yours will actualize itself. It is not an easy way. Practice *zazen* and make karate-do your life by making your life karate-do. Discipline your mind and live fully the experience of the eternal *now*. The actualization of enlightenment in everyday life is the true teaching of all the patriarchs. There is nothing besides this.

Dirk Mosig, Ph.D., is a professor of psychology at Kearney State College in Kearney, Nebraska. He is one of only eight chief instructors in the Shuri-Ryu *system of karate in the world. A Seventh-Degree Black Belt, he maintains a karate and* Kobudo *(Okinawan weaponry)* Dojo *in Kearney. The same facilities are shared by Kearney Zendo, which is affiliated with the Minnesota Zen Meditation Center, under the direction of Dainin Katagiri-Roshi. Dirk Mosig believes that karate-do is a form of Zen practice, and that ninety-five percent of karate is mental discipline, which is accomplished, above all, through the practice of* zazen.

The Way of Zen Sword*

BY MARIA KIM

The techniques of Shim Gum Do are an extension of the natural movements of the body. Motions we use to eat, wash ourselves, or read a book are already martial art techniques.

In the clear space between waking and sleeping, a vision arose and took form. Thousands of techniques organized themselves into a system of martial arts known as *Shim Gum Do*. The creator, Chang Sik Kim, had a vision to revive Zen sword and held that vision through eight years of Zen training at the *Hwa Gye Sa* Korean Buddhist Monastery. His work at the *Hwa Gye Sa* was demanding: cooking, pounding laundry, washing floors. In winter the water he got at the nearby stream was so cold that when he dipped a rag into it and ran it across the floor, the thin film of moisture would freeze, burning and cutting his bare hands and feet. Yet there were never complaints from him, even when his arduous work schedule deprived him of sleep. He was thirteen when be began Zen training, an austere childhood, yet he developed compassion rather than bitterness. He paid attention, worked hard, and never gave up his ambition. One might try this formula without significant results, but there is such a thing as fate, and it has been said that Chang Sik Kim was born with a sword in his hand. Certainly his facility and mastery of it confirms this. The severe conditions of his life made possible his achievement, at age twenty-one, of martial arts enlightenment.

The Founding Master's martial inspiration took form during a one hundred-day retreat. Not only did he give birth to an intricate pattern

---

*American Buddhist Shim Gum Do, Brighton, Massachusetts

Life-size, carved wooden guardian in Shim Gum Do Temple.

of martial art techniques, he also discovered the *Mind Sword Path*, the meditative discipline which sharpens the mind like a sword. This came to him fifty days into his retreat, during midnight meditation, when an apparition entered his retreat house and spoke to him. The following excerpt from *THE ART OF ZEN SWORD: THE HISTORY OF SHIM GUM DO, PART I*[1] tells of his vision, one of many during the retreat. The apparition spoke first:

"Hello, Won Gwang (Chang Sik Kim's Dharma name), are you having a good *Yong Maeng Jong Jin*?" (Korean term for retreat)

"Yes, sir," Won Gwang prostrated himself three times to his teacher.

"Look at the ceiling."

Looking up, he saw a sharp, steel sword protruding through the ceiling of the hut.

"Break the sword with your stick," his teacher commanded.

With his wooden stick, Chang Sik Kim struck the steel blade with all his might, but it did not move an inch. Taking up the stick from his student, the Zen Master gave the blade a light tap, and it shattered into pieces.

"What does this mean?" the Master asked.

"Please teach me, sir."

But (the apparition) just said, "Goodbye," and walked out of the room.

"Come back, come back, tell me the answer, what is it?" Groveling after the vanishing form, the dreamer awoke from the vision with a start. He pondered the meaning of his dream, wondering, "How can you break a real sword with a stick?" In a flash the answer came, "Mind-Sword can break the steel blade!" The mind is limitless and perfectly free and complete; it is the source of infinite energy. Chang Sik Kim had found many sword forms, but when he discovered Mind-Sword, he tapped into the essence of Zen Sword. . . . On the last day of his retreat, Chang Sik Kim wrote his enlightenment poem:

The mind of giver and receiver must become the same.
A fish who rejects the water dies.
A flower cannot proclaim its beauty until it dies.

---

1. Chang Sik Kim and Maria Kim, *The Art of Zen Sword: The History of Shim Gum Do*, Part I (Brighton: American Buddhist Shim Gum Do Association, Inc., 1985).

Founding Master Chang Sik Kim.

Translating the Founding Master's experience into a school of Zen practice known as *American Buddhist Shim Gum Do* has been an ongoing process. The original austerity of the Founding Master's life is not easily duplicated in the easy-going American life style. But then again, one might repeat the Sword-Master's formula and gain nothing. How can any discipline guarantee enlightenment? Looking for it is like a man pursuing a woman; he must not give up even though she discourages him. When he finally gets her, he finds she is quite ordinary, gets in moods, loses her temper, sometimes is selfish. More important than winning her is his ordeal . . . and not giving up. Shim Gum Do training puts the student through hardships to make him want to give up and go away. Sitting meditation, bowing, training in martial arts, getting up early, eating in a disciplined way, conserving energy, working hard and sometimes going on retreats and redoubling the hardships—these pains are worth little in themselves. It is the struggle with ourselves that turns lead into gold.

A teacher is someone who gives you little rest, and the Founding Master makes every attempt to keep his students out of breath. He has a relentless energy, being stern one moment and radiating warmth the next. I met him in 1975 in Boston, one year after he had emigrated from Korea. I was not looking for a spiritual path or a teacher, so expecting nothing, the relationship developed without expectations. The Founding Master did not speak English at that time and taught martial arts and the traditional formalities of practice by example. Even without language he was charismatic and won respect from his students. Slowly I fell in love with him, and we became lovers; later we became husband and wife and made a family together. As his English improved, my endless questions began. I had to keep a mantra of my own making: "shut up . . . wait . . . find out for yourself." That managed to keep the questions down to a minimum. I idealized him and tried to mimic his every move. I ate what he ate, sat the way he sat, cut everything out of my life except for following his every move, while *he* criticized *my* every move. I could do nothing right. If I put off making a phone call or putting my bowls away after washing them, or if I didn't make my bed right away or left a light on, he would fuss. "Do it just now," he would insist. I would become flustered, angry at myself, and repeat my home-made mantra. Eventually I became a Sword-Master and found that everything had to come from me—most importantly, my direction. I discovered that the Founding Master was not a god, a great shock at first but part of growing up; and it only made his achievements more amazing in my mind.

Sometimes training in the Shim Gum Do Center seems like housework or torture; the tendency is to fight the order and discipline. But only if our life becomes clear at the primary levels—cooking, cleaning, energy conservation—can our mind be freed on other levels—creativity, compassion. Basic motions become forms, scales become symphonies. It is hard to believe that making your bed relates to anything but bed making, but mindfulness means paying attention to everything.

On the other hand, if you train hard and become very disciplined, you might become a robot or a rock, and lose feeling or humanness. The remedy is to mess things up a bit! So when should it be clear and when messed up? Balance is a part of Zen martial arts, and if you train for a long time, you become imbued with this sense of correct proportion. It is not only the body that gains coordination, that learns when to relax and when to tighten. What differentiates Shim Gum Do from non-meditative martial arts is mind training. One cannot progress far in Shim Gum Do without practicing the martial art forms mentally during sitting meditation. The system of forms is so complex that once you know fifty forms you begin to forget them unless you practice them mentally. When one knows hundreds of forms, it is impossible to practice them physically in order to retain them, and only by training forms mentally can the progression of techniques be learned and remembered. The mental training sharpens the mind and keeps the memory alive. Memory is a great key to life. Without it we become demented. The training in Shim Gum Do is like a shower. It cleans out your body and mind and, as a daily practice, prepares you for all the complicated facets of your life—work, study, relationships.

In Shim Gum Do the restless, unchained spirit of Mars is combined with the control of meditation and thus releases creativity. The simplicity and austerity of Zen combine with art in a most pleasing manner. Zen art is close to nature. The techniques of Shim Gum Do are an extension of the natural movements of the body. Motions we use to eat, wash ourselves, or read a book are already martial art techniques. Already we all have the thousands of techniques of Shim Gum Do in our mind, and already we are all enlightened. The raw material is all there; it is up to each person to use it and realize its potential. That is the great challenge which gives meaning to life.

Each night beginning at midnight the Founding Master begins his session of sitting meditation, sometimes not moving for four or five hours. His students follow his lead, once a month sitting for one hour at midnight for seven days. This hour is one of the most difficult times to overcome drowsiness and concentrate. If you can do it, your power is increased. Already the Founding Master has attained his goal of martial arts enlightenment. What more is there for him? **A flower does not proclaim its beauty until it dies.**

Maria Kim has studied Shim Gum Do *for the past fifteen years. She is an instructor of martial arts, a short story writer, and a mother of three. She lives at the Shim Gum Do Zen Center in Brighton, Massachusetts.*

East Moving West: Theravada Buddhism Grows in Britain

BY AMARAVATI BUDDHIST COMMUNITY

For the laity, unselfish giving is an active, joyful part of their spiritual life, and the monastic order acts as a source of spiritual guidance and encouragement to them, through its teachings and living example.

There is a tranquil serenity about the beautiful English countryside. Its rolling, green hills provide a perfect setting for cultivating the Way of the Buddha. This ancient teaching has long interested many British people, an interest that has flourished over the last few years. One of the more recent developments, however, has a particular significance: men and women born in the West are now able to become Buddhist monks and nuns in Britain. They shave their heads and wear the traditional robes of the Theravada, but receive instruction in *Dhamma-Vinaya* in the English language. This is a sign that the lotus flower of the Dhamma is truly able to grow and be cultivated here in the West.

Four Theravada monasteries have now been established in Britain by an American-born monk, Venerable Ajahn Sumedho. At the invitation of a trust set up to establish the *Bhikkhu sangha* (community of monks) in England, he came in 1977 with three other Western monks to live in a small house in London. Ajahn Sumedho had been a monk for ten years in the forest monasteries of northeast Thailand, training with Venerable Ajahn Chah—a highly respected teacher there. (*Ajahn* means

Teacher in Thai.) From that modest beginning has grown a mon-astic order of thirty-three monks (*bhikkhus*), twelve nuns (*siladhara*), and sixteen male and female novices (*anagarikas*) of over fourteen nationalities.

Besides being places for the monastic *sangha* to live and train, the four monasteries—two small *viharas* (monastic residences), a training monastery, and a larger Buddhist center—act as focal points for the wider Buddhist community in Britain. People of many cultures, back-grounds, and affiliations gather to hear and practice the teachings, and to reaffirm their faith in the Triple Gem—the Buddha, Dhamma, and *sangha*. These are the rare and precious jewels of true wisdom, a way of cultivating it, and a living religious tradition in which it is practiced and perpetuated. The three refuges of Buddha, Dhamma, and, *sangha*—Wisdom, Truth, and Virtue—form the foundation of the traditional Buddhist approach to life.

As Buddhism filters from East to West, differing cultural perspectives can affect each other in beneficial and sometimes unexpected ways. It can be helpful to reflect upon such differences. For the rational West-erner, there can be mixed feelings towards the traditional Asian ap-proach to Buddhism. As Wes Nisker described in his recent *Inquiring Mind* travelogue: [1]

> Buddhism in Asia is not synonymous with meditation practice as it is here in the West. In Theravadaland most lay people pray to the Buddha as a god and often ask the Buddha for favor or merit. Buddhism in Asia is a *religion*. It feels alien to me, having rejected all that, but I am touched by this lay worship and sometimes wish it were more a part of my life . . .

Eastern and Western minds can display very different tendencies, as was once observed by an English monk living in Sri Lanka:

> In Europe intellectualism takes precedence over tradition; in the East it is the reverse. In Dhamma terms, the European has an excess of *panna* (wisdom) over *saddha* (faith), and he tends to reject what he can-not understand, even if it is true; the Oriental has an excess of *saddha*

1. See *Inquiring Mind* 4, No. 1 (Summer 1987): 19.

over *panna*, which leads him to accept anything ancient, even if it is false.[2]

Joseph Goldstein, also writing in the *Inquiring Mind*, sees some danger in the Western tendency to pick and choose:

> A great concern is that this profound teaching of liberation will be diluted in the transmission of the Dharma to the West. If we pay attention only to those aspects of the Dharma which conform to our established world view, then our practice may become a matter of simply feeling good or even just doing good, and thus fail to at least test the waters of a more comprehensive understanding.[3]

However, when people of East and West are open to learning from each other, they can discover qualities that strengthen and balance their different approaches to Buddhism.

In the sixties and seventies, many Westerners, disillusioned with materialistic values, were attracted by the spirituality of the East. Some, including Jack Kornfield, Christopher Titmuss, and John Orr, found their way to the forest monasteries of Thailand to become *bhikkhus*, and a few decided to stay. Ajahn Chah in particular, although he spoke no English, seemed to be especially gifted at teaching Westerners. So many gathered around him that an international monastery was set up, where *Dhamma-Vinaya* could be taught in the English language. (Ajahn Sumedho was the abbot there for its first two years, just before he came to England.)

At that time, when their own country was undergoing a period of rapid modernization, many Thais hoped that America would lead the way towards a secure future of material plenty. That young people from the West should spurn such apparent riches, and journey to Thailand to live with old forest monks in the most down-home rural areas, intrigued the Thais. Many turned to take a fresh look at their own religious traditions and culture and developed a new interest in the practice of meditation. In the past this had been generally left to those in the monasteries.

2. Ven. Nanavira, *Clearing the Path* (Colombo, Sri Lanka: Path Press), p. 305.
3. *Inquiring Mind* 4, No. 1 (Summer 1987): 12.

Many Westerners who went to Thailand to explore the practice of meditation, were, in turn, influenced by Eastern ways. The generosity, faith, and devotion that permeates Thai culture taught them a more graceful way of living—one of joy, respect, and concern for others. Traditionally, the Buddhist Path is separated into three aspects—*Dana* (generosity), *Sila* (virtuous conduct), and *Bhavana* (cultivation of the heart, or meditation). When Ajahn Chah started teaching Westerners, Thai people often asked why he just taught them meditation without stressing the first two steps. He replied that it would be impossible for Westerners to make progress without cultivating generosity of heart and a good moral foundation. He was, however, content to let them find this out for themselves.

On beginning to practice, many Westerners often thought that meditation meant sitting for long periods in quiet places, with no disturbances. Ajahn Chah's frequent response to this was to frustrate their efforts to seek out tranquility. The emphasis in his monasteries was to surrender to a community life style, and this could sometimes be quite busy. Investigation of Dhamma in *all* situations was encouraged, not just in formal meditation practice, and great stress was placed upon careful and attentive observance of the *Vinaya*—the monastic rule. Ajahn Chah described the practice in the following way:

> Our practice really isn't that difficult; there's not much to it . . . simple things like cleaning basins and washing bowls, performing one's duty to one's elders. Keeping rooms and toilets clean are important. This is not crude or menial work. Rather you should understand [that] it is the most refined. . . . Take care of moral discipline as a gardener takes care of trees. Don't discriminate between big and small, important and unimportant. Some people want short cuts. They say "forget concentration, we'll go straight for insight" or "forget moral discipline, we'll go straight for concentration." Westerners are generally in a hurry, so they have greater extremes of happiness and suffering. The fact that they have many defilements can be a source of wisdom later on. . . . Don't be concerned with how long it may take to see results, just do it. Like growing a tree, you plant it, water it, feed it, keep the bugs away. If these things are done properly, the tree will grow naturally. The speed of the growing is something you can't control . . .

The *Vinaya* is a detailed code of conduct that forms an elaborate system of training. Its fundamental principles are contained in the Eight Precepts:

The Eight Precepts
(These are observed by the novices and resident lay visitors to the monasteries.)

Harmlessness: to refrain from intentionally taking the life of any creature.

Trustworthiness: to refrain from taking anything which is not given.

Chastity: to refrain from sexual activity.

Right Speech: to refrain from false, abusive, or malicious speech.

Sobriety: to refrain from taking intoxicating drink or drugs.

Abstinence: to refrain from eating after noon.

Renunciation: to refrain from entertainments, self-adornment, and provocative dress.

Moderation: to refrain from over-indulgence in sleep.

Such guidelines encourage simplicity, honesty, and restraint, and they help to free the mind from unnecessary entanglements. Their emphasis on personal integrity and responsibility promotes harmonious relationships with others and helps to cultivate a sense of self-respect. This forms a firm foundation for the development of meditation practice.

As one surrenders to the monastic form, letting go of personal preferences and desires for the sake of community harmony, many manifestations of selfishness are brought up into consciousness. The task of meditation is then to accept, investigate, and let them go. As this process unfolds, it becomes clear that understanding is not something that comes through exertion of willful effort alone; it is less a matter of *doing* than of *undoing*. Gradually there develops a peace of mind which does not depend upon external conditions and gives rise to joy and gratitude. Such is the training of the heart; it continues, under the guidance of Ajahn Sumedho, at our monasteries in Britain.

In addition to promoting harmony within the order, the *Vinaya* was established by the Buddha to help protect and sustain the teachings, and it has been a key factor in their survival over the last twenty-five centuries. It also creates a firm bond between the monastic order and the laity, based upon mutual respect and generosity, which supports the application of the teachings to both ways of living.

The relationship is one of interdependence. The monastic order does not possess any means of independent support, as the monks and nuns are prohibited from keeping money or from growing, storing, or cooking food. (In fact, they are only allowed to eat food directly given to them between dawn and noon of the same day.) So without daily contact with supportive lay people, the monastic order cannot continue. Their dependence upon others inspires the monks and nuns to be worthy of the faith and generous offerings they receive by applying themselves wholeheartedly to their training. They are thus freed from most of the burdens of ordinary life and are enabled to live simply in a way which supports the cultivation of the Path.

For the laity, unselfish giving is an active, joyful part of their spiritual life, and the monastic order acts as a source of spiritual guidance and encouragement to them, through its teachings and living example. Entering into this relationship draws people close to the living teachings and helps to strengthen their practice of Dhamma. To have more contact with the monasteries and with other Buddhists, many families come to live nearby, where their children can grow up in an environment in which wholesome values are encouraged. The sense of community that develops can thus support, balance, and nourish both sides in a beautiful way, beneficial to everyone.

Guests are also welcome to come and stay with the monastic community at most times of the year, living and practicing alongside the monks and nuns. A daily rhythm is set by the three formal meetings— morning and evening *pujas* (periods of devotional chanting followed by a silent meditation and sometimes a Dhamma Talk)—and the main meal offering. Other activities include periods of work and informal gatherings for tea.

The atmosphere is one of supportive friendship in which silence is very much valued. There is no attempt to press the teaching upon anyone, and in fact much of the transmission of Dhamma happens by osmosis. Many aspects of monastic form can seem new or unusual, and visitors frequently comment upon the things they notice, like the joy that comes in offering food, the power of the chanting, the gentle humor, and the resident cats.

Contact with Asian Buddhists presents many other facets of Buddhist life. Thais, Sri Lankans, Laotians, and Cambodians often turn up in large numbers on weekends. Mostly they come to offer alms food to the monks and nuns—ceremonially dedicating the goodness of their acts of generosity to the memory of departed friends and relatives. Some, however, also come to practice meditation, and this interest is gradually growing. The preservation of the familiar Asian Buddhist rituals provides a focus for their widely-dispersed communities and helps to sustain their sense of cultural identity.

The Asian community has, in fact, provided a large proportion of the financial and material support for the monastic *sangha* in Britain during its development over the past ten years. In the beginning, life in the West was quite difficult for the newly-arrived forest monks, who suddenly found themselves living in urban London. However, their training and the practical wisdom of Ajahn Sumedho helped them to adapt to their new surroundings, and a few more Western monks came from Thailand to join them. Interest in the fledgling monastic order grew, and in 1979 they were able to move to a larger house in the countryside of southern England. This was the first step towards the creation of a proper monastery.

Shortly after the move, despite the fact that there were no nuns yet, four women expressed interest in joining the monastic community. In Thailand there are white-robed nuns holding the eight precepts; however this form carries little of the social status of the *Bhikkhu* in Thai society (the *Bhikkhuni* Order, the womens' equivalent, disappeared in the Theravada over one thousand years ago). Although Ajahn Sumedho had no experience of training nuns, he was impressed by their determination and sincerity and decided to make use of this form for the time being. So these four women, of very different ages and backgrounds, took a step into the unknown and became the first Theravada Buddhist nuns in Britain.

One of these nuns continues the story:

When I first took ordination, Chithurst Buddhist Monastery had just started and was still little more than an old, crumbling stone house. Besides the four new nuns, there were eight monks and a handful of laymen and *anagarikas*, men who were training in the monastic form and, like ourselves, holding the eight precepts.

It took a good five years of hard physical labor to renovate the house. At first there was no proper kitchen, and we cooked in a tent; there was little electricity, no hot water, limited heating, the gardens were completely overgrown, and the building itself was riddled with dry-rot. Regardless of the obstacles facing us as a community, we had a lot of determination to carry on. Although there were problems on the material level and inevitable interpersonal difficulties that arose with the mostly untrained community, there was a wonderful spirit and enthusiasm amongst the group. The strength needed to carry us through these early difficulties came largely from the teaching and leadership of Ajahn Sumedho, the structure provided by the *Vinaya* discipline, and the daily monastic routine, which was very grounding and helpful in focusing people's energies.

As time went on, more people started to come, some to take ordination, others to stay as guests. The community grew in strength as people started to understand how to apply the teachings, letting go of their personal desires, ambitions, and negativities for the good of the whole. As support and interest grew, it seemed as though this new undertaking would be a viable proposition after all.

After a few years living as white-robed, eight-precept nuns, we were attracting a lot of attention from other women wishing to live with the monastic community. However, at that time our facilities were limited. We were living very frugally in a small cottage, which was a ten-minute walk from the main house and had no electricity, only rudimentary heating, and very little space. By 1982 the number of nuns had increased to ten. It was becoming clear that, for the sake of harmony, there was a need for larger facilities and for a more evolved system of training than the eight-precept form allowed. The next year, after consulting the elders of the Thai Sangha, Ajahn Sumedho gave us the ten precepts. This was a very big change. Surrendering the use of money—by which people manipulate life for comfort, convenience, and security—enabled us to live as true alms-mendicants, dependent upon the goodwill and generosity of others.

In taking this step forward, we had no set precedent or senior nuns to follow. In response to our difficult predicament, Ajahn Sumedho appointed a senior monk, experienced in *Vinaya* discipline, to help train and guide us. Using the ten precepts as a foundation, the nuns' discipline has been gradually evolving to fulfill the same detailed training and support functions as the traditional *Vinaya*. At present it is still in the very early stages of development, and the first brown-robed, ten precept nuns, grateful for the opportunity to be able to live and train in this way, are just beginning to accept invitations to teach.

By 1983 it had become clear that more space was needed. Chithurst could no longer cope with the increasing numbers wishing to join the community and with the widening of interest in the teachings. Although two small *viharas* had been set up in the southwest and in the north of England, accommodating the expansion of the monastic *sangha* was not the only consideration. Ajahn Sumedho felt that the needs of the time required a larger place that would greatly broaden opportunities for Dhamma practice.

After a search, a former school was purchased, set in the Hertfordshire countryside quite close to London. The name chosen, "Amaravati," meaning "the deathless realm," echoes an oft-quoted stanza attributed to the Buddha: "Open are the doors of the deathless, let those who can hear give forth their faith." This reflects the spirit of openness and optimism which characterize the intention for the new center.

In the three years since the opening of Amaravati Buddhist Centre, support and interest have blossomed, and large numbers of people now come to visit, stay, and practice. A variety of teaching activities are offered—including beginners' meditation classes, public talks, and family days—and retreats are held at a self-contained retreat facility on part of the site. Outside teaching invitations are also accepted. Behind all the comings and goings, however, the steady rhythm of monastic life continues, imparting a sense of tranquility to the many facets of Amaravati.

As we are often reminded, the future is uncertain. In Thailand, Ajahn. Chah now lies paralyzed from a stroke and is not expected to live much longer. Further developments have occurred in the West: new *viharas* have been set up in Australia and New Zealand, and one is due to start in Switzerland in 1988. Recently there has been much talk of American interest. But, as Ajahn Sumedho used to remind the monks during the early days in London, "We didn't come here to build monasteries or to spread Buddhism or for any other reason. Our duty is to do the practice, that is all. Everything will flow from that in its own time, according to its own nature. We don't need to concern ourselves with anything else."

In September 1987 Joseph Goldstein, Sharon Salzberg, and Howard Cohn visited Amaravati Buddhist Centre in Hertfordshire, England. During a warm and informal meeting with the Abbot, Ajahn Sumedho, they reaffirmed the interest that has been growing in establishing branches of the monastic sangha in America. Joseph asked if we would write an article describing how Theravada Buddhism is lived and practiced at our monasteries here in England. We would like to extend a welcome for all interested people to visit and experience our life style and practice first hand. (Copyright Amaravati Publications. To visit, write to: The Secretary, Amaravati Buddhist Centre, Great Gaddesden, Hemel Hempstead, Herts, England HP1-3BZ.)

The Nonsectarian Buddhist Centers of North America

Centers are listed alphabetically first by state, then by city and should there be more than one within a given city, by the names of the centers themelves.

CALIFORNIA

Buddhist Peace Fellowship

The Buddhist Peace Fellowship was founded in 1978 by Robert Aitken-Roshi and some of his students to bring a meditative dimension into the peace movement and to bring awareness of social and ecological issues to the Buddhist community. In ten years, BPF has grown into an active network of twenty-five chapters with nearly two thousand members worldwide. Thich Nhat Hanh, Christopher Titmuss, Joanna Macy, and others lead retreats on meditation and social action, known as "engaged Buddhism." A variety of meditation techniques are offered. They all emphasize meditation in daily life—mindful awareness in each activity. Days of Mindfulness include tea meditation, mindful discussions, group outdoor walking meditation, and quiet sitting. Sitting meditation may include following the breath, concentrating on a *gatha* (short verse), or any other practice the retreatant does elsewhere (e.g., koan study, insight meditation, or "just sitting"). BPF's excellent quarterly newsletter is included with $15 per year membership. Buddhists of all denominations and also non-Buddhists are encouraged to join the Buddhist Peace Fellowship.

ADDRESS: P.O. Box 7355, Berkeley, CA 94704
PHONE: (415) 525-0101
LINEAGE: Members from all sects
ESTABLISHED: 1978
FACILITIES: Retreats at various sites throughout the United States
RETREATS OFFERED: A "Day of Mindfulness," interfaith retreats, other retreats integrating meditation and social action.
OPEN TO: General public

College of Buddhist Studies

The College of Buddhist Studies was instituted in 1983 by the Buddhist Sangha Council of Southern California in answer to the growing desire for more Buddhist education than the temples themselves could provide. The college offers students of Buddhism a unique opportunity to experience a comprehensive in-depth study of Buddhism from a nonsectarian point of view, while also promoting knowledge and undersanding of the different schools and cultural traditions within Buddhism. Courses are taught by scholars and masters of a variety of traditions, taking advantage of Southern California's uniqueness: the only place in the world where all Buddhist ethnic practices and denominations are found, allowing the student the chance to study not only the philosophy and psychology of Buddhism, but also to experience its richness of practice.

ADDRESS: 933 South New Hampshire
Avenue, Los Angeles, CA 90006
PHONE: (213) 739-1270
LINEAGE: Nondenominational
SPIRITUAL HEAD: Dr. Ratanasara
RESIDENT DIRECTOR: Teachers are
recruited to give classes.
AFFILIATED WITH: Autonomous
ESTABLISHED: 1983
FACILITIES: Urban meditation center.
We share premises of IBMC, so their
meditation hall is used for regular
practice.
RETREATS OFFERED: The college itself
functions as a nucleus and offers retreats
through its affiliated groups.
OPEN TO: General public

The Community Meditation Center of Los Angeles (CMC)

The CMC training program is designed
for those who wish to seriously pursue
meditation while continuing to live and
work as members of society. Weekly Sunday lectures provide a public forum for ex-
plaining and discussing the process. For
those who want to make this practice part
of their life skills, we offer beginning and
advanced classes. After completing this
course of study, one may become a regular
participant, attending retreats each month.
Regular participants receive personalized
continued guidance from CMC teachers
and a network of peer support. The dis-
tinctive style of meditation taught at
CMC is based on a Buddhist technique
called Vipassana or insight meditation. It
is presented as a clear and powerful trans-
formative process without dogma, ritual,
or cultural trappings.
ADDRESS: 1041 Elden Avenue, Los Angeles, CA 90006
PHONE: (213) 384-7817
LINEAGE: Burmese Vipassana
SPIRITUAL HEAD: Shinzen Young
RESIDENT DIRECTOR: Shinzen Young

AFFILIATED WITH: Autonomous
ESTABLISHED: 1982
FACILITIES: Urban meditation center.
RETREATS OFFERED: Shorter Vipassana
courses, weekend sittings, supervised
solitary retreats.
OPEN TO: General public

COLORADO

Chan-Nhu Buddhist Pagoda

Chan-Nhu Buddhist Pagoda is a Buddhist
nunnery, women's retreat, and conference
center. Emphasis is on Vipassana practice.
Men are welcome Sundays, 8:00−11:00
A.M. Experienced women meditators from
various Vipassana and Zen backgrounds
may do self-retreats. Ajahn Sobin Namto
offers training based on an adaptation of
the Mahasi Sayadaw technique. Individual
thorough preliminary instruction is emphasized before entering "intensive" Vipassana retreat. Adaptation of the Mahasi
Sayadaw method is further refined in accordance with commentaries to the Satipatthana Sutta. Special step-by-step slow
movements are taught without compromise of technique. Attention is on "non-
stop" complete focusing on mind-body
objects to realize balance of meditation
"faculties." Frequent personal interviews
are given to correct initial confusion or
long-standing problems. Individualized
training is emphasized. Teacher-supervised "intensives" are offered during the
year. Spiritual guidance is offered to the
Vietnamese community.
ADDRESS: 7201 West Bayaud Place,
Lakewood, CO 80226
PHONE: (303) 238-5867
LINEAGE: Burmese Mahasi Sayadaw and
Vietnamese Mahayana
SPIRITUAL HEAD: Rev. Chan-Nhu
(Vietnamese), and Rev. Martha
Dharmapali (American). Ajahn Sobin
Namto teaches at this temple from time
to time.

Chan-Nhu Buddhist Pagoda, Women's Retreat Center and Nunnery, Lakewood, Colorado.

RESIDENT DIRECTOR: Same
AFFILIATED WITH: Autonomous
ESTABLISHED: 1986
FACILITIES: Urban meditation center. Vietnamese community temple. Some facilities for solitary retreats.
RETREATS OFFERED: Short Vipassana courses, day-long and weekend sittings. Supervised and unsupervised solitary retreats. Retreats are offered three or more times per year or upon request.
OPEN TO: Primarily women. Some events also open to men.

NEW HAMPSHIRE

Friends of the Western Buddhist Order—Aryaloka Community

Aryaloka is a residential community and retreat center of the Friends of the Western Buddhist Order (FWBO), an international Buddhist movement founded in 1967 in the United Kingdom by Ven. Maha Sthavira Sangharakshita. The FWBO encourages the study of all Buddhist traditions. We offer a number of meditation techniques and engage in various devotional practices. The FWBO offers facilities to those who wish to commit themselves to the Buddhist spiritual life, and who wish to express that commitment through a life of meditation, study, socially-oriented work, artistic pursuits, direct Dharma teaching, support of public centers, or any combination of these. At Aryaloka Community members engage in a daily program of meditation, work (in a business that supports the community), study, and general community life. The two basic practices taught at our classes and retreats are "Mindfulness of Breathing" and "Metta Bhavana." The former is an awareness meditation based on the

Aryaloka Community—view of east dome.

breathing process, and the latter—also called the "Development of Universal Loving-kindness"—is concerned with the development of positive emotional states. More experienced meditators are introduced to other meditation practices from the Theravada, the Mahayana, and the Vajrayana traditions.

ADDRESS: Aryaloka Community, Heartwood Circle, Newmarket, NH 03857
PHONE: (603) 659-5456
LINEAGE: Nondenominational
SPIRITUAL HEAD: Ven. Maha Sthavira Sangharakshita (English)
RESIDENT DIRECTOR: Manjuvajra, Ratnapani (English)
AFFILIATED WITH: An autonomous center but part of an international movement of the same name.

ESTABLISHED: 1980 (in the United States)
FACILITIES: Urban meditation center; country retreat facility
RETREATS OFFERED: A "Day of Mindfulness," weekend sittings, study retreats, and FWBO-style retreats, which are a mixture of meditation, study, and devotional practice.
OPEN TO: General public

NEW MEXICO

Jacqueline Mandell: Independent Teacher

Jacqueline Mandell is one of the teachers featured in Lenore Friedman's book *Meetings with Remarkable Women—Buddhist*

Jacqueline Schwartz-Mandell as a nun at Taungpulu Kaba Aye Monastery, Boulder Creek, California. Photo courtesy of Rameshwar Das.

Teachers in America (Boston: Shambhala, 1987). She began her formal training in India under S. N. Goenka in 1972. Continuing to practice intensively at Mahasi Thathana Yeitktha Meditation Center in Rangoon, Burma, she took formal ordination as a nun with the Ven. Mahasi Sayadaw as her preceptor. She has also practiced under the guidance of the Ven. Taungpulu Sayadaw at Taungpulu Monastery in Boulder Creek, California. In 1979 she was one of four Americans (Jack Kornfield, Joseph Goldstein, and Sharon Salzberg were the other three) sanctioned to teach by the late Ven. Mahasi Sayadaw. She does not maintain a meditation center per se but travels internationally, giving Vipassana retreats to all who request them. She supervises solitary retreats for meditators who are willing to set up their own accommodations near her home.
ADDRESS: 23 Encantado Loop, Santa Fe, NM 87505 (Mailing address: 3220 East Galbraith Road, Cincinnati, OH 45236
PHONE: (505) 982-8775
LINEAGE: Several Vipassana traditions, including those taught by Taungpulu Sayadaw and Mahasi Sayadaw.
SPIRITUAL HEAD: Jacqueline Mandell (American)
RESIDENT DIRECTOR: Same
AFFILIATED WITH: Autonomous
ESTABLISHED: 1976
FACILITIES: Facilities are rented for each retreat.
RETREATS OFFERED: Individuals and small or large groups invite the teacher to lead retreats.
OPEN TO: General public

NORTH CAROLINA

Southern Dharma Retreat Center
Southern Dharma Retreat Center is a nonprofit educational foundation, eclectic in nature, whose purpose is to offer medi-

tation retreats. Our goal is to provide a comfortable gathering place, removed from the everyday hassles of life, and to create an atmosphere of tranquility where one can nurture a sense of peace and uncover the truths within the heart. It is our intention to sponsor teachers from a variety of traditions (Buddhist, Christian, and Native American), to maintain a supportive environment for meditation, and to keep costs to participants as low as possible.
ADDRESS: Route 1, Box 34-H, Hot Springs, NC 28743
PHONE: (704) 622-7112
LINEAGE: We honor all.
RESIDENT DIRECTOR: On occasion a teacher will be in residency here for a week or so. Those teachers are from a variety of traditions.
AFFILIATED WITH: Autonomous
ESTABLISHED: 1978
FACILITIES: Country retreat facility. Solitary retreat facilities.
RETREATS OFFERED: Weekend sittings, unsupervised solitary retreats, seven to ten-day meditation retreats. Retreats are held twice per month. Teacher-supervised private retreats are always available.
OPEN TO: General public

PENNSYLVANIA

Won Buddhism of Philadelphia
Won Buddhism aspires to establish a harmonious, peaceful world that integrates body and mind, science and religion, secular life and religious practice, and differences among races, nations, or religions through right faith in truth and the sincere practice of morality. Thus, Won Buddhism actively participates in the ecumenical movement of world religions as well as Buddhist ecumenical studies. The activities of Won Buddhism in America are at

present generally confined to three major works: missionary work for Korean adults and children in Sunday services; training programs for spiritual cultivation, such as sitting meditation and yoga classes; educational institutions, especially Korean language schools, for second-generation Korean Americans.

ADDRESS: 6523 North 3rd Street, Philadelphia, PA 19126
PHONE: (215) 548-6463
LINEAGE: Reform Buddhism in Korea
SPIRITUAL HEAD: Rev. Chun Sik Park
RESIDENT DIRECTOR: Rev. Young Bong Song
AFFILIATED WITH: Won Buddhism in Korea
ESTABLISHED: 1987
FACILITIES: Urban meditation center
RETREATS OFFERED: Meditation every morning for two hours, weekend retreats depending on need.
OPEN TO: General public

TEXAS

Quantum Dharma Center

John R. B. Whittlesey was a Zen student of Nyogen Senzaki (1954–1958) and a non-Tantric student of Chogyam Trungpa, Rinpoche, of the Kagyu lineage (1971–1977). Since 1971 he has practiced meditation as taught by his teachers, sharing his sitting practice with any who care to attend.

ADDRESS: 5439 Del Monte, Houston, TX 77056-4211
PHONE: (713) 621-5933
LINEAGE: Japanese Rinzai-Soto Zen and Tibetan Kagyu
SPIRITUAL HEAD: Root teacher Nyogen Senzaki; second teacher, Chogyam Trungpa, Rinpoche (both deceased).
RESIDENT DIRECTOR: John R. B. Whittlesey
AFFILIATED WITH: Autonomous
ESTABLISHED: 1973

FACILITIES: Meditation at our home
OPEN TO: General public

Triyana Meditation Group of San Antonio

Triyana is a Buddhist organization originally formed by members of other Buddhist groups. Because each of our own local groups was small, we felt it made more sense for all of us to practice together, and so we formed Triyana. Our purpose is to: practice mindfulness meditation, sponsor retreats, share a resource library, engage in peace promotion, and to study and instruct others in Buddhist precepts and practices. Respect for heterogeneous Buddhist meditation styles is observed. Our basic form of mindfulness meditation, Shamatha/Vipassana, consists of: observing one's moment-to-moment mind/body process (one's thoughts, feelings, physical sensations, and perceptions) as they arise, with the breath serving as the focus for cultivating mindful awareness.

ADDRESS: 406 Olney Drive, San Antonio, TX 78209 (Mailing address: 318 Eleanor Avenue, San Antonio, TX 78209)
PHONE: (512) 826-1971; 826-4251; 558-8111
LINEAGE: Kagyu, Zen-Lin Chi, Theravada
SPIRITUAL HEAD: (1) Ven. Thich Nhat Hanh (Vietnamese Zen of the Lin Chi Sect) (2) Vajra Regent Osel Tendzin (Tibetan Kagyu Lineage) (3) Alan Clements (Burmese Theravada Vipassana)
RESIDENT DIRECTOR: These students have been given permission to give meditation instruction in their respective traditions: (1) Mobi Ho (Thich Nhat Hanh) (2) Elisa Gonzalez (Vajra Regent Osel Tendzin) (3) Dawna Wright (Alan Clements)
AFFILIATED WITH: Individual, non-affiliated practitioners, as well as members of organizations.
ESTABLISHED: 1985

FACILITIES: We use space at a local school for practice and at a member's home for study.
RETREATS OFFERED: *Nyinthun*, a "Day of Mindfulness," weekend sittings
OPEN TO: General public

WASHINGTON

Friends of the Western Buddhist Order, Seattle

Sangharakshita founded the FWBO in 1964 in England. Currently there are seventeen centers in Europe, a center in Australia and New Zealand, and a center in New Hampshire. The Seattle branch is maintained in a private residence, and the program is limited. On a regular basis there is a weekly meditation night, beginning meditation class, and occasionally retreats are offered. Aryaloka is the Seattle order member that leads these activities. Any correspondence is welcome.
ADDRESS: 2410 East Interlaken Boulevard, Seattle, WA 98112
PHONE: (206) 325-3196
SPIRITUAL HEAD: Ven. Sangharakshita
RESIDENT DIRECTOR: English
AFFILIATED WITH: Friends of the Western Buddhist Order
ESTABLISHED: 1985
FACILITIES: Urban meditation center
RETREATS OFFERED: Weekend and week-long meditation; study retreats.
OPEN TO: General public

Nonsectarian Centers— Canada

BRITISH COLUMBIA

Karuna Meditation Society Formerly Vipassana Meditation Society)

Karuna Meditation Society is a nonsectarian Buddhist organization which offers both nonresidential weekend and residential week-long Vipassana retreats led mostly by teachers affiliated with the Insight Meditation Society in Barre, Massachusetts. Day retreats of *Metta* (loving kindness) meditation and introductory and intermediate classes in insight meditation, as well as a meditation group for people with AIDS, are led by the local teacher. We also sponsor periodic weekend retreats of study and practice with Zen teachers. KMS publishes *Karuna: A Journal of Buddhist Meditation*.
ADDRESS: P.O. Box 24468, Station C, Vancouver, B.C., Canada V5T-4M5
PHONE: (604) 872-0431
RESIDENT DIRECTOR: Kristin Penn (Canadian)
ESTABLISHED: 1984
FACILITIES: Urban meditation center. We rent facilties for retreats and classes, and are currently looking for space.
RETREATS OFFERED: Weekend Vipassana retreats with various teachers, yearly residential Vipassana retreats (five to eight days), Soto Zen weekends, and retreats of practice and study.
OPEN TO: General public

ONTARIO

Dharma Centre of Canada

For nearly twenty-five years Buddhist Western Mysteries and Universalist teachings have been given in constantly changing programs at this four hundred-acre wooded retreat center. Three years of academic, structured study are combined with short, intensive meditation retreats. Most retreats are open. Some programs are also offered in Toronto and Ottawa.
ADDRESS: R.R.1 Galway Road, Kinmount, Ontario, Canada K0M 2A0 (Mailing address: Box 5549, Station A, Toronto, Ontario, Canada M5W-1N7)
FACILITIES: Country retreat facilities
RETREATS OFFERED: Short intensive meditation retreats

OPEN TO: Most retreats open to the
general public

YUKON

Yukon Dharma Society/ Northern Meditation Center

We offer weekly meditation and sponsor teachers who come to do three-day to two-week courses here a few times a year. Our level of activity is very much dependent on the number of people around and the level of interest at the time of each event. We also have a retreat center out of town, but it has not been actively used for some time.

ADDRESS: 2 Redwood, Whitehorse, Yukon, Canada Y1A 4B3
LINEAGE: Nonsectarian
AFFILIATED WITH: Autonomous
ESTABLISHED: Reopened 1987
RETREATS OFFERED: Weekly meditations. We sponsor teachers who come to lead three-day to two-week meditation courses.

APPENDIX: *Unconfirmed Centers*

The following centers did not respond to our survey. However, we believe that at least some of them do exist. If you know anything about them, please let us know so that we can update our listings in future editions.

California

Lopsang Khemdup
1540 Richmond Street
El Cerrito, CA 94530

Rinzai Zen Dojo
14912 Mariposa Avenue
Gardena, CA 90247

Karma Triyana Choling
P.O. Box 701
Idylwild, CA 92349

Gelugpa Society of Yamantaka
1439 E Street
Napa, CA 94559

Advaitayana Buddhist Communion
750 Adrian Way
San Rafael, CA 94903

Santa Barbara Zendo
333 East Anapamu
Santa Barbara, CA 93101

Santa Cruz Zen Center
113–115 School Street
Santa Cruz, CA 95060

Florida

Insight Meditation Group
2220 Southwest 34th Street #186
Gainesville, FL 32605

Hawaii

Situ Choling Retreat Center
53–086 Halai Street
Hau'ula, HI 96717

Taishoji Soto Mission
275 Kinoole Street
Hilo, HI 96720

International Zen Dojo
3565 Kalihi Street
Honolulu, HI 96818

Daifukuji Mission
Honalo
Keauhou, HI 96751

Society of Egalitarian Buddhists
P.O. Box 205
Kula/Maui, HI 96790

Indiana

Chambaling Inc.
Rt. 1, Box 9
Nashville, IN 47447

Maryland

Washington, D.C. Zen Group
C/O Strauss
Rt. 1, Box 604
Accokeek, MD 20607

Massachusetts

Sayagi U Ba Khin Memorial
C/O Stein
Roaring Brook Road
Conway, MA 01314

Vipassana Fellowship of America
41 Stearns Avenue
Medford, MA 02155

Boston Buddhist Center
Dr. Giac Duc
72 Shirley Avenue
Revere, MA 02151

Michigan

Shin Gum Do Zen Group
6 Geddes Heights
Ann Arbor, MI 48104

Detroit/Toledo Zen Group
7908 Reuter
Dearborn, MI 48126

New York

Zen Center of Annandale
C/O R. Clark
Bard College
Annandale-on-Hudson, NY 12504

Zen Group at Annandale
C/O Dan Sedia
Box 5
Annandale-on-Hudson, NY 12504

Kagyu Pende Kunchab
P.O. Box 39
Annandale-on-Hudson, NY 12504

International Meditation Center
415 Franklin Street
Buffalo, NY 14202

Bodhi House
619 Pulaski Road
East Northport, NY 11731-2141

Kagyu Osal Do Nga Choling
6 Seasongood Road
Forest Hills, NY 11375

Longchen Nyingthig Buddhist Society
P.O. Box 302/ Big Woods Road
Harris, NY 12742

Kagyu Thubten Choling
P.O. Box 112
New Hamburg, NY 12560

Jampal Cho Ling
C/O N. Clark
343 Bleecker Street #1
New York, NY 11114

Kagyu Dzamling Kunchab
C/O C. Cannon
35 W. 19th Street, 5th floor
New York, NY 10011

Lama Pema Wangdak/Jetsun Sakya
4 West 101st Street #63
New York, NY 10025

Buffalo Zen Group
629 Deerfield Drive
North Tonawanda, NY 14120

Kagyu Thubten Choling
127 Sheafe Road
Wappingers Falls, NY 12590

Beech Hill Pond Meditation Center
P.O. Box 64
West Danby, NY 14896

New Jersey

Gaden Chophel Ling
331-D West 6th Street
Howell, NJ 07731

Lamaist Buddhist Monastery of America
281 Hamilton Street
New Brunswick, NJ 18901

Princeton Zen Center
317 Mt. Lucas Road
Princeton, NJ 08540

Oregon

Ashland Zendo
125-A Scenic Drive
Ashland, OR 97520

Women's Sangha
90 North Lawrence
Eugene, OR 97401

Texas

Buddhist Cultural Institute
C/O Mrs. Sujatha Nadarajah
3708 110th Street
Lubbock, TX 79423
(806) 745-4452

Chua Buu Mon
2701 Procter Street
Port Arthur, TX 77640
(409) 982-9319

Virginia

Rock Creek Buddhist Temple of America
1823 North Lincoln Street
Arlington, VA 22207

Washington

Washington Buddhavanaram
C/O Ven. Sukhadhammo
4401 South 360th Street
Auburn, WA 98010
(206) 927-5408

Kachap Ling
P.O. Box 95
Blue Diamond, WA 98010

Cho Bo Ji
3010 South Edmunds
Seattle, WA 98108
(206) 633-0214

Khentse Choling
East 507 Shinto
Spokane, WA 99202

Karma Nordup Dorje
9621 Seeley
Tacoma, WA 98499

Canada

British Columbia

Sakya Buddhist Society
7340 Frobisher Drive
Richmond, B.C. V7C 4N5

Bodhi Dharma Society
7011 Marguerite Street
Vancouver, B.C.

Buddhayana Educational Association
3813 West 21st Avenue
Vancouver, B.C.

Ontario

Kadam Zhenphen Thaye Ling
133 St. Lawrence Street West
Madoc, Ont. K0K 2K0

Gaden Phen De Ling
P.O. Box 414
Orleans, Ont. K1C 1S8

Gampo Gangara Wang Du Ling
1290 Dorchester Avenue
Ottawa, Ont. K1Z 8E7

Kampo Gangra Drubgyud Ling
200 Balsam Avenue
Toronto, Ont. M4E 3C3

Karma Kagyu Centre
C/O C. Peterson
8 Everingham Court
Willowdale, Ont. M2M 2J5

About the Editor

Don Morreale received his undergraduate degree in religion from the University of Denver and has been a "Dharma Bum" since 1968. In 1986 he journeyed to Asia for a period of extended retreat in the monasteries of Thailand. He has worked as a glove packer, fruit picker, hospital attendant, printer's apprentice, trail cook, deckhand, sandwich man, pushcart vendor, racetrack gambler, sign painter, figure model, building wrecker, electrician, architectural designer, house renovator, landlord, English teacher, meditation instructor, juggler, courier, exhibit co-ordinator, hand shadowist, artist, radio producer, disk jockey, world traveler, sacred cowboy, and cosmic troublemaker. This is his first book.

About the Conspiracy of Silence

Conspire, L. *conspirare*, com- + spirare, to breathe together, harmonize, agree. To concur or work to one end: act in harmony.

"The Conspiracy of Silence" was originally the name given to a performance piece by Don Morreale, in which 130 people from around the world were invited to maintain silence for ten minutes each day for a year. The concept has since been expanded to encompass a wide range of creative enterprises. In the planning stages are a National Day of Buddhist Meditation and a series of radio documentaries on contemplative religion. All authors' profits from the sale of this book will go towards the establishment of a Buddhist retreat scholarship fund—The Conspiracy of Silence Trust—and towards financing other creative projects of the Conspiracy. Inquiries are invited and contributions welcome.

PUBLICATIONS

People's Guide to Mexico, Carl Franz $14.95 (99-0) 600 pp.

Now in its 13th printing, this classic guide shows the traveler how to handle just about any situation that might arise while in Mexico. "...the best 360-degree coverage of traveling and short-term living in Mexico that's going." - *Whole Earth Epilog*

People's Guide to RV and Adventure Camping in Mexico, Carl Franz $13.95 (91-5) 356 pp.

The sequel to *The People's Guide to Mexico,* this revised guide focuses on both the special pleasures and challenges of RV travel in Mexico and on the excitment of non-vehicle adventure camping in Mexico. An unprecedented number of Americans and Canadians has discovered the advantages of RV and adventure travel in reaching remote villages and camping comfortably on beaches.

The On and Off the Road Cookbook, Carl Franz $8.50 (27-3) 272 pp.

Carl Franz, *(The People's Guide to Mexico)* and Lorena Havens offer a multitude of delicious alternatives to the usual campsite meals or roadside cheeseburgers. Over 120 proven recipes.

The Heart of Jerusalem, Arlynn Nellhaus $12.95 (79-6) 312 pp.

Denver Post journalist Arlynn Nellhaus draws on her vast experience in and knowledge of Jerusalem to give travelers a rare inside view and practical guide to the Golden City—from holy sites and religious observances to how to shop for toothpaste and use the telephone.

Buddhist America: Centers, Retreats, Practices, Don Morreale $12.95 (94-X) 356 pp.

The only comprehensive directory of Buddhist centers, this guide includes first-person narratives of individuals' retreat experiences. Invaluable for both newcomers and experienced practitioners who wish to expand their contacts within the American Buddhist Community.

Catholic America: Self-Renewal Centers & Retreats, Patricia Christian-Meyers $12.95 (20-3) 356 pp. April '89

The only comprehensive directory of Catholic self-renewal centers and retreats. Also includes articles by leading Catholic teachers.

A Traveler's Guide to Healing Centers & Retreats, Martine Rudee & Jonathan Blease $12.95 (15-7) 320 pp. April '89

A resource guide for travelers and any person wishing to locate and/or obtain detailed information about healing centers and retreats within North America.

Gypsying After 40, Bob Harris $12.95 (71-0) 312 pp.

Retirees Bob and Megan Harris offer a witty and informative guide to the "gypsying" lifestyle that has enriched their lives and can enrich yours. For 10 of the last 18 years they have traveled throughout the world living out of camper vans and boats. Their message is: "Anyone can do it!!"

Complete Guide to Bed & Breakfasts, Inns & Guesthouses, Pamela Lanier $13.95 (09-2) 520 pp.

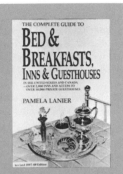

Newly revised and the most complete directory, with over 4800 listings in all 50 states, 10 Canadian provinces, Puerto Rico and the U.S. Virgin Islands. This classic provides details on reservation services and indexes identifying inns noted for antiques, decor, conference facilities and gourmet food.

All-Suite Hotel Guide, Pamela Lanier $13.95 (08-4) 396 pp.

Pamela Lanier, author of *The Complete Guide to Bed & Breakfasts, Inns & Guesthouses,* now provides the discerning traveler with a list of over 800 all-suite hotels, both in the U.S. and internationally. Indispensable for families traveling with children or business people requiring an extra meeting room.

Elegant Small Hotels, Pamela Lanier $14.95 (10-6) 224 pp.

This lodging guide for discriminating travelers describes 204 American hotels characterized by exquisite rooms and suites and personal service *par excellence.* Includes small hotels in 39 states and the Caribbean, Mexico and Canada.

Mona Winks: Self-Guided Tours of Europe's Top Museums, Rick Steves $14.95 (85-0) 450 pp.

Here's a guide that will save you time, shoe leather and tired muscles. It's designed for people who want to get the most out of visiting the great museums of Europe. It covers 25 museums in London, Paris, Rome, Venice, Florence, Amsterdam, Munich, Madrid and Vienna.

Europe Through The Back Door, Rick Steves $12.95 (84-2) 404 pp.

Doubleday and Literary Guild Bookclub Selection.

For people who want to enjoy Europe more and spend less money doing it. In this revised edition, Rick shares more of his well-respected insights. He also describes his favorite "back doors"—less-visited destinations throughout Europe that are a wonderful addition to any European vacation.

Europe 101, Rick Steves & Gene Openshaw $12.95 (78-8) 372 pp.

The first and only jaunty history and art book for travelers makes castles, palaces and museums come alive. Both Steves and Openshaw hold degrees in European history, but their real education has come from escorting first-time visitors throughout Europe.

Asia Through The Back Door, Rick Steves & John Gottberg $11.95 (76-1) 336 pp.

In this detailed guide book are information and advice you won't find elsewhere—including how to overcome culture shock, bargain in marketplaces, observe Buddhist temple etiquette and, possibly most important of all, how to eat noodles with chopsticks!

Traveler's Guide to Asian Culture, Kevin Chambers $12.95 (14-9) 356 pp. Spring '89

Veteran traveler in Asia, Kevin Chambers has written an accurate and enjoyable guide to the history and culture of this diverse continent.

Bus Touring: A Guide to Charter Vacations, USA, Stuart Warren & Douglas Bloch $9.95 (95-8) 192 pp.

For many people, bus touring is the ideal, relaxed and comfortable way to see America. The author has had years of experience as a bus tour conductor and writes in-depth about every aspect of bus touring to help passengers get the most pleasure for their money.

Road & Track's Used Car Classics, edited by Peter Bohr $12.95 (69-9) 272 pp.

Road & Track contributing editor Peter Bohr has compiled this collection of the magazine's "Used Car Classic" articles, updating them to include current market information. Over 70 makes and models of American, British, Italian, West German, Swedish and Japanese enthusiast cars built between 1953 and 1979 are featured.

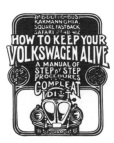

Automotive Repair Manuals

Each JMP automotive manual gives clear step-by-step instructions, together with illustrations that show exactly how each system in the vehicle comes apart and goes back together. They tell everything a novice or experienced mechanic needs to know to perform periodic maintenance, tune-ups, troubleshooting and repair of the brake, fuel and emission control, electrical, cooling, clutch, transmission, driveline, steering and suspension systems, and even rebuild the engine.

How To Keep Your Car Alive: A Basic Sanity Saver $14.95 (19-X) 208 pp. April '89

If you don't know a spark plug from a soup spoon, this book is for you. Gives the basic of how a car works, where things are and what they're called. Demystifies your auto and allows you to drive or talk to your mechanic with confidence. Color illustrations to enhance descriptions.

How To Keep Your VW Alive $17.95 (12-2) 384 pp. (revised)
How To Keep Your VW Rabbit Alive $17.95 (47-8) 440 pp.
How To Keep Your Honda Car Alive $17.95 (55-9) 272 pp.
How To Keep Your Subaru Alive $17.95 (49-4) 464 pp.
How To Keep Your Toyota Pick-Up Alive $17.95 (89-3) 400 pp.
How To Keep Your Datsun/Nissan Alive $22.95 (65-6) 544 pp.
How To Keep Your Honda ATC Alive $14.95 (45-1) 236 pp.
How To Keep Your Golf/Jetta Alive $17.95 (21-1) 200 pp. April '89

ITEM NO.			TITLE	EACH	QUAN.	TOTAL
		-				
		-				
		-				
		-				
		-				
		-				
		-				
		-				
		-				
		-				

Subtotals _____

Postage & handling (see ordering information)* _____

New Mexicans please add 5.625 % tax _____

Total Amount Due _____

METHOD OF PAYMENT (circle one)   MC   VISA   AMEX   CHECK   MONEY ORDER

Credit Card Number   Expiration Date

Signature X _____
Required for Credit Card Purchases

Telephone: Office (   ) _____ Home (   ) _____

Name _____

Address _____

City _____ State ____ ✓ ____ Zip _____

*See reverse side for Ordering Information

ORDERING INFORMATION

Fill in the order blank. Be sure to add up all of the subtotals at the bottom of the order form, and give us the address whither your order will be whisked.

Postage & Handling

Your books will be sent to you via UPS (for U.S. destinations), and you will receive them in approximately 10 days from the time that we receive your order.

Include $2.75 for the first item ordered and add $.50 for each additional item to cover shipping and handling costs. UPS shipments to post office boxes take longer to arrive; if possible, please give us a street address.

For airmail within the U.S., enclose $4.00 per book for shipping and handling.

ALL FOREIGN ORDERS will be shipped surface rate. Please enclose $3.00 for the first item and $1.00 for each additional item. Please inquire for airmail rates.

Method of Payment

Your order may be paid by check, money order or credit card. We cannot be responsible for cash sent through the mail.

All payments must be in U.S. dollars drawn on a U.S. bank. Canadian postal money orders in U.S. dollars also accepted.

For VISA, Mastercard or American Express orders, use the order form or call (505) 982-4078. Books ordered on American Express cards can be shipped only to the billing address of the cardholder.

Sorry, no C.O.D.'s.

Residents of sunny New Mexico add 5.625% to the total.

Backorders

We will backorder all forthcoming and out-of-stock titles unless otherwise requested.

Address all orders and inquiries to:

JOHN MUIR PUBLICATIONS
P.O. Box 613
Santa Fe, NM 87504
(505) 982-4078

All prices subject to change without notice.